Political Geography

Critical Introductions to Geography

Critical Introductions to Geography is a series of textbooks for undergraduate courses covering the key geographical sub-disciplines and providing broad and introductory treatment with a critical edge. They are designed for the North American and international market and take a lively and engaging approach with a distinct geographical voice that distinguishes them from more traditional and outdated texts.

Prospective authors interested in the series should contact the series editor:

John Paul Jones III
School of Geography and Development
University of Arizona
jpjones@email.arizona.edu

Published

Political Geography: A Critical Introduction
Sara Smith

Political Ecology: A Critical Introduction, 3e
Paul Robbins

Economic Geography: A Critical Introduction
Trevor J. Barnes, Brett Christophers

Health Geographies: A Critical Introduction
Tim Brown, Gavin J. Andrews, Steven Cummins, Beth Greenhough,
Daniel Lewis, Andrew Power

Urban Geography: A Critical Introduction
Andrew E.G. Jonas, Eugene McCann, Mary Thomas

Environment and Society: A Critical Introduction, 2e
Paul Robbins, John Hintz, Sarah A. Moore

Geographic Thought: A Critical Introduction
Tim Cresswell

Mapping: A Critical Introduction to Cartography and GIS
Jeremy W. Crampton

Research Methods in Geography: A Critical Introduction
Basil Gomez, John Paul Jones III

Geographies of Media and Communication
Paul C. Adams

Social Geography: A Critical Introduction
Vincent J. Del Casino Jr.

Geographies of Globalization: A Critical Introduction
Andrew Herod

Cultural Geography: A Critical Introduction
Donald Mitchell

Political Geography

A Critical Introduction

Sara Smith

WILEY Blackwell

This edition first published 2020
© 2020 John Wiley & Sons Ltd

Registered Offices
John Wiley & Sons, Inc., 111 River Street, Hoboken, NJ 07030, USA
John Wiley & Sons Ltd, The Atrium, Southern Gate, Chichester, West Sussex, PO19 8SQ, UK

Editorial Office
9600 Garsington Road, Oxford, OX4 2DQ, UK

For details of our global editorial offices, customer services, and more information about Wiley products visit us at www.wiley.com.

Wiley also publishes its books in a variety of electronic formats and by print-on-demand. Some content that appears in standard print versions of this book may not be available in other formats.

Library of Congress Cataloging-in-Publication Data

Names: Smith, Sara, 1974– author. | Wiley-Blackwell (Firm)
Title: Political geography : a critical introduction / Sara Smith, University of North Carolina
  Chapel Hill Chapel Hill, USA. Other titles: Critical introductions to geography.
Description: First Edition. | Hoboken : Wiley-Blackwell, 2020. | Series: Critical introductions to
  geography | Includes bibliographical references and index.
Identifiers: LCCN 2019053535 (print) | LCCN 2019053536 (ebook) |
  ISBN 9781119315186 (Paperback) | ISBN 9781119315148 (Adobe PDF) |
  ISBN 9781119315155 (ePub)
Subjects: LCSH: Political geography–Textbooks.
Classification: LCC JC319 .S5685 2020 (print) | LCC JC319 (ebook) | DDC 320.1/2–dc23
LC record available at https://lccn.loc.gov/2019053535
LC ebook record available at https://lccn.loc.gov/2019053536

Cover Design: Wiley
Cover Image: © cloverphoto/Getty Images

Set in 10/12.5pt Minion by SPi Global, Pondicherry, India
Printed and bound in Singapore by Markono Print Media Pte Ltd

10 9 8 7 6 5 4 3 2 1

Contents

Acknowledgments

Sallie Marston laid the foundations for this book many years ago as my graduate advisor and the first person to teach me about political geography. Paul Robbins encouraged me to say yes to the book and generously shared advice.

I am deeply grateful to the series editor, John Paul Jones, III, for his advice and extremely helpful feedback on the earliest version of this manuscript. Justin Vaughan was an endlessly patient and supportive editor through every step of this process, and provided clear and useful guidance at our annual conference meetings. Liz Wingett, Merryl Le Roux, and Sarah Keegan at Wiley were likewise lovely, kind and patient. I am also in debt to the two reviewers who read this manuscript, and to the copyeditor, Carol Thomas, not only a patient saint, but also witty. Siobhan McKiernan kindly provided the index.

I could never have written this book without the support of friends who have not only heard out my deepest insecurities but also patiently offered strategies, very close and generous readings, and laughter. In particular, I owe a debt of gratitude to our "dangerous playground" writing group: Lilly Nguyen, Maya Berry, Banu Gökarıksel, and Andrew Curley. Banu has been a mentor to me since I first came to UNC. Andrew kindly provided feedback on many more chapters than necessary. Erika Wise and Jocelyn Chua listened to too many of my complaints. Other encouragement and advice came from Jenny Tone-Pah-Hote, Jennifer Ho, Sarah Shields, Jecca Namakkal, Annette Rodriguez, Danielle Purifoy, and Jean Dennison. Malinda Maynor Lowery very kindly provided feedback and advice on thinking about UNC's relationship to Indigenous land. Other colleagues and friends who generously read chapters include Mike Hawkins, Michelle Padley, Altha Cravey, Sathyaprya Mandijny, and Jill Williams.

Ideas in this book were deeply informed by my current and former graduate students Working with them has profoundly shaped my outlook on the discipline, how I live in the world, and given me strength. As if this wasn't enough, they also read the book proposal and commented on chapters. I can never repay Mabel Gergan, Pavithra Vasudevan, Mike Dimpfl, Chris Neubert, Carlos Serrano, and Pallavi Gupta. I am so grateful for their intellectual community, humor, and solidarity. My scholarship has been fundamentally influenced by our conversations. Other UNC graduate students have provided everything from good humor to critical insight to inspiration when I needed it, including, but not limited to Mike Hawkins, Willie Wright, Adam Bledsoe, Stevie Larson, Priscilla Vaz, Lara Lookabaugh, Nathan Swanson, Batool Zaidi, Dayuma Alban, and Anusha Hariharan. I have been fortunate to listen to a number of student activists here at UNC speak about their experience, both at public events and smaller meetings, and this has been transformative. FLOCK, our feminist collective, has been a home at UNC. I'm especially grateful to have learned from student activists including Omololu Babatunde, June Beshea, Crystal Yuille, and Jayna Fishman, and so many others. I am also endlessly grateful to UNC undergraduate students, for their enthusiasm and support for this project, and for their insight, wit, and earnest desire to fix our broken world.

The staff in our department, Nell Phillips, Barbara Taylor, and Dan Warfield put up with my book-induced forgetfulness with charm and patience. I couldn't have written at all without the coffee from our student-run Meantime Café.

My family has both encouraged me and also put up with me despite my many absences, for which I am thankful, particularly Teresa Swingle, the most loyal and caring sister anyone could hope for, my mom, Kiki Atkinson, and my dad and stepmom, Peter Smith and Dana Smith. Our family back in Ladakh, especially ama-le Dolma Tsering and my sister-in law, Stanzin Angmo, have always been a source of comfort.

Our daughter, Sasha Kunzes, age seven now, has been not only a source of delight but also endless encouragement, telling me to set realistic goals, asking if my book would include pictures, and telling me about the books she has written. I look forward to all the books she plans to write on animals and art. My husband, Stanzin Tonyot, supported my odd writing habits despite being deeply skeptical of academic work, and our conversations about why he left academia have fundamentally shaped the approach taken here. As I finished up this book, he was distracting Sasha with swimming and learning to ride her bike. Her joy makes everything possible.

Chapter 1

Introduction

This book was written inside Carolina Hall, a stately three story brick building at the University of North Carolina (UNC) at Chapel Hill, in the United States (US) South. With high ceilings, tall windows, and hardwood floors, the building can be a source of delight – a quiet space to stare out at the oak trees, with sunny classrooms where students laugh, debate, take exams, or daydream. It is also a wound that cannot be healed. When I began working here in 2009, the name inscribed in stone above the entrance was not Carolina, it was Saunders. In February 2015, Black students stood on the steps of this building with nooses around their necks, chanting "This is what Saunders would do to me!" in reference to the building's then-namesake. William Laurence Saunders had been a Ku Klux Klan (KKK) leader, as well as a lawyer and Secretary of State (Commemorative Landscapes of North Carolina 2010). Saunders's KKK position was one reason the university honored him with the name in 1920 (as activists discovered through archival research). As you begin to read this book, you might be in an academic building or a campus library. Have you considered the political geography of the little piece of the world that you currently inhabit? What stories might it have to tell you about state power, nations, and difference?

The students on the steps were part of the Real Silent Sam Coalition (RSSC), one in a series of organizations that have worked to bring the university to terms with its white supremacy, in part through analysis of and intervention into the racialized landscape. The RSSC had suggested renaming the building after Zora Neale Hurston, a Black folklorist, playwright, and novelist. Hurston, now hailed as a luminary of the Harlem Renaissance, wove ethnographic work with Black people in the US South into plays, short stories, and

Political Geography: A Critical Introduction, First Edition. Sara Smith.
© 2020 John Wiley & Sons Ltd. Published 2020 by John Wiley & Sons Ltd.

novels, such as *Their Eyes Were Watching God* (Hurston 1937). Hurston had audited a UNC course with playwright Paul Green while teaching at the North Carolina College for Negroes in 1939–1940. She had to attend class off campus: segregation laws prohibited Black students from enrolling in white schools such as UNC, and a white student had registered a complaint (Harvey 2016). The first Black student admitted (after a lawsuit to integrate) was Gwendolyn Harrison Smith in 1951 and she had to struggle to attend even after being admitted (Graham 2017). In 2015, activists like Omololu Babatunde, Blanche Brown, and others, put forward Hurston's name to celebrate Hurston's intellect and fearless approach to the barriers in her way, but also in allusion to all the Black scholars who were unable to participate in the life of the university due to the structures of racism (Butler 2014). In May 2015, forced to act and reluctant to take up Hurston's name, the Board of Trustees renamed the building "Carolina Hall," but also put a 16-year moratorium on further building renaming. That summer, the state legislature passed a law requiring their approval of changes to monumental landscapes – likely in reference to the Confederate monuments scattered across the state and in particular to "Silent Sam," the Confederate memorial on our campus at that time. The name of Hurston still haunts the building in ephemera and conversation, and in the ways that students and faculty refer to the building.

Political geography is the study of how power is spatial: how power struggles both subtle and spectacular are shaped by and shape the places in which they occur. The layers of meaning and experience embedded in the history above demonstrate the approach taken in this book, which is to bring political geography to life by asking us to reflect on how it shapes our life and how we are part of political geography through our daily actions. The experience of the building is intensely personal; for students, faculty, and staff, it is a space of labor (from cleaning toilets to answering email), pleasure, conversation, boredom. For some, it is a place they enter with great pride: UNC draws some of the highest-achieving students from across the state. Many of these top students are also first generation college students, from economically constrained families, or the first children of immigrants to attend a US institution. Their college years can be a turning point not only for them, but also for their families, who hope this will lead to a new economic status or broader horizons for their children. These students often approach their first classes with great trepidation – writing on anonymous notecards on the first day of class that they feel anxious, excited, or concerned that they may have been admitted by accident.

The place that generates excitement and anxiety for bright-eyed first year students is also a place where student activists experienced tears, anger, frustration, or indifference. Consider a student who had stood on the steps with a noose around her neck, or one who had smiled and laughed or even sung when students gathered the following week to read Zora Neale Hurston's writing on those same steps. This student might recall those moments walking through the front doors to class, carrying the tension, anger, or weariness that is the struggle to remain upright in a world seeking to knock you down. At other times (or maybe even in the same moment) they might recall with joy the solidarity of working for change. In conversations with student activists from the RSSC and the Silent Sam Sit-In (Figure 1.1), what has struck me most is the amount of emotional labor that they had put into this work, at the cost of leisure and pleasure. They keep up with their schoolwork, but skip parties to work for justice. We see then that the building as a place has meaning and political importance that is tied not only to its history, but also to how people experience it and the political actions they take in it: naming, re-naming, studying, protesting.

Figure 1.1   Students stage a sit-in at the Confederate Monument in August 2017.

So: why start with this story? With a building and university students – isn't this a book about political geography? Aren't we here to learn about world leaders, political economy, war, and military strategy? Of course, the answer is yes, but the premise of this book is that your everyday life and the world of global conflict and nation-states cannot be separated from one another. Each classroom is both a microcosm of economic processes and gendered and racialized interpersonal dynamics *and* a potential site of transformation and learning. The story of Hurston Hall is about student activists, but it is also a story about the history of the world that we live in. It is a global story of forced migration through enslavement, the invention of race, and fundamental questions about whose interests are served by the modern creation of the nation-state. The building's presence on a lawn named after the US President James Polk, known for territorial expansion through settler colonialism, points to the further layers in this story (to which we will return). The Hurston Hall story is about the critically creative manner in which people come together to transform the world.

University campuses (and even high school campuses) are also places where we witness both economic anxiety and class turmoil, as students work to prepare themselves for an unknown economic future, wondering which major will provide them with job security. These concerns are both everyday and mundane; they are worked out in daily life in interactions between students, parents, faculty, and also tied into formal political structures – in the determination of who attends what schools and whose children attend public institutions versus private schools. In the US, campuses are also sites of activism and discussion about gun violence and the role of young people in shaping political discourse on the topic Globally, young people are also a driving force in shifting conversations on global warming. Political geography gives us tools to think through the complex entanglement between these processes, sites, and the people who navigate them.

Space, Place, and Power

As political geographers, we seek to understand how power is manifest in and through space and place, at scales large and small. Political geography gives us a means to understand the *spatial* power relations we find on the college campus. We might ask why the once predominantly Black housekeeping department at UNC is now staffed mainly by refugees from Burma and elsewhere in Southeast Asia (Dimpfl 2017; Dimpfl and Smith 2018). We might also ask why most UNC faculty are white, from outside the state, and from middle-class backgrounds, while the students and staff are both mostly from North Carolina, and comprise a more diverse population, while the students are still not as diverse as the state population. In conversation with theories of feminism, decolonization, and critical approaches to race, political geography also gives us tools to understand why so many syllabi used on college campuses include the writers that they do, and why the racial, ethnic, socioeconomic class and gendered composition of students, staff, and faculty are so different from the makeup of the state and the nation. Perhaps most tantalizingly, in this book, we will think through critical understandings of what makes the relationships between micro-political interactions and spaces and large-scale phenomena. In other words, how can people like us try to change the world? As we begin this book, let us consider a few of geography's key terms.

Space is where things happen in the world. Spaces are political because they have been *produced* through political processes, and because they reinforce, reinscribe, or destabilize power hierarchies. **Spatial relationships** or the relationship between spaces, are likewise political – think of the movement of labor mentioned above. Can we untangle that movement from political histories connecting the United States to Southeast Asia? Or from global labor prices? Flows of people or money are never accidental – they are always tied to other political relationships, and we understand these better by understanding the spatial aspect of such relationship – or how these relationships happen through spatial practices. What happens when money flows rapidly into a city for instance? Does it displace the urban poor, as though they were so many branches and leaves swept out to the sea? Does it change the shape of the skyline, with high-rises reaching up to the sky like spindly plants growing toward the sun? These are the spatial expressions of economic and social processes.

Think of the urban space generated by the university. The university creates a specific form of capitalist space that we witness on the streets near campus, which inevitably house pizza shops, bookstores, and places to get t-shirts with the university logo. These spaces, though they are unique, also bear the marks of global capitalism – spaces determined in part by the logics of economies of scale and designed to be reassuring, familiar, and efficient (Lefebvre 2004). Chain shops like Subway or McDonald's are this kind of global capitalist space: familiar, repetitive, profit-maximizing. But we can think of other familiar spaces within the university itself: the lecture hall or podium is a familiar space that reflects traditional European ideas of knowledge: that students are containers to be filled with knowledge by the teacher. Classrooms and lecture halls train us to focus on the front of the room, computers and screens lead us to expect PowerPoints and passive learning. The space sets up the power dynamics of what then occurs, and if we seek to change what happens in classrooms, we might need to reconfigure the space itself.

Through a different lens, spaces are also **gendered**, that is, the widespread gender binary of male and female shapes the spaces we inhabit, both public and private. For **cisgender** people who comfortably perform the gender they were assigned at birth, this has profound effects – as, for instance, due to the ways that patriarchy is enforced, men can be made to feel uncomfortable in spaces that are gendered as feminine (for instance, if they choose traditionally feminine careers) and women can feel unsafe in spaces coded as masculine. For men and women who are transgender, or people who are gender nonconforming or nonbinary, the stakes can be very high, as they are more likely to be the victims of hate crimes if people perceive them to be invading spaces not meant for them. They may be at risk in public space because of harassment or threat of violence (Browne 2004; Browne, Nash, and Hines. 2010; Doan 2010). As we discuss in a few chapters, experiences of citizenship can also be tied to sexual orientation in both subtle and explicit ways, such that those of us who are LGBTQ+ may have to struggle to access rights.

Place is a related but different way to understand where things happen in the world. Places are sites that have been given cultural meaning by the people who inhabit them. A place could be a monument or it could be where everyone lies in the grass on the first warm day of spring. It is the campus as a place where we expect some things to happen: students to study but also to express their youth and socialize. Places are given meaning through our cultural practices: a mosque, temple, or church, could be where we *feel* the presence of the sacred if we have been raised in that cultural tradition, it could also be a political site vulnerable to attacks or prone to visits by politicians seeking election. It is a place that might have meaning for a local but also for a traveler (though those meanings might be different). First-generation college students, children of immigrants, non-traditional students will re-experience in the place of campus the ways that they are marginalized elsewhere, and they may find or develop their own means to articulate and challenge those processes of marginalization.

A sense of place is created through ascribed meanings over time. Let us return to UNC to consider the statue of a nondescript Confederate soldier known as Silent Sam. While I was writing this book, a group of student and community activists, in a daring and heist-like operation, pulled the statue off the base and down onto the ground, forcing the university administration to grapple with its landscape and history and foreclosing their default position of deferral. This statue had one meaning in 1913 when it was erected by the North Carolina Division of the United Daughters of the Confederacy and some alumni, during a wave of commemoration that was part of a broader project of validating white supremacy and the Jim Crow regime of segregation (Leloudis 2017; Sturkey 2017). That meaning remains, but is now also layered with other meanings that students, faculty, staff, administrators, and community members have ascribed to it over the last one hundred years. In just the nine years I have worked for this institution, I have already seen the meanings change. In 2018, Maya Little, a graduate student in history, mixed her own blood and red paint and poured it on the statue. In an interview the next day, Little was asked: "What would you say to those who are criticizing what you did yesterday?" She replied:

> I guess, for them, a lot of people say, "Well look at the statue, the statue shouldn't be moved, it's history." Well, as someone who's a Ph.D. student in history, you can't call something history without showing the real history of it. The blood of Black people is the real history of that statue.

White supremacy was built on violence toward Black people. To have a white supremacist mon-
ument sitting on our campus without that context, standing there, kind of sanitized by the
University as it was yesterday when they power-washed it, is not history at all. It's against history.
It's against the study of history. (Quoted in Blake 2018)

In her honor court hearing, interviews, and articles, Little and her advocates argued that she
improved and *contextualized* the statue, using blood and paint to reveal the statue's deeper
meaning and make visible to all what had already been visible to her. While place is experienced differently, power relations also structure places. Some had the power to keep the
statue in place, while many students agitate for it to be removed. Place is made through
interaction. Imagine this statue on the day it was dedicated, with white elite local residents,
faculty and administrators from the university crowded around, including the local chapter
of the Daughters of the Confederacy (Figure 1.2). They were there to hear a speech that
hinged on respect for tradition, culminating in the speaker, Julian Carr, bragging that he
had "horse-whipped a negro wench until her skirts hung in shreds," because she had
"publicly insulted and maligned a southern lady" (Commemorative Landscapes of North
Carolina 2010). Now imagine it in fall of 2017, surrounded by students and faculty,
some identifying as people of color, immigrants, and queers, others white southerners with
confederate heritage, but with signs reading "#SilenceSam," and "Black Lives Matter." In
these two different times and places, the meaning of place is itself quite different. In both
cases, people are united for a common goal, but these goals are radically divergent and the
atmosphere at the site is also transformed.

Figure 1.2   "Unveiling of the Confederate Monument, June 2, 1913" in Orange County, North
Carolina Postcard Collection (P052), North Carolina Collection Photographic Archives, Wilson
Library, UNC-Chapel Hill. Reproduced with permission of Wilson Library.

Place is political: the presence of the statue on the lawn makes it a political site, where student activists call attention *not* only to the values of the university, but to social problems that transcend the campus. Consider summer 2015, when someone spray-painted the statue on multiple nights, writing things like "Black Lives Matter," and "Who is Sandra Bland?" (Figure 1.3). Also, consider the intent behind Maya Little's public act of civil disobedience in paint in 2018. These activists were making an explicit connection between anti-Black violence on the national stage, the symbolic landscape, and history of the university. This might remind you of the students on the steps with nooses around their necks in 2015. By choosing the setting (right beneath the main entrance where Saunders's name is engraved into the stone), and then enacting the visually arresting image of young Black women with nooses around their necks, these activists made passerby *feel* the shock of history and its links to the present. These student activists remind us of the ways that place can be used in the service of a political point. But even in these moments when the history of white supremacy is made visible through public protest, erasure and silence is also an important part of the meaning of place. In an op-ed in the *New York Times*, UNC historian Malinda Lowery, a member of

Figure 1.3   The confederate monument spray-painted with "Who is Sandra Bland?" in August of 2015. Courtesy of Nathan W. Swanson.

the Lumbee Tribe reminds us that it is her people who were the original Southerners, and that these original Southerners were also subject to erasure, racially segregated after being classified as "colored" in 1924, and then subject to projects of eugenics and cultural assimilation (Lowery 2018). Lowery writes "Those who wish to keep the monuments argue that tearing them down would erase Confederate history. But the distorted history that Confederate monuments symbolize will always be with those it did not favor. American Indians will never forget it."

The observations of these scholars and activists can push us to think about **scale** (the relationship between local and micro-expressions of processes and larger national or global processes), or beyond scale entirely. We can understand political processes differently by thinking about how the tension felt in the body of a student entering Hurston Hall or passing by Silent Sam is symptomatic of and symbolic of wider networks and structures of oppression, but that *beyond individual experience of injustice,* it is through embodied experience in multiple sites that power functions and is challenged. The members of the Board of Trustees, who make decisions regarding naming on campus, are tension-bearing, angry, sad, joyful, and complacent bodies, as are those who walk through the halls of the US legislature, as was Saunders himself. That is, we cannot hold up the "global," or "national" scale of political power as though they were separate from the embodied life in the various rooms and sites that enact this political power (Marston 2002; Marston, Jones, and Woodward 2005). Everything happens in a place: even global meetings of world leaders happen in rooms in which gestures, handshakes, and casual comments may have global significance. As we will discuss later in the text, it is important not to think of "the global" as existing out there somewhere apart from these local spaces.

Conflict over the racialized landscape of my campus resonate with national discourses on place and belonging. We might think of extraordinary moments such as the "Unite the Right" rally in Charlottesville, Virginia in 2017, in which a crowd of white supremacists converged shouting, "You will not replace us, Jews will not replace us." These protests resulted in the death of Heather Heyer (run over by a car driven into a crowd of counter-protestors), and the ensuing political commentary, in which the US president declared there were "good people" on both sides at the protest. This of course is part of a global turn to the right that manifests in a variety of locally-specific nationalisms in places like the United Kingdom (UK), Turkey, Brazil, and India (Burrell et al. 2018; Gökarıksel, Neubert, and Smith 2019). We can also connect this struggle to quite different impulses: global conversations about the future of nation-states, and the role of education in shaping the future in the wake of colonialism and empire. These include a recent set of conversations in the UK about race in higher education (Johnson, Joseph-Salisbury, and Kamunge 2019; Joseph-Salisbury 2019; Noxolo 2017a; 2017b) and the colonial nature of neoliberal education today in places such as South Africa (Elliott-Cooper 2018). We will return to these connections in chapters on nationalism and on the prospects of decolonizing the discipline.

How do we think about power across spaces without thinking in a scalar manner? How do we better understand what is meant by citizenship, nationalism, and the state by thinking about their others, excesses, and exclusion zones? Who can truly be called a citizen? How are ideas of national belonging constructed? How do different people experience place? In this text, we will seek to understand these political entities, processes, and categories, through an approach that begins from our day-to-day lived experience as a means to understand political geography. This chapter has begun from a few ideas that will be expanded on in the pages to come.

al Intro

a *critical* introduction to political geography, this text foregrounds not the most conventional historical origins and architecture of political geography (though that in itself is valuable work), but rather furthers the potential of political geography through the academic margins that have begun to fundamentally shape and shift what counts as knowledge (hooks 1984). This *critical* approach should not be read as a condemnation of the discipline. Growth comes from an acknowledgment of shortcomings and erasures, and movement toward different ways of thinking that enable us to more fully understand our world. When someone provides us with criticism of our thinking, our writing, or our theories about the world, we can react defensively, or we can take on that criticism as an act of generosity, one in which the critic has put faith in our ability to grow and change.

It is in this spirit that this text, in addition to the fundamental analyses provided by Marxist theorists and the ways they underpin much of political geography's core tenets, works to engage intentionally with both academic- and social-movement-based critical thought and theorizing on power. These engagements emerge from feminist, Black, Indigenous, de-and post-colonial and queer geographies (and those working the intersections of these geographies), as well as the materialist/non-human geographies that destabilize the subjects and analysis of political geography. This text begins from the assumption that the literature many of us read, the lenses we might use to see the world, and our mechanisms for understanding it have been *anemic* (Domosh 2015; Gilmore 2002; Jazeel 2014; Mahtani 2014; Noxolo 2017a; 2017b; Peake and Kobayashi 2002; Pulido 2002). That is, our descriptions and theorizations of the world have been shaped by the **positionality** of those who produced these theorizations. Positionality refers to our social, racialized, gendered, and class positions within existing power structures. Knowledge builds on that which came before it, and places that produce knowledge, such as universities, book presses, and laboratories, have not, and still do not, represent the full breadth of humanity, but have usually excluded or only marginally included the working class, people of color, Indigenous people, white women and genderqueer people, (and of course the various intersections of these positionalities). This means that if we inhabit that space we should take seriously the challenge of decolonizing the multiple sites through which power is produced through the production of knowledge. To **decolonize** in this context is to ask questions about this knowledge production and what is the relationship between the ideas produced and the political context from which they emerge, though later we will also interrogate the language of decolonization itself (Tuck and Yang 2012). For now, let us begin by reflecting: who is in our classrooms? Among those, who feels they can speak? Who is at the front of the room? Who is in our canon? Among those, who are foundational and who are optional or last-week-of-the-semester reading?

The logic of this book is not only to trace the lineage of concepts, but rather to begin from their edges and their breaking points: When does citizenship fail us? In what way is the concept of sovereignty (self-governance) and the state an illusion? These chapters will start from these breaking points rather than push them aside or create a coherent narrative that makes things appear more functional than they are. A second logic is to begin from what have historically been the margins of our discipline, rather than beginning from the center and then turning to critiques and criticism (hooks 1984).

Professors often build our syllabi around foundational concepts (state formation, nationalism, electoral politics), while reserving a week for "gender and political geography" or other ways of representing and capturing difference within a specific demarcated space (for more on these ideas, Weheliye [2014] is an excellent starting point). And yet the foundational concepts are themselves fraught with an unmarked Euro-American white masculinism. What would it look like to destabilize those assumptions? Where would we start? This is not to suggest that the foundational ideas of political geography are not important – they certainly are – but they become even more helpful in our attempts to understand the political world when they are put in conversation with their critics from the beginning.

Could we start with the current state of the field in all its messiness and disagreement? Could we begin with where the critiques have taken us, rather than coming to them at the end? Many students go into the study of political geography because they are deeply invested and interested in the state of the world. The challenges we face in making the world more just and equitable are thus foregrounded in this book, as are the ideas of people working to change the world. To engage critically with the theories and advances of political geography is not to devalue or criticize the content of the subdiscipline, but rather to work to make the ideas that are central to the field sharper and more inclusive. It is to point to the ways that scholars have sometimes missed crucial points of engagement because their experiences or their chosen topics of study did not present these points of engagement as pressing and central. The key tenets and debates of political geography remain crucial to our times: how is power manifest in space? What is the state and how does it relate to class processes? What is the relationship between cultural and societal belonging and the governance of nations? How do we make the world by writing its geopolitical categories? In the context of this book, a critical engagement with political geography centers the ways that theorizations from many margins have pushed (or could push) political geographers to think more deeply and to broaden what counts as political geography. The categories that we think with matter deeply and shape what we are and are not able to understand about the world. By broadening the voices we listen to within the discipline, we have the opportunity to think with greater clarity about our chosen topic.

This book is intended to give you the lay of the land, so that you may figure out which ideas and concepts help you to better understand the world or your research. To do so, the book begins with a political geography that foregrounds this diverse set of voices, and asks what we learn by beginning from the margins, as generations of feminist and subaltern scholars have suggested we do. You will notice that this book is written in first person and as you have seen, it begins from grounding in the context from which I write. This is not by accident, but rather is an intentional technique to remind you, the reader, that all knowledge is generated by real people who are located in a particular time and place – that is, all knowledge is situated (Haraway 1991). To understand this, **situated knowledge**, that is, to know the ways in which the author is situated is to better be able to evaluate and understand what they are trying to tell you. In fact, when you read texts in which the author *does not* reveal or interrogate their relationship to the subject matter, you might wonder why that is or how that act (not-revealing) has shaped the material.

To enable the reader to get a glimpse into some of the thought processes of geographers grappling with the challenges of research today and the excitement of approaching political geography from a variety of angles, most chapters will include a short section called, "geographer at work," which features first person writing about a current project. This first chapter begins from my own perspective to ground the themes of the book and to explain how I arrived at the perspectives deployed in the text.

Geographer at Work: Sara Smith

When I began my graduate research in 2004, I labeled myself a political geographer. When I was in Ladakh, a mountainous region of India bordering Tibet, I began my research asking questions about formal politics. In response, people told me stories about love affairs and dinner parties. This was a revelation, particularly as I could begin to understand differently the ways this politics played out because of my own marriage to a Ladakhi man, and the ways that I had been accepted over time (as a white foreigner from a nominally Catholic family) even when Buddhist-Muslim marriages seemed impossible. This was an immediate signal to me that the way I understood the political through the macro lenses of the nation state and citizenship was not sufficient to understand what was happening on the ground. I needed new ways of thinking that could transcend the global and national scale. By listening to the women and men I interviewed, I learned that politics was something that was experienced in daily life, in interactions between neighbors and friends, and that this was related to and as important as electoral politics. To communicate this to academic audiences, I turned to the language of feminist geopolitics (described in Chapter 11). In writing about my research, during my dissertation, I began to struggle with the relationship between how India is represented in academic literature and how this reinforces the stereotypes and misconceptions that we will dismantle in later chapters, drawing on postcolonial and decolonizing scholarship. As I read more, the feminist perspectives continued to be useful, as they not only drew attention to the embodied and everyday experience of the state, but also insisted that all knowledge (including that of the researcher) is situated, that is, there is no neutral vantage point from which to understand the world.

In proceeding with my next research project, I began to think more about the meaning of "race," as I worked with students from India's Himalayas who face racialized discrimination when they attend university. They receive messages that they do not look Indian, but rather that they look Chinese or Japanese; simultaneously their mountain origins become part of this harassment as the British colonial narratives about mountain "tribal" people being backward and closer to nature persist in India today (Gergan 2014, 2017; Smith and Gergan 2015). As I was working on this project, the issues of racial justice that opened this chapter became more and more pressing on my campus, and I also was working with graduate students researching racial justice and difference both in the US context (Gergan, Smith, and Vasudevan 2018; Smith and Vasudevan 2017; Vasudevan 2019) and in the context of South Asia. As I read, I began to realize how much had been missing from my own reading of political geography, and in particular, the ways that we as political geographers often assumed that we could use concepts such as "the state," or "citizenship," as universal categories that could be understood outside or beyond questions of race, gender, or sexuality. More recently, as I have been working on research that asks about the future, my understandings of political geography have been further destabilized by reading queer critiques of the future, and by reading Indigenous critiques of how settler colonialism has shaped our understandings of past and future. I start with this first person narrative because I want you, the reader, to think of the concepts in this book in relation to "real life," and to emphasize that theory and concepts are not abstract, but are the lenses through which we see the world. This means that they can either sharpen or blur our vision.

In the chapters to come, we will explore central political concepts like citizenship and territory, through a geographic lens. The following core ideas animate the book.

- Our political institutions (e.g., the modern sovereign state) are not natural or pre-given. When we encounter an institution, we should consider its origins, and the differential way these institutions (such as the state and citizenship) work in everyday life.
- The state is both more and less than its components – ordinary people produce it in everyday life.
- When you encounter a key category (development, modernity, tradition, homosexual), consider how this category was created, who upholds it, and what political function it plays.
- We must grapple with difference (e.g., class, gender, race) and politics at a structural level, and not only through individual relationships or events.
- Identity is intersectional and performative, and is created in part through political processes.
- Knowledge is situated and is inseparable from power relations. We must take this into account when we produce and consume language.
- Power is spatial. It plays out at different scales, and scale itself is a product of power relations. Power is resisted and is never completely hegemonic. It operates in our daily lives and relations to one another.
- Nonhuman actors also play a role in politics – the qualities of nature, water, drones, and social media, for example, have profound political effects that sometimes exceed our expectations or design.

What Have We Learned and What Is Next?

In the next chapter, we will begin from the idea of citizenship, and consider how this concept works in our lives, that is, how we relate to state forms of power. This will lead us to think about the role of nationalism in shaping our allegiances in the world, in Chapter 3. After these chapters set the stage for us, we will take a step back and turn to broader questions of power and state formation – asking first how power operates spatially, and then going back in history to trace the development of the contemporary state form. This will bring us to chapters on urban politics and social movements, before we re-evaluate political geography as a discipline. In the last chapters of the book, we will consider the relationship between international relations and security, and the messy and complex ways these processes play out for ordinary people. We will close the book by considering how people long for, fear, and work toward the future.

Keywords

Cisgender   People who comfortably perform and identify with the gender they were assigned at birth.

Gendered   The ways that places, people, and objects, are made and read through the widespread gender binary of male and female shapes the spaces we inhabit, both public and private.

Place   A way to understand how sites have been given cultural meaning by the people who inhabit them.

Positionality   Our racialized, gendered, and class positions within existing power structures.

Situated knowledge   How our knowledge of the world is shaped by our positionality.

Space   Where things happen in the world. Geographers understand space to be made through environmental, political, and social practices. That is, our way of being in the world creates the world that we inhabit.

Spatial relationships   The relationship between spaces, which is also created through political and social practices

Further Reading

Further reading on the racialized landscape at the University of North Carolina at Chapel Hill

Charlotte Fryar has created an archive of activism and writing about the university's racialized landscape, including oral histories, statements, and images. It is available at https://uncofthepeople.com (accessed September 10, 2019).

Bledsoe, A. 2015. Why Does the University of North Carolina at Chapel Hill Continue to Honor the KKK? *Counterpunch.* March 15.

Menefee, H. 2019. Black Activist Geographies: Teaching Whiteness as Territoriality on Campus. *South: A Scholarly Journal* 50(2): 167–186.

On monumental and commemorative landscapes

Alderman, D. 2000. A Street Fit For a King: Naming Places and Commemoration in the American South. *The Professional Geographer* 52(4): 672–684.

Hoelscher, S. and Alderman. D. 2004. Memory and Place: Geographies of a Critical Relationship. *Social & Cultural Geography* 5(3): 347–355.

Inwood, J. and Martin, D. 2008. Whitewash: White Privilege and Racialized Landscapes at the University of Georgia. *Social & Cultural Geography* 9(4), 373–395.

Rose-Redwood, R., Alderman, D., and Azaryahu, M. 2008. Collective Memory and the Politics of Urban Space: An Introduction. *GeoJournal* 73: 161–164.

On place and space

Cresswell, T. 1992. *In Place-Out of Place: Geography, Ideology, and Transgression.* Minneapolis: University of Minnesota Press.

Hubbard, P. and Kitchin, R. (eds.). 2010. *Key Thinkers on Space and Place.* Thousand Oaks, CA: Sage.

Lefebvre, H. 2004. *The Production of Space.* Oxford: Blackwell Publishing.

Massey, D. 2005. *For Space.* Thousand Oaks, CA: Sage.

McKittrick, K. 2006. *Demonic Grounds: Black Women and the Cartographies of Struggle.* Minneapolis: University of Minnesota Press.

Chapter 2

Citizenship Fails

"You need to have a green card if you are going to be in the United States longer than x amount of time," she said, to which I replied:

"Look, I was born down there; I don't need a green card; I am not an immigrant; I am part of a *First Nation*, and this is the card that proves it!"

Upon hearing this her posture complete changed, she pushed my card to me, and said, "well then,

> *You*
> Are an American."
> To which I said,
> "*No*, I am not,
> *I*
> Am a *Mohawk*."
> I walked away from her. But as I was walking toward the door, she yelled across
>   the border house to me,
> "*You are an American*."
> And I yelled back,
> *I am a Mohawk*."
> And she yelled
> "*No*
> You are an American."

Audra Simpson, *Mohawk Interruptus* 2014, p.119

Political Geography: A Critical Introduction, First Edition. Sara Smith.
© 2020 John Wiley & Sons Ltd. Published 2020 by John Wiley & Sons Ltd.

Are you a citizen? Try to remember when you realized that you had citizenship, or when you realized your citizenship was compromised. Was there a day in your life when you contemplated what it means to have a Singaporean or Brazilian passport (or the right to apply for one)? If your citizenship is compromised, think about when you first realized this. It might be when you applied for a passport, when you enlisted in military service, or when you first learned your parents do not have legal documentation for your country of residence. In the world we live in today, our rights and our ability to be mobile, to attend school, to seek protection from the state are contingent upon citizenship. This has been highlighted in the so-called "refugee crisis," in the conversations over the "Windrush Generation," of immigrants from the British Empire, who arrived in the UK before 1971 and who sometimes lack documentation for citizenship claims. It has also been a topic of conversation for academics and workers of all kinds living in the UK as Brexit approaches. We can learn a lot by thinking back on when and how we are faced with our citizenship. Was it a moment when citizenship status facilitated accomplishing something you wanted to do (going on a big international trip with a passport that guarantees entrance on arrival – or traveling across Europe as a citizen of the EU)? Or when it hindered you in your goals and desires (not being able to apply for government assistance, not being able to get a visa to travel to a country because of your passport, having to be careful when you see a police officer)? If you have waited in an immigration line, was it boring? Or did your heart beat fast, and your palms sweat? Did you scan the row of state officers, wondering which might be the most empathetic? Were you certain you would be able to walk past the official with the badge?

Citizenship is a legal relationship with a state in which there are both rights and responsibilities – laid out in the state's constitution. Citizenship is the "right to have rights" (Arendt 1973). This means citizenship will *always* fail to protect some people. We can challenge the ways that citizenship has structured our lives and our ways of thinking about the world by considering both the ordinariness of citizenship and the exceptional cases in which we founder on the structure of citizenship as a means for protecting people's basic human rights. Throughout the chapter, it will be helpful to keep in mind one of the themes introduced in the Introduction: that categories structure our thought and sometimes obscure things that are right in front of us.

If the question: "Are you a citizen?" surprised you, you might think about why this is, *especially* if you realize it is only because of an accident of your birth that you have never had to be concerned about whether you are or are not a citizen. How is it that for some of us, citizenship is an unquestioned site of stability and a natural state of being? For some of us a lack of state citizenship may be a daily hurdle is an illuminating truth that this chapter will argue teaches us quite a bit about the framework of citizenship itself. When people's lives and livelihoods, education and safety, health and wellbeing depend on citizenship, as it is currently configured, the heartbreaking truth is that *citizenship fails us*. We have only to recall the men, women, and children who have lost their lives in the Mediterranean or in the Sonoran Desert of the US Southwest as they left a state that could not or refused to care for them to travel toward a place where they believed they and their children could survive. When we consider citizenship and its limits, we would do well to keep in mind the circumstances that may lead people to take a risk on the citizenship-less living of refugees and asylum-seekers. British poet Warsan Shire writes:

no one leaves home unless
home is the mouth of a shark
you only run for the border
when you see the whole city running as well
your neighbors running faster than you
breath bloody in their throats
the boy you went to school with
who kissed you dizzy behind the old tin factory
is holding a gun bigger than his body
you only leave home
when home won't let you stay.

no one leaves home unless home chases you
fire under feet
hot blood in your belly
it's not something you ever thought of doing
until the blade burnt threats into
your neck
and even then you carried the anthem under
your breath
only tearing up your passport in an airport toilets
sobbing as each mouthful of paper
made it clear that you wouldn't be going back.

Shire described her writing about refugees as being inspired by her own family's experiences, but also by time spent with young undocumented refugees in Europe, who had fled their homelands in Somalia, Eritrea, Congo, and Sudan (Bausells and Shearlaw 2015). The poem reflects on the circumstances through which an asylum-seeker or refugee might end up on the borders of another country or slipping across, and the reasons they might risk this position. But our chapter began with a different circumstance: a refusal of citizenship.

In the epigraph for this chapter, Simpson (2014) describes her aggravation at being told she is an American citizen, and her own desire to refuse that citizenship and forcefully claim instead *Mohawk* citizenship, that she belongs to her Indigenous community, not to the United States. This is a means to declare ongoing Mohawk **sovereignty** in the face of settler colonialism. When Simpson shouts "Mohawk!" She is affirming that the belonging that matters to her is that of her community, and that it exists prior to, and in defiance of the **settler colonial** state. Asserting her Mohawk identity declares that it cannot be subsumed into US citizenship, but rather, that the Mohawks of Kahnawà:ke, a region that crosses the US-Canada border, maintain sovereignty – the right to govern themselves. We will return to the question of Indigenous sovereignty and citizenship at the end of this chapter. Part of the premise then of this chapter is not to celebrate or normalize citizenship, but to try to understand citizenship through its complications, edges, and failures. What is citizenship to a father holding his child in a boat, hoping to cross a sea for her safety? What is citizenship to the border guard and to the Mohawk woman who yells at the guard even when she knows this may impede her travel?

Citizenship has never been neutral or universal; for instance, it has often been enmeshed in the creation of racial categories. Mae Ngai (2014) begins her book, *Impossible Subjects*, by tracing the stories of two people classified as "illegal aliens" in the United States: Rosario Hernandez, deported from Texas to Mexico in 2001, and Lillian Joann Flake, whose deportation was canceled by the Secretary of Labor in the 1930s. Both Hernandez and Flake had been convicted of crimes: Hernandez for driving while intoxicated and Flake for theft. Hernandez, married to a US citizen and two US citizen children, had been sober for years, and continued to participate in Alcoholics Anonymous; he was deported. Laws enacted in 1996 in fact meant that his deportation could not have been stopped. Ngai argues that the operation of race in the United States has changed over time (for instance, with Hernandez receiving sympathetic media attention, while during the 1930s the deportation of Mexican and Chinese "aliens" usually went unremarked). *However,* race still plays a powerful role, with significant focus on the US-Mexico border and undocumented immigrants entering from Mexico and Central America. Undocumented immigrants are "woven into the economic fabric of the nation," as "labor that is cheap and disposable," and "might be understood as a caste, unambiguously situated outside the boundaries of formal membership and social legitimacy" (Ngai 2014, p.4). Flows and movement across the border and blocked by the border are structured by the racialization of people, and this racialization in turn structures the border itself.

In this way, the border is a traveling site of multiple forms of violence – a theme we will return to across chapters on security, biopolitics, and geopolitics. Borders become a site through which racialized and gendered national identity is made, and this making of identity is also an unmaking of those who are excluded, in ways that drive home the importance of intersectionality in analysis. First, the securitization of the border creates violence and insecurity for migrants (Slack 2016; Kocher 2017; Torres 2018; Williams and Boyce 2013) Second, as people without documentation, migrants' other vulnerabilities are heightened, for instance for undocumented queer Latinx migrants (Sandoval 2019; see also Cahuas 2019a; Cahuas 2019b). Movements like that of the UndocuQueers both highlight and refuse this violence through forms of world-making – an opening up of "citizenship" that we will return to later in this chapter. Sandoval (2019, p.3) describes a performance by Jacque Larrainzar:

> As the music concludes, I watch as Jacque proclaims, "Being undocumented and gay, just like death, means having to navigate between two worlds," after concluding her performance for the Día de los Muertos benefit for Entre Hermanos, an LGBTQ Latinx nonprofit in Seattle. To the right of Jacque – above an altar that honors the deceased with gifts, stories, and music – sit 49 photos of the victims of the Pulse nightclub shooting in Orlando, most of whom were queer and trans Latinxs.

Sandoval describes the experiences of UndocuQueers as one in which their lives are shaped by violence of bordering and absent citizenship, but he stresses that people who identify as UndocuQueer also use a "cartography of social practices" to make a life that is livable, in part by questioning the meaning of citizenship.

Legal scholar Michelle Alexander (2012) begins *The New Jim Crow: Mass Incarceration in the Age of Colorblindness* with a story of five generations of American men who could not vote. Jarvious Cotton's great-great-grandfather could not vote because, as an enslaved person, he was not considered a full citizen under the law – until the late nineteenth century in most states only white men owning property could vote. In 1870 the 15th amendment to the US Constitution extended the right to vote, prohibiting the denial of voting rights based on "race, color, or previous condition of servitude," however, this was the **de jure** right (rights according to law), not, the **de facto** or everyday experience of having access to those rights. Cotton's great-grandfather was killed by members of the Ku Klux Klan for trying to vote, and his grandfather and father were also prevented from voting by intimidation and so called "Jim Crow," laws that made voting difficult for minorities. Jarvious Cotton, a felon convicted of murder, cannot vote because of Mississippi's laws, which disenfranchise felons (these laws vary state by state). Alexander uses this example to begin an argument that mass incarceration of Black people in the United States has meant that even though minority voting is protected under the law, anti-Black institutional violence has meant that Black people are disproportionately affected by mass incarceration (and the United States has the highest percentage of its population incarcerated than has any other country in the world – see Walmsley 2013). Geographer Ruth Gilmore describes this mass incarceration as part of a Prison Industrial Complex, in which, "The way the system works is to move the line of what counts as criminal to encompass and engulf more and more people into the territory of prison eligibility" (Loyd and Gilmore 2012, p.43). We will return to these questions in Chapter 10 on security.

Alexander's argument is too important and layered to be adequately addressed here, but two points are very helpful with our goal of understanding the uneven nature of citizenship. First, she argues that the citizenship accorded Black Americans throughout the country's history has been limited (or nonexistent, under slavery), but that this curtailment has taken different forms at different times. While the disenfranchisement of felons is an instance of the de jure (legal) relationship of citizenship, it is also a case in which the structure of the law has reflected racialized ideas of order – for instance the increasing criminalization of specific drugs and harsh punishment for small amounts, and the racialization of specific *kinds* of drugs like crack (versus other forms of cocaine). In tandem with this means of criminalization through the law was a de facto citizenship that continues to be different for Black Americans (and other racialized people, specifically Latinx Americans and Native Americans). This means that though Black Americans are statistically less likely to use illegal substances, they are *more* likely to get in trouble with the law if they do use illegal substances Why? Because Black communities are disproportionately policed (meaning, under increased surveillance), *and* struggle with disproportionate sentencing. Geographers have explored spatial dimensions of this policing, approaching it as foundational to the structure of US cities (Shabazz 2015; Nast 2000; Jefferson 2018, 2016; Cahill et al. 2017), something to which we will return. This means that though Black Americans have the right to vote under the law, *as a population* they are disproportionately disenfranchised, through a combination of restrictions on both their de jure and de facto citizenship. As you will no doubt realize, this is not a universal experience for Black Americans, but the structuring of citizenship as a framework is mediated through these racialized processes.

In this chapter we will consider the boundaries of citizenship and how we might reconceive of it through considerations of "ordinary" citizenship, its uneven qualities, de jure vs. de facto citizenship, and the paradoxes and failures of citizenship.

Ordinary and Extraordinary Citizens: Justice, Care, and the DREAMers

A group of North Carolina college students recently took time from their busy days of work and study to teach faculty and staff about life as DACA (Deferred Action on Childhood Arrivals) students under the Trump administration. DACA is a special program for people who crossed the border as children without paperwork. The students helped faculty and staff understand what life is like for them as they move through the campus and the town carrying the uncertainty of their immigration status with them. They pay out-of-state tuition, but often lack resources due to their parents' compromised visa status. These students are members of the North Carolina Dream Coalition (and you can read about some of their stories at https://ncdreamcoalition.wordpress.com/). Students described themselves as "undocumented" and "unstoppable." Their parents traveled across the border at great personal risk and enduring physical hardship often with the sole purpose of securing safety and a future for their young children. Some of the students could not remember the places where they were born and asked what would happen to them if they were forced to return. Another had been desperate to visit her ailing grandmother one more time before she passed away, and had been unable to do so since the Trump administration had thrown DACA into uncertainty.

The DACA program means recipients are in an intermittent state of anxiety, not only for themselves, but for their parents or loved ones who did not even have DACA. They also fear family separation – as sometimes their parents did not have DACA protection, they had the temporary status, but their siblings might be US citizens. This led them to wonder: "What would happen to my five-year-old sister if my parents and I were to be deported? Why am I struggling to get a degree when my future is uncertain?" While political rhetoric portrays immigrants as burdens on the social welfare systems, these students were eager to point out that they do not qualify for financial aid or in-state tuition, pay out of pocket, and are ineligible for most social services even though they and their parents pay taxes.

What does citizenship mean in this complicated web of obligations, rights, and responsibilities? Research on "Dreamers" complicates straightforward definitions of citizenship.

In a revealing analysis of the case of Jesus Apodaca and other "DREAMers," that is young people brought across the US border as children, Staeheli et al. (2012) ask us to think of citizenship as more than a legal category. Citizenship is also an ordinary web of connection that links people in a community through ethical engagement. They argue that Jesus, the valedictorian of his high school with a scholarship to the University of Colorado, was a citizen of his hometown, Aurora, Colorado, through his engagement in the community and through fulfilling the responsibilities of citizenship. When his status as an undocumented person was revealed, his scholarship was revoked. Suddenly, his "ordinary" dream of going to a public university became extraordinary – even impossible. Paying out-of-state tuition was financially impossible: "something that [had] become an expectation as a social right of citizenship for American teenagers is not available to those who *are citizens in all but legal status*" (Staeheli et al. 2012, p.629). Jesus's case became a flashpoint for the state, with Tom Tancredo, a member of the US House of Representatives calling for his deportation and Senator and Representative Ben Nighthorse Campbell and Mark Udall introducing bills in support of his case.

Young people like Jesus have inspired a push for legislation like the DREAM Act (Development, Relief, and Education for Alien Minors). The DREAM Act has thus far failed to pass, and the Deferred Action for Childhood Arrivals (DACA) program, went into effect in 2012, but is currently in limbo due to recent policy changes made by the Trump administration. The DREAM Act was proposed so that children brought into the country could seek conditional residency and eventually even permanent residency. The DACA legislation allows minors to have a two-year deferral of action on their cases, which they can seek to renew, and eligibility for a work permit. Under the Trump administration at the time of this writing, two DACA recipients have been detained and released, raising questions about its future. Staeheli et al. want us to understand the complex nature of citizenship by thinking about "ordinary" citizenship: that is, how laws are inseparable from ordinary daily life, and hence that citizenship, daily life, and exclusion are all entwined. One question at stake is whether we choose to consider citizenship only as a legal framework, or to consider it as a substantive part of daily life that is more than a legal relationship between people and the state.

At first, the question of legal citizenship might seem quite straightforward – you either are or are not of legal status, and accordingly you either have the rights and responsibilities of citizenship or you do not. But Staeheli and others make clear that in the case of undocumented immigrants, they have the burden of citizenship – following laws, having responsibilities to the state, paying taxes for social security and so forth – but they do not have the rights that other citizens have – such as collecting government benefits from systems they have paid into. The result is, "a hodgepodge of rules" inconsistently applied (p.633). This hodgepodge is further complicated by the spatiality of law and legality, as overlapping jurisdictions of the US Constitution, and federal, state, and local laws may all have slightly different limits and constraints. Staeheli et al. frame citizenship differently for us by introducing the concepts of justice and care: justice pointing to the ways each layers onto the existing story: legally the state may deport those who violate its territorial sovereignty, but from a justice framework, Jesus himself was a child and not responsible. From the perspective of care, there are ethical relationships between Jesus and his family and the other members of the community, and a citizenship based on care would extend protection to Jesus.

The ordinariness of citizenship is also pertinent when we think back to the questions that opened this chapter. If we are lucky enough to be born into citizenship status within the country in which we reside, we have privileges that ease our daily life. If we are the victim of a crime, we do not need to worry that reporting it to the authorities will lead to our paperwork being called into question (though we might have other concerns based on race or gender identity). If we can afford it we can travel back home to family events like weddings or funerals without worrying that we may be detained or unable to return to our workplace.

The intensity of meaning over citizenship and belonging comes into focus when we consider contestations over *jus soli* or **birthright citizenship**. *Jus soli* citizenship is the form granted to babies born in a state, regardless of the citizenship of their parents. Sean Wang's (2017) research on "fetal citizens," has drawn out how political narratives about birthright citizenship connect the intimate and embodied (the space of the womb) to the local. He researched how a Chino Hills California neighborhood, in which one house was accommodating Chinese citizens hoping to give birth in the United States, became connected to the national (the discourses and laws on birthright citizenship) and to the transnational (these Chinese women's desires to provide the *option* of multiple citizenships to their children). Wang connects space to time or temporality in his analysis, showing how an outsized reaction to the discovery of a "maternity hotel," in Chino Hills leads to a controversy that entangles interpretations of the past and concerns about **reproductive futurity**, or the ways that reproduction engenders particular kinds of futures (for instance, a changing demographic makeup). Wang (2017, p.264) argues that anti-immigration politics, "are conducted through a temporal mode of control that relies on anxieties about the future," which brings "the figure of the fetal citizen to the forefront of immigration politics." We will return to the ways that babies and demographic change draw political attention in later chapters.

What then do we make of the spatiality of citizenship? Must it be linked to the state as a natural location? Can we think of forms of citizenships that challenge state borders? That is what some theorists have been trying to do as they work to conceive of transnational forms of citizenship that cross borders (e.g., Leitner and Ehrkamp 2006), and of migration as a fundamental human right (Casas-Cortes, Cobarrubias, and Pickles 2015; Jones 2016). We will return to these questions in a few pages, but for now let us shift to other questions of place and citizenship, now as they are tied to sexual orientation.

Uneven Citizenship, Sexual Citizenship, and Gender Identity

The case of Jesus Apodaca's complex legal relationship to nested jurisdictions of Aurora, the state of Colorado, and finally the US government reveal to us the ways that geography complicates citizenship. For the DACA students and the DREAMers, the *problem* of citizenship is in its attainment, and one potential solution is a path to obtain citizenship. However, this is not the only way that citizenship jostles up against people's daily lives. While for some, it is the process of gaining citizenship that is an obstacle to a full life, for others, their experience is one of **uneven citizenship**, that is, they do not have full access to the rights of citizenship because they are discriminated against due to their racialized identity, gender identity, sexual orientation, or other factors. As we will discuss in further chapters, the state is both an abstract idea, and part of the fabric of our everyday life. In some cases, uneven citizenship is written into the law (for instance, where same-sex marriage is prohibited). Even when people are protected under the law, the law is carried out by all of us from schoolteachers to police officers to the neighbor who calls (or does not call) the police to report your loud party or a teenage boy in a hoodie walking through a neighborhood (Painter 2005). In this section, we will consider this uneven nature of citizenship. First, we will consider this through sexual citizenship and the uneven policing of public displays of affection, and then we will more briefly consider uneven citizenship as it relates to racialization, and to people who consider themselves transgender, gender queer, gender nonconforming or nonbinary.

Sexual orientation offers another example of the unevenness of citizenship from which we can further interrogate citizenship's boundaries and limitations. Hubbard (2013) demonstrates this nicely through a simple example of physical affection. In 2011, journalist Jonathan Williams was kicked out of a pub in central London's Soho neighborhood for kissing his date, also a man. This occurred *despite* the existence of laws meant to protect the inclusion of sexual minorities. Even though these legal codes recognize and prohibit homophobic acts as a form of discrimination, Williams was still kicked out of the pub. For Hubbard, this case allows us to think of citizenship being a process and a negotiation that operates differently at different scales. What does he mean by this? On the one hand, sexual minorities have a right under national law to be protected from discrimination. On the other hand, in this case, the pub owner pointed to a right to regulate conduct within private property. Citizenship is necessarily exclusionary, as we have observed in the cases above in which citizenship is a boundary between those who can be protected and those who are not. However, here even those afforded citizenship under the law experience that citizenship differently, with their rights protected in some spaces and at some scales but not at others.

As Hubbard explains to us, the rights secured at the national level ought to be available in our daily (or "ordinary") lives. However, the nuances of intersecting jurisdictions and the ways that citizens treat one regulate rights and conduct at the "street level." This may mean that heteronormative moralities supersede the rights afforded by national anti-discrimination law for sexual minorities. Hubbard's (2013, p.230) argument is not that we ought to privilege the local over the national, but rather that we ought to "consider the geographies of sexual citizenship and the ways these are determined *through* jurisdictional scale." Anti-discrimination laws are meant to protect evenly across state territory, but in practice they are contingent on the micro-politics of exclusion that vary and are spatially uneven.

Through this example, Hubbard deploys the idea of **sexual citizenship**. Bell and Binnie (2000, p.10) have observed that "all citizenship is sexual citizenship." That is, "the ideal citizen is normatively gendered and sexualized; a subject that exhibits the proper gendered (masculine or feminine) behaviors required of a biologically unambiguous body" (Nash and Browne 2015, p.368). How else does sexual orientation impinge upon the ability to access citizenship? We can think of many: inheritance rights, the right to be with a loved one in the hospital or make decisions on their behalf, the right to marry, the right to have children or to adopt children, or the simple right to consensual sexual activity with someone of the same sex. Discriminatory laws have in different places and cases compromised all of these. In this way, citizenship is *uneven*. As we discussed above, legal citizenship might seem to be a clear-cut distinction that affords rights and responsibilities to those who fall within the citizenship category, along many axes of identity and position in society, from sexual orientation and racial identity to class privilege or disadvantage, *access* to citizenship is not uniform. Barriers to voting may be higher for those with low socioeconomic status or those who are differently abled. Participation in political processes is facilitated by wealth and in some places by gender and race. Following Hubbard, we can see a spatiality to these across geographic locations and also shifting over time. We can think of this unevenness and the gap between law and *experience* of the law in the distinction made between de jure citizenship and de facto citizenship.

De jure citizenship refers to citizenship rights under law. The two gay men on a date have the same rights as a heterosexual couple to freedom of sexual expression and freedom from discrimination based on sexual orientation. However, they do not have the same access to these rights as a heterosexual couple. Their de facto experience is of uneven citizenship and is a reminder to us that citizenship in practice is contingent and relational – that is, it is not evenly experienced by all people and is formed in relation to the institutions, societal structures, and people who make up our daily lives.

Aside from sexual orientation, citizenship is also entangled and uneven for people who identify differently from the sex they were assigned at birth, or people who are nonbinary or gender fluid. How easy does the state make it to have your appropriate gender listed on your passport or other identification? Can you change your birth certificate so that it reflects your gender rather than the gender you were assigned at birth? Do exclusionary laws make even the most mundane moments of your day difficult – such as using the bathroom? Are you at greater risk for physical violence? Does the state police force adequately understand your risks (especially for people of color who are transgender or gender non-conforming)?

Petra Doan (2010) has argued that the pervasive **binary gender system** is experienced as a "gender tyranny," not only for people who are transgender, but also for all people who are affected by the rigidity of these norms. Petra Doan, writing from her own expertise in urban planning, but also as a self-identified trans woman, has honed a research agenda on the ways that gender binaries are entrenched in the urban landscape (e.g., Doan 2010, 2007), and today there is a small but growing literature on trans and genderqueer geographies. The binary gender system sets up gender as a dichotomous or binary system of two opposed, rigid, and distinct poles: male and female. The pervasiveness of the binary system is difficult and even dangerous for those who are **transgender**. For people who are transgender, their gender identity does not match up with the gender they were assigned at birth, while some of us may have a **nonbinary** or **fluid gender identity**, and not easily identify with either gender or identify with both. It is important to note here the culturally constructed nature of gender, and thus its contextually grounded specificity: in many times, places, and languages, gender has been less rigid, more varied, or simply different. In South Asia, for example, *hijra* or *kinnar* or other variants refers to a third gender that could be intersex (having both "male," and "female," qualities), transgender, or eunuch. In North America, many Indigenous groups have specific gender categories that do not fit the male/female binary. Sometimes the modern category "two spirit," is used to signal "a varied and complex array of gender and sexual identities rooted in Indigenous worldviews and lived experience" (Hunt and Holmes 2015, 160; see also Thomas and Jacobs 1999).

As the struggle for transgender rights has become more visible, paradoxically, in some cases, transgender people may become more vulnerable due to backlash and legislation intended to prevent the protection of their rights. This has been evidenced by laws passed (and challenged or repealed) in the US states of Texas and North Carolina, which sought to limit access to restrooms based on people's assigned gender at birth, despite any steps someone has taken to affirm their gender identity (Cofield and Doan in press). That is, even if someone has been a woman for most of their life, they would have to use the men's restroom if "male," is written on their birth certificate. This kind of legislation has paradoxically been promoted as a "safety issue," with ads incorrectly portraying women and girls vulnerable to sexual predation due to "men," being in women's spaces – a rhetorical move that obscures the actually existing violence against transgender and genderqueer people (Bender-Baird 2016).

But is Citizenship the Goal?

Struggles over citizenship are not always uniform and are not always a quest for inclusion. **Sexual citizenship** provides a lens for us to understand how people with minoritized sexual orientations or gender identities might seek equality – for instance by demanding the right to marriage, the right to correct a birth certificate that lists gender assigned at birth, or to have a gender neutral birth certificate. Thinking of sexual orientation in relation to citizenship provides us with a language for people who are LGBTQ+ to seek equality and the same rights that heterosexual couples have. As we proceed in this book, we will unpack some of the related conceptions of power, hegemony, and the social order that are entangled here. To seek the legitimacy of the state is to affirm the legitimacy of the state. For some, citizenship issues like the right to marry are founded in two institutions – the state and marriage itself – that are profoundly **patriarchal** and **heteronormative**. Patriarchy refers to institutionalized governance by men in arenas from government to the business and home, accompanied by cultural explanations for this dominance, and some would argue patriarchal values are embedded in the marriage contract's history as the exchange of a woman as property between father and husband. Heteronormativity refers to ways that the assumption of heterosexuality is embedded into day-to-day life from laws that benefit heterosexual married couples (tax breaks, inheritance laws, immigration legislation) to the ways this assumption is embedded in how people interact and socialize children. We see this in nonchalant interactions like asking your son if he wants to marry any of the girls in his class to children's films in which every central character has a love interest that is not their gender (a prince for every princess).

Some queer theorists, like Jack Halberstam (2008) argue explicitly against inclusion and assimilation for queer people, finding solace and autonomy instead in a rejection of these terms. This could include the abandonment of what Lauren Berlant (2011) has called **cruel optimism**: the ideal of a perfect storybook family that keeps us pursuing a life we can ultimately never obtain in our current economic structure, and thus a dream that hurts us. If citizenship is de facto heterosexual citizenship, then does the pursuit of parallel citizenship for queers suppress the potential for a truly radical queer life that challenges gendered and patriarchal norms around sexuality and private property. That is, does it the normalize of the property-owning nuclear family as natural and ideal? Some scholars and activists have argued just that (Halberstam 2008, 2005; Berlant 1997; Berlant and Warner 1998; see also Sycamore 2008; Conrad 2014), making the case that seeking greater inclusion in the existing structures of government and citizenship upholds and legitimizes historically oppressive and exclusionary structures and defers more radical change.

Building on a different tradition, these rejections of queer assimilation also evoke decolonial theorizations of gender, which suggest that gender itself is part and parcel of the fabric of colonial encounter, and that to accept the gender binary and patriarchal structures of the law is to be colonized (Lugones 2010). Given the challenges of citizenship outlined earlier, what happens at the edges of citizenship? Next, let us consider insurgent or active citizenship, in which those excluded from citizenship create new spaces of political engagement both within the spheres of **formal politics** and in the **informal politics** outside elections and political lobbying. After this, we will consider the politics of refusal.

Citizens Insurgent

After Jonathan Williams spoke out on Twitter about his experience in the Soho Pub, the story was featured in *The Guardian*. A few days later, 300 people showed up at the pub for a "kiss-in," as a way of demanding rights in such spaces (Hubbard 2013). This is an example of what has been called **insurgent citizenship**: citizenship that creates new spaces of political action for the marginalized, rather than citizenship given freely from the state (Holston 2008, p.313). We can find examples of insurgent citizenship across the globe as people have struggled for inclusion or for the transformation of their governmental structure. Holston's work on urban Brazil and the marginalization of squatters in São Paulo shows how demands for existence translate to a demand for citizenship, "a struggle for rights to have a daily life in the city worthy of a citizen's dignity." Holston's language of "insurgent citizenship," reconceptualizes citizenship as a site for struggle. It is important to note, however, there are a host of scholars who have been studying in particular Black women's struggles for citizenship, solidarity, and life, in the context of anti-Black state violence (e.g., Caldwell 2007; Perry 2013; Smith, C.A. 2015; Bledsoe 2017, 2016), some of which we will return to in subsequent chapters.

The work of Holston (2008) and many others, such as Simone (2011), Anand (2017), Sultana (Sultana 2009; Sultana and Loftus 2013), and Valdivia (2008), shows us that citizenship can be active and enacted through engagement with the material world, and bolsters the complexity of such struggles. In this framing, poor people are not passive victims of their marginalization; instead they transform society through their efforts to thrive in an unjust world (Ballard 2015).

Refusal: Indigenous Citizenship Politics

Thus far, much of this chapter has explicitly or implicitly presented citizenship in an existing nation-state as a norm or an aspiration. That is, by reading this chapter, we could arrive at the conclusion that a solution to some of the challenges above – refugees seeking safety, Jesus Apodaca and the DREAMers seeking education, stability, and a future, and the men on a date in a London pub – is a more inclusive citizenship. In this last section of the chapter, let us consider just two ways in which citizenship itself might be considered a problem.

What is citizenship in the context of settler colonialism? If you are the original inhabitant of a place, and a foreign power has come and subjugated your people, made their own laws into the conditions of citizenship, and their state is founded on the elimination of your people (even if the means and terms have changed from outright genocide to assimilation to a multiculturalism that still does not repatriate the land to your people), can you then accept that citizenship? On what terms is it offered? This is the refusal that the chapter begins with, in which Audra Simpson tells an exchange she had with a border guard. Simpson (2014, p.1) writes on the ways that Mohawk nationhood interrupts or refuses to participate in the citizenship practices of the United States or Canada, and begins by asking: "What does it mean to refuse a passport – what some consider to be a gift or a right, the freedom of mobility and residency?"

In the context of settler colonial states, the Mowhawks of Kahnawà:ke are "nationals of a precontact Indigenous polity that simply refuse to stop being themselves" (Simpson 2014, p.1). Simpson's scholarship works to explain the difference between politics of recognition and sovereignty, concepts we will take up again in the next chapter. Recognition seeks to see and honor difference in a multicultural society, but stops short of sovereignty – the autonomy to determine one's own or one's people's affairs. When called to be part of a multicultural society that does not recognize pre-existing Indigenous sovereignty, the Mohawks that Simpson works with may instead enact refusal. Settler colonialism sets up settlers to desire legitimacy on the land, to claim and displace original inhabitants and position settlers as legitimate; paradoxically, multicultural forms of citizenship facilitate this, "through the language and practice of, at times, nearly impossible but seemingly democratic inclusion" (Wolfe 2011, p.32). A refusal to be recognized, whether by anthropologists (Simpson 2007), or through a stubborn consciousness and maintenance of cultural practices and histories and management of membership in Indigenous nations thus sustains sovereignty.

Most of the forms of citizenship and claims to citizenship we have seen in this chapter so far are in explicit relationship to the state. Jesus and his advocates seek for him to be able to obtain state education and for more general rights afforded to the citizen, Jonathan speaks out when his national rights are not protected in a pub, Alexander argues that Black

Americans do not have the same citizenship rights as white Americans, and Holston shows Brazilians demanding rights in the city. Here, let us continue to consider what we learn about citizenship through a refusal of settler state citizenship for Aboriginal and Torres Strait Islanders. We begin with the Aboriginal Tent Embassy in Canberra, Australia.

> Tony Coorey was talking on the way down, he said, "What do we call this demonstration?" We said, "Land rights now." "No that don't sound good." So we kept talking about this in the car. And then we said, "Well there was the Indian fella burnt himself to death in the street over there, poured petrol over him." And Tony says, "Fuck that, you are not going to pour petrol on me and burn me." So that was out of the question. And I remember Billy Craigie saying, "Well there's no good us going on a starvation diet because we have been on that bastard all our lives. So that's not going to work." And we had no idea, absolutely no idea. But it was just land rights. Land rights and sovereignty. Sovereignty was a key issue. Because the two go together, as far as we are concerned. Anyway, we are sitting down there and we are debating this you see. And Tony Coorey went down the hall to the toilet. And he is sitting there with the door open, obviously because he is listening to everything we are saying. And we are in this discussion in the lounge room saying, "Well, what are we going to call it?" There's got to be some name. And out of the blue from the throne, deep down, in the hallway, there's Tony Coorey sings out and he says, "Well this is the home of the embassies, why don't we call it the Aboriginal Embassy?" Done. It snapped like that. It was just wonderful. You know, it was the thing. So Tony Coorey called that out and we said, "Yes, that's the name for it. We'll set up an Aboriginal Embassy."

In this account above, Michael Anderson (2013), a Gamilaroi man from New South Wales, Australia, recounts the 1972 founding of the "Aboriginal Tent Embassy," in Canberra (Figure 2.1). Anderson is recounting in detail the night of January 26, when after a series of longer conversations that sprang from meetings related to Prime Minister William McMahon's January 26 "Australia Day" statement (Anderson, M. 2013). Gary Foley, a member of the Gumbainggir nation, was expelled from school at 15, took part in the Tent Embassy protests, and later returned to school to complete a PhD and become an academic while continuing his activism. He is now a Professor at Victoria University and has also written about the events. In his account, it was Chicka Dixon who proposed the idea, after first floating the possibility of "tak[ing] over Pinchgut Island [like] the Indians in America had taken over Alcatraz. So I wanted to put it in the eyes of the world" (Dixon 1984 in Foley 2013, p.27). Considering the practicalities of this – given the sharks in Sydney Bay – Dixon then recalled how an earlier activist, Jack Patten, had said, "we should be setting up an Aboriginal mission station in front of this white man's Parliament House." Foley describes a series of events that unfolded both as the outcome of years of dedicated activism for Aboriginal rights as well as a stroke of luck, namely, that a loophole meant there was no law against setting up camp on the Parliament House lawn. The cleverness of the staging and fortunate timing meant that they could count on public support from Australians who had voted for the 1967 Referendum in support of Aboriginal rights, and, in Foley's words, "A large segment of the Australian people also appreciated the gentle irony that enabled the activists to make pompous government officials look like fools" (Foley 2013, p.23).

Australia Day celebrates the 1788 date on which the British Royal Navy arrived to establish a colonial settlement in what is now New South Wales; it is also called "Invasion Day" or a Day of Mourning by Aboriginal Australians (Foley 2013, 24; Iveson 2017, p.538). McMahon's statement was a reaffirmation that the Australian state would not bend to the

Figure 2.1 Aboriginal Tent Embassy, 27 January, 1972. Reproduced with permission of State Library of New South Wales and Courtesy Tribune.

demands of Aboriginal and Torres Strait Islander peoples for land rights. This followed a Northern Territory Supreme Court Case that had ruled against the Yolgnu people of Yirrkala, who were trying to prevent a Swiss company from bauxite mining in their land, and a growing Aboriginal Black Power movement that had been staging demonstration (Foley, Schaap and Howell 2013). McMahon's statement declared the mine to be in the nation's interest, and rather than granting land rights for Aboriginal Australians, he proposed land be *leased* to them in the Northern Territory, only temporarily, and only if they made judicious use of the land according to the government (Foley 2013). Thus, this was a denial of land rights *and* sovereignty, the right to determine your own people's affairs.

Before we continue tracing this story and its implications, consider the simple brilliance and spatial strategy of this series of actions. To set up an Aboriginal Embassy is to not only demand, but to enact nation-to-nation contact on equal terms, *not* on the terms of colonizing state to colonized subject. This act is in its own right a refusal to be citizens of a colonizing state (Simpson 2014). An embassy is many things: the place of ambassadors in a city abroad, the place where you get your visa and passport, a place of refuge and negotiations. The Embassy signals that Aboriginal Australians and Torres Strait Islanders have their own sovereignty and exist outside the purview of the Australian state.

At the Aboriginal Embassy, Anderson made the first statement: "As soon as they start tearing up Arnhem land we're going to start tearing up bits of Australia … the land was taken from us by force … we shouldn't have to lease it … our spiritual beliefs are connected with the land" (Canberra Times January 26, 1972, cited in Robinson, S, 1994, p.5). By another fortuitous happenstance, members of the National Council of Aboriginal and

Torres Strait Island Women had been attending a conference at Australia National University: they visited the Embassy immediately and then used the platform provided by the conference to amplify and build on the message sent by the establishment of the Embassy. White students and anti-apartheid activists began helping with logistics, and the Embassy activists also hoisted both Marcus Garvey's flag for international Black consciousness and a flag of their own design (Foley 2013). Even local police became sympathetic to the cause, and landscapers conceded to demands not to turn sprinklers on the lawn. By February 5, a five-point plan was written, focusing on sovereignty, land rights, the right to protect sacred places, and compensation for land that could not be returned.

At stake in the accounts above is the question of the citizenship of the Indigenous people whose ancestors lived in Australia prior to 1788. As we have discussed, **settler colonialism** is a distinct form of colonialism that usually operates as imperial authority (here, Great Britain), sending groups of people to a place to "settle," or colonize that space and slowly replace the Indigenous population. This form of colonization, which is typified by the cases of the United States, Canada, and Australia, is distinct from other forms, such as the British colonization of India, the French in Vietnam, or the Dutch colonization of the islands that would become Indonesia. As the outsiders – here, all Europeans – begin to formalize rule and set up the kind of sovereign state form familiar from Europe, they are violently imposing this sovereignty upon an already-existing Indigenous sovereignty and set of relationships. Wolfe (2006) has argued that the long-term logic of settler colonialism is toward elimination: "to get in the way of settler colonization, all the native has to do is to stay at home" (Wolfe 2006, 388 paraphrasing; Rose 1991, p.128).

Wolfe's argument begins from an analysis of the foundational forms of racism that underwrite settler colonialism. To make his argument, he contrasts, as one example, the **racial capitalism** of slavery and the racial formation that created the category of "Indian," in the United States context – to point to the process of elimination as central to settler colonialism. Racial capitalism (Robinson, C.J. 1983) refers to the ways that the racialization of Black people supports capitalism by deepening differences that create low-cost labor and differential markets that capitalism requires to thrive. **Racial formation** (Omi and Winant 2014) refers to the specific, economically and contextually situated creation and maintenance of racial categories and relationships (which vary across time and space). While Black people who were enslaved and their ancestors were defined as Black through the "one drop rule," meaning that any African ancestry defined a person as Black. The enslavement of Black people added to the wealth of the white state and its white land-owning citizens, while on the other hand the resilience and survival of the Indigenous inhabitants constituted a barrier and problem. Thus, argues Wolfe, the racialization of Native peoples came instead to be defined by the concept of blood quantum, in which you could be ½ or ¼ Indigenous, or, with assimilation, gradually not Indigenous at all (which he argues is the end goal of settler colonialism; for a more thorough unpacking of blood quantum see Dennison 2012). It is important to take care not to think of these racial categories as given – rather the political context of the settler state claiming land and extracting wealth creates them. Wolfe writes:

> Indigenous North Americans were not killed, driven away, romanticized, assimilated, fenced in, bred White, and otherwise eliminated as the original owners of the land but *as Indians* ... Whatever settlers may say – and they generally have a lot to say – the primary motive for elimination is not race (or religion, ethnicity, grade of civilization, etc.) but access to territory. Territoriality is settler colonialism's specific, irreducible element. (Wolfe 2006, p.388)

Figure 2.2   Saif Azzuz, Clarion Alley, San Francisco. 2017. Reproduced with permission of Saif Azzuz. https://clarionalleymuralproject.org/mural/no-ban-stolen-land/

The Embassy enacted the refusal that Simpson describes. Distinct from this form of refusal (which is a refusal to engage on the terms set by the settler), it also created policy change. In February, the opposition leader, Gough Whitlam paid the Embassy a visit, considered the positions of the protestors, and conceded that changes needed to be made to Australian policy on Aboriginal Affairs (Foley 2013). He was elected later that year and officially disavowed the policies of assimilation. Aboriginal groups in Australia continue to work for their future, in opposition to the settler state.

The refusal of citizenship may also be directly related to the refusal to legitimate the sovereign state. We see this in coalitional movements or in the support given by Indigenous activists for refugees and immigrants, summed up in the phrase "no ban on stolen land," (Figure 2.2) and "Refugees welcome on native land," in reference to the Trump administration's efforts at a Muslim ban (e.g., Monkman 2017). In this way, it can also be a call for a different form of citizenship or an abolition of citizenship altogether, as we will explore further in the chapter on security.

What Have We Learned and Where Do We Go From Here?

In this chapter, we have learned both that citizenship can be defined in a straightforward way, as the "right to have rights," and a legal relationship to a state. However, we have also learned that this vision of citizenship does not account for its varied dimensions, the ways it fails, and the ways that sometimes people refuse citizenship itself. For some groups, citizenship may be a partial or temporary answer to their difficulties: a path to citizenship for DACA recipients and their parents, or for refugees, could provide safety and stability. For LGBTQ+ people, equal access to the rights that citizenship provides could enable them to live their lives more fully and safely. That does not mean that all LGBTQ+ individuals desire the same things – so some may lean instead toward the abolition of marriage itself as a patriarchal institution and some may embrace being able to marry a person of their choosing and have the state affirm their choices. We have also learned that the material world – from water pipes to oil wells – can be a site where citizenship is contested. Finally, we have learned that citizenship may also be refused when to accept it means accepting the terms of your own elimination.

In the next chapter, we will turn from citizenship to nationalism, in order to understand how states become tied to a sense of collective belonging.

Keywords

Birthright citizenship   *Jus soli* or birthright citizenship is the form granted to babies born in a state, regardless of the citizenship of their parents.

Citizenship   A legal relationship with a state in which there are both rights and responsibilities – laid out in the state's constitution.

Cruel optimism   The ideal of a perfect storybook family that keeps us pursuing a life we can ultimately never obtain in our current economic structure, and thus a dream that hurts us.

De jure rights   Rights according to law

De facto rights   Actually existing everyday experience of having access to those rights

Formal politics/informal politics   Formal politics refers to engagement with the political system, such as elections and political lobbying. Informal politics refers to political engagement that happens outside this formal sphere.

Heteronormativity   Heteronormativity refers to ways that the assumption of heterosexuality is privileged and embedded into day-to-day life.

Insurgent or **active citizenship**   Citizenship in which those excluded from citizenship create new spaces of political engagement

Nonbinary gender/genderfluid   People who are nonbinary do not comfortably fit in either of the two common gender binaries (male/female), while people who are genderfluid may identity as both at different times or simultaneously.

Patriarchy   Patriarchy refers to institutionalized governance by men in arenas from government to the business and home, accompanied by cultural explanations for this dominance.

Racial capitalism   Refers to the understanding of how capitalism developed alongside and profits from the creation of racialized difference, particularly the institution of chattel slavery and subsequent anti-Black racism.

Racial formation   The specific economically and contextually situated creation and maintenance of racial categories and relationships (which vary across time and space).

Reproductive futurity   How reproduction creates particular kinds of futures (for instance, a changing demographic makeup).

Settler colonialism   A form of colonialism in which the colonizers occupy stolen land and create their own system of laws and governance, displacing or seeking to eliminate local people and their culture.

Sexual citizenship   The ways that citizenship is related to normative ideals of gender and sexuality.

Sovereignty   The right and recognized ability to determine ones own affairs and the affairs of one's people.

Transgender   People who are transgender have been assigned a gender at birth that does not match their gender identity.

Uneven citizenship   Citizenship that is not uniform but varies according to one's position in society, for example due to discrimination.

Further Reading

On migration, the US–Mexico border, and migration activism

Chávez, K.R. 2013. *Queer Migration Politics: Activist Rhetoric and Coalitional Possibilities.* Urbana: University of Illinois Press.

Coleman, M. 2007. Immigration Geopolitics beyond the Mexico-US Border. *Antipode* 39(1): 54–76.

Williams, J. and Boyce, G.A. 2013. Fear, Loathing and the Everyday Geopolitics of Encounter in the Arizona Borderlands. *Geopolitics* 18(4): 1–22.

Ybarra, M. and Peña, I.L. 2017. We Don't Need Money, We Need to Be Together: Forced Transnationality in Deportation's Afterlives. *Geopolitics* 22(1): 50.

On LGBTQ citizenship

Bell, D. and Binnie, J. 2000. *The Sexual Citizen: Queer Politics and Beyond.* London: Polity.

Brown, G. and Browne, K., eds. 2016. *The Routledge Research Companion to Geographies of Sex and Sexualities.* London: Routledge.

Browne, K. and Ferreira, E. eds. 2015. *Lesbian Geographies: Gender, Place and Power.* London: Ashgate.

Hubbard, P. 2001. Sex Zones: Intimacy, Citizenship and Public Space. *Sexualities* 4: 51–71.

Hunt, S. and Holmes, C. 2015. Everyday Decolonization: Living a Decolonizing Queer Politics. *Journal of Lesbian Studies* 19(2): 154–172.

Puar, J. 2013. Rethinking Homonationalism. *International Journal of Middle East Studies* 45(2): 336–339.

On settler colonialism and Indigenous sovereignty

Byrd, J.A. 2011. *The Transit of Empire: Indigenous Critiques of Colonialism.* Minneapolis: University of Minnesota Press.

Coddington, K. 2017. The Re-Emergence of Wardship: Aboriginal Australians and the Promise of Citizenship. *Political Geography* 61: 67–76.

Coulthard, G.S. 2014. *Red Skin, White Masks: Rejecting the Colonial Politics of Recognition.* Minneapolis: University of Minnesota Press.

Dennison, J. 2012. *Colonial Entanglement: Constituting a Twenty-First-Century Osage Nation.* Chapel Hill, NC: University of North Carolina Press.

Pasternak, S. 2017. *Grounded Authority: The Algonquins of Barriere Lake against the State.* Minneapolis: University of Minnesota Press.

Simpson, A. 2014. *Mohawk Interruptus: Political Life across the Borders of Settler States.* Durham, NC: Duke University Press.

Simpson, L. 2011. *Dancing on Our Turtle's Back: Stories of Nishnaabeg Re-Creation, Resurgence and a New Emergence.* Winnipeg: Arbeiter Ring.

Wolfe, P. 2006. Settler Colonialism and the Elimination of the Native. *Journal of Genocide Research* 8(4): 387–409.

On trans geographies

Abelson, M.J. 2016. "You Aren't from around Here": Race, Masculinity, and Rural Transgender Men. *Gender, Place & Culture* 23(11): 1535–1546.

Browne, K. 2004. Genderism and the Bathroom Problem:(Re) Materialising Sexed Sites,(Re) Creating Sexed Bodies. *Gender, Place & Culture* 11(3): 331–346.

Browne, K., Bakshi, L., and Lim, J. 2011. "It's Something You Just Have to Ignore": Understanding and Addressing Contemporary Lesbian, Gay, Bisexual and Trans Safety Beyond Hate Crime Paradigms. *Journal of Social Policy* 40(4): 739–756.

Browne, K., Nash, C.J., and Hines, S. 2010. Introduction: Towards Trans Geographies. *Gender, Place & Culture* 17(5): 573–577.

Doan, P.L. 2007. Queers in the American City: Transgendered Perceptions of Urban Space. *Gender, Place and Culture* 14(1): 57–74.

Doan, P.L. 2010. The Tyranny of Gendered Spaces – Reflections from Beyond the Gender Dichotomy. *Gender, Place & Culture* 17(5): 635–654.

Halberstam, J. 2005. *In a Queer Time and Place: Transgender Bodies, Subcultural Lives.* New York: New York University Press.

Lombardi, E.L., Wilchins, R.A., Priesing, D. et al. 2002. Gender Violence: Transgender Experiences with Violence and Discrimination. *Journal of Homosexuality* 42(1): 89–101.

Moran, L.J. and Sharpe, A.N. 2004. Violence, Identity and Policing: The Case of Violence Against Transgender People. *Criminal Justice* 4(4): 395–417.

Nash, C.J. 2010. Trans Geographies, Embodiment and Experience. *Gender, Place & Culture* 17(5): 579–595.

Rosenberg, R. and Oswin, N. 2015. Trans Embodiment in Carceral Space: Hypermasculinity and the US Prison Industrial Complex. *Gender, Place & Culture* 22(9): 1269–1286.

Chapter 3

Living the Nation

Ask a college student from a small town in India's Himalayan region of Ladakh where they get their ideas about style and they may well mention Korean movies, soap operas, and pop-stars. South Korea is nearly 3,000 miles from Leh, the largest town in Ladakh, and most Ladakhis will never visit. If they did, the language, cultural practices, and food would be quite new to them. Why do not these young people turn to India's own wildly influential global film and music industry, which generates $2 billion a year with up to 2,000 films annually? If you are already a fan of addictive Korean dramas like *Boys over Flowers*, maybe you are not surprised. You might already have songs like Subin's "Circle's Dream" on your phone, and love the cutesy-edgy aesthetics of Heize's "Don't Know You" video in which she torments a giant teddy bear, and the winking perfection of Girls' Generation. But even if you are familiar with K-pop, Korean drama, or have a 10-step K-beauty routine, you might be surprised it is so popular in this region of India. One reason is tied up with India's racial politics and young people's identity strategies (and this case will be described in detail in the chapter on intimate geopolitics). The appeal of the Korean Wave, often referred to as *hallyu*, is also a global story of national identity and soft power (defined below) that impacts not only young people's hairstyles but also understandings of the nation itself (Joo 2011; Kim 2013; Shim 2006).

Distinct from the concept of the state, the nation is a collective of belonging, defined through language, religion, ethnicity, place-based ties, shared history, or some combination of these. The **nation-state** is an ideal form: meaning, not one to aspire to but one that does

Political Geography: A Critical Introduction, First Edition. Sara Smith.
© 2020 John Wiley & Sons Ltd. Published 2020 by John Wiley & Sons Ltd.

not exist in ordinary life. As Gilmartin (2009, p.20) describes, the idea of the nation-state "suggests that the borders of the nation and the borders of the state coincide, so that every member of a nation is also a member of the same state, and every member of a state belongs to the same nation. In practice, this is impossible to achieve."

In this chapter, we will think more about how abstractions such as "Korean," "Sudanese," "French," or "Brazilian," come to mean something in our everyday life. When does a group of people who have never met one another become a "we"? And what are the political effects that emerge when they become a nation? Let us think a bit how these examples connect to and diverge from the previous chapter on citizenship. In this chapter we will seek to understand the nation, the nation-state, and nationalism, with special attention to the embodied and lived experience of the nation.

What does pop culture have to do with politics? Apparently, quite a bit. The Korean wave exists as a form of **soft power**, or power wielded through cultural influence. Korean cultural productions have shifted neighboring countries' perceptions and raised its profile on the global stage; created new forms of hybrid identities; and undermined US- and Euro-centric conceptions of globalization as the global spread of "Western" culture (Joo 2011; Kim 2013; Shim 2006). These arguments point to the ways that the idea of national identity is tied up with culture, but not in a fixed or rigid way – K-pop, for instance, is both a fundamentally global and local entity, consumed in an uneven manner by different people (sincerely, ironically), and profoundly tied to the contemporary moment – not to a distant past. In the late 1990s, consumption of Korean pop culture, particularly television dramas, began to spread across East Asia as residents of Taiwan and China were drawn into watching long-running serials with attractive stars. Soon these shows were popular across East and Southeast Asia and even began to gain traction further afield in India. More broadly, *hallyu* emerges in the context of the broader narratives of cultural independence, decolonization, and the "reassertion of 'Asian' identities that function as a social and cultural response to the global hegemony of the West" (Yin and Liew 2005, p.208). The media and technology-mediated ways that we live today mean that both those in the Korean diaspora and those who have other reasons for enjoying Korean cultural products can engage with and enact imaginary geographies of "Korea" (of course quite rooted in the urban cultural hub of Seoul), through consumption.

By 2005, Yin and Liew (2005, p.207) describe scenes in which Singapore's President S.R. Nathan declared that Singapore's residents are "in contact with Korea in their daily lives," through Korean-made phones and dramas. When Korean President Roh Moo-hun hosted Vietnamese Prime Minister Phan Van Khai at a diplomatic event in South Korea, a rush of Vietnamese officials seeking the autograph of a Korean TV star overshadowed the diplomats' presence. The prioritization of television stars over political leaders may be read by some as unfortunate – a symptom of the overwhelming saturation of global celebrity culture. But perhaps this is not the most helpful way to think about the scene of diplomats lining up to get Kim Hyun-joo's signature, especially given how the Korean state has bolstered this culture through tax incentives and government funding. Instead, what if we were to think about the political implications of the idea of "Korean" pop-culture. Perhaps the ways that diplomats' impressions of Korea, and thus their political actions as well, were in fact shaped by their emotional reaction to the beauty of Kim Hyun-joo and their empathy for her orphan character on *Glass Slippers*. This possibility is captured in the idea of **emotional and affective politics**, or the ways that *feelings*, and *sensory experiences* may influence our political orientations, even before we speak them aloud or articulate them.

Twenty years after the initial waves of diffusion, K-Pop, or Korean pop music has a global following. In 2012, Psy's "Gangnam Style" (ironically, a class critique of one of Seoul's wealthy neighborhoods) exceeded one billion views on YouTube to become the most viewed video of all time (at the time of writing, it is over 3.2 billion views and remains among the most viewed). Since 2017, Seoul-based boy band BTS has risen to the top of global charts, and in 2018 was second in a global list of recording artists based on sales. The global consumption of Korean culture is *also* not a straightforward case of one-way transmission. *Hallyu* studies suggest that K-pop, K-drama and other products are picked up to different results in different contexts. Yin and Liew (2005) demonstrate that the consumption of Korean pop culture reinforces divisions between Singapore's ethnic Chinese majority and Singapore's other major ethnic groups. But K-Pop's following of course has transcended East and Southeast Asia.

In Sweden, K-pop has been described as a racializing force of whiteness, a radical and queer (and sometimes kitschy) embrace of alternative gender roles, and a cultural resource for ethnic minority Swedes who embrace it (Hübinette 2012). Meanwhile, across the border, Norway is one site for K-pop production, and the connections between the K-pop industry and Norwegian music producers and songwriters reflect the inherently globalized industry and how its specific aesthetic relies on and defies tropes of globalization and reflects Korea's globally oriented national industries (Rånes 2014). This allows for these national industries to facilitate culture-based capitalism, made spectacular in scenes like the crossover performance of comedy group Ylvis performing "What does the fox say," with girl group Crayon Pop at the 2013 MAMA music awards in Seoul – in which the kitsch and the reification of national culture is part of the subtext. Even ironic, tongue-in-cheek, or kitschy iterations of national identity shore up the outlines of that identity.

In India, the Korean wave began in the Northeast, a region of considerable ethnic diversity and Indigenous minorities. The spread of (pirated) Korean films was related to animosity toward Indian nationalism and the incursions of the Indian state into the Northeast: in 2000, for instance, an insurgent organization in Manipur sought to ban Hindi films, leading to the increased appeal of alternative media forms (Kuotsu 2013; Srinivas 2016). Residents of the Northeast (and India's Northwestern Himalayan region as well) experience racial discrimination when they are told that they do not "look Indian." Some people belonging to these ethnic minorities feel an affiliation with the aesthetics and facial features of characters in East Asian cinema and this enables a cosmopolitan sense of self and community that escapes the Indian orbit (Srinivas 2016; Wouters and Subba 2013). Paradoxically, then, these trends that are transnational in nature also relate to national identity – as young people describe their embrace of such fashions in relation to feelings of being excluded from the Indian nation (Smith, S. and Gergan 2015). Of course, part of defining the nation is determining who does not belong. Now, we turn from music and film to beauty.

In her work on beauty, geographer Caroline Faria (2010, 2014) takes these ideas further, by demonstrating how concepts of beauty and gender are central to nation-building as evidenced by discourses surrounding South Sudanese beauty pageants held by diaspora, and in the movement of beauty products and beauty ideals that make transnational journeys in the service of the nation. In the case of the beauty pageant, Faria observes how Miss South Sudan beauty pageants, held in 2006 and 2007 in the US Midwest, were about gender and beauty, but also about nationalism. South Sudanese refugees living in the United States were creating a South Sudanese nationalism through voicing national ideals via the contestants, who were hailed as potential role models for a new nation. That meant they had to meet certain criteria, such as Christianity and patriotism, but also embrace of a particular racial identity (for instance through beauty choices such as twists or cornrows rather than a weave). In a series of email exchanges on a diaspora listserv, one woman writes:

> One of the contestants was asked, if I can remember correctly, "What do you see or like when you look yourself up in the mirror?" She replied, "I see my beautiful black skin." It was a powerful message to our young girls to preserve their natural beauty given to them by God. We have much to learn from these young beauty queens. (Faria 2010, p.232)

In another forum, a conversation emerges about hair politics, with one member asking, "Why do they make their hair straight? Are they denying their African beauty?" (Faria, 2010, p.232). As Faria explains, "Here *self*-representation, how a woman wears her hair, clothes and makeup and whether she chooses to use skin-lightening creams, is seamlessly connected to her representation of the *nation*" (Faria 2010, p.233).

I began our discussion of the nation with K-pop and Gangam style, South Sudanese beauty pageants and hair styles in order to forefront the very ordinary and everyday way that an abstract idea like national identity comes to feel real to us. The "Korean wave," K-pop, K-drama, and K-beauty turn up here, in this chapter, as though they were instantly digestible, and referred to a singular "Korean" identity that we could grasp and think about together. *And yet*, what makes a national identity? Within each **nation**, aren't there far more differences than there are similarities? Think of your own sense of national identity, or those with which you are familiar. Does that sense of belonging to the nation (if you feel it) mean you ascribe to a particular set of ethical or aesthetic values? Or that you are just like all the others who identify with that nation? And what does the idea of a nation mean if we are living in a multicultural country?

Imagining Community and Everyday Nationalism: Modernist Theories

In *Imagined Communities*, Benedict Anderson (2006) made what would become a foundational argument for the study of nations. Basing his work on the development of postcolonial nation-states, Anderson pushed for an understanding of nations as imagined communities. In using the word "imagined," he did not intend to dismiss the importance of nations, but rather to emphasize that nations are *created* rather than discovered, and that they have far-reaching political and social effects. For Anderson, key features of the nation are that it is both inclusive *and* exclusive – that is, it must have limits to membership, it is *imagined* because the members of this community do not have personal relationships with one another but feel that they do and it is imagined to be sovereign – that is, to be able to determine its own affairs. These characteristics enable people even to be ready to die for the sake of the nation. In Anderson's (2006, p.6) words, the nation is "*imagined* because the members of even the smallest nation will never know most of their fellow members, meet them, or even hear of them, yet in the minds of each lives the image of their communion." While Anderson drew on many place-based examples in his book, Indonesia, the country that was the focus of his research career, is a startling example of his premise.

An archipelago in Southeast Asia made of more than thirteen thousand islands with approximately 700 spoken languages, the idea of Indonesia as a nation emerged during the twentieth century and was the results of concerted efforts by nationalists to develop a common sense of belonging in opposition to Dutch and in the wake of the Japanese occupation during World War II. Though it is complicated by contradictions and the subsequent treatment of minorities by the Javanese, the official ideology of Indonesia, *Pancasila* (five principles), was developed as a means to unify this diverse collection of places and people by bringing together ideas from the nationalist movement.

Anderson developed his theory of the nation and nationalism as a counter to assumptions that nations simply exist "naturally," and that they emerged in Europe. Rather, he suggested that the nation developed in the eighteenth century as a complement to state sovereignty, and was influenced by the development of nationalist movements in colonized places, in which ideas of community and belonging were developed and spread through key mechanisms of print capitalism – which enable newspapers or other print sources to give people across a region a feeling that the day's news was relevant to them. In 1991, in a new edition of the book, Anderson added technologies such as maps, the national census (which we will return to in the chapter on colonialism), and national museums. All of these build a sense of national belonging. The national map, in outline, for instance, is instantly recognizable to its residents – a "logoization" of the space that calls us to see ourselves within the nation.

If this seems abstract or theoretical, take a moment to envision yourself in a distant place that you have never been, whether that is a major world city on the other side of the world or a distant mountain range where the local folks will not speak your language. You hear someone using the slang from back home or talking with an accent that recalls your own country – do you turn to them to chat? Do you introduce yourself and try to establish familiarity through things you miss from back home? Or expect them to have a similar reaction to the place you are both visiting? Where does this feeling come from? Surely you do not do this in the corner shop near your home. Why do you expect that you have something in common with a stranger? Part of this feeling may come from the exclusionary and inclusionary aspects of community that Anderson points to: in which you form a new sense of collective identity by expecting to share things in common through a belonging that occurs even with those that you have never met. And yet perhaps this feeling of belonging occurs more readily when you are in a context where you feel you may not belong.

But can these feelings of belonging bring us to violence? What is the link between a flag in a classroom or at an automobile dealership and a flag on a battlefield or bomber? To understand this question, the work of Michel Billig (1995) is helpful. Billig asks us to consider how belief in the nation leads to acceptance of violence, or how the "cool nationalism," of flags on a t-shirt or at a picnic can suddenly turn "hot." Billig begins his book on *Banal Nationalism* with a description of US president George H Bush declaring war on Saddam Hussein's Iraq: this is an intentional choice because, as he puts it, "in both popular and academic writing, nationalism is associated with those who struggle to create new states or with extreme right-wing politics" (Billig 1995, p.5). His argument is that there is a tendency to relegate hot or dangerous forms of nationalism to the periphery – to new and thus fragile democracies, to developing countries, or to problem cases of separatism. This is a mistake, because the nationalism that we acquire through our habitus, that is, our daily practices that become part of who we are (Bourdieu 1990), can ultimately snowball into more dangerous forms of nationalism. As Billig (1995, pp.5–6) states, when the troops or Americans back home (or both) saw US flags during the war in the Gulf, they "did not have to remind themselves what this arrangement of stars and stripes was. The national anthem, which topped the US music chart during the Gulf war, was recorded at a football final. Each year, whether in peace or war, it is sung before the game," thus, "crises do not create nation-states as nation-states." Billig's point here is that the nationalism of sporting events or the personalization of the nation into a collective "we" as in, "we won the gold medal," is not so far from hot forms, and in fact it is this very banality of nationalism that makes it so powerful.

This taken-for-grantedness makes the study of the nation more difficult, as nations and national identity may seem "natural." As Gellner observes, "having a nation is not an inherent attribute of humanity, but it has now come to appear as such" (1983, p.6). These theories of nationalism (from Anderson, Billig, and Gellner) emphasize the constructed nature of the nation: that is, a nation is not something that simply exists; rather, it is both consciously and unconsciously created by political actors and ordinary people, and is tied to broader social, cultural, and political developments. Thinkers theorizing the nation in this manner include scholars like Gellner and Hobsbawm, both of whom tie nations and nationalism to capitalism and industrial development in the modern era. Gellner's scholarship is focused on the ways that systems of education and the spread of labor markets through capitalism, industrialization, and urbanization, paved the way for a homogenization of cultural identity, which in turn served a political purpose in supporting the rise of the modern state system.

Anderson's, Billig's, and Hobsbawm's theorizations of nationalism fit under a broad umbrella described as modernist in order to distinguish them from primoridialist theories. Though they are not uniform, modernist theories link the nations and the ideal of the nation-state to the modern era and emphasize its constructed nature, while primordialists believe that nations are natural human phenomena that derive from inherent cultural differences going back to early human communities. For primordialists, contemporary forms of nationalism are the extension of early ethnic conflict. For modernists, nationalism is a political strategy that came into being when it was necessary as a political tool in relation to state-building. Ethno-symbolism or perennialism is a third way to understand the nation which is modernist in its inclinations, but also locates the origin of nations in historical entities (Smith 1991).

National belonging might take varied forms but always contains the threat of violence. It is the drive to purify nations and make them homogenous that has resulted in some of the most violent state actions of recent history. The logic of genocide is grounded in the abstract ideal of a homogenous and unified nation-state, as we see in Hitler's genocidal quest to purify Germany of its Jewish population and all demonized and scapegoated others, as well as genocidal violence during the colonization of the Americas by Europeans, and more recently in Rwanda, Yugoslavia, Cambodia, and Sudan.

Embodying Nations

Most political geographers begin from the idea that nations are created, maintained, and contested by political actors for political purposes. They then take on the question of *how* this happens and what the implications are. For instance, Jason Dittmer has explored how the superhero Captain America has served as a protagonist to tell US citizens stories about themselves. By tracing these stories we can learn about both nationalist values, and about geopolitical conflicts and antagonisms over time (Dittmer 2012). Natalie Koch (2013) has demonstrated how nation-building through sport is part of the "tool-kit" of soft authoritarian regimes such as that of Nursultan Nazarbayev in Kazakhstan. As we will explore in more detail later in the text, feminist scholars have called attention to **embodied nationalism**, that is, the body itself as a site at which nationalism plays out (Mayer 2000; Oza 2007). These scholars attend to how people's bodies are read in relation to the nation, as symbols (like in Faria's work discussed earlier), but also as potential targets of violence. In other cases, "strongmen" embody the kinds of masculinity expected to govern (Foxall 2013; Gökarıksel and Smith 2016).

The bodily experience of the nation can be understood in relation to affect and emotion, or the feelings and sensations of belonging or exclusion, comfort or pain. **Affect** specifically signals the way our bodies know something before we put it into words. **Emotion** is used to indicate feelings, but can be distinct from affect in the theories that scholars draw on to understand what it means to "feel," and how we can communicate about feelings and sensations, albeit in language that does not always adequately express what we mean. Sara Ahmed (2004) has written of the ways that emotions like love and hatred are linked and part of the ways we become part of the nation – learning who we hate and who we love orients our bodies toward some people as a shared identity, which requires us to turn our backs upon others. In the context of Azerbaijan, Elisabeth Militz and Carolin Schurr (2016), for instance, observe youth in Baku becoming part of the nation through participating in exhilarating Azerbaijani dances that enact the nation through the synchronization of bodies in movement.

In the United Kingdom, Azeezat Johnson (2017) and Hannah Lyons (2018) have written about British Muslim women and their feelings for the nation. For Lyons, diasporic Muslims' sense of belonging to more than one place and their affective atmosphere in which they are embedded serves as material that they must engage with and draw on as they work through their understanding of national identity. Johnson's (2017) research with Black Muslim women in Britain understands comfort as a feeling through which they navigate their relationship to a place in which they are often perceived as different or "strange." Johnson attends to the comfort work of clothing practices – from the home comfort of what one of her participants calls "pyjama time," to the practices of "visibly Muslim" women wearing everything from "hip, colorful bricolage," to the black abaya. Johnson observes that Black Muslim women work to create comfort in the spaces they inhabit. Simultaneously, they carry the knowledge that they are perceived as Other, and thus, that they "need to 'know' themselves (in part) through this process of Othering" (Fanon 2008; Johnson, A. 2017, p.282). Johnson describes her research for us as the "Geographer at work," in Chapter 5.

Ideals of gender, religion, race, and heteronormativity unfurl from the centering anchor of the nation. Thus, people understand themselves in relation to these ideals, understanding themselves and others as fundamentally belonging, excluded, or aspiring to belong to the nation, or any other manner of reaction. Jasbir Puar (2007) adds much-needed nuance to this conversation on embodied nationalism through her concept of **homonationalism**. Puar traced the entanglement of sexual orientation, queerness, and racialization in the ideal of the nation and the liberal subject, and observed that it is too simple to say that queer people are always cast out as the Other to a fundamentally heteronormative nation. Puar points to, for instance, **pinkwashing**: using protection of LGBTQ+ people to entrench territorialization of the state and justify imperialism most notably in the case of Israel and Palestine (Puar 2013). Pinkwashing operates along the same tracks as the trope of "saving Muslim women," in which Muslim-majority countries are portrayed as premodern patriarchies in contrast to an enlightened Europe, justifying colonial intervention (Abu-Lughod 2013). In pinkwashing it is queers who are portrayed as culturally aligned with Europe and the US, and in need of rescue. Puar (2013, p.336) argues that queerness operates in and is picked up in multiple ways and can be deployed in orientalist fantasies of Muslim men as "simultaneously excessively queer and dangerously premodern," justifying queered forms of torture and violence (Puar 2007; see also Ahuja 2011).

What Does Nationalism Do?

In the following quote, María Pérez (2016) describes accompanying Ramón Alberto Hernández on a visit to Venezuela's landmark Guácharo Cave in 2008 (Figure 3.1). Hernández, 79 years old at the time of the visit, traveled 472 meters into the cave to cover the same ground that had been covered by Prussian explorer Alexander von Humboldt – known as both an explorer and a key figure in the development of geography as a discipline (Cresswell 2012). At the point in the cave that Humboldt reached, there is a marble plaque that Hernández had helped to place, marking the one hundredth anniversary of Humboldt's death.

Figure 3.1 María Perez in the Guácharo Cave in 2008. Source: Photograph by Alan Warild. Reproduced with permission from María Perez.

The transition from the outside to inner darkness is gradual. Guácharo Cave's first and largest gallery, named after Humboldt, is relatively straight and horizontal, although the path itself sways, climbs, and drops throughout. This twilight zone extends to almost 400 m. More than the darkness, it was the loud cackle of guácharos [oilbirds] that inhabit this first large passage that often overpowers visitors. Indeed, upon exiting the grotto, Humboldt describes being 'glad to be beyond the hoarse cries of the birds, and to leave a place where darkness does not offer even the charm of silence and tranquility'... Hernández recounted memories of past explorations and experiences with de Bellard. And then there was that pungent smell of mud mixed with mounds of the guácharos' regurgitated seeds. Many of these seeds have lanky whitish plants sprouting from them, defying the lack of light. (Pérez 2016, p.702)

Pérez (2016, p.696) herself has her own relationship to the cave, entangled through yearning, and binding substances that "include love, blood, mud, and/in space," as her godfather and father were speleologists who had been part of cave exploration, and she had known of the cave from a young age. We learn of a young Venezuelan girl who grew up hearing about and even yearning for, and thus moving toward, a cave known for being home to nocturnal oilbirds – the guácharos for which it is named. But what do we learn about the nation from this quite intimate geography?

Guácharo Cave became Venezuela's first natural monument during the Pérez Jiménez regime, fitting into Jiménez's vision of "Venezuelan spirit" based in "history, religion, and popular culture" (Pérez 2016, p.708) here this was materialized in the cave, as a site of Indigenous and Catholic culture. The exploration of the cave by scientific associations, and the legitimation of its importance by Humboldt's visit, are events that mark Venezuela as a modern nation – its natural monument status being parallel to some of the mechanisms such as the state's census and national museums that Anderson argues create a sense of community. Pérez describes these as being not background to, but entangled in, yearnings (Pérez, 2016, p.708). Thus, the cave is in national atlases, high school students lead tourists through the cave, and in the variety of yearnings and visits to the cave, it is also placed within a national imaginary and strengthens the idea of Venezuela as a nation. Particularly in the post-colonial context, investments in science and infrastructure are entangled into narratives of progress and modernity.

Nationalism is the belief in the nation and in the right for members of the nation to have sovereignty and be able to determine their own affairs – but this can take many forms and result in different outcomes, from patriotism to genocide to liberation from colonialism. During the twentieth century, nationalism was a driving force in decolonization, as waves of liberation movements rose up to take control of their own lands and expel the Europeans who had colonized most of Africa and Asia (independence movements in the previous century in North and South America had been fundamental to the development of the idea of the nation itself).

The nationalist movements that were a fundamental force in this historic transformation were complex and often fraught with consequences that went beyond independence. Colonial India is a prime example – a diverse region with over 800 major languages and a patchwork of semi-autonomous kingdoms even under British colonialism, how were the residents to form a unified sense of national identity? The lead up to independence from the mid-nineteenth century to 1947 when it was achieved included debate, discussion, and violence in the process of determining what would be meant by Indian nationalism, and it was only in the last decade of the struggle for independence that it became clear India would be partitioned into India and Pakistan (now Pakistan and Bangladesh). From the first war of rebellion in 1857 until 1947, nationalism sometimes served as a unifying force (for instance when Indian nationalists, regardless of religious identity, supported the decolonial khilafat movement that sought to restore the power of the Ottoman caliph in opposition to British imperialism in the Middle East). But the politics of divide and rule that were integral to British governance of India had sown seeds of religious nationalism that came to fruit in the "two nation" theory, which held that, as a good example of the primordialist understanding of the nation, there was a fundamentally Hindu nation distinct from the Muslim nations of South Asia – the regions with a higher percentage of Muslim population.

By 1940, efforts to collaborate and build a secular and multi-faith state that would encompass the region from Dhaka to Karachi had been pushed aside in favor of the plan to partition the region into Hindu-majority India and Muslim-majority Pakistan. By the 1970s, East and West Pakistan could no longer be held together across cultural, environmental, economic, and linguistic differences, and this was demonstrated by the war of independence in which East Pakistan became Bangladesh. We can also interpret active movements for indigenous sovereignty in places from Brazil and Ecuador to the United States to Canada to Australia and New Zealand in part through the lens of nationalism, though it is important to recognize that this can comprise diverse, complex, and distinct ways of belonging that are distinct from the theories of the nation emerging from Europe, even as they confront the European state form that holds nationalism at its center (Barker, 2015; Simpson, 2011; 2014; Trask, 1996).

Can Nationalism be Multicultural in Conditions of Settler Colonialism?

Multiculturalism has acquired a quality akin to spectacle. The metaphor that has displaced the melting pot is the salad. A salad consists of many ingredients, is colorful and beautiful, and it is to be consumed by someone. Who consumes multiculturalism is a question begging to be asked. (Davis 1996)

Nationalist movements seeking independence from existing state forms are not, however, a thing of the past, nor are they exclusive to decolonial movements in the Global South. Let us explore a few examples that show us that belonging to a nation is often not fixed, but is rather a fluid and ambiguous pull that ebbs and flows; nationalism is both inclusive and exclusive (Botterill et al. 2016; Lyons 2018). Multiculturalism is sometimes put forward as a way to escape exclusionary nationalism described above, but this too can be complicated.

Civic nationalism refers to state-based nationalism that can be multicultural in nature, while **ethnic nationalism** is tied to cultural belonging. As you will imagine this distinction is quite tricky in practice – but have it in mind for a moment. In December 2015, Canadian Prime Minister Justin Trudeau was quoted in the *New York Times Magazine* saying:

There is no core identity, no mainstream in Canada … There are shared values — openness, respect, compassion, willingness to work hard, to be there for each other, to search for equality and justice. Those qualities are what make us the first postnational state. (Lawson 2015)

Trudeau's comments are an embrace of civic nationalism – a celebration of **multiculturalism**: the ideal of bringing together people of different cultural backgrounds without expecting assimilation. This idea of the "postnational" state has drawn attention, particularly declared and affirmed as it was amid a perceived global rise in more exclusionary forms of right-wing nationalism signaled by increasingly authoritarian regimes in Turkey and the Philippines, and escalating cultural nationalism in places from India to the United States, not to mention the cultural politics of Brexit (Burrell et al. 2018). A 2017 article in *The Guardian* highlights Canadian exceptionalism, its title asking, "Is this the world's first 'postnational' country?" and opening lines weaving this question into a description of immigration policy and diversity:

> As 2017 begins, Canada may be the last immigrant nation left standing. Our government believes in the value of immigration, as does the majority of the population. We took in an estimated 300,000 newcomers in 2016, including 48,000 refugees, and we want them to become citizens; around 85% of permanent residents eventually do. Recently there have been concerns about bringing in single Arab men, but otherwise Canada welcomes people from all faiths and corners. The greater Toronto area is now the most diverse city on the planet, with half its residents born outside the country; Vancouver, Calgary, Ottawa and Montreal aren't far behind. Annual immigration accounts for roughly 1% of the country's current population of 36 million. (Foran 2017)

Foran argues that Canada's nationhood is partly multicultural and open because it is "incomplete," and that incomplete identity is "a spur to move forward without spilling blood, to keep thinking and evolving – perhaps, in the end, simply to respond to newness without fear." Justin Trudeau's rise has been portrayed as return to an embrace of multiculturalism and other progressive values, and away from the conservative politics espoused by Stephen Harper (Lawson 2015):

> The younger Trudeau has appointed a cabinet from a wide sweep of ethnic groups and made a point of choosing equal numbers of men and women. Virtually every Trudeau initiative, from tax policy to an embrace of the L.G.B.T.Q. community to relations with China, seemed a rebuke to the previous administration. Government scientists, who had been effectively prevented from talking to the press lest they contradict Harper's skeptical view of climate change, now shared their research with reporters in tones of relieved amazement.

Some of this ethic of multiculturalism draws from decisions made during the 1980s. In 1982, under the government of Justin Trudeau's father, Pierre Trudeau, the British Parliament formally passed the Canada Act, which patriated the Canadian Constitution, meaning that from that point forward the political ties between Britain and Canada were severed and the Canadian government could from that point forward change its own constitution without British approval. The Charter of Rights and Freedoms in this 1982 Constitution includes the values of multiculturalism in Section 27. Building on this foundation, the 1985 Multicultural Act (*Consolidated Federal Laws of Canada, Canadian Multiculturalism Act* 2014) declares that multiculturalism is a "fundamental characteristic of the Canadian heritage and identity and that it provides an invaluable resource in the shaping of Canada's future."

The act also recognizes the rights of Canada's First Nations, declares social equality for Canadians of all races, religions, ancestries, and ethnic origins, and guarantees minority rights to cultural differences. The emphasis on difference as something to be maintained or celebrated, in contrast to ideals of assimilation (in which differences are lessened or erased as immigrants or minorities take on the values and practices of the dominant culture) has been described as a "cultural mosaic" or a "salad bowl," as described by Angela Davis in the opening to this section. These approaches are in contrast to the twentieth-century imagery in the United States of the "melting pot," a term popularized after a 1908 play. In a salad, each ingredient remains distinct and identifiable, retains its own characteristics, but in a melting pot these differences disappear.

The values of respecting and protecting cultural differences, as well as the potential for tensions, are encapsulated in an example given by Trudeau in relation to Canadian identity:

> When a mosque was vandalized in a small rural community in Cold Lake, Alberta – which is as conservative as you can imagine in Canada, with the stereotypes around that – the entire town came out the next day to scrub the graffiti off the walls and help them fix the damage ... Countries with a strong national identity – linguistic, religious or cultural – are finding it a challenge to effectively integrate people from different backgrounds. In France, there is still a typical citizen and an atypical citizen. Canada doesn't have that dynamic. (Lawson 2015)

And yet, is Canada's multiculturalism the panacea that is may appear in these representations? It may not surprise you that scholars question many of the assumptions implicit in the discourse of multiculturalism. Drawing on the context of relationships between the Australian state and Indigenous life, Elizabeth Povinelli (2002) argues describes multiculturalism as the **cunning of recognition**. Why? Under a multicultural state, Indigenous people's authenticity must be recognized and legitimated by the state. Through this process they are also acknowledging the legitimacy of the state, and the state is the arbiter of their authenticity. Back in the context of Canada, Himani Bannerji (2000) points to multiculturalism as a strategy of governance that reifies or simplifies ethnic, religious, and other forms of difference into distinct and manageable categories that are then rendered as malleable political objects. In her words, "third world or non-white peoples living in Canada become organized into competitive entities with respect to each other. They are perceived to have no commonality, except that they are seen as, or self-appellate as, being essentially religious, traditional or pre-modern, and thus civilizationally backward" (Bannerji 2000, p.7). The multicultural policies of the 1980s were savvy political moves that defused threats of linguistic separatism and sidestepped First Nations' sovereignty. In her reading, "An element of whiteness quietly enters into cultural definitions, marking the difference between a core cultural group and other groups who are represented as cultural fragments" (Bannerji 2000, p.10).

As Povinelli's work suggests, multicultural forms of national identity pose specific issues for Indigenous people. First, Indigenous people *already* comprise nations that pre-exist settler states like Canada and the United States. Relations between Canada and these First Nations are then meant to be on equal footing, not to be folded into an umbrella nation-state. The logic of settler colonialism is to eliminate Indigenous people, understood to be a barrier to the interests of settlers (Simpson, A. 2014; Wolfe 2006). Thus, lands to be colonized were represented as empty, and perverse logics of elimination even operate through legal frameworks in settler states to reduce the number of people who can identify as Indigenous (Robinson 1983; Wolfe 2006). This means, for instance, that supposedly scientific state definitions of blood quantum are designed to lead toward erasure as fewer and fewer people might "count" as members of specific tribes due to intermarriage (Dennison 2012; Wolfe 2006), while on the other hand, the relationship between whiteness, the state, and enslaved (and their descendants) Black people was figured differently, so that those with any Black heritage were defined as Black (the "one-drop" rule). Indigenous people's pre-existing national sovereignty complicates multicultural conceptions of nationhood, which do not necessarily allow room for *national* sovereignty, only *cultural* difference.

Michelle Daigle's (2016) research on Indigenous–state relations with Canada thwarts an easy acceptance of multiculturalism and the potential of civic nationalism by showing us that there are challenges that are harder to reconcile. The Canadian state has changed its approaches to Indigenous nations, shifting from treatment of them as "wards of the state," to a nation-to-nation approach, acknowledging their right to sovereignty in theory. But Daigle joins other scholars in suggesting that the politics of recognition in which these moves to reconciliation are based are limited (Coulthard 2007; Daigle 2019; Simpson, A. 2014). Daigle's engagement with Omushkegowuk Cree ontologies of self-determination complicate how we might think of the definitions of the nation that we have already encountered. If becoming part of a nation is imagining yourself as a member of a bounded community and if we come to this through many kinds of banal encounters – such as seeing a flag and knowing it stands for our country of citizenship, then we can perhaps think of civic nationalism in a multicultural form. That is, civic nationalism could be a promising alternative to the kinds of **ethnic nationalism** that have the potential to lead to the persecution of minorities or even ethnic cleansing. *But* this is still quite tricky. Even within civic or multicultural nationalism, we might still ask what space is there for other forms of community? What are the limits? Ethnic difference and Indigenous belonging in a nation are not equivalent, to begin. If we take questions of **ontology** seriously, then this becomes even more difficult. This is particularly true if we consider that nationalism is not just about a sense of belonging, but also affirming the idea that nations should have sovereignty – control over their own affairs. This discussion is going to get a little abstract, but we will quickly turn to more grounded discussions of grandmothers' languages, blueberries, and practices that connect to sovereignty in non-state forms.

Ontology is the study of existence or being itself. To say that the nature of existence is something that we can study is perhaps already a strong statement about being itself – it suggests that there are different ways to look at the question of existence – that our assumptions about existence itself may be wrong or that there may be more than one way that the world exists. Daigle is asking us to think about ontology in connection with **relational** approaches to geography; that is geographies that are relational – that make one another through their relationship. The idea of **relational space**, propounded by Doreen Massey (1994, 2005) is that space is made through relationships and cannot exist outside that network of relationships. This suggests a primary interconnectedness of space, as well as a heterogeneous and unfinished nature: specific places or space itself can never have a fixed set of characteristics if it is formed only in relation to other spaces and places. This is a different understanding of the world than an ontology that understands the world as **discrete space** that can be separated from other spaces – for instance, a private property view of the world that understands space through a grid of land ownership. We will come back in a moment to how these ideas – ontology and relational space – may shape what we do with the idea of the nation. Let us return to Daigle's research on the case of Canada and Indigenous relations to explore this further. Daigle lays the ground for us on what she refers to as **Turtle Island** (an Indigenous term for North America, though this term is not used by all Indigenous scholars):

> My argument begins with the affirmation that, prior to colonial settlement, Indigenous peoples on Turtle Island existed as diverse nations defined by their ancestral lands, kinship relations, governance structures, economic trading networks and well-established yet fluid legal orders. (Daigle 2016, p.260; citing Borrows 2010; Napoleon 2013)

Forms of Indigenous erasure and assimilation policy have had profound impacts on Indigenous people in Canada, however, Daigle asserts that, nevertheless,

> Indigenous peoples have remained diverse by continually transmitting and renewing their ontologies though their languages, artistic and storytelling traditions, spiritual ceremonies, annual community gatherings, and through the harvesting and sharing of their local food (Hunt 2014; Napoleon 2013; Simpson, L. 2011; Stark 2010). It is these ontologies and the practices in which they are transmitted, I argue, that cultivate an alternative politics for Indigenous self-determination. (Daigle 2016, 260)

Daigle's argument is important for our consideration of the nation, as well as how a longing for multicultural nationalism to map onto the Canadian state cannot accommodate Indigenous ontology. She joins other Indigenous legal scholars in arguing that pre-colonial ways of being in relation to the land are not commensurable, that is, they cannot be measured by the idea of the nation, nor compatible with the legal form of the Canadian state. The relationship between the Canadian state and Indigenous people has of course been changing over time. In the nineteenth century, Canadian policy was unapologetically geared toward assimilation – for instance in 1857 the "Gradual Civilization Act," spelled out terms of assimilation through which Indigenous people could become "civilized," in order to become fully enfranchised Canadian citizens with the right to vote. The Indian Act of 1867 consolidated policies into one act, outlined responsibilities of Canada to First Nations, and set out the determination of status (that is, ways to define who is and is not Indigenous). Subsequent amendments to the act outlawed some Indigenous religious practices, and required attendance at residential schools intended to break connections to First Nations languages and practices and replace them with supposedly superior languages and cultural traditions that had been based in Europe.

In the mid-twentieth century, new policies, debates, and protests began to change the bounds of this conversation, shifting the discourse from one of assimilation to the framework of nation-to-nation recognition and reconciliation. While this may be viewed as an improvement over explicitly racist policies of the nineteenth century, which intentionally sought to break First Nations identities and traditional practices, some members of Indigenous nations, activists, and scholars call for a **refusal** of recognition. That is, they suggest a political position of refusing to comply or be categorized within this framework itself, suggesting it is only a means of furthering the interests of the state, enabling resource extraction, and managing an intransigent population (Coulthard 2007; Daigle 2016; Simpson, L. 2011; Simpson, A. 2014). This language, of refusal, should recall Audra Simpson's shouted refusal of "American" identity in Chapter 2: "I am Mohawk."

In Daigle's words,

> in order for Indigenous peoples to make claims for self-determination that will be recognized by the Canadian government, they must mobilize through state-sanctioned spatio-legal identities such as "Aboriginal," which are tied to colonial spaces such as treaty territories. (Daigle 2016, p.255)

To make this less abstract, consider the nation of the Omushkegowuk Cree, of which Daigle is a member. Within this nation, the law of *awawanenitakik* asks community members to uphold land-based and place-based responsibilities such as "learning and speaking Omushkego, the Cree language, taking part in our annual ceremonies, and harvesting and sharing our local foods" (Daigle 2016, p.261). This includes Indigenous kinship networks that extend to the land as one form of kin. For Omushkegowuk Cree living on *Treaty 9* territory in Ontario, in the Achikamaw reservation, both assimilation and regenerative practices have defined their experience. The laws of Omushkegowuk Cree such as *awawanenitakik* require locally grounded practices, such as blueberry picking, and hunting and trapping of beaver, goose, and moose, as well as storytelling traditions, spiritual ceremonies, and speaking Omushkego (Daigle 2016). This conception of national belonging thus is woven into conceptions of sovereignty – for instance, think of the right to speak your own language versus being forced to attend a residential school in English *and* the right to maintain a relationship to the land that enables food practices to continue – something that could be compromised by activities like logging or resource extraction.

Here, sovereignty and national belonging are contingent on ontology. Though we might wish to translate ideas easily from one context to another, two ideas presented in this chapter about national belonging and sovereignty may not be commensurable. One suggests that to belong to a nation is to speak a language, eat specific foods, and maintain the environment and kin relationships that enable these practices (for instance, maintaining connections to grandparents who can teach you your languages, and understanding the land as being "an animate being, a relative, a food provider, and a teacher of law and governance to whom we are accountable" (Daigle 2016, p.267). Though there are overlaps, this is a different model of the nation than one that understands national belonging to emerge in the modern era with literacy, decolonization, censuses, flags, and museums that lead to a *feeling* of belonging.

It is easy to see that the goals of the settler state are in direct opposition to the law of *awawanenitakik*. Policies of assimilation and the gradual incorporation of First Nations people into the Canadian state, accompanied by the conversion of territory into private property through treaties and sale or the granting access to resource extraction, all comprise a threat to the practices outlined earlier. In Achikamaw, the 1990s were a period of regeneration, beginning with just one woman, Taryn (a pseudonym), who was a member of the community seeking to revive Cree and Anishinaabe ceremonies, despite resistance on the part of some residents. This involved renewing connections to the land, but also to other lands beyond the territory and to community members who had moved away. Her work and the labor of those who joined her meant that, "While Taryn had grown up, as did her son, in a community where ceremonies were not being practiced, her granddaughter was immersed in these practices from very young age, which she is now passing down to her own children" (Daigle 2016, p.268).

As Daigle observes, the kinds of sovereignty and self-determination expressed here are "not simply different opinions." State relations to Indigenous people that are based on recognition can merely facilitate Canada's own sovereignty, so it is important to grapple with the larger ontological issues at stake in mediating between nations. The question of how First Nations identity is lived for those who have been displaced from their lands for generations remains.

Geographer at Work: Michelle Daigle

Michelle Daigle is an Assistant Professor of Geography and Indigenous Studies at the University of Toronto. She received her PhD in Geography from the University of Washington in 2015. Dr. Daigle is Mushkegowuk (Swampy Cree) and a member of Constance Lake First Nation.

The Relational Geographies of Indigenous Polities and Colonial Violence

Kishiichiwan is one of Canada's largest rivers. It is part of the Albany river watershed, and spans 928 kilometers flowing northeast from Cat lake in northwestern Ontario, into the James Bay. At one time, Kishiichiwan was a fur-trading route, with the first Hudson's Bay Company post erected along the river in 1675 (Long 2010). In 1683, the British named the fort and river after James, Duke of York and Albany, who later became King James II of England.

Mushkegowuk (Cree) people, the original inhabitants of this place, know Kishiichiwan and the interconnected waterways of the Albany river watershed through embodied and storied practice. My kokom (grandmother) and moshoom (grandfather) grew up on the river. Throughout the summer, they would visit many place-names on Kishiichiwan, and would gather with other Mushkegowuk and Anishinaabe (Ojibway) families at "the forks," where Kishiichiwan meets the Kenogami River. There they would visit with relatives, harvest and trade food, get local news updates, discuss pressing political concerns, and renew diplomatic relationships. Kishiichiwan, along with other rivers in the region, were highways for Indigenous peoples, connecting different families, communities, and nations to one another. These rivers activate the relational geographies of Indigenous political, legal, and economic life.

Throughout the twentieth century, as Canada was establishing itself as an independent settler nation, it became increasingly difficult for Indigenous peoples to maintain their relationships with local waterways and thus with each other. Many Indigenous men became increasingly integrated into the settler economy, working in the lumber and infrastructural development industries. Indigenous women were relegated to the domestic sphere, taking on social reproductive labor for the household. Meanwhile, Indigenous children in Mushkegowuk territory and across Canada were forced to attend Indian residential school, an assimilative and genocidal system that was administered under the Indian Act for more than 100 years. During this time, my grandparents returned to Kishiichiwan whenever they could. At times, they paddled down the river to visit their children who were attending St. Anne's residential school in Fort Albany, several hundred kilometers north from my family's community.

Indigenous relational geographies were also severely ruptured as Indigenous peoples were forcefully relocated to reserves in the nineteenth and twentieth centuries. They became increasingly subjected to settler colonial jurisdictions, including private property laws that restricted their movement and mobility within and beyond their home territories. Settler colonial laws and jurisdictions were pivotal technologies of power that violently dispossessed Indigenous peoples of their human and non-human relations, to secure the Canadian government's access and control of Indigenous land for settlement and capitalist developments. These colonial laws, including the Indian Act, still exist today with the aim of controlling and disciplining Indigenous peoples in Canada.

Today, Kishiichiwan and Mushkegowuk land and waterways are entangled in mining developments. De Beers, an international company specializing in the mining and trading of diamonds, opened the Victor Mine outside of Attawapiskat First Nation in 2008. Proposed mining developments dubbed the "Ring of Fire" are reported to contain the largest chromite deposit in North America, with an estimated value of 30 billion dollars. These mining developments, which Indigenous communities have not provided full, informed, and prior consent for, are tied to rising levels of mercury and methylmercury in the Albany and Attawapiskat rivers. This is disproportionately impacting Indigenous women and children, as well as pike, pickerel and caribou. Indigenous women, for example, are experiencing higher cases of infertility, miscarriages, and birth deformities (Daigle 2018).

My research brings Geography into critical dialogue with Indigenous Studies to examine colonial capitalist violence on Indigenous lands-waters-bodies reproduced through mining extraction in my home territory. I do this research as a member of the Mushkegowuk nation, by seeking out the knowledge and expertise of land and water caretakers and defenders in my home territory. While I interview people, much of my work is grounded in practice, by taking part in community events, including land-based practices through which I learn about Mushkegowuk diplomacies and law.

One strand of my research examines how Mushkegowuk waterscapes re-activate Indigenous political geographies and accountabilities that counter the divisive colonial politics that is reproduced through current extractive developments. In recent years, Mushkegowuk people have organized community paddles on regional waterways, to teach youth about Mushkegowuk conceptualizations of territoriality and kinship relationships with human and non-human relations. Many of these paddles are aimed at educating community members about the impacts of unconsented and unsustainable resource extractive developments. I am particularly interested in how Indigenous movement on waterways activates a terrain of political agency that ruptures colonial framings of Indigenous space as solely confined to reserves. Simultaneously, I am interested in how Indigenous movement and mobility expands conceptualizations of Indigenous peoples as tied to particular places (for example, sacred place-names, and even our home territories), to more expansive and relational framings of Indigenous space.

The second stream of my research draws on Indigenous feminist and youth scholarship and activism to examine the hetero-patriarchal workings of extractive mining developments, and the disproportionate impacts embodied by Indigenous women and youth. I am specifically interested in expanding conceptualizations of extractive violence on Indigenous lands – and specifically on Indigenous lands in rural areas – to center everyday experiences embodied by Indigenous women and youth, and how those can be traced to interconnected forms of state-sanctioned violence in urban areas, such as in the northern city of Thunder Bay (Talaga 2017). In examining this violence, I center the resistance and resurgence these women and youth embody on an everyday basis, and the political and transformative visionaries that they are.

Separatism, Regionalism, and Independence Movements

Separatism is when people in one region create a movement to break away from the country in which they reside due to a sense of national belonging. Separatist movements can be found across the globe, from places like the Basque region between France and Spain to the Kashmiri separatist movement in India (Behera 2000; Duschinski et al. 2018; Rai 2004; Zutshi 2010). Related to separatism is **irredentism**, in which one country makes a claim that part of another country is rightfully theirs. The case of South Ossetia, in the former Soviet republic of Georgia, is a case of irredentism as the separatists remain entangled in Russian politics, and bolster Russian claims to Georgia (Kabachnik 2012; Toal and O'Loughlin 2013). These kinds of disputes can contain multiple layers. For instance, in the case of the state of Jammu and Kashmir, Pakistan and India both claim the entire state (and national maps of each country generally include the entire state as part of their territory, while in the Srinagar Valley, some Kashmiris have demanded independence, while majorities in the Jammu and Leh-Ladakh regions wish to remain with India. As may already be evident, these conflicts often stem from historical connections or are the artifacts of colonization or decolonization.

Nationalism on Edge

In 1906, a young British gentleman returned from a long journey in the upland reaches of what is now northern Iraq and Syria. During his travels he wandered in extravagant style between Mosul, Aleppo, and southern Anatolia for some time, venturing even into the Kurdish mountains at Jabal Sinjar. Returning to England, he followed the fashion of the times for a man of his position, writing up his exploits as a window onto the state of the Ottoman Empire. This he presented to the Royal Geographical Society in London in 1907, where it was popularly received and helped launch a career in the British Foreign Office, one with far-reaching consequences for state-formation in the Middle East. His name was Mark Sykes.

> More than a century later, a militant, garbed in black and sporting a dusty black baseball cap, speaks Sykes's name into a camera. The man is Chilean, and his English is peppered with religious utterances in Arabic. Smiling meaningfully, he ambles up an earthen berm that rises unnaturally above the sun-blasted scrub of eastern Syria. With apparent ease he crests this modest heap of soil, calling it the "barrier of Sykes-Picot," the material contour dividing one state (Syria) from another (Iraq). The usual performances of state sovereignty are conspicuously absent, all save a few: the sign identifying the quarters of a commando unit, its soldiers long gone; the patches they cut from their uniforms as they fled, strewn across the dirt floor; an Iraqi flag. Each of these he proceeds to tread on in turn with a studied, theatrical indifference. "They say that [Caliph] Abu Bakr al-Baghdadi is the breaker of barriers," he says. "God willing, we will break the barrier of Iraq, Jordan, *Lubnan* [Lebanon] … all the countries."

In this quote, Ali Nehme Hamdan places two moments in tension: the drawing of borders through the Sykes-Picot line, and the work to undo borders by Islamic State (IS) militants (Hamdan 2016, p.605). Hamdan simultaneously demonstrates the aspirations to grand narrative in the rhetoric of IS, as well as the "slapdash" ways that this takes place and also fails on the ground (Clark 2017; Hamdan 2016). Nationalism references history but it is critical to attend to the omissions and selective politics of how that history is referenced. In the 2016 US presidential election, then candidate Donald Trump ran on the slogan, "Make America Great Again."

The past decade has been one in which some forms of communication and mobility have increased alongside a transformation of nationalism. From Brexit and the intensification of debates about migration and cultural transformation in Europe to the (to some) surprising rise of Trump's "America First" nationalism, to the Islamic State's declaration of an alternative form of political organization, understandings of the process and consequences of "imagining community," are as relevant as they were during the period of decolonization or the beginnings of the modern nation-state system. To understand these phenomena we have to go further than Anderson's conceptions. To understand the idea of the nation as it relates to and complicates state formation, let us consider the case of the IS through the work of Ali Hamdan.

Though the promotional materials of the IS are intended to counter the modern nation-state, we can learn about processes of nationalism through the strategies that IS has used to create a novel and destructive territorial and political strategy. The emergence of IS must be placed in context of the ongoing history of what Ann Laura Stoler (2013) has called colonial ruination. IS did not emerge in a vacuum, but in the context of the "Global War on Terror," that has been ongoing since 2001, and which is of course framed even by its proponents as an endless war – as it has been named in response to a *tactic*, unbounded by time or space, and then, potentially, without end. That is, terror is a *method*, or *mode*; it cannot be eradicated, and thus can serve as justification for a war that can likewise never end.

In June 2014, The Islamic State in Iraq and Syria, also referred to as Daesh, ISIS or IS, proclaimed that there was a new Caliphate based in Syria and Iraq, with Abu Bakr al-Baghdadi as Caliph. These are the same terms used by the Indian nationalists in the historical moment of nationalist and anti-imperial unity in the early-twentieth century and have some resonance with discourses of anti-imperialism, but in the worldview of IS they have a quite different formulation in regard to religious difference. Before we think about what IS teaches us about nationalism, it is important to note a few things about the political use of Islam *and* the way that political Islam is represented in global media.

First, and likely most obviously, Al-Baghdadi's views and those of his followers diverge dramatically from mainstream Islam (see, e.g., Hamdan 2016; Pelletier et al. 2016). Second, even while we acknowledge the fundamental differences between Islam as practiced globally and the political actions and idiosyncratic interpretations of Islam propounded by IS, we must take care not to fall into what Mamdani (2004) has demonstrated to be a false dichotomy between modern and secular "good Muslims," and traditional and dangerous, "bad Muslims," as this is a historical misreading of the origins of radical Islamism. Furthermore, as Asad (2003) has demonstrated, the representations of Islam often rely on a fundamentally misleading distinction between secularism and religion, which he argues is a political move that favors European formulations of "East vs. West," and "Tradition vs. Modernity." These connections, which posit Europe as the source of rational and secular thinking, in opposition to the Middle East, which is constructed as being bound to religion, have roots in what Edward Said (1979) has termed **Orientalism**. Orientalism is ways of representing "the East" as static and trapped in the past, which justifies the colonial intervention of "the West." We will return to these themes in subsequent chapters, but it is important to keep them in mind when considering the actions of IS, as well as the context of the development of IS.

The use of the caliphate language by IS calls to mind the historical caliphates such as the Abbasids and the Ottoman Empire, thus echoing on a global scale the kinds of vague allusion to historical greatness we find in "Make America Great Again" rhetoric. Hamdan (2016), writing on the geopolitics of IS both engages with IS rhetoric and demonstrates how we err by privileging this rhetoric over practices on the ground. At stake is the IS narrative around the Sykes-Picot lines that divided the Ottoman Empire in the wake of World War I. As Elden (2009) and Culcasi (2014) (among others) have observed, these lines were drawn according to European colonial logics, but Hamdan (2016) points out that we can fault imperial arrogance without ascribing to a belief that there were more "'natural" pan-ethnic nation-states that would have inevitably formed instead.

The rhetoric of IS presents its regime as, "the inevitable, singular alternative to colonial boundaries in the region" and "claims to reject the bounded territoriality of the Westphalian [modern nation-state] order writ large," contrasting it with the caliphate as a "global political order characterized by the bound*less* sovereignty of God" (Hamdan 2016, p. 608). *Dabiq*, the IS magazine, contains repeated iconography of "border-smashing," but Hamdan contends that these are rhetorical gestures, and that any analysis of IS that focuses on a specifically *Islamist* territoriality "edges uncomfortably to essentialism," as though Islamism is always already a challenge to sovereign territoriality and could not be a response to other questions or a means to other purposes. For Hamdan, ISIS's politics are not a coherent philosophy, but are more of a "slapdash," and pragmatic set of strategies in reaction to neoliberal economic change and the ongoing ruination (Stoler 2013) of American imperialism. This reaction set the stage for ISIS institutions to gain traction. For Hamdan (2016, p.620), "the politics of place in the Jazirah have greatly shaped ISIS's political practice more than its vision does." Here, he asks us to go beyond thinking only of questions of territory and political Islam, and to think instead of the politics of *place* that offer to create an alternative form of belonging, one which "poses a very tangible, murderous alternative to the contemporary states of the Middle East in ways that have irrevocably transformed the everyday life of thousands already" (Hamdan 2016, p. 626). Hamdan asks that we not unduly perpetuate grand narratives that ISIS propounds (as in the Sykes-Picot line video above), but rather understand the ways that ruination on the ground enables haphazard tactics of oppositional place-making to gain traction.

Military strikes in Syria, Iraq, and Afghanistan have had profound effects in the region, decimating cities, creating ontological insecurity, that is fear of extinction, and contributing to a swell of refugees fleeing the region (Basham 2018; Johnson, C. et al. 2011; Jones 2016; Kovras and Robins 2016). We will return to these lives in the chapters on security and critical geopolitics.

What Have We Learned and Where Do We Go From Here?

In this chapter, we have learned about the ideas of nation and nationalism as political tools that forge group identity across a wide array of contexts, from independence movements to conceptions of native sovereignty. We learned that nations are "imagined communities," that can change over time and be used to different purposes, and that they have embodied and material effects. In the chapters that follow we will pick up on these themes of belonging, exclusion, and sovereignty, as we explore how ideas of difference fit into the concepts and legal frameworks of citizenship and the material realities of the city.

In the next chapter, we will build on what we have learned so far by thinking more broadly about power and how it is deployed through spatial relationships.

Keywords

Affect   How our bodies know or experience something before we put it into words.
Civic nationalism   State-based nationalism that can be multicultural in nature.
Discrete space   Space that can be separated from other spaces.
Embodied nationalism   The body as a site at which nationalism plays out.
Emotion   Feelings, but can be distinct from affect in the theories that scholars draw on to understand what it means to "feel," and how we can communicate about feelings and sensations, albeit in language that does not always adequately express what we mean.
Emotional and affective politics   The ways that *feelings*, and *sensory experiences* may influence our political orientations, even before we speak them aloud or articulate them.
Ethnic nationalism   Nationalism tied to cultural belonging.
Homonationalism.   How sexual orientation, queerness, and racialization (and "tolerance" of these differences) are bound in representations of the nation.
Irredentism   A political situation in which one country makes claim that part of another country is rightfully theirs.
Ontology   The study and understanding of existence or being itself.
Pinkwashing   The use of purportedly LGBTQ-friendly policies to justify imperialism.
Nation   A collective of belonging, defined through language, religion, ethnicity, place-based ties, shared history, or some combination of these.
Nation-state   A state (political entity) in which national boundaries match political boundaries. That is, one in which a nation is homogenous and has self-governance.
Nationalism   The belief in the nation and in the right for members of the nation to have sovereignty and be able to determine their own affairs – but this can take many forms and result in different outcomes.

Multiculturalism   The ideal of bringing together people of different cultural backgrounds without expecting assimilation.

Relational space   The idea that space is made through relationships and cannot exist outside that network of relationships.

Refusal   A political position that does not agree to comply or be categorized within the legal or political framework itself, suggesting it is only a means of furthering the interests of the state.

Separatism   When a group of people in one region create a movement to break away from the country in which they reside due to a sense of national belonging.

Soft power   Power wielded through cultural influence.

Turtle Island   An Indigenous term for North America, though this term is not used by all Indigenous scholars.

Further Reading

Affect and emotion

Ahmed, S. 2004. *The Cultural Politics of Emotion*. New York: Routledge.

Nayak, A. 2011. Geography, race and Emotions: Social and Cultural Intersections. *Social & Cultural Geography* 12(6), 548–562.

Pile, S. 2010. Emotions and Affect in Recent Human Geography. *Transactions of the Institute of British Geographers* 35(1): 5–20.

Thien, D. 2005. After or Beyond Feeling? A Consideration of Affect and Emotion in Geography. *Area* 37(4): 450–454.

Indigenous sovereignty

Coulthard, G.S. 2007. Subjects of Empire: Indigenous Peoples and the "Politics of Recognition" in Canada. *Contemporary Political Theory* 6(4): 437–460.

Daigle, M. 2016. Awawanenitakik: The Spatial Politics of Recognition and Relational Geographies of Indigenous Self-determination. *The Canadian Geographer/Le Géographe Canadien* 60(2): 259–269.

Daigle, M. 2018. Resurging through Kishiichiwan: The Spatial Politics of Indigenous Water Relations. *Decolonization: Indigeneity, Education & Society* 7(1): 159–172.

Dennison, J. 2012. *Colonial Entanglement: Constituting a Twenty-First-Century Osage Nation*. Chapel Hill, NC: University of North Carolina Press.

Hunt, S. 2014. Ontologies of Indigeneity: The Politics of Embodying a Concept. *Cultural Geographies* 21(1): 27–32.

Pasternak, S. 2017. *Grounded Authority: The Algonquins of Barriere Lake Against the State*. Minneapolis, MN: University of Minnesota Press.

Simpson, A. 2014. *Mohawk Interruptus: Political Life across the Borders of Settler States*. Durham, NC: Duke University Press.

Simpson, L. 2011. *Dancing on Our Turtle's Back: Stories of Nishnaabeg Re-Creation, Resurgence and a New Emergence*. Winnipeg: Arbeiter Ring.

Multiculturalism

Bannerji, H. 2000. *The Dark Side of the Nation: Essays on Multiculturalism, Nationalism and Gender*. Toronto, ON: Canadian Scholars' Press.

Davis, A.Y. 1996. Gender, Class, and Multiculturalism: Rethinking "Race" Politics. In A. Gordon and Ch. Newfield (eds), *Mapping Multiculturalism*. Minneapolis, MN: University of Minnesota Press, pp.40–48.

Mitchell, K. 2004. Geographies of Identity: Multiculturalism Unplugged. *Progress in Human Geography* 28(5): 641–651.

Povinelli, E.A. 2002. *The Cunning of Recognition: Indigenous Alterities and the Making of Australian Multiculturalism*. Durham, NC: Duke University Press.

Nationalism

Anderson, B. 2006. *Imagined Communities: Reflections on the Origin and Spread of Nationalism*. London: Verso Books.

Billig, M. 1995. *Banal Nationalism*. Los Angeles: Sage.

Dittmer, J. 2012. *Captain America and the Nationalist Superhero: Metaphors, Narratives, and Geopolitics*. Philadelphia: Temple University Press.

Gilmartin, M. 2009. Nation-State. In C. Gallaher, C.T. Dahlman, M. Gilmartin et al. (eds), *Key Concepts in Political Geography*. Thousand Oaks, CA: Sage, pp.19–27.

Mayer, T. 2000. *Gender Ironies of Nationalism: Sexing the Nation*. Hove, UK: Psychology Press.

Mountz, A. 2004. Embodying the Nation-State: Canada's Response to Human Smuggling. *Political Geography* 23(3): 323–345.

Puar, J.K. 2007. *Terrorist Assemblages: Homonationalism in Queer Times*. Durham, NC: Duke University Press.

The "war on terror"

Abu-Lughod, L. 2013. *Do Muslim Women Need Saving?* Cambridge, MA: Harvard University Press.

Amoore, L. 2007. Vigilant Visualities: The Watchful Politics of the War on Terror. *Security Dialogue* 38(2): 215–232.

Culcasi, K. 2014. Disordered Ordering: Mapping the Divisions of the Ottoman Empire. *Cartographica* 49(1): 2–17.

Elden, S. 2009. *Terror and Territory: The Spatial Extent of Sovereignty*. Minneapolis: University of Minnesota Press.

Gregory, D. 2011. The Everywhere War. *The Geographical Journal* 177(3): 238–250.

Mamdani, M. 2004. *Good Muslim, Bad Muslim: America, the Cold War, and the Roots of Terror*. New York: Pantheon Books.

Said, E. 1979. *Orientalism*. New York: Vintage.

Chapter 4

Power/Territory

In an article titled "If Trayvon were Pakistani", analyst Micah Zenko contrasted President Obama's sensitive approach to domestic racialized killing with his notorious campaign of drone attacks in the highlands of northwest Pakistan. Especially controversial were the so-called "signature strikes" Obama repeatedly authorized – drone killings based on "appearance, associations, and statistical propensity to violence" (Zenko 2013) of racialized target populations. While the situation of young men in northwest Pakistan and the urban US are different in a multitude of ways, Zenko noticed a common thread. Populations in both instances were subject to violence based on racial and geographical assumptions – who and where they were (or were not supposed to be).

(Akhter 2019, p.1)

In the above excerpt, Majed Akhter reflects on the relationship between populations, territory, and violence. Akhter (2019) connects violence to people understood to be out of place: the anti-Black violence in a Florida neighborhood that killed teenager Trayvon Martin and drone strikes in Pakistan (a topic to which we will return in a few chapters). Power and violence are spatial phenomena and practices, from the macro space of a globe, which we currently understand to be divided into the sovereign territory of states, to the space of neighborhoods and cities, which we expect to be governed by property law or codes of public conduct. Here we unpack spatial power relations. We will consider power not as a thing that one can possess, but rather a web of relationships between people and the non-human world from animals to oil. We will consider how territory is fundamentally space in relationship to power and distinguish between the fundamental concepts of human geography: space and place.

The operations of power in space affect every aspect of our lives. Perhaps this occurs most profoundly through the ways that we do not come to think of power relations at all, but perceive them as normal or natural states of being in the world. Does it seem natural to you that there are wealthy neighborhoods and poor neighborhoods in your town? When you imagine the world, is one of the images that comes to mind that of the political map, with the earth divided into colored shapes denoting the countries? These are both the manifestations of political, economic, and social power in space, but seem quite natural to us, such that now we begin even our imagining of the world as already compartmentalized into jurisdictions. The world that we imagine is **territorialized**. It has been demarcated into spaces that are under the jurisdiction of the state: **territory**. Land and water are then further internally demarcated into publically and privately held entities, in which the enclosed nature of private property is emphasized through the proliferation of gated neighborhoods discussed later. As we will discuss in this chapter, the territorialized space discussed is not natural; it is an active archive of power struggles.

Carl Dahlman (2009, p.77) defines territory most crisply as "the spatial extent of the state," meaning that it is a "portion of the earth's surface claimed by or associated with a particular group or political entity." This definition is thus caught up in the historical origins of the European state form and its theorization, which will be discussed in greater detail in the next chapter. Territory is land or water that has been acted upon as an exercise of power (Cowen and Gilbert 2008). This could entail walling, fencing, or the stationing of military troops, but these physical manifestations of power are founded upon a host of other technologies such as mapping, census-taking, surveillance, and the production of knowledge. Territory can also take on a livelier and embodied form in the ways that bodies stake out territory or exclude others, or in the way that the body itself can become a kind of territory, as discussed in the intimate geopolitics chapter.

Stuart Elden (2009; 2013b) tells us we cannot understand territory without understanding a fundamental but also shifting relationship to **terror**. Elden (2009, p.xxi), asks us to think of terror not only as nonstate actors (terrorist organizations) but also as state actions, "from the bombs, missiles, and bullets of death and destruction to the imagined geographies of threat and response." Elden (2009) changes how we think about terrorism: what if terror is not an aberration, but is rather central to the definition of territory itself? Elden uses Giorgio Agamben's (2005) idea of the **state of exception**. The state of exception is a moment when the sovereign (the decision-maker, whether king or governing body) declares an exception to the ordinary rules of law. This is usually done in a moment of crisis. After the attacks of September 11, 2001, for instance, the US government pushed through the enactment of the Patriot Act, which enhanced surveillance and limited civil liberties. This act might have faced more resistance had it not come in the wake of the terrorist attack. The power to create an exception to the rule is the sign of the sovereign, a sign of power more so than the ability to make the rules. Elden demonstrates the pervasiveness of the exception. In our next chapter, on state formation, we will pursue Elden's work and this train of thought further to consider why and how territorial sovereignty was embraced at the moment that Europeans undermined the sovereignty of others.

There are a few ways we might understand the operation of power, but by distinguishing them the intent is not to suggest that power is operating in one way or another – people may be using multiple strategies at one time or engaged in what we might think of more as a web of power relations. Thinking about the forms that power takes will enable us to gain a clearer understanding of its processes, even as we know that things are always more nuanced in life than in the theorization of life. In the following sections we will consider theoretical frameworks for understanding power, and then we will turn to two case studies for understanding the relationship between power, territory, and space: the indeterminate landscape of the Arctic, and the case of neighborhoods in the United Kingdom and South Africa.

Power

Power has been approached by political geographers along a number of axes. Allen (2003), distinguishes between **inscribed power** – power individuals possess in relation to other individuals or entities, power as a resource to make a specific thing happen (for instance through military action) and **power as technique** (for instance, strategies of knowledge production as a form of power). Being the president gives you inscribed power. In that role you may use various techniques or methods of power, from military coercion to the production of knowledge that persuades citizens of your country to agree to your policies. We will begin to understand power here by thinking through some of the forms that power takes. We will return to these over the course of the book and add nuance and depth, and think more specifically about how they play out in relation to politics and to our spatial understandings of the world. In this chapter, we will sketch out how these dynamics play out spatially. Let us start with five (intersecting) lenses:

- power as coercion
- power as ontological or epistemological action
- power as technique
- power and class conflict
- power as desire

Power as coercion

In thinking of political geography and power, we might first think of military might. The number of ships in a navy or bombers at air bases signal the power that a country has to dominate others or protect itself from incursions. This is power as violence or threat of violence. At other scales, we might think of law enforcement in cities or towns as the threat of force to maintain law and order. Power as coercion is also street crime (give me your wallet or I will hurt you), or physical bullying on the playground. Physical force and threat of damage or harm is an important form of power, but not all power operates this way – in fact this might be understood as a last resort or a symptom of other kinds of violence. This form of power is expensive, cannot be enacted without evoking deep ethical questions, can lead to loss of life, and backfires frequently, whether in war or through police security practices. Perhaps most importantly, the *possibility* of physical violence *and* the likelihood that it will be used against specific classes and identity groups is created by political, social, and cultural processes.

When is violence is considered legitimate? Max Weber distinguishes the state (which will be covered more thoroughly in the next chapter) as the institution that claims legitimate use of violence (Weber 1946, p.78). Police and military are expected to use violence in ways that civilians are not. The role of state institutions and law in determining who can and cannot use violence are foundational to our expectations about life in a state, and the functioning of a state is likewise often judged by its ability to maintain that monopoly over violence. It is not only that the state can deploy violence (for instance during arrests or even in administering death for states with the death penalty), but also that the state adjudicates whether violence used by its citizens was legitimate (for instance, justified by self-defense). In this chapter, we will attend less to physical violence itself than to the structural forces that enable it, such as those that structure our understanding of the world and our relationship within it.

Power as ontological and epistemological action: Power/knowledge

What sets the stage for violence to occur? Whether it is state violence or interpersonal, *something* enables that violence and makes it possible. When we think of the foundations of modern nation-states (described in detail in the next chapter), *epistemological* and *onto-logical* **violence** were foundational to violence itself (and we might ask if this is also our current condition). **Epistemology** is the study of knowledge, or how we know what we know, and ontology is the study of being. Epistemological questions include: how do we know what we know? How do we know when something is true? And ontological questions include: what is reality? What categories can we use to understand reality? These philo-sophical underpinnings may initially seem abstract, but when we reflect on the history of violence, they become urgent.

Consider how important categories become when we think about violence: does vio-lence only include physical harm? When is physical harm justified, if ever? Can we use the term violence for harm done to nature? We must attend to epistemological and ontological violence from the moment that the question of violence is placed on the table, because these have been fundamentally linked to the deployment of all forms of violence in ways we will explore below.

Sylvia Wynter, Hortense Spillers, and Frank Wilderson, III, and others (sometimes referred to as Afro-Pessimists – though this label is too broad) have argued that a profound ontological violence originating in Europe's colonization of the world is foundational to Western understandings of what it means to be human. The Transatlantic trade in enslaved people attempted to render 10 to 12 million human beings, with lives, ancestries, and lan-guages, into a living form of property. This was an ontological form of violence in that it created persistent categories through which the world was understood. Wynter, Spillers, and others, argue this violent ontology is fundamental to our world today in the ways it structured both thought and economic and political processes. That ontological violence (turning humans into property) enabled devastating forms of physical violence, and we cannot really separate these from one another. The ontological and physical violences of slavery enabled and fed on each other: it was only through the dehumanization of West African people that the violence *legally* permitted against them could be enacted. Once they had been dehumanized, the ethos of white modernity was created in opposition to those who had been unmade as people. The legacies of slavery persist in modified form in the present in justifications for racism as well as in generational wealth gaps and differential health expectations (Sharpe 2016). Scholarship on these ontological questions has informed Black Geographies in productive ways (e.g., McKittrick 2006; 2011; McKittrick and Woods 2007). It is important to note that this is only one strand of theorization in Black Geographies, which is a complex and nuanced field, but here, this perspective offers us a helpful way to understand ontological violence.

To understand ontological power, it is helpful to begin from the work of Sylvia Wynter (1994; 2003). Wynter demonstrates that philosophy and theory central to European thought relied implicitly on a foundational distinction between human/non-human, which was always figured with the white male body at the center. This is how the US constitution was written ensuring equal rights of (white, property-owning) men, while the authors upheld violence against Native people, the enslavement of Black people, and for white women to be subject to discipline by their fathers and husbands. Please take care to note that the intention here is *not* to suggest that the experiences of Black women and men, Indigenous women and men, and white women are equivalent – as white women simultaneously materially benefited from and propagated a racial hierarchy of humanity even when they were constrained or targeted by the violence of patriarchy. The framing of history around an unmarked white European body is a form of ontological violence (violence through categories used to understand the world) that then enables the physical violence and death that was necessary for the enslavement of human beings.

In March 1991, taxi driver Rodney King was pulled over after a high-speed car chase that ended in an LA neighborhood. After King had been subdued by force, including tasering and being hit with police batons, two of the five officers at the scene continued to beat King repeatedly, reportedly aiming for his joints. Bystander George Holliday videotaped the incident from his apartment, and the video was later aired on local and national television. This incident sparked riots in 1992, when a jury acquitted three of the officers and failed to make a decision i=on the fourth. The Los Angeles riots that resulted ended with 53 deaths, over 2,000 injured, and a great deal of damage to property. Subsequently, in 1993, Officer Laurence Powell and Sergeant Stacey Koon were found guilty in a federal court but received mitigated sentences. Twenty-three years later, the city of Ferguson, Missouri was the site of mass demonstrations by Black residents after a young Black man named Michael Brown was shot in the street by police. Subsequent protests have occurred in most major US cities as part of the Movement for Black Lives – sometimes in response to local incidents (as in New York, Baltimore, and Charlotte). Activists Alicia Garza, Opal Tometi, and Patrisse Cullors began this movement after the 2012 death of Black teenager Trayvon Martin, shot in a Florida suburb by a vigilante who was acquitted of his death.

Returning to the events of 1991, after the jury's initial acquittal, Sylvia Wynter, at that time a professor of Spanish at Stanford University, wrote an open letter to her academic colleagues titled, "No Humans Involved" (Wynter 1994). Wynter begins from a radio news report after the local jury's acquittal; the report reveals that public officials in the LA judicial system used the acronym "NHI," or "no humans involved," to describe "any case involving a breach of the rights of young Black males who belong to the jobless category of the inner city ghettoes," (Wynter 1994, p.42). Wynter directs her letter toward her colleagues, her fellow professors, because she wants to draw attention to their role in educating young people into foundational ways of thinking about the world around them and their fellow human beings. Her argument is that the education system has in fact been complicit, through the education of young people, in enabling the kind of violence that Rodney King endured. She asks how not only the police who beat King, but also the jury that acquitted the police "[came] to conceive of what it means to be both *human* and *North American* in the *kinds of terms* (i.e., to be White, of Euroamerican culture and descent, middle-class, college-educated, and suburban) within whose logic, the jobless and usually school drop-out/push-out category of young Black males can be *perceived*, and *therefore behaved towards*, only as the *Lack* of the human, the Conceptual Other to being North American?" In this question, she also evokes the work of Zygmunt Bauman (1989) in showing how German Jews were made into a dehumanized other under the Nazis, and the rendering of the world's "damned," under colonization in the terms of Frantz Fanon (1963).

Following Wynter, we would do well then to consider how someone's humanity becomes a justification for their protection, or how they are portrayed as not fully human in order to justify violence against them.

Epistemological violence is violence through the production of knowledge, and this itself constitutes one field of power. This is related to the earlier discussion, but we can think of other ways in which it occurs, both through absences and through specific stories that are told about the world. Indigenous writers and theorists of colonialism have argued that there is a "coloniality of power" through which European systems of knowledge, such as the classifications of races (and their relationship to gender and sexuality), justified and enabled colonial domination (Quijano 1992; 2007; Mignolo 2002; Lugones 2010; Said 1979; Wynter 2003). This **coloniality of power** was ontological in that it included a fundamental understanding of how the world is.In this case, this ontology was premised on a racial hierarchy that justified colonialism by classifying the colonized as not fully human. This enabled other kinds of spatial practices, such as the labeling of inhabited land as *terra nullius* (or, "nobody's land," in Latin), an idea that was used by white European settlers to justify invasion and expansion, for instance in what is today Australia, or the principle of "manifest destiny" in the case of the United States in North America.

Power as technique

Supplementary to forms of ontological power above, we can engage with the work of Michel Foucault on technologies of power. Foucault's work helps us to think about ontological and epistemological violence through attention to power as something that is everywhere, that is diffused, and that is part of our knowledge of the world and our regimes of truth (Foucault 1978a; 1980). For him, power is not something that one has; rather it is a relationship in which we enact technologies of power in relation to one another. Foucault describes power in sometimes-counterintuitive ways that enable us to denaturalize things we had considered natural. For example, writing on sexuality, Foucault (1978b) flips the script on ideas of repression, arguing that the rhetoric of repressing and disciplining sexual desire that we associate with the Victorian era was instead an "incitement to discourse," that is, it was actually an invitation to talk more in a confessional manner about supposed perversions, such that repression in fact made these impulses and discussions flourish. In essence, talking a lot about the dangers and evils of sex and how to control and manage sexual impulse, is, in fact, talking a lot about sex.

Foucault thus emphasizes that power is based in **discourse**. That is, that power regimes emerge through how we understand and see the world. Discourse is the language we use to describe a phenomenon, which in turn becomes the only way we can communicate about that phenomenon, and thus shapes our thinking. Discourse can include individual words or phrases (e.g., the difference between referring to a person as an "illegal alien," or as an "undocumented person"), but these also fit patterns of logic and larger storylines (the "illegal alien," as a security threat, the "undocumented person," as someone with rights). While discourse is grounded in language, it is also manifest in physical spaces: the prison, the mental asylum, the school. Wynter's earlier example is a demonstration of the discourse of "no human involved" and shows that young Black men in zones of police surveillance are denied humanity in order to excuse the inexcusable violence enacted upon them. This evokes the Combahee River Collective's statement about Black queer women's liberation. In their groundbreaking feminist statement from 1977, they stated, "We reject pedestals, queenhood, and walking ten paces behind. To be recognized as human, levelly human, is enough." In both these cases (Wynter's NHI letter, and the Collective's statement) the category and discourse of humanity is a reference point for rights and inclusion. To think about this further, let us expand this discussion of epistemology and ontology by turning to power as legibility.

The work above is work to create categories, and we can think of the creation of categories and discourses as fundamental to the operation of power. We have seen how Wynter and others center the definition of the human as a powerful means through which violence might be enacted. Foucault, writing in late-twentieth-century France, sought to understand how various categories of abnormality, the criminal, the "madman," the pervert, or the diseased, were used to discipline all members of society into "normality," which was then defined against these categories. Part of Foucault's work then was to demonstrate that these categories change over time and were thus shifting, such that people who were sick, mentally different, or with disabilities were gradually moved out of public view as requiring special treatment, but simultaneously excessively documented and studied.

Foucault was also invested in understanding the ways that we are enmeshed in disciplinary techniques that are deployed in settings from prisons to schools. These techniques are related to discourses about childhood and criminality. Techniques of power ensure compliance to social norms through language and discourse, and are material and physical. Think of surveillance and adherence to a strict schedule. These are techniques of power that impact the body: the gaze of teacher for instance, reminding us to sit up straight, be quiet, and behave, study, get up early, arrive at school on time, keep your handwriting neat. Though children are sometimes represented as innocent, these forms of power resonate with those of the prison in which the guard keeps watch, the schedule is regimented, and prisoners fear punishment. The techniques share a goal of creating docility, which translates into daily life as a worker. The built environment of schools and prisons are created for visibility, and for docility, with the roles of teacher and student, prison guard and prisoner written into the structures of the buildings. We will return to Foucault's perspectives on power in relation to desire, later, as part of Foucault's argument is that power operates most smoothly *not* through physical violence per se, but rather through instilling in us technologies of self-governance.

Power operates in part through the creation of knowledge about people and places. It is both intensive, in that it is deeply intimate, and extensive, in that it involves the management of populations. James Scott has described this as *Seeing like a state* (1998) and has also discussed the ways that peasants, workers, and others elude and escape logics of legibility by refusing to be easily managed, categorized, or otherwise captured through practices of legibility and governance (Scott 2009). Geographer Matthew Hannah (2000) has applied Foucault's work on governmentality to the expansion of mapping and censuses in the nineteenth-century United States. Hannah follows in particular the figure of Francis Walker, an influential census director and commissioner of Indian affairs, who sought to deploy discourses of modernization through geographic means. Hannah argues that Walker, and his approach to immigration and the nation were also tied to ideas of race and gender.

Power and class conflict

The perspectives on power discussed earlier complement Marxist analyses of power, which in turn built upon Georg Wilhelm Friedrich Hegel's vision of history (which was itself profoundly influenced by the work of Immanuel Kant). Hegel, a nineteenth-century German philosopher, was influential in the development of later social theory, and Friedrich Engels and Karl Marx's theorization of history began from Hegel's **teleological** understanding of history. For Hegel, the history of the world was a process in which the (internal and collective) human spirit was increasingly realized in the external world through a process of dialectics, in which opposing ideas came in conflict and resulted in something new. Karl Marx famously wished to turn Hegel's dialectics "on its head" and to begin with the material world, where, for him, class conflict was the primary driver of social change. For Marx, position was primarily determined by your relationship to the means of production – do you sell your labor? Or profit from the labor of others? Do you own the means of production? These place you in a particular economic class, and conflict between these classes was driving history.

Marx understood history as a series of different socio-economic states that drove history forward. In this way, he carries forward Hegel's teleological views – that history has been leading us to this point in a way that was destined. Thus, for Marx, we move from the primitive communism of early human life into slave society, in which civilization is formed but concentrates power in the hands of urban aristocrats, and then into feudalism, in which aristocrats rule over peasants. It is during feudalism that small merchants began to expand their power and develop a new system: capitalism. Because of Marx's ultimately optimistic teleological view of the world, capitalism is a way station on the road to socialist revolution, part of history being made through a series of dialectical conflicts between groups defined by their relationship to the means of production and one another.

Marx and Engels's theories begin from a foundational critique of capitalism, which is crucial to understanding how political geographers have theorized power as a form of class conflict. Under capitalism, power is part of a structure that is greater than any one individual. We can later return to this idea and the question of how much of our lives and actions are determined by structure rather than individual **agency**, or the ability to enact your own desires in the world. For Marx and Engels, power is in the material world, and it is by understanding the material world that we better understand history and our place in it. Their analyses emerge from Engels's observations of the industrial revolution, in which thousands of rural poor moved into the urban workforce to labor in factories owned by capitalists. Engels spent two years in Manchester, where he observed the desperate conditions of the working poor. This was at the height of the social change wrought by the industrial revolution. Engels was influenced by the bleak conditions of the working class in England, also captured by the novels of Charles Dickens (who had firsthand experience as a child worker in a factory after his father was sent to debtors' prison). Engels documented excessive death rates, higher than in the countryside, and he pointed to unfair wages and dangerous living and working conditions.

Marx and Engels turned to a structural analysis of power operating through economic and political mechanisms to understand these societal changes and their importance. For them, power could be possessed by those who held the means of production, who consolidated and deepened their class position through the working of **capital**, money and goods that could be invested. The **bourgeoisie** are those who own the means of production, and they are able to make a profit only by alienating workers, the **proletariat**, from their labor. That is, they buy labor and materials and make products that then are sold for more than the cost of the labor or the materials. In doing so, they have extracted surplus value from the laborer, who is not paid a fair price, but is rather separated from the thing that they have created. In doing so, people are exploited through the theft of the value of their work.

For Marx and Engels, this labor/capital relationship defines power relations between individuals and classes, and contemporary Marxist or historical materialist geographers will begin from this relationship as a means to understand power relations. Of course, economic conditions have changed since the nineteenth century. In today's global labor market there are new sectors of labor (for instance the growth in the service and technology sectors), and we can now read the division of labor across the globe. Marx's analysis has also been further developed and deepened. Through the work of Cedric Robinson (1983), Robin D.G. Kelley (2015), and others often left out, such as Claudia Jones (Davies 2007), **Black Marxist** approaches have demonstrated the ways that capitalism's spread was underwritten by racial categories and the labor of enslaved and subjugated Black people. As capitalism thrives on differential labor prices and markets, so the racialization of people into the categories of Black and white sustains an inequality upon which capitalism relies. **Marxist feminists** have built on Marx and Engels' analyses to consider the unpaid labor of the household (e.g., Federici 2012). Other forms of analysis we will consider later in the book draw on all these approaches, exploring the ways that class, gender, race, and sexual orientation work together (e.g., among many others Davis 1996; hooks 1981; Combahee River Collective 1977).

Antonio Gramsci, the Italian Marxist theorist whose *Prison Notebooks* (Gramsci 1992), are foundational to a wide swath of theorizations of power across the social sciences and humanities, built on the work of Marx and Engels in order to understand the mechanisms through which class privilege is maintained and consolidated. As we have already begun to explore, power is not only exerted on people through violent means or physical coercion. That is *not* to underplay the role that coercion plays – Gramsci himself was imprisoned by Benito Mussolini's fascist regime until his body broke down and he died after being transferred from prison to clinic after eleven years. But, as we ask earlier: what are the conditions that set the stage for this physical violence – here, the imprisonment of a person for dissent? In Gramsci's theorization, this occurs through **hegemony**: the production of ideology that allows repressive governments to rule through consent, rather than through violence.

Gramsci's insight was to ask: why hadn't the socialist revolution predicted by Marx and Engels come to pass? The expected crisis that would bring us to a new era in which workers themselves took control of the means of production, ushering in a more just and equitable future had not come into being – instead, the bourgeoisie maintained control through generative ideology. Gramsci posited a relationship between the base (the workers and relationships between workers and the means of production) and a superstructure. The superstructure is the cultural and political aspects of society – the political and cultural institutions and civil society that, in Gramsci's explanation, perpetuated the violence embedded in class-based society. Like other Marxists, Gramsci was not interested in abstract reasoning for the sake of it – he wanted to change society. If hegemony was part of the problem, what was the solution?

For Gramsci, in order to transform relations between worker and the bourgeoisie, we need cultural change, which could only come from intellectual labor and new ideologies that could lead to a more just world. But when Gramsci was referring to intellectuals, he did not want to maintain the status quo by having the same upper class elites who had always been part of the superstructure continue to dominate ideological and cultural knowledge. Instead, he believed that all people could be intellectuals, theorizing and producing new kinds of knowledge in the world, which could in turn lead to radical social and political change. Such **organic intellectuals**, Gramsci believed, could speak better on behalf of the **subaltern**, or dominated classes, and through their advocacy could change the world.

Power as desire and self-governance

Describing a scene from a 1999 Belgian film, *Rosetta*, Lauren Berlant (2011, pp.161–162) writes about a young girl in a "utopian moment" of a core desperation and desire for connection. In this moment, the possibility of connection, even with a stranger, feels like it could change the girl's relation to the whole world.

> We find Rosetta at the end of a very long day. She has made a friend, Riquet, and through that friendship found an off-the-books job at a waffle maker, escaped her alcoholic and sexually profligate mother, and, with Riquet, spent the evening imitating what it might be like sometime to have fun with a friend or in a couple. She is awkward at this thing called relaxing, but she is game; she'll take the risk of submitting to someone else's pleasure economy in order to get that *thing* she wants, whose qualities she describes as she goes to sleep: "Your name is Rosetta. My name is Rosetta. You found a job. I found a job. You have a friend. I've got a friend. You have a normal life. I have a normal life. You won't fall through the cracks. I won't fall through the cracks. Good night. Good night." (Berlant 2011, p.162)

Berlant describes a profound desolation that she terms cruel optimism: the desire for a future that compels us to continue participating in neoliberal economic systems that can never give us that future of connection we yearn for, but may instead destroy us. Here, Berlant suggests that the form of neoliberal capitalism that Rosetta is enmeshed in means that individuals are always chasing the possibility of the "good life," of economic security and loving connection to family and friends, but that the atomistic world we inhabit makes it impossible that we would achieve it. She asks:

> Why do people stay attached to conventional good-life fantasies – say, of enduring reciprocity in couples, families, political systems, institutions, markets, and at work – when the evidence of their instability, fragility, and dear cost abounds? (Berlant 2011, p.2)

She is asking us to consider the possibility that the fabric of our lives will make it very difficult to achieve the future life we imagine, but that as long as we maintain that fantasy, we will individualize our own sense of failure, and try to work harder in order to have what we want – in Rosetta's case, just a job and a friend. For others, this cruel optimism may be attached to the idea that we can buy a house, win the girl (or boy), secure our future, go on vacation, be loved, lose weight. Instagram is perhaps the social media of cruel optimism: both pleasurable and mindless scrolling through charming pets, softened light and radiant faces on beaches and in candlelight, and a curation of impossible perfection that could lead someone to debt or despair. The idea that we can achieve our dreams of perfection through individual striving, may, however, cause us to lose sight of the ways that our society is fraying around the edges: "Cruel optimism exists when something you desire is actually an obstacle to your flourishing. It might involve food, or a kind of love; it might be a fantasy of the good life, or a political project. It might be simpler, too, like a new habit that promises to induce in you an improved way of being" (Berlant 2011, p.1).

In a parallel register, Sara Ahmed (2010) writes on "the promise of happiness," asking us to consider ways that the idea that we could be happy if we only wanted the right things, is what binds us to repetitive behaviors and an acceptance of systems of domination. She asks us to consider, "what are we consenting to, when we consent to happiness?" In Ahmed's analysis, figures like the "feminist killjoy," the "melancholic migrant," and the "unhappy queer," demonstrate an inability or refusal to be happy, even as those around them insist on their happiness. Telling a story of a daughter who buries her own frustration in order to be happy for others, Ahmed (2010, p.64) writes, "The mother can thus love the daughter who is becoming like furniture, who can support the family by staying in the background." In opposition to acquiescing to happiness, Ahmed (2017) embraces the figure of the feminist killjoy, who is willing to risk breaching silence in order to create a different world. The feminist killjoy speaks an unpleasant truth that might spoil the party: the woman who doesn't laugh at the joke, the woman of color who speaks about racism in a moment of colorblind sisterhood. Ahmed has embraced this role in her own life, notably by quitting a prestigious job at Goldsmiths College, University of London, to protest sexual harassment of students by faculty and the administration's failure to protect the students.

What is "power" in the desire of a young woman to have a job and a friend? What is power to the daughter who agrees to narrow her horizons in order to please her family? Power is not wielded by any one person over others. Nor is there an intact and intentional system of suppression based on violence (in its most overt form). Rather, people are enmeshed in economic and interpersonal relations that cause them to sometimes desire things that betray them or keep them working within a system that will not meet their desires, or when they do not desire the right things they find themselves cast out of interpersonal relationships. Here, people govern themselves and manage their own desires in ways that are fraught with power relations, but also tricky and hard to pin down.

Foucault overturns more conventional understandings of power as power over, by focusing more on "power to," power as a set of relationships, and on fields of power. For Foucault, power is less a question of physical force, than of the ways that power operates in a positive sense, by making us want to be a certain kind of person. This means that power is diffuse, but also that our very sense of ourselves as individual subjects is tied up in power relations. One of Foucault's central contributions related to his lifelong study of power is to center how we learn self-governance. Why is it that each day we rise from our beds, brush our teeth, and (for the most part) do what is expected of us? Why do we self-regulate and follow societal norms? Why do not we all just do our own thing?

For Foucault, the answer is both quite simple and very complicated. We are engaged in a web of **capillary power**, that is, power that is exerted through our own and others' bodily comportment – how we move through space, the people that we imagine ourselves to be, and so forth. If we do not want to be among the classes of so-called "abnormal" people mentioned earlier (the supposedly mad, criminal, perverted, or diseased), then do we imagine ourselves to be self-actualizing, healthy, free, effective, strong, and capable people? If so, we have absorbed these societal values into our very sense of who we are as people. No one must then tell us to work hard or get up on time – we *want* to, because these things are inseparable from the person whom we want to be. This is why then power is capillary, in the sense that we act as little conduits of power moving through the world but often repeating the actions of others and reinforcing societal norms through our own self-governance. There is also then a kind of pleasure to the operation of power – the pleasure of being good and being rewarded for being normal as opposed to the abject of society who are cast aside. This pleasure even may extend to measuring one's own propensity for good behavior. We might track calories, count steps, wear a Fitbit or Apple watch: we monitor and surveil ourselves and may even take pleasure in this governance.

Power, Politics, and Relations in Space, Place, and Territory

What are politics in relation to power? We might begin from acknowledging that we can understand politics most broadly as power relations. Power then operates through the micro-scale of interpersonal relations into the state-oriented space of formal politics. Formal politics are those that are managed through regularized and structured institutions and society: participation in civil society organizations, voting and everything that goes along with electoral politics, the movement of policy and law through bodies of government, treaties, and negotiations at the United Nations – all these are elements of formal politics.

Though this book certainly engages with formal politics, it also argues that informal politics, all that which happens outside the formal political sphere, is equally important and has lasting and crucial impacts on the things that are marked as formal. Think of how societal change often comes from outside formal institutions of governance. It might begin from the conversations around the dinner table that might change your political views, or from the frustrations of everyday life: high unemployment, low wages, sexual harassment, inaccessible healthcare, bad schools for your child, or encounters with the police. These are the material of everyday life, but they also profoundly shape our decision making as we interact with formal political systems.

As geographers, we wish to understand how power operates in space, through the built environment, through the uneven distribution of resources, through the mapping of power relations onto neighborhoods or the structuring of relationships between spaces. How can we understand the sometimes-abstract theories of power above as they relate to geography? How are power relations also spatial relations? Doreen Massey (e.g., 1993; 2005) foundationally argued that "space matters," and that there is a geometry of power, a power-geometry produced by capitalism's uneven generation of inequality in space: rich regions and poor regions, rich neighborhoods and poor neighborhoods. As we proceed into the next chapter and talk about processes of state formation, we will focus on some of the historical events that led her to make this argument. Here, we will just discuss a few examples of power relations as spatial relations before we explore these ideas through the complicated case of the Arctic region. The spaces around us not only *make* but also are *made by* power relations.

Henri Lefebvre was a French philosopher and sociologist active during the late twentieth century, and though he himself was not a geographer, his ideas have been very influential for some strands of political geography and urban theory. Lefebvre's key insight was to see space itself as a product of social and economic relations; we can refer to this as the **social production of space**. Consider the shopping mall as a very particular space that is immediately recognizable whether it is in Lima, or Lagos, or Jakarta, it is a space that is fundamentally a product of capital. The components of the space are interchangeable – it is often made of pre-fabricated parts, for instance, from ceiling tiles to drywall. The signage indicating store brands and fast food shops is likewise mass-produced, with imagery that is recognizable across the globe (from the Nike logo to the McDonald's sign). There are welcoming entrances meant to establish class privilege through aspirational signaling of expensive materials like marble in some places or faux versions of these materials in others. In many countries, you might find security guards who keep out those without means to shop. There will also be a messier side of the mall, where the garbage, food waste, and packaging exits, and you find only workers, never shoppers, as though you had stepped behind the curtain of a theater upon which consumption had been staged, or witnessed Mickey Mouse and Cinderella remove their costumes after work at Disneyland.

This is how capitalism takes material shape in our cities or towns. Capitalist spaces such as the mall are likely so familiar that we might not ask: how did this instantly recognizable space proliferate? We might not frequently think of how this is a place that could only exist under this mode of social relations in which capitalist firms use economies of scale and attempt to expand into new products and new markets to increase their rate of profit. This is quite different from older settlements based in rural or agricultural areas. In such a setting, whether in France or Tanzania, Vietnam, or Nepal, you are less likely to find that components of the built environment (the human-made structures) rely on pre-fabricated components or globally recognizable iconography. You are more likely to find building components that have been made by hand, by a local craftsperson, or even by the family living in the house. This difference leaves its mark in the material world in the shapes and forms that buildings and their interiors take. In this way, our spaces reveal our economic power relations. Why can we think of this as a form of power relations? In part because these relations can over-determine these spaces, until they crowd out alternatives. Nowadays, for most it would be *too expensive* to build your own home or place of business by hand – cheaper to acquire one made through economies of scale. We will return to this way that power is embedded in subsequent chapters, such as the chapter on cities.

In these examples, we understand capitalism to be enacted within the city. But the geographer David Harvey gives us a means to think about the spatial implications of capitalism at a different scale through the idea of the **spatial fix**. Capitalism is understood to be confronted with a series of crises. These crises might be resolved or might stage the way for evolution into a new economic system. The bourgeoisie naturally strive to perpetuate capitalism and enable it to survive – sometimes through concessions to the working class. Harvey observed that it is also possible to postpone crises through a spatial fix – that is, by expanding into new markets or seeking out new sources of cheaper labor. In the chapter on biopolitics, we will consider whether and when our own bodies can become the spatial fix that Harvey describes. There is another conversation to be had here about the ways that capitalism initially functioned and spread through the dispossession of Indigenous people as a form of primitive accumulation (Byrd 2011; Coulthard 2014; Curley 2019b), a topic we will return to later in the book.

Contingent Territory: The Governance Of Ice

We have defined territory as space that is acted upon, and earth claimed by sovereign states. But these definitions assume a certain stability to territory – that it is fixed, that we know what and where it is – thus the technologies of mapping and quantification are central to the governance of territory. But what if we are confronted by what Hannes Gerhardt et al. (2010) refer to as "territorial indeterminacy"?

In a study of Arctic politics, Gerhardt et al. (2010) suggest that global climate change is raising new and challenging questions about the meanings of territory and sovereignty. Paradoxically, while much of the world fears negative ecological, human, and economic effects of climate change, Arctic States such as Canada, Norway, Russia, the United States, and Denmark (Greenland), as well as the Inuit Circumpolar Council (which will be discussed later) are also strategizing how they might capture economic opportunities (though these may be exaggerated) but also how they might handle state sovereignty in a deeply unstable region. As Gerhardt et al. argue, much of state law is based in an assumption that we can distinguish between land and water, but in the Arctic, this distinction gets confusing: ice is a little bit like water, a little like land (Gerhardt et al. 2010, pp.993–994). In addition to legal assumptions that we can distinguish between water and land, many of the conversations about the Arctic as territory draw on the assumption of terra nullius (Steinberg, Tasch, and Gerhardt 2015), which was the justification for settler colonialism in what is now Australia.

Paradoxically, as concerns grow about our planet under conditions of global warming, this future also reveals potential economic and geopolitical possibilities. In fact, this generates a new "icy geopolitics" in which a future in which the North Pole might thaw means Arctic states look to make illegible subterranean territory legible and define liminal places (Dodds 2010a, p.66; 2008). Unraveling the implications of the Russian flag that was planted at the bottom of the Arctic Ocean in 2007, Dodds points to the ways that legibility and calculability (Scott's "seeing like a state" and Hannah's use of governmentality) play out in how knowledge of the Arctic is being produced as part of its claiming and bounding.

Governance of the Arctic attempts to reconcile law with the icy waters melting and refreezing – an impossible task as in this space, the division between land and water is complicated by this fundamental instability. Our rapidly changing climate has made this yet more complex and volatile (Gerhardt et al. 2010, p.994). This has resulted in questions around the Northwest Passage and control of the Arctic Ocean, but it has also led to the possibility of new forms of multilateral governance. With regard to the Northwest Passage, the reduction of sea ice has meant that a once difficult and seasonal passageway between the Atlantic and Pacific Oceans has now become navigable year-round for ships with special ice equipment. In 2013, a large cargo ship made it through the Northwest Passage without icebreakers. The United States claims it is an international strait while Canada claims it as its own internal waters.

In this discussion, we find that the ambiguity of water, ice, and land, and places that are not quite any of these entities but rather move back and forth between them complicates the regulation of that space, and reveals the illusory nature of the assumption embedded in territory: that one state or entity can exert power evenly over a given and demarcated space. Added to this are the private entities such as oil and gas companies that seek to extract untapped mineral resources in the Arctic, and the presence of their lobbyists and people of influence at the doors of governance in each of the five Arctic countries – and questions of capital, class, and hegemony, broached earlier in the chapter, loom large.

Now, take a step back. In portraying a kind of "scramble for the Arctic" narrative as I have until this point, we risk imposing an overwhelmingly settler state focused narrative onto questions of Arctic sovereignty (Barkan in Nicol et al. 2016, p.176). The material qualities of water – freezing, thawing, changing with human intervention making territorial questions difficult to answer – is only part of the story. Because the narrative above – in which nature challenges governance – already assumes that these states have authority to negotiate rights among themselves. However, these are **settler states**, that is, states formed through a process of external or internal **colonization** of **Indigenous** people and land. Along with the so-called "Arctic Five" (Canada, Denmark, Norway, Russia, and the United States), there is the Inuit Circumpolar Council.

The Inuit Circumpolar Conference's origins date back to 1977, when it was founded as a response to colonial governance in the region. As the Inuit Circumpolar Council (henceforth ICC), it now represents 160,000 Indigenous people across the Arctic region. Due to the legal structures in place, "Inuit people are engaged in an anticolonial struggle for self-determination that is centrally about the control of land, territory, and resources," but the struggle must rely on "modes of representation that are colonial and imperialist" (Barkan in Nicol et al. 2016, p.176). Through other lenses, we could read a proliferation of actors as Inuit and other Indigenous groups mobilized in opposition to the 2008 Ilulissat Declaration (a declaration of the Arctic Five forestalling new governance regimes in the Arctic) because of its disregard of Inuit sovereignty (Nicol 2010; Heininen 2004). In the words of a statement released by the ICC in 2009, the Arctic five "in their discussions of Arctic sovereignty, have not referenced existing international instruments that promote and protect the rights of Indigenous peoples. They have also neglected to include Inuit in Arctic sovereignty discussions in a manner comparable to Arctic Council deliberations" (Inuit Circumpolar Conference 2009). As Mountz summarizes in regard to territorial rights in the Arctic:

> Nation states hold power to make claims in their representations of the interest of large, territorially bound, and internationally legible populations associated with sea and the Arctic; and yet these claims to sovereignty are being challenged as political and physical geographies combine in the Arctic region and Indigenous sovereignties challenge state sovereignties. (Mountz 2013, p.836; Nicol 2010; Powell 2010)

To understand the claiming and bounding of space in the Arctic, we must at minimum seek to understand:

- How categories and discourses shape thinking and policy at the Arctic
- How prior histories of colonial conquest shape current practices
- How legibility of sovereign Indigenous rights to the land and water are or are not able to disrupt settler state claims
- How the material qualities of land that is sometimes ice and sometimes water shapes policy
- How techniques of mapping are tied to governability and territory-making practices

As we unravel claims to control the Arctic, or the process of making and contesting territory in the Arctic, any simple sense of territory unravels. But perhaps there is more uncertainty to all forms of territory than we might expect.

Neighborhoods as Territory

Moving from the indeterminacy of ice and water in relation to sovereignty, let us consider now the territoriality of urban life. Writing in the 1990s, Jennifer Robinson (1997) argued that the planning of urban space in South African cities was "central to the exclusion of African people from citizenship," and that in the post-apartheid era, the segregated spaces of apartheid became significant for understanding the future of citizenship. In the following decade, Charlotte Lemanski (2004, p.101) analyzed fear of crime in Cape Town, South Africa, suggesting that fear was creating fortified enclaves and a "withdrawal from public space." Lemanski contended this "architecture of fear," (Agbola 1997) was sustained in the post-apartheid era, and that such architecture comprised a "new apartheid." A decade later, Paasche, Yarwood, and Sidaway (2014) point to a splintering of the city of Cape Town into private enclaves and spaces of consumption, and the increasing use of private policing of demarcated territories in the city.

After the end of apartheid, planning in the city of Cape Town, South Africa, has come to revolve around a perceived security crisis understood to delay the city's progress and development (Paasche, Yarwood, and Sidaway 2014; Miraftab 2007). In what has been argued to be a continuation of the colonial legacy, now with differently assembled transnational connections, city managers imported a system developed in a segregated country across the Atlantic – the North American City Improvement District (CID), which created formal associations of business and property owners to invest in private provision of services from street-cleaning to security. This entails the territorialization of space as these associations seek to create, "a clean, attractive, fashionable and, above all, safe place to shop, in contrast to other parts of Cape Town" (Paasche, Yarwood, and Sidaway 2014, p.1564). If more than half of the businesses in a district vote for the CID, one can be established and begin developing a firm grasp over the territory demarcated by its formation; this includes use of city by-laws and enforcement of laws in order to criminalize disruption in ways that also criminalize homeless people.

That the urban form in South Africa is an archive of segregation technologies relocated across an ocean, and that this is now taking new shapes through neoliberalization and the privatization of public space is perhaps not surprising. Across the globe, scholars have studied the political geography of gated communities. These accounts find territorialization in the material architecture of neighborhoods and urban spaces, and in the policing of these spaces. Consider though, that the spaces of territorialized neighborhoods might not always be so spectacular, and the ways that they are made into territory might be emotional rather than through bricks and metal fences.

Anoop Nayak does just this by understanding territory through the "seemingly ordinary landscapes of English suburbia" (Nayak 2010; see also Tolia-Kelly 2006; see Kobayashi and Peake 2000 for how this plays out in the United States). Turning away from urban centers, which have been the center of much conversation about race and ethnicity, Nayak wants to understand how rural and suburban places become described as "idyllic, pastoral English retreats far removed from the multicultural city where different bodies throng together and rub up against one another" (Nayak 2010, p.2371). Nayak's starting point is that some neighborhoods are understood to be "ethnically marked terrain," (Figure 4.1) but the

Figure 4.1   English Defence League Blackburn protest on April 2, 2011. Reproduced with permission of b3tarev3. https://www.flickr.com/photos/28310050@N02/5581953575

process through which other everyday spaces become "white territory," is not marked (see also Lipsitz 2011). Nayak finds these expressions in graffiti, clothes, and lampposts, in the suburbs that are imagined as "the last bastions of whiteness."

In a photo taken by Nayak, white letters on blue metal shutters assert "North side last white man's stand," and include the BNP acronym for the far-right British National Party. Other graffiti contains code terms for Adolph Hitler, or reads "England for whites." Nayak describes a fieldwork moment as follows:

> We sit in silence. Numbed by the sensory overload of raw encounter we remain stuck to the seats of a small Vauxhall Metro resting motionless on the Kempton Dene estate. Occasionally the windscreen wipers flick into life but the sleet of a dark December day has long dissipated. This small metallic vehicle has carried us on our night flight from inner-city Birmingham across amber-lit dual carriageways, beneath long echoing tunnels and over tongue-arched flyovers towards our eventual destination. My friend and colleague Les Back usually exudes serenity, but just now he is sat beside me mildly perspiring and looking distinctly unnerved. For a few still moments we maintain a monastic silence. Les is the first to speak: "I've never experienced anything like that", he splutters, breaking the cotton-wool quietness we are cocooned within. We have just had our first encounter with the young Skinhead "gang" who were to become a formative part of our ethnography on racist violence. (Nayak 2010, p.2380)

Nayak's interviews with skinheads take place as the young men experience unemployment, partial employment, or, in one case, are expelled from school for "paki-bashing." They complain about the local South Asian shopkeepers, saying things like, "It's our country, not theirs," "They've got all the jobs, like me and Mark could be working now but fucking two pakis have jumped in our place haven't they?" (Nayak 2010, p.2382). Nayak observes not only displays of racism, but also "a marked sense of hypermasculinity, and an obsession with the local estate as 'territory'" (Nayak 2010, p.2382). The skinheads describe Asian shopkeepers as "territorial infiltration," and also display this animosity to Nayak (2010, p.2385) himself, as in this exchange:

ANOOP: Is it Asians that you hate more or black people?'
DANIEL: Pakis.
ANOOP: Why?
LEONARD:' Cos they smell.
ANOOP: Who told you that?
DANIEL: Fucking smell it! No one has to tell us. Fucking can smell it.
YOUTH WORKER [INTERVENING]: When you go into an English person's house…
DANIEL: It smells of nice air-freshener … If you go into a Paki's house stinks of curry
        and shit.

In the case of the Arctic, the indeterminacy of ice and water complicate questions of sovereignty. Here, in the suburbs in England, young white men work to maintain their neighborhood as a white territory even as whiteness itself is a fiction mediated through class and empire. What resonates through both these cases, however, is a territorializing impulse to mark, measure, and contain the globe.

Geographer at Work: Azeezat Johnson

Azeezat Johnson is a Leverhulme Early Career Fellow in the School of Geography, Queen Mary University of London.

Beginning from the Margins: The Clothing Practices of Black Muslim Women in Britain

What happens if our explorations into spaces *began* from the complex and "messy" lived experiences of racialized persons?

This question frames a lot of the work that I do: it reflects the words of Audre Lorde (1996, p.163) who has time and again urged us all to use our differences as "a springboard for creative change." Instead of minimizing the differences between us, or locating specific experiences as the strange or marginal, we can understand how constructions of space shift across different experiences of being.

I think of this "creative change" as I focus on the clothing practices of Black Muslim women in Britain: my interest in addressing this topic came from the absence of work that addressed my experiences, and the many other Black Muslim women that I knew. Research on British Muslims tended to focus on Muslims with some form of South Asian heritage ties, and research about Blackness and religion focused on the role of Christianity and churches. Both these linkages worked to essentialize race and religion, and limits an exploration into how Blackness, anti-Black racism, Muslim identity, and Islamophobia alter as they are constructed with and through different social and economic factors. This prevents us from addressing how Blackness and Muslim identity shifts across different contexts; we need to understand these social processes as continuously being developed as we interact with different objects, bodies, gazes, and spaces.

Importantly, clothing practices allowed me to focus on these broader social processes through mundane, everyday practices. It is commonplace knowledge that we all – whether Muslim or not – change clothes (often several times within a day) as we move through homes, workplaces, schools, etc. However, research (and public narratives) around Muslim women has been fixated on the role of the headscarf (and niqabs, burqas, etc.) within public spaces. This stops an understanding of the diversity of clothing practices that Muslim women engage with for any number of reasons. Rather than paying attention to the differences within Muslim women, we are fixed as a homogeneous Other.

I wanted to move beyond this Othering and marginalization by highlighting how different Black Muslims negotiate objects, bodies, gazes, and spaces. By focusing on the changing clothing practices of Black Muslim women across homes, prayer, and workplaces, I wanted to highlight how processes of categorization (i.e. race, religion, gender, nationalism) are intertwined and produce our embodied experiences across different spaces. This, in turn, tells us a lot about how different spaces are organized as particular (white, male, CIS, straight, and/or Christian) bodies are imagined as the norm, and how those of us who deviate from these social norms find our own ways to negotiate these spaces.

By starting from the critical knowledges that Black Muslim women develop to negotiate our surroundings, I wanted to show how research on the construction of different spaces can end up limiting itself by treating racialized bodies as a homogeneous and/or fixed Other. This is what Noxolo, Raghuran, and Madge (2008, p.157) speak to when criticizing Geography as a discipline that "attempts to theorize a globalized world of flows and multiple perspectives, whilst denying the multivocal, decentralised, postcolonial discipline that is inside its own belly."

So to answer my original question: by beginning from the lived experiences of racialized persons, we can move beyond this Othering of such experiences, and develop tools that allow us to recognize (and relish in) all of our similarities and differences. By centering the experiences of Black Muslim women, research on race, religion, gender, nationalism, and material culture is expanded upon and understood through their entwinements. This is part of a larger task across the Social Sciences to move beyond tools that have been used to fix and homogenize racialized bodies.

What Have We Learned and Where Do We Go From Here?

By seeking to understand how power operates in space even within one particular region, we see that we cannot really begin to understand politics without close attention to the spatial ways that power is enacted and challenged. Furthermore, my hope is that this text will not only help you to pass your class but also change the ways that you think about the world. As you proceed in life, consider the ways that you are engaged in strategies and practices of power and the ways that they impinge on your own life. Consider how you might be more conscious of your role in the web of power relations in which we are all enmeshed.

Keywords

Agency   The ability to enact your own desires in the world.

Black Marxism   An approach to understanding economic systems that includes attention to how capitalism's spread was underwritten by racial categories and the labor of enslaved and subjugated Black people. Part of the Black Radical Tradition.

Bourgeoisie   Those who own the means of production (such as factories), and are able to make a profit by alienating workers from their labor.

Capital   Money and goods that can be used to generate production and profit.

Capillary power   Power that is exerted through our own and others' bodily comportment, power that is diffused through society.

Coloniality of power   The power of European systems of knowledge (such as the classification of race and gender), which goes hand in hand with colonialism and imperialism.

Discourse   The language we use to describe a phenomenon, which in turn becomes the only way we can communicate about that phenomenon, and thus shapes our thinking.

Epistemology   The study of knowledge (how do we know what we know?).

Feminist Marxism   Approach to Marxism integrating the analysis of the unpaid labor that occurs in the household and elsewhere due to patriarchal labor systems.

Hegemony   The production of ideology that allows repressive governments to rule through consent, rather than through violence.

Inscribed power   Power that individuals possess in relation to other individuals or entities, power as a resource to make a specific thing happen (for instance through military action).

Power as technique   Power that is not inscribed but rather is a technology or method of making things happen in the world, for instance, strategies of knowledge production.

Proletariat   The working class in Marxist analysis.

State of exception   A period of time or even in which a sovereign (a decision-maker, whether king or governing body) declares an exception to the ordinary rules of law.

Territory   Land or space that has been acted upon, made into discrete entities under the jurisdiction or control of a person or group of people.

Teleological   An understanding of time or history as unfolding in a linear way toward a defined goal, the idea of natural progress.

Subaltern   The dominated classes.

Social production of space   The ways that space is made through social relations.

Spatial fix   How capitalist crises are resolved through spatial means: firms expanding into new markets, of moving in search of cheaper labor.

Further Reading

Marxism and power relations

Combahee River Collective. 1977. *A Black Feminist Statement*. https://americanstudies.yale.edu/sites/default/files/files/Keyword%20Coalition_Readings.pdf (accessed September 17, 2019).

Davies, C.B. 2007. *Left of Karl Marx: The Political Life of Black Communist Claudia Jones*. Durham, NC: Duke University Press.

Davis, A. 2011. *Women, Race, & Class*. New York: Vintage.

Federici, S. 2012. *Revolution at Point Zero: Housework, Reproduction, and Feminist Struggle*. Oakland: PM Press.

Gramsci, A. 1992. *Prison Notebooks*. New York: Columbia University Press.

Harvey, D. 2002. *Spaces of Capital: Towards a Critical Geography*. London: Routledge.

Harvey, D. 2018. *The Limits to Capital*. New York: Verso.

Herod, A. 1997. From a Geography of Labor to a Labor Geography: Labor's Spatial Fix and the Geography of Capitalism. *Antipode* 29(1): 1–31.

hooks, b. 1981. *Ain't I a Woman: Black Women and Feminism*. London: South End Press.

Kelley, R.D.G. 2015. *Hammer and Hoe: Alabama Communists during the Great Depression*. Chapel Hill, NC: University of North Carolina Press.

Robinson, C.J. 1983. *Black Marxism: The Making of the Black Radical Tradition*. Chapel Hill, NC: University of North Carolina Press.

Neighborhoods and urban space as territory

Agbola, T. 1997. *The Architecture of Fear: Urban Design and Construction Response to Urban Violence in Lagos, Nigeria*. Ibadan: Institut français de recherche en Afrique (Ifra).

Bonnett, A. and Nayak, A. 2002. Cultural Geographies of Racialization – the Territory of Race. In K. Anderson, M. Domosh, S. Pile et al. (eds.), *Handbook of Cultural Geography*. London: Sage, pp.300–312.

Derickson, K.D. 2016. The Racial State and Resistance in Ferguson and Beyond. *Urban Studies* 53: 2223–2237.

Hook, D. and Vrdoljak, M. 2002. Gated Communities, Heterotopia and a "Rights" of Privilege: A Heterotopology of the South African Security-Park. *Geoforum* 33(2): 195–219.

Jürgens, U. and Gnad, M. 2002. Gated Communities in South Africa– Experiences from Johannesburg. *Environment and Planning B: Planning and Design* 29(3): 337–353.

Le Goix, R. and Webster, C.J. 2008. Gated Communities. *Geography Compass* 2(4): 1189–1214.

Lemanski, C. 2004. A New Apartheid? The Spatial Implications of Fear of Crime in Cape Town, South Africa. *Environment and Urbanization* 16(2): 101–112.

Lipsitz, G. 2011. *How Racism Takes Place*. Philadelphia: Temple University Press.

Nayak, A. 2010. Race, Affect, and Emotion: Young People, Racism, and Graffiti in Postcolonial English Suburbs. *Environment and Planning A* 42(10): 2370–2392.

Shabazz, R. 2015. *Spatializing Blackness: Architectures of Confinement and Black Masculinity in Chicago*. Chicago: University of Illinois Press.

Van Houtum, H. and Pijpers, R. 2007. The European Union as a Gated Community: The Two-faced Border and Immigration Regime of the EU. *Antipode* 39(2): 291–309.

Ontological and epistemological power
Fanon, F. 1963. *The Wretched of the Earth*. New York: Grove Press.

Lugones, M. 2010. Toward a Decolonial Feminism. *Hypatia* 25(4): 742–759.

McKittrick, K. 2006. *Demonic Grounds: Black Women and the Cartographies of Struggle*. Minneapolis, MN: University of Minnesota Press.

McKittrick, K. 2014. *Sylvia Wynter: On Being Human as Praxis*. Durham, NC: Duke University Press.

McKittrick, K. and Woods, C. eds. 2007. No One Knows the Mysteries at the Bottom of the Ocean. In *Black Geographies and the Politics of Place*. Cambridge, MA: South End Press, pp.1–13.

Mignolo, W.D. 2002. *Local Histories/Global Designs: Coloniality, Subaltern Knowledges, and Border Thinking*. Princeton, NJ: Princeton University Press.

Quijano, A. 1992. Colonialidad y Modernidad/Racionalidad. *Perú Indígena* 13(29): 11–20.

Quijano, A. 2007. Coloniality and Modernity/Rationality" *Cultural Studies* 21(2–3): 168–178.

Sharpe, C. 2016. *In the Wake: On Blackness and Being*. Durham, NC: Duke University Press.

Spillers, H.J. 2003. *Black, White, and in Color: Essays on American Literature and Culture*. Chicago: University of Chicago Press.

Weheliye, A. 2014. *Habeas Viscus: Racializing Assemblages, Biopolitics, and Black Feminist Theories of the Human*. Durham, NC: Duke University Press.

Wilderson III, F.B. 2010. *Red, White & Black: Cinema and the Structure of US Antagonisms*. Durham, NC: Duke University Press.

Wynter, S. 1994. "No Humans Involved." An Open Letter to My Colleagues. *Forum N.H.I. Knowledge for the 21st Century* 1(1): 42–73.

Wynter, S. 2003. Unsettling the Coloniality of Being/Power/Truth/Freedom: Towards the Human, After Man, Its Overrepresentation--An Argument. *The New Centennial Review* 3(3): 257–337.

Power in geography

Allen, J. 2003. *Lost Geographies of Power*. Malden, MA: Blackwell Publishing.

Cowen, D. and . Gilbert, E. eds. 2008. *War, Citizenship, Territory*. New York: Routledge.

Elden, S. 2016. *Space, Knowledge and Power: Foucault and Geography*. New York: Routledge.

Gilmore, R.W. 2002. Fatal Couplings of Power and Difference: Notes on Racism and Geography. *The Professional Geographer* 54(1): 15–24.

Sharp, J. 2009. Geography and Gender: What Belongs to Feminist Geography? Emotion, Power and Change. *Progress in Human Geography* 33(1): 74–80.

Chapter 5

State/Borders

Where is the border? In classrooms around the world, children memorize colorful shapes and associate them with languages, histories, and cultures. When our daughter was four, she pointed to the globe asking, "Where is India? Where is France?" "India is the pink one, your friend Cedric's mama is from the yellow one." I answered. These colors trick us into picturing fixed borders and homogenous interiors. But the border is also the Mediterranean Sea that swallows the vulnerable. The border is also the color of your passport, which discourages you from waiting in line at the embassy, where expats from the country that colonized your own home many years ago will weigh and judge your life and perhaps deny your visa request because they deem you to be a potential permanent settler. The border is your name, which places you on a no-fly list that immobilizes you, or identifies you as a member of a given ethnicity to be treated with suspicion at the consulate. Borders are a material manifestation of the power of the state, a complicated entity that shapes our day-to-day life. In this chapter, we will define the state and state formation, beginning from its borders.

Borders are intense, material, violent, and ghostly presences in our lives. And borders are a distant abstraction … there are places where you might accidentally cross from one country to another without noticing or filling out a visa form. A winding line at the end of a long trip marks a crossing over from one place to another. The border agent might laugh and make small talk, might make eye contact in ways that are welcoming or in ways that make your palms sweat. Their judgment of whether to allow you to cross the border could be based on a complex algorithm of how long you have been in what place and for what reason, your age, your skin color, the way you speak, your marital status, your gender.

Political Geography: A Critical Introduction, First Edition. Sara Smith.
© 2020 John Wiley & Sons Ltd. Published 2020 by John Wiley & Sons Ltd.

In other sites, you might not know exactly where the border is – crossing a desert, walking through a forest – but that crossing could take your life. Through state efforts to prevent terrorism, borders of one country – the United Kingdom, the United States, could be extended or serve as invisible bubbles around individuals thousands of miles away, on no fly lists or banned from entry. The border is a force field that fails to recognize or destroys the humanity of some people. Where is the border, then? The border then is an experience as much as a material site and our knowledge of the border depends on our positionality. But as we grow up, from a small child pointing at a globe to an adult voting in an election, the existence of borders comes to be taken for granted. In nearly every moment of our existence, we will be within the territory of a sovereign state, and it is in fact difficult to imagine otherwise. In this, we find ourselves enmeshed in the **state effect,** the feeling that the state is more than it is – more coherent, more necessary, and more natural. How might we unravel this sense of taken-for-grantedness and thus come to better understand the workings of the state? One way is to trace back the birth of the state, both in our own life history, and in the history of the world.

In 1999, four boats crowded with migrants from the Fujian province of southeast China arrived off the west coast of Canada's British Columbia. These migrants had been brought across the ocean by smugglers, and their arrival and the subsequent legal cases created a wave of conversations about the migrants, about Canada's identity as a nation-state, and about policy (Mountz 2004). Of the 599 migrants, 500 sought asylum, so their ability to remain in Canada or the possibility of their return to China would be based on legal adjudication of their claims. Unlike its neighbor, the United States, Canada does not usually detain migrants arriving by plane or boat, but in this case, they did detain the migrants from all but the first boat. In subsequent media coverage, the bodies of the migrants took center stage: as young children in some cases, signaling innocence and the need for care, as dehydrated and ill due to their struggle to get to Canada, or as evidence of Canada's borders being leaky, unprotected, and insecure (Mountz, 2004).

Most likely, this story brought to mind for you more recent images of boats full of migrants trying to make it across the Mediterranean Sea to get to Europe from North Africa or the Middle East. The perils of the transit was made clear in the devastating 2015 image of three-year-old Aylan Kurdi on a Turkish beach after his family tried to reach Greece on a small inflatable boat (Austen 2015; King and Johnson 2015). This was part of their family's quest to seek asylum in Canada, where Aylan's aunt was living, and subsequently became part of Canada's national election story. His death is also part of a larger crisis of migrants seeking safety and security in Europe or even farther from home. As I write this chapter, I can recall the faces of two young children, Jakelin Caal and Felipe Gomez Alonzo who died in detention facilities after crossing the US-Mexico border between December 2018 and January 2019. Both children were from families that speak Q'eqchi' and Chuj, Indigenous Mayan languages in Guatemala, both children arrived in the United States with their fathers, who were seeking safety and survival across the border.

We live in a paradoxical world. Not too long ago, theorists and op-ed columnists wondered if we were facing the decline of the state, as the rise of very powerful multinational corporations meant that some companies have larger economies than states, and these economic, social, and political entities can have outsized influence on our daily lives – putting them at times at odds with government policies. Is the state now less important than it was 50 years ago? Some may argue as such, but when we see a hardening of borders and escalation of rhetoric of national purity and tightening immigration controls, we must question whether the death of the state is exaggerated.

The stories above are stories about the state. The world as we know it today is territorialized by the state form: a presumption that all spaces on earth are sovereign, or self-governing, states, with definable borders, government institutions, and populations of citizens. But how did this world come to be and could it have been (or in the future, be) different? If our current state system often fails people like Aylan Kurdi, Jakelin Caal, and Felipe Gomez Alonzo, are there alternative ways of being in the world that would have protected them? In this chapter, we will trace the history of the sovereign state and other governmental forms, and then return to these questions of the everyday nature of the state and its consequences for our lives and the lives of those we care for. But the state is also quite difficult to study in its own way. As has been argued by a range of sociologists, political theorists, and geographers, whether we want to smash the state or study it (paraphrasing Abrams 1988), we must know what it is – and to know it is quite difficult as it becomes part of what sociologist Pierre Bourdieu calls our habitus, or our way of being in the world (Bourdieu 1990). This makes it more crucial to work to understand the state's origins and its components, since in allowing the state to exist as an un-interrogated entity, we risk granting it rather too much power and agency, seeing it as a unitary and intentional actor without understanding its contingent history or the ways that it is internally fragmented, disjointed, and fractious.

We can call this difficulty the **state effect** (Mitchell 1999; 1991). What does it mean to refer to a state effect? This means that the state is not in fact one thing – rather it is a conglomeration of agencies, people, and other entities, but because of how it operates in our lives, we begin to think of it as a structure, as a powerful and unitary force in our lives. We might read along similar lines the observations of Agnew (1994) on the territorial trap. Agnew points out that of the two defining features of the state (its political institutions and its sovereign territory), the territory component of the state is less fixed than we often assume. Under the Westphalian model of the state the assumption is that there must exist a "clear spatial demarcation of the territory within which the state exercises its power" (Agnew 1994, p.53–54): these are the colorful and confidently demarcated shapes on the globe I showed my child. We know, however, that, "even when rule is territorial and fixed, territory does not necessarily entail the practices of total mutual exclusion which the dominant understanding of the territorial state attributes to it" (Agnew 1994, p.53–54). Let us explore the history of this institution and then return to this idea of the state effect.

Is The History of the World the History of the West? Sovereignty's Origin Story

Every book on political geography refers to the Treaty of Westphalia: it is non-negotiable, and yet, this is also a very fraught and complex history. Here, let us rehearse this history but also add some crucial footnotes on its development. For the irony of global history is that the Treaty of Westphalia in the seventeenth century and subsequent understanding of the world as ideally divided into mutually acknowledged sovereign territories also took place on the eve of imperialism and colonialism. This meant that the birth of sovereignty was inextricable from exclusions and exceptions from sovereignty. Thus, we cannot consider the sovereign state without considering the Indigenous people that Europeans sought to eliminate, those who were enslaved in the service of state expansion, or those who were denied participation in the subsequent mechanisms of governance until only the last hundred years, and then only partially and contingently. So what do we do with the history of the sovereign state, which is both dry and simultaneously bloody? In this text, we will certainly trace how the discipline has understood the development of the state, but will also complicate this by thinking through both other state forms that emerged outside Europe and by pointing out how Europe's history cannot be separated out from the history of the rest of the world.

But before we get into this set of questions that require historical context, let us begin a little more abstractly. What do we need to be part of the state system? Can I start my own sovereign state? Let us consider what I would need. First, I need territory. Not just territory that I own as private property but territory over which I have sovereignty. These are perhaps the two most crucial elements that define what we think of as the state today: sovereign territory, over which only the state has legal jurisdiction in order to determine its own affairs. We will complicate this in a while, but for now let us be comically simplistic. What else might we consider as integral parts of a state? We will definitely need a government and some formal institutions of governance, and it is also conventional to have a military to defend our borders. All this would be rather pointless without a population to govern and defend. So in most states today we expect to find all of the following:

- Territory with defined and internationally recognized borders (though some may be in dispute);
- Sovereignty within that territory – that is, the power to make laws and govern its own people;
- Formal systems of governance that may take different forms;
- Government institutions and public infrastructure;
- A population; and
- A military and police force, and a monopoly on the legitimate use of violence.

You likely live inside an entity with the characteristics above. Does this mean that this is the ideal form of human existence? The pinnacle of civilizational development? Of course not. It is very important not to take a **teleological** view here, that is, not to assume that history was necessarily driving us to the point at which we now find ourselves, and that each step was preordained or indicated progress. Rather, we can understand our current political forms to be the outcomes of processes and events that could have happened differently, not something that was natural or without alternatives. This is just one reason that political geographers often refer to "state formation" rather than "the state." This is not only because academics seem to enjoy wordiness and jargon, but because what seems to be jargon at first can in fact just be more precise language. State *formation* emphasizes that the state is never fixed or complete, but is a process that is always contested and changing. Referring to state formation rather than the state chips away at the state effect discussed earlier – it reminds us that states are in process, contingent, less solid than they seem.

For this reason, Painter (2006, p.758) suggests that we think not of the state, but focus instead on **statization** as the "intensification of the symbolic presence of the state across all kinds of social practices and relations." As he clarifies, institutions such as schools and police stations are certainly real, but we cannot easily classify all state functions as being the

work of the state, nor all state institutions as being separate from the social. We will elaborate on this later, but for now let us return to the idea of the Westphalian state.

In 1644, in the Westphalian towns of Münster and Osnabrück, meetings began in an
attempt to end chronic war and territorial disputes that had been ongoing for 30 years
across central Europe, and longer in the case of the 80-year conflict between Spain and
what was to become the Netherlands. The Holy Roman Emperor Ferdinand II of the
Habsburg family had attempted to regain influence in a period of chaos with Protestantism
and sectarianism gaining strength and territorial struggles on multiple fronts. By 1648, the
"Peace of Westphalia," comprised of a series of smaller treaties, had been negotiated
through a series of meetings between parties representing European interests. Foundational
to this peace was recognizing the rights of sovereign rulers to determine affairs within
their own lands, and the recognition therefore of territory as an organizing principle of
peace. That is, by agreeing not to interfere or intervene in other princes' territory, peace
was established, and boundaries were fixed, and a new map of Europe was born. Tilly
(1975) thus points to a simplification in Europe from 500 small kingdoms clamoring to
"about 25" states.

This model of statehood is often referred to in an ideal form as the **Westphalian model**.
"Ideal," doesn't mean "the best we can come up with," but rather refers to a model or
type – the abstract version or concept that we use to understand a phenomenon. The
Westphalian ideal, then, is a system of states in which borders are clearly defined and do not
overlap, and within these borders there is independence from external interference. This
also imagines that the state is the most important actor in international relations, and
assumes a level playing ground. In other words, the assumed integrity, autonomy, and internal governance that is implied by the colorful patchwork of states that we see when we look
at a political map. On a political map, it is not that the color is deepest in the middle of the
country, and then blurs out to blend into other countries at the edges. Rather, each state is
defined by thick black lines, and colors are chosen so that the borders are easy to see. This
is the Westphalian model that much political theory and indeed diplomacy rests on – a kind
of shorthand through which we think about the world, even as we recognize that things are
not as clear or straightforward.

Elden's (2013b) genealogy of territory pushes the origins of the Westphalian model
deeper into the history of Europe, arguing that the seventeenth-century developments were
built upon earlier processes of territorialization. This reading of territory is at the heart of
our understanding of the Westphalian state form, as the idea of the relationship between
sovereignty and territory is crucial for the Westphalian formulation. Elden is careful to
distinguish between territory and land (defined as property) or terrain (defined as the space
of military engagement). For Elden (2013b, p.2), questions of nationalism, geopolitics, and
terror, which we will grapple with in later chapters, must begin with questions about sovereign territory: "What is being fought over, divided, mapped, distributed or transformed?
Where did this idea of exclusive ownership of a portion of the earth's surface come from?"
and, "Is the standard story that it emerged with the Peace of Westphalia in 1648 sufficient?"
For Elden, the seventeenth-century outcomes were rooted in a deeper history, beginning
from the Greek ideas of *koinon*, "a place and the people who inhabit it," and the *polis*, the
community of people in that site who have status as citizens (that is, "not foreigners, not
slaves, and only men" (Elden 2013b, p.48). In other words, the polis "excludes any who do
not rule themselves" (Elden 2013b, p.48).

Elden traces the meaning of territory under the Romans, with a particular focus around the limits of empire, and then the later history of Europe through its land politics, both familial and geopolitical. These earlier histories build through European history, into, Elden argues, the fifteenth-century landing of Columbus in North America and the subsequent dividing lines of the Treaty of Tordesillas. These were critical moments in the theorization of territory, the establishment of dividing lines that parsed the places that were supposedly "newly discovered" (of course this would be a peculiar idea to the people living there). These were "an attempt to break with the idea that simple occupation led to possession; rather, it divided lands that were not yet known by a calculative measure" (Elden 2013b, p.243). Crucial to note, and something requiring elaboration, is that "It was not a case of a Europe with nation-states with fixed territory as a model that was exported to the rest of the world; rather, the New World proved to be a laboratory where ideas were tried out, concepts forged, and techniques tested and perfected, which were then carried back to Europe" (Elden 2013b, p.245). In Elden's reading, then, this is not unlike the thinking of Wynter (2003) that we encountered in Chapter 4 – that is, though the idea of the sovereign state emerges in Europe, it is unthinkable without Europe's relationship to the rest of the world. This echoes the ways that the ideas of modern humanity, with roots in the same historical moment, also required at the time a hierarchy of humanity that in fact excluded much of the world's people.

Shortly after the Peace of Westphalia, Thomas Hobbes published the *Leviathan*, with its famous frontispiece, which is included in many political geography textbooks. The image depicts a king presiding over fields and a walled city. As you look closely at the king, you see that his body is made of his people. Writing perhaps in response to the years of war and conflict, the *Leviathan* is an argument for civil peace through the centralization of power in the sovereign ruler of the state; symbolized by the king who is literally embodied by his subjects (the gendered language here is intentional). The thinking of John Locke, "cement[s] the relationship between political power and territory," by arguing for the state to rule by consent in order to protect private property (Elden 2013b, p.308).

If we take the idea of the sovereign state at face value, then in this period, a container-like state begins to emerge. But is sovereignty quite so neat as all that? We must be careful not to assume this ideal is so simple, cohesive, or consistent in daily practice. The Westphalian model has an appealing origin story, but one may be taken in by the story and misled, thus overlooking "situations in which rulers have, in fact, not been autonomous" (Krasner 2001, p.17). Perhaps the treaty was more important in the limitations it placed on princes through the protection of religious minorities (Krasner 1999). Or perhaps the importance of 1648 is overwrought, and the treaty marked not the birth of the modern state system, but rather the consolidation of absolutist sovereignty for France and Sweden (Teschke 2003). Remember that sovereignty was clearly articulated in the context of Europe just at the moment when exclusions from sovereignty proliferated under European empires.

Turan Kayaoğlu and others have questioned the starring role that the Westphalian state narrative has played in over-determining political theory and international relations. Along the same lines as Elden's inquiry into the deployment of territorial sovereignty of some places as a means to undermine the territorial sovereignty of others, Kayaoğlu dismantles the idea of the sovereign state through a focus on its outside: the extraterritoriality that was deployed through legal imperialism. As he observes, the consolidation of Westphalian sovereignty is depicted as a two-step process, "the emergence of norms in Europe and their subsequent diffusion to non-European entities through state socialization. Sovereignty norms emerge from the norm-generating European core, and then diffuse into the norm-receiving non-European periphery" (Kayaoğlu 2010, p.9). Kayaoğlu writes against this narrative.

First, the telling and re-telling of the birth of the modern state as a European practice reinforces a Eurocentric view of the world in which European ideas drive history (this echoes Elden's points about the European ideas being generated through encounter). Secondly, this obscures the way that the birth of sovereignty went hand in hand with the birth of **extraterritoriality**: the extension of sovereignty beyond its delimited borders and the spaces of exception that are not granted sovereignty at all. Sovereignty and extraterritoriality spread together. That is, the entrenchment of mutually-exclusive territories as the hallmark of the modern state happened in conjunction with "a legal regime whereby a state claims exclusive jurisdiction over its citizens in another state," and such courts, "embodied the semicolonial status of non-Western states such as China" (Kayaoğlu 2010, p.2). Thus, at the same time that the rights of others outside Europe to govern themselves were violated – consider Elden's point that the "discovery" of the Americas was a means through which Europe theorized territory. A little more than two centuries later, we find ourselves in the midst of imperial resurgence during the "Scramble for Africa." Kayaoğlu's research examines the spread of British courts outside Britain during the late nineteenth and twentieth centuries. In these courts, which Kayaoğlu documents in China and the Ottoman Empire, Europeans abroad were able to seek trials under British law, clearly violating the ideal of the sovereign state that we have laid out earlier (in which sovereigns or governments define legal jurisdiction within their territories).

Consider the case of Henry Demenil, a US citizen who killed a Tibetan monk in Yunnan Province in 1907. Demenil was traveling along the Tibetan frontier, in violation of the terms of his visa, and the Viceroy of Szechwan had sent two Chinese soldiers with him for protection. Court documents record that, upon being frustrated about delays, Demenil seized one of the soldier's guns, and shot at him apparently to scare him into moving more quickly through the village. Though Demenil did not hit the guard, one bullet hit and killed a Tibetan monk in the village. In his diary, he recorded this as an accident, and this same diary became evidence of his innocence when he was tried for murder not in a Chinese court, but rather in a US Court in Shanghai. Both Judge Wilfey and Demenil were from the US state of Missouri. Wilfey ruled that Demenil's peculiar actions of firing upon his own escort were caused by nerves and "the rarefied mountain air of the locality, the loneliness of the place, and the wilderness of his surroundings" (Scully 2001, p.129; see also, Williams 1922 for accounts reflecting on the incident; Huang 1925). As part of a symposium on "What China Demands," Robert Huang (1925), a law student at the University of Chicago declared such courts in China to be "a legal joke," by recounting as evidence several cases, including Demenil's, in which Chinese citizens had been killed and US or British courts had found the defendants not guilty on quite suspect evidence.

Kayaoğlu describes **legal imperialism** as a means through which imperial practices take the shape of the operations of the law – that is, through the operations of courts such as the Shanghai court that dismissed charges against Demenil. Beyond this East Asian case, Kayaoğlu also describes the "Ottoman Empire's Elusive Dream of Sovereignty," that is, its over-60-year quest to abolish the sovereignty-compromising extraterritorial courts of the Europeans within their borders, a goal finally reached in the Lausanne Treaty of 1923. You will recognize here that these conversations are continued today, though in different forms – consider, for example, Chapter 3's discussion of the Islamic state.

From these histories, we ought to take a few points. First, the state form we assume is natural is an artifact of history and could have been different. Second, we ought to take care when we think about this history and sovereignty's relation to imperialism. The history of the world, the use of terms like, "failed states," and "developing countries," appears very different if we try to trace the history of the development of the modern state form alongside the history of its exceptions.

The Everyday State

Let us return to the question from the early pages of this chapter on the reasons that the state is so difficult to study, and also consider this question of the state effect more carefully.

In the 1980s, anthropologist Akhil Gupta was conducting research in a small village in North India, and noticed how much of ordinary conversation was about corruption and bureaucracy. The way they talked about the state was quite different from how it was described in state theory. And: they weren't wrong! In their lives, the state was encountered through frustrating negotiations with petty bureaucrats or police officers. They were not crossing a national border or meeting the Prime Minister. Gupta (1995, p.375) writes:

> Most of the stories the men told each other in the evening, when the day's work was done and small groups had gathered at habitual places to shoot the breeze, had to do with corruption (*bhashtaachaar*) and "the state." Sometimes the discussion dealt with how someone had managed to outwit an official who wanted to collect a bribe; at other times with the "going price" to get an electrical connection for a new tubewell or to obtain a loan to buy a buffalo … Sections of the penal code were cited and discussed in great detail, the legality of certain actions to circumvent normal procedure were hotly debated … at times it seemed as if I had stumbled in on a specialized discussion with its own esoteric vocabulary, one to which, as a lay person and outsider, I was not privy.

What Gupta begins to see emerging, and then to pursue in a more focused way, is an **ethnography** of the state. An ethnography is a methodology developed in anthropology but now also commonly deployed by human geographers. In this research method in which an anthropologist spends a significant amount of time in a place living with and in conversation with the people who live there, until they come to understand the logics and aesthetics of how life is understood and "what makes sense" in that context. Historically, ethnography was part of imperial and colonizing knowledge production – collecting information and documenting the lives of "exotic" others in ways that were used to bolster now discredited racial science. In the twentieth century, ethnography often involved privileged and usually white academics traveling to supposedly exotic (to them) locations in distant lands in the Global South. Yet we should work against holding this idea in our mind. Reconsidered and approached carefully, the tools of ethnography could be used to understand business executives in a global technology firm in South Korea or New York, the housekeepers in your university's student housing, or small town teenagers, whether in Laos or Bolivia or Portugal. And the researcher using the tools of ethnography could be from the community itself, picking up tools developed in an imperial frame but repurposing them now for self-determination. We will return to these questions of research methods. For now, consider the ideas that Gupta was able to derive from listening to these conversations. He realized that he was creating an ethnography of the state from the point of view of people just getting by. What might we learn from this?

Gupta learns (and teaches us) that the state is not just one thing, and is not a unified actor. We also cannot abstract the state from these mundane interactions. Think of the recently renewed conversations on police violence in the United States. If people of color, especially in particular cities or neighborhoods, experience negative, violent, or even deadly use of force by the police, this is the reality of the state in their lives. On the other hand, if the state brings much needed infrastructure, new roads, or electricity to your village, you might say "give thanks to god and the government," which is a phrase I've often heard in kitchens up in the Himalayas (though, to be clear, this might be part of a longer conversation in which the government is also criticized!). Gupta learned to his surprise that the residents of this village felt that Indira Gandhi, who was running under a "get rid of poverty" campaign, cared for them, but that her care and initiatives could not reach them through the tangled and twisted lines of power that run through bureaucrats. In this way, he observed, the state is embodied in its public servants, and in the forms and infrastructure, which either get you to the place that you want to be, and deliver services and rights to you, or do not.

Let us build on these ideas by thinking about the work of Joe Painter (2006) on Anti-Social Behavior Ordinances (ASBOs). In 1998, a new Crime and Disorder Act was introduced in the United Kingdom, with the ASBO as one component, and 2003 saw the introduction of the Anti-Social Behavior Act. These pieces of legislation enabled ordinary citizens to report anti-social behavior. The kinds of behavior could include things like public drunkenness or brawling, littering, or letting your dog poop in the road. What Painter so presciently observes is that in these cases, it is not only that the state is comprised of individual people working on its behalf such as bureaucrats and mail carriers, but that its reach extends to our neighbors and people we meet on the street: for when they report our drunken night out or call about our loud music, in fact they are in that instance performing the work of the state in determining what is and is not antisocial behavior. In his words, "everyday life is permeated by the social relations of stateness."

As examples, Painter draws on a series of election posters put out by the UK Electoral Commission, which encouraged people to participate in the formal politics of elections by demonstrating the degree to which state policy shapes daily life. The posters begin with "How politics affects," and then go on to give examples for one component of daily life, so in the poster on "your night out," examples are given such as "[politics] decides where and when you can buy an alcoholic drink. Says at what age you can buy an alcoholic drink … Says what substances are illegal and what will happen to you if you're caught with them. Decides what time trains and buses stop running and whether or not there will be a night service …" (Painter 2006, p.754).

Painter observes that the characterization of state violence and law as legitimate is undercut by the ways that both violence and laws are contested. In fact, as we will explore in the chapter on social movements, the work of activists in drawing attention to state violence as unjust and mobilizing to change state law is part of the process of state formation itself. Painter also observes that the territoriality of the state is also questionable, due to its unevenness and the ways that its sovereignty over a given territory is never absolute, but is rather imagined to be stronger than it is.

On the Margins of the State

We began this chapter with the image of a child learning the colorful shapes on a globe, and then turned to thinking through how we came to think of these shapes as a natural backdrop to our daily existence. The history of state sovereignty we have covered tells a different and more complicated story, but we can likewise understand the state further by thinking about the complicated relationship between the state and displaced people. What is the state to the refugee or internally displaced people? And how is the state formed in relation to the presence of refugees, internally displaced people, and the humanitarian groups that seek to provide assistance to them? Patricia Daley's (2013) work on citizenship and refugees in the African Great Lakes region provides new ways to consider both citizenship and the state that defines it. The Great Lakes region's combination of both refugees and displaced people in a post-conflict setting raises questions about how such people will relate to the states, particularly in conditions of neoliberalism, in which even citizens face a rollback of state protections. When humanitarian groups intervene, this further complicates the relationship between displaced people and the state. Here, a politics of indigeneity has come to define citizenship rights, and defined many displaced Africans as "foreigners" to be excluded from national belonging (Daley 2013b; Nugent, Hammett, and Dorman 2007).

Following on our consideration of the possibility that citizenship fails the vulnerable, Daley (2013b, p.894), observes that citizenship rights "secure the holder in the territorial space of the state that confers those rights." Citizenship rights in the colonial era were by nature discriminatory. Now, even in peacetime, when refugees "return" home, neoliberal reconstruction priorities, xenophobia, and even the well-intended humanitarian interventions "create new categories of people, who despite having acquired or reactivated legal citizenship are exposed to exclusionary practices precisely because of the nature of their prior displacement" (Daley 2013b, p.895). This is complex. The drive to achieve refugee status itself legitimates the state by acknowledging its importance, even as it also acknowledges a liminal group of people who are "positioned in opposition to the citizen; represented as a victim, outcast, and in need only that which maintains 'bare life'" (Daley 2013b, p.896; Agamben 1998). At the same time, internally displaced people, even when they have citizenship, may be placed in the position of being refugees, without state protection. Daley suggests that displaced people's fate is shaped by the diversity politics of specific states, entitlement protection, and the role of humanitarian aid.

As in so many colonized places, ideas connecting citizenship rights and difference can be traced to the colonial state, whose legal systems inculcated differential citizenship, and created the idea of the foreigner through the foundation of the sovereign state we have discussed earlier (Daley 2013b; Herbst 2014). In the contemporary context, rights are secured through property, ethnic backgrounds can be mechanisms of exclusion, and some people can spend their lives as exiles, without a means to claim rightful citizenship. Humanitarian aid recognizes state sovereignty and both legitimates state regimes, while also working to depoliticize refugees, ironically rendering them as abject and vulnerable subjects without agency.

The Great Lakes region has complex layers of displacement: political opposition exiles from Rwanda and Burundi, internally displaced people within the Democratic Republic of Congo (DRC), efforts to force the repatriation of refugees from Burundi and Rwanda, and attempts to remove refugee status from those who refuse to repatriate. As a result, Daley observes that displaced people often end up being repatriated without integration, as in the case of Burundians in Tanzania, particularly since 2002. In 2012, Tanzania began forcibly repatriating Burundian refugees based on security concerns. Those who were repatriated faced difficulty in integrating, particularly in having access to land and food security. On the other hand, those who remained in Tanzania, face a complicated terrain of economic marginalization and displacement or resettlement across the state, which portrays them as competing for resources with citizens.

A differently troubling situation occurs for internally displaced people. In the case of the DRC, people from the Eastern DRC, counting in the millions, were displaced to other regions during fighting between Rwandan-backed Congrès National pour la Défense du People and the Congolese Army followed by further Congolese military actions in 2009 and 2012. In this case, as the state itself is part of the violence leading to displacement, people have to turn to family or to United Nations High Commissioner for Refugees (UNHCR) camps, while the government places pressure on them to return home. Some remain as internally displaced, some cross the border into Rwanda, Burundi, Tanzania, and Uganda. If citizenship is the means to obtain rights in relation to the state, and states uphold exclusionary forms of citizenship, displaced and marginalized groups will be without protection. This precarity is inseparable from citizenship debates, property-based citizenship, and neoliberal approaches to governance (Daley 2013b).

Geographer at Work: Ali Hamdan

Ali Hamdan earned his PhD in Geography from the University of California-Los Angeles in 2019. He is a Mount Vernon Society Fellow at George Washington University, where he is affiliated with the Department of Geography and the Institute for Middle East Studies.

My paternal grandfather was born in Lebanon in 1905. He lived through an unimaginable wave of political change, from the collapse of the Ottoman Empire to French Mandate rule, independence, civil war and eventually, postwar reconstruction. His youngest son – my father – fled Lebanon as a young man in the 1970s, meeting my American mother in Germany. It was impossible, growing up, to not feel some immediacy to events happening "back in Lebanon," to not imagine it as center of a unique political world. Memories of violence, transmitted through the generations, meant that figures like my father and grandfather come to dramatize for me the political stakes of "knowing" the Middle East, and of knowing the Global South in general.

Political geography can benefit, I believe, in returning some humility to the work that our ideas do in the world – to center different stories. Arguably, one of the greatest challenges for the field today is not empathizing with the political struggles of the Global South as such, but how to transcend a minimalist conception of solidarity that is mired in a navel-gazing idiom of Northern guilt. This conception has, in my experience, motivated a good deal of critical writing on the Middle East in geography. I find that I struggle to recognize the region at all in the many tired descriptions of victimhood and suffering, the stories of millions like my father and grandfather boiled down to epiphenomena of political geographies whose centers lie, inevitably it seems, in the Global North.

For those of us with a foot in both worlds, there is something unsatisfying about forms of critique that leave their object of solidarity with space for only two modes of politics: resignation to American Empire, or resistance to it. Neither affords a politics that is *about more* than how one relates to the Global North, or envisions a political geography in which the Middle East is not just part of the "global borderlands" of an American planet. I agree with Katherine McKittrick that accounts like this "leave little room to attend to human life" as it can be productively engaged, as she has so persuasively noted of Black geographies (McKittrick 2011, p.954). We might extend her insights to more distant corners of the globe that know other forms of domination. As geographers, our accounts do places like this a disservice when they are so darkly overshadowed by the forces of domination to which they are subjected. They preclude the possibility of "a more hopeful politics for a place that is, as every place, both flawed and deeply beautiful" (Clark 2017, p.10).

This concern for returning "human life" to a flawed but beautiful region deeply informs my work on the transnational dimensions of Syria's civil war. For the last several years I have been following a network of displaced Syrians who constitute an opposition movement-in-exile operating from Turkey and Jordan (among other countries), seeking to oust the autocratic Assad regime in Damascus. This movement-in-exile is the natural outgrowth of the 2011 Syrian Uprising, which saw waves of popular protest shake this government to its foundations. After several years of struggle, peaceful social contention degenerated into a violent contest for sovereignty that has transformed lives, communities, and arguably, the political geography of the entire Middle East.

This movement has attracted little interest among geographers. Geographers have shown far more interest in the threat of the so-called "Islamic State" and in the Syrian Kurdish autonomy movement led by the *Partiya Yekitaya Demokrat* (PYD), two actors who speak quite explicitly to the Northern impulse of self-critique. Both are cast as avatars of response to the imperial hubris (and folly) of the Global North, presenting European imperial intervention in 1919 as an original sin that offers a ready-made toolkit for understanding, even justifying their actions. For many, one deserves solidarity, the other our morbid curiosity. But the repeated framing of the region as trapped in the never-ending machinations of Others offers a painful reduction of its political field. It leaves a solidarity that is so awkwardly curated that it encourages US military intervention to protect "Rojava" while dismissing calls for the same to protect civilians in Idlib (Letter 2018). It is accompanied by a suspicion that Islam is necessarily at odds with the territorial state, and implies all too often that Islamism represents a coherent political ideology. The shortcomings of this frame spring less from malice than from a knee-jerk gaze to the navel. All the same they nonetheless leave much to be desired.

In all fairness, the revolutionaries from Syria whom I came to know simply did not speak in an idiom that geographers in the Global North would find immediately recognizable. But nor have geographers shown much concern for their plight beyond a throwing up of hands in acknowledgment of the sheer "complexity" of the subject – as if politics in Syria are so fundamentally Other that even our analytical categories cannot travel there. But Syria's conflict is not beyond our comprehension. I would actually argue that our conceptual tools are uniquely well-suited to untangling the complex, the overlapping, and the interconnected political geographies of the Middle East. Rather, Syria's conflict lies beyond what is familiar.

A political geography that is sensitive to these concerns is one that foregrounds different centers, gives voice to alternative agents, and breathes life into the unfamiliar. In short, it is critique that bridges space and is wedded to life in its vibrant multiplicity. For this reason, I am deeply inspired by the wave of feminist scholarship that has revitalized the subdiscipline, advocating intimate engagement with research subjects, ethnographic methods, language training, and above all, the kind of intellectual humility that enables us to see in the field what we cannot from the university campus (Koopman 2011; Massaro and Williams 2013). These methods are by no means value-neutral or beyond reproach, but they are the most effective for arriving at a political solidarity that is grounded in a kind of empathy that my grandfather might recognize as such.

Reflecting on the prospects of progressive politics in the region, Gilbert Achcar (2016) argues that Syria's uprising, like so many of its neighbors, is caught in a struggle against two counter-revolutions: one jihadi, the other fascist. In this simple formula, Achcar captures the stakes of politics in the entire Middle East in a way that does not deny the significance of American empire. But it does deflate its centrality to the story. There is plenty of room for other stories to be aired, for other projects to see daylight, for us to meet unexpected subjects. I write about Syria's opposition because who we write about matters.

What Have We Learned and Where Do We Go From Here?

As we move forward through the concepts that are to come, keep the ideas of sovereign state formation in mind, and do not be afraid to trouble them or to ask: what is this thing called sovereignty that spirals out of Europe in waves, enveloping the world in a colorful but deceptive patchwork that both affirms self-rule and simultaneously undermines it and diminishes it? As we transition to the next chapter, we will take some of the concepts we have encountered thus far: citizenship, state formation, and national belonging, and consider how they animate the landscape of cities and the lives of those who inhabit them.

Keywords

Ethnography An ethnography is a methodology developed in anthropology but now also commonly deployed by human geographers. A process by which an anthropologist spends a significant amount of time in a place, living with and in conversation with the people who live there, until they come to understand the logics and aesthetics of how life is understood and "what makes sense" in that context.

Extraterritoriality   The extension of sovereignty beyond its delimited borders and the spaces of exception that are not granted sovereignty at all.

Legal imperialism   How imperial practices take the shape of the operations of the law.

State effect   The state is not in fact one thing – rather it is a conglomeration of agencies, people, and other entities, but because of how it operates in our lives, we begin to think of it as a structure, as a powerful and unitary force in our lives.

Statization   An intensification of state presence throughout our lives, making it difficult to separate out state and social processes.

Westphalian model   A system of states in which borders are clearly defined and do not overlap, and within these borders there is independence from external interference.

Further Reading

Everyday states

Anand, N. 2017. *Hydraulic City: Water and the Infrastructures of Citizenship in Mumbai.* Durham, NC: Duke University Press.

Cowen, D. 2014. *The Deadly Life of Logistics: Mapping Violence in Global Trade.* Minneapolis, MN: University of Minnesota Press.

Gupta, A. 1995. Blurred Boundaries: The Discourse of Corruption, the Culture of Politics, and the Imagined State. *American Ethnologist* 22: 375–402.

Gupta, A. 2012. *Red Tape: Bureaucracy, Structural Violence, and Poverty in India.* Durham, NC: Duke University Press.

Marston, S.A. 2004. Space, Culture, State: Uneven Developments in Political Geography. *Political Geography* 23: 1–16.

Mountz, A. 2010. *Seeking Asylum: Human Smuggling and Bureaucracy at the Border.* Minneapolis, MN: University of Minnesota Press.

Painter, J. 2006. Prosaic Geographies of Stateness. *Political Geography* 25: 752–774.

Questioning Westphalia

Abraham, I. 2014. *How India Became Territorial: Foreign Policy, Diaspora, Geopolitics.* Palo Alto, CA: Stanford University Press.

Benton, L. 2009. *A Search for Sovereignty: Law and Geography in European Empires, 1400–1900.* Cambridge: Cambridge University Press.

Chen, C.-C. 2012. The Im/Possibility of Building Indigenous Theories in a Hegemonic Discipline: The Case of Japanese International Relations. *Asian Perspective* 36(3): 463–492.

Kayaoğlu, T. 2010. *Legal Imperialism: Sovereignty and Extraterritoriality in Japan, the Ottoman Empire, and China.* Cambridge: Cambridge University Press.

Krasner, S.D. 1999. *Sovereignty: Organized Hypocrisy.* Princeton, NJ: Princeton University Press.

State formation

Abrams, P. 1988. Notes on the Difficulty of Studying the State. *Journal of Historical Sociology* 1: 58–89.

Agnew, J.A. 1994. The Territorial Trap: The Geographical Assumptions of International Relations Theory. *Review of International Political Economy* 1: 53–80.

Agnew, J.A. 2013. *The Birth of Territory*. Chicago: University of Chicago Press.

Mitchell, T. 1999. Society, Economy, and the State Effect. In G. Steinmetz (ed.), *State/Culture: State-Formation After the Cultural Turn*. Ithaca, NY: Cornell University Press, pp.76–87.

Sparke, M. 2000. Graphing the Geo in Geo-Political: Critical Geopolitics and the Re-Visioning of Responsibility. *Political Geography* 19: 373–380.

Tilly, C. 1975. *The Formation of National States in Europe*. Princeton, NJ: Princeton University Press.

Chapter 6

Urban Politics

I have been told that villagers are eggs, and those powerful are rocks, that we cannot win against them. But I don't think that way. It is probably true that we are the eggs, and they are the rocks, however we have to clash against the rocks even though we might be crushed. At least I shall make those rocks smell badly.

> (Srey Pov, housing rights activist in Phnom Penh, quoted in Brickell [2014, p.1264]).

What are the politics that enable cities to take the shape that they do? And why do we associate certain forms of political action with cities? What does it mean to be the egg that breaks itself upon the rocks in an effort to survive in an urban world? We will start this chapter by briefly considering two cases in which people claim life and belonging in the city simply by continuing to exist. In the first case, residents in Sanjay Nagar, an informal settlement in Mumbai, find ways to get water despite bureaucratic and logistical hurdles. For them, water becomes a form of hydraulic citizenship. In the second case, families who have built a livelihood along Boeung Kak Lake in Phnom Penh fight to retain their homes and livelihoods in the face of Chinese-backed investments seeking to redevelop their neighborhood. Women like Srey Pov, quoted above, become activists emphasizing home as a universal need. After these vignettes call us into an urban frame of mind, we will step back to consider the tools urban theorists, political geographers, and others have given us to think about the relationship between politics, space, and place in the city. Today, more than half of our world lives in urban settings, and beyond the simple fact of this urbanity, cities shape the countryside as well – requiring the water, labor, food, and energy resources that flow from the countryside into the city.

Political Geography: A Critical Introduction, First Edition. Sara Smith.
© 2020 John Wiley & Sons Ltd. Published 2020 by John Wiley & Sons Ltd.

Water and Life in Mumbai

In the short film *4:30 pm*, two young women walk through the neighborhood of Sanjay Nagar in Mumbai, chatting with neighbors as they collect in lines and groups to fill steel containers with water from the taps that have just come on. A young boy flits in and out of the picture, eager to be part of the film as he eats his package of chips, and the narrator asks us to look for the woman in the yellow sari moving from one tap to another to speed the process of water collection and get home. For these residents, the fact of getting water each day is not exceptional: it is part of a daily routine that is both pleasant (laughing with your friends, speculating on the latest gossip), and a frustrating and unjust set of demands on your labor, time, and energy (waiting in line, hauling heavy plastic or steel containers). Because the film was captured, edited, and narrated by local young people, the camerawork presents all of these aspects, and neither romanticizes this labor *nor* depicts it through the "poverty porn" lens familiar from charity commercials or representations like *Slumdog Millionaire*. For this reason, the scenes of neighbors chatting, water splashing, and the joking boy with his snacks bring us a different message. They assert: we have a right to be in this city, we will survive and thrive, and if the city infrastructure does not support our survival, we will affirm our citizenship through our own skill and ingenuity in the claiming of space and water.

4:30 pm is one of a series of 12 films, called *Ek Dozen Paani* (available on Vimeo), produced by young people from community organizations based in Mumbai – Aakansha Sewa Sangh and Agaaz Arts Collective Camp and anthropologist Nikhil Anand (Anand et al. 2008). These films follow water through the life of the city, and in particular, how water becomes a site through which citizenship is negotiated in the city. The urban residents who appear in the films confront politicians, petty bureaucrats, engineers, and their fellow residents as they work to ensure their own existence in the city. The uneven provision of water across the city reflects the city's particular geography, and the qualities of water, but also differences of class, religious identity, and migrant status in the city (Anand 2011; 2017). To claim water is to claim a "right to the city," that is, "far more than a right of individual access to the resources that the city embodies: it is a right to change ourselves by changing the city more after our heart's desire" (Harvey 2008, p.272). In the full series of films, we also see the interwoven nature of rural and urban, as the camera follows one of the water pipelines from farms on the outskirts into the city, and Anand as the narrator explains that farmers outside the city are affected by the diversion of water to feed the urban environment. Later in this chapter we will go further to understand this relationship between the cities and the countryside. Writing about water in the city, Anand describes water's material qualities – it leaks, it is heavy, it requires infrastructure to get uphill. These qualities intersect with the forms of difference that matter in the city, such as economic class, religion, and migrant status. This may recall for you the icy geopolitics of Chapter 4. Engineers explain to the residents of Prem Nagar, a longstanding migrant settlement, that because of water's material qualities, it is hard to get water up the hill to their homes. And yet, at the same time, water always flows uphill to Malabar Hill, where wealthy citizens and movie stars reside.

Why choose water as a site of urban citizenship? As an urgent daily necessity that requires complex systems of infrastructure, the politics of water are one way we can begin to understand who is included and excluded in urban settings, and how claims to the right to water provide a vector through which people claim citizenship and belonging. But there are many ways that claims to the city are made – a rich body of literature has explored these themes – in India alone there is a wealth of literature on how the mediation of everyday life and the flow of material entities (such as water or waste) through urban settings is constitutive of larger processes of capitalism, development, colonial legacies, and differences of gender and religion. Just as a few of many examples of this rich literature, Vinay Gidwani and Rajyashree Reddy (2011) trace the afterlives of waste through the colonial era into the management of present day solid waste in Delhi and Bangalore: the uneven ways in which wealth and poverty are co-produced from global to neighborhood scales are evident in the ways that people and places are marked as "waste," and yet indispensable to the process of capitalism signals not only local difference but also global and colonial processes. Wealthy urban residents strive to preserve green zones and historic areas and to "clean up the streets," but waste remains and even takes new forms, such as electronic and toxic waste. In the dangerous process of recycling e-waste, class differences are again intensified as the labor is performed mainly by poor members of Bangalore's marginalized Muslim communities. In Mumbai, Doshi (2013) demonstrates that the differential displacement of the poor is not incidental to wealth creation, but rather that the dispossession of the poor is part of how land markets are socially created. In Bangalore, Ranganathan (2015; 2018) works through the idea of risky urban socionatures of flooding in relation to capitalism, and framings of "improvement," that rely both on colonial legacies and liberal understandings of the city and its residents.

Of course, water and infrastructure are not the only ways to understand a city! Ayona Datta (2016), through her work in Delhi, has argued for an understanding of the "intimate city," in which gendered violence is ascribed to public space, but made more complex if we seek out claims for intimate spaces as fundamental to the city, and the biopolitical city structure as a lasting example of what Stoler (2013) calls imperial ruination. Elsewhere in India, Ananya Roy (2003) has demonstrated the ways that poverty is made relationally between rural and urban spaces, and gendered through the ways that services and infrastructure are managed. In *Why Loiter*, Shilpa Phadke, Sameera Khan, and Shilpa Ranade (2011) call for us to understand the city of Mumbai as a thriving place of both pleasure and risk, and, in particular, for women and marginalized others to demand not only existence in the city but also leisure and pleasure. Activist groups based in this philosophy now organize night time pleasure strolls, napping in parks, and drinking tea at roadside stalls as profoundly political acts (on social media, search for Why Loiter, Girls at Dhabas, and Blank Noise, among others). These reflections on urban life demonstrate the ways that political processes, with all their complexity, are manifest and contested in city infrastructure and in the ways that people navigate the city. In this chapter, we will explore politics in the city, as well as the role that cities play in politics. To begin, let us turn again to activists like Srey Pov, to understand the conditions that prepare her to fight a battle she knows she will likely lose.

The Intimate Geopolitics of Home in Phnom Penh

Like us, housing rights activists in Phnom Penh can easily see connections between global patterns of wealth and poverty and the conditions in their own neighborhood. In one protest, women wear t-shirts with the slogan, "The Whole World is Watching," to protest forced eviction in 2012 (Brickell 2014). In a neighborhood of Phnom Penh, informal settlements became claims to land and home to 20,000 people, whose livelihoods depended on fish, agriculture, and tourism centered on Boeung Kak Lake (Figure 6.1). But in 2007, the municipality leased 133 hectares of the lake and land to a Chinese-backed private developer, one of the developments leading to mass evictions. Brickell's (2014) research suggests that of 4,000 families, by 2014, only 794 remained. These figures, and the women's struggles to remain in their community and fight eviction, reveal how the city is both a lens through which to understand broader political forces such as neoliberalism, and a special site through which these forces play out. One theme of this chapter will be that the city is a crucial and critical site of geopolitics. Here, Brickell is also building on the ideas of Casolo and Doshi (2013, p.800), who propose that "Geopolitics today is increasingly marked by the violent convergence of (in)security, market integration, and dispossession." Brickell's work demonstrates the value of understanding intersecting forms of violence as a site of vulnerability but also a means through which organizing occurs, as women join together to

Figure 6.1   Tep Vanny in Boeung Kak, Phnom Penh in 2011. Reproduced with permission of Katherine Brickell.

understand the role that violence plays in their life, whether through the form of spousal violence or forced eviction.

These activists are women who also struggle for the right to be in the city, and do so in part by dramatically staging the injustices of their eviction. They strip themselves naked in front of the Cambodian parliament and grieve their homes at the American Embassy. They design elaborate hats with eggs in nests to symbolize the universal need for home. They collectively strategize and use their bodies to demand justice and rework intimate relations of the home by asking their male partners to work in the background rather than be the public face of this struggle. When the activists demand housing, they frame it as a "gateway right" to "normative values of privacy, security, intimacy, comfort, belonging, and control accorded to home" (Brickell 2014; see also Datta 2016).

When the Boeung Kak Lake activists speak out, they are addressing processes of state oppression, but simultaneously they are taking on a global pattern: the accumulation of wealth by global elites through dispossession in the name of development (Harvey 2003; Doshi 2013; Casolo and Doshi 2013). Accumulation by dispossession means that projects of development or urban renewal are a way to target the most vulnerable people in a city (such as those in informal settlements) for removal. This enables speculative capital (wealthy land developers with sums to invest or loans at their disposal) to take over to build more lucrative housing for the wealthy (Casolo and Doshi 2013; Doshi 2013). In the quest to develop and demonstrate signs of economic growth, government power in Cambodia (as well as elsewhere, such as China and India), has sought to capture wealth from urban zones of potential and also from natural resources or potential sources of electricity (for instance, the large dam projects in India, China, and Egypt), and has utilized demolition and the bulldozing of homes as a means to this end. When communities are resettled, it is into less desirable land, and often lacks the services such as education and health, that were available in the city, and yet the "annihilation of home," is still seen as being in the "public interest" (Brickell 2014, p.1261). Brickell's work (2014, p.1261) hones in on the intimately political way that this structural work reshapes the city through the haphazard destruction of individual lives, as in the testimony of Phorn Sophea, a woman in her forties:

> My situation is cruel [crying]. I had to tear down my own house to receive compensation. Later, when I went to the City Hall for help, the authority said that I had come only to annoy them … that I had already gained compensation. They did not want to listen to my miserable life after I had left … Why do the authorities treat us badly this way? Honestly speaking, my husband blames me every day that I was wrong to accept compensation; he blames me for being too impatient. On the other hand, my children begged me to accept the compensation and leave. They didn't want me to face arrest and detention. I cannot even describe how I felt after leaving my home.

Phorn Sophea's downward trajectory demonstrates the workings of accumulation by dispossession. While she struggled to retain her home and livelihood, the development company set up an office in the neighborhood and offered compensation below market value and relocation 20 km outside the city. As the families banded together and tried to retain their right to live in the neighborhood, the company filled the lake with sand until families like hers feared for safety, especially given the danger of electrocution. Once relatively secure with publishing machines and a successful small business, since Phorn Sophea was forced to dismantle her own home to receive compensation, and then agree to be displaced and relocated. Her family has been unable to adjust. Her children dropped out of school or took low-wage work, her marriage became consumed with conflict resulting from the economic stress, and she describes herself as experiencing torture and misery. Even her internal life is now "penetrate[d] and haunt[ed] in ways that we can only intimate, and there is no territorial defense of privacy or domesticity that protects the intimate from the global" (Pratt and Rosner 2006, p.18; cited in Brickell 2014, p.1262).

The destruction of home, or **domicide**, as labeled by Porteous and Smith (2001, p.63), comprises not only a loss of housing, but is also

> the destruction of a place of attachment and refuge; loss of security and ownership; restrictions on freedom; partial loss of identity; and radical de-centering from place, family and community. There may be a loss of historical connection; a weakening of roots; and partial erasure of the sources of memory, dreams, nostalgia and ideals.

The women that Brickell speaks with theorize this domicide as sharing the fabric of earlier histories of domicide, drawing analogies between the genocide of Pol Pot's regime, and the ways that this history reinserts itself into their lives when they see echoes of it in the "demonization of urban dwellers, the annihilation of familial intimacy, and the complete disregard for emotional and personal attachments in the pursuit of (agrarian) progress and forced eviction" (Brickell 2014, p.1263). The women's analysis is reminiscent of Tyner's (2008) description of the "unmaking of space" in Cambodia, and the ways that people's connections to the land were severed and urban dwellers were expelled from the city. Under the Khmer Rouge, the unmaking of space was meant to "[usher] in a communist society" (Tyner 2008, p.106). Today, the Cambodian People's Party unmakes the homes of urban dwellers to enable large-scale infrastructure projects: an embodied and material **creative destruction** (Schumpeter 1942; Harvey 1999; Marx and Engels 1967), in which old ways of life and economic systems were devastated in order to make room for new ones. If you have ever lived in a city undergoing rapid **gentrification** – from Mumbai to San Francisco to Hong Kong, some of these processes will feel familiar to you – but in each place they unfold they are entangled in local histories, memories, and power dynamics. Broadly, gentrification refers to the ways that an influx of capital into low-rent areas ushers in new classes of people and displaces lower-income residents – we will return to this idea in a few pages.

Strikingly, for Boeung Kak Lake activists, the emotional bonds to home are a source of resistance to neoliberalism that they relate back to earlier experiences during the Khmer era. It is these emotional bonds that make women like Srey Pov (quoted at the beginning of the chapter) willing to be the eggs that break upon the rocks. The work of these activists makes vivid and compelling links through imagery of their bodily protest and their lost homes, the history of genocide, and the domicide of the contemporary neoliberal flows of capital that remake and restructure place. For a moment, take a breath, and imagine money not as zeros and ones in a computer, as change in your pocket, or as your credit card. Imagine money as a river, as a fluid: it flows into urban settings, to increase and double itself and multiply, but like a river, it oversteps banks, runs a little bit wild, and reshapes the earth itself. So money in the form of investment capital flows into urban settings, and pushes out some residents so that those who can pay higher rents take its place. Once this dangerous and desired substance fills the city, those from the rural areas are drawn there as they must be for survival, but the city has been shaped by forces beyond their control and they must seek to live and thrive in the sandbanks and reshaped shores of the ever-changing landscape. Does water flow downhill? Or does it flow toward money? For residents of Prem Nagar, water is the sustenance that is being pumped up other hills to the stars on Malabar Hill, but for which they must scramble and fight. For the Boeung Kak Lake activists, Chinese capital flows into the city with the intent of replacing them, and literally displaces water into their homes until they reluctantly flee.

Beyond the ways that money in the form of capital shapes our cities, there are other influences at play as well. The city can be a place where fights about who belongs in the nation play out in disagreements about water. It can be a place where women gauge their gendered safety through risk assessments of going out at night, and a place where they find freedom to challenge gender norms and embrace new visions of their own sexuality and sexual orientation. It can be a place of suffering and vulnerability, and of interethnic solidarity and **subaltern cosmopolitanism** (Gidwani 2006; Yeh 2009). That is, a place where marginalized groups and poor migrants interact, develop worldly skills befitting their mobility, and deploy them both in the realm of politics and within their own life trajectories. The city is a space where landless rural migrants find space to thrive, *and* where they find a new sense of self, new tastes in food, and become a different person. It is a landscape of capital and dispossession. But it can also be "an organ in your body": the place you met the person you love, acquired your political orientation, and developed a taste for food not found back home (Mehta 2009).

What Do We Learn About Politics from Urban Spaces?

In primary school, we learn about cities as centers of political organization – though perhaps we do not remember it that way. We learn that early civilizations, art, and culture emerged in cities, as conglomerations of urban people began sustaining themselves from the labor of the countryside, and urban centers began to thrive with more concentrated population centers and an elite class that developed cultural, religious, and political power, first in the Indus Valley (present day India and Pakistan) and in Mesopotamia (present day Iraq), and in Egypt and China. Geographers initially drew their theorizations of the city from European city development, in which population clusters grew up around free citizens that were part of larger feudal territories, and the development of cities often grew around trade, or cultural or political power sources, such as churches or early universities (Keil 2009). Over the course of the twentieth century, influential theorizations of urban politics increasingly skewed toward justice-oriented and Marxist analyses, and thus drew on some of the ideas emerging from critical understandings of the industrial revolution, *and* the affiliated social movements. Harvey (e.g., 1973), Lefebvre (e.g., 2004, 2003) and others (Castells 1977; Smith, M.P. 1979) began approaching the city as a product of social relations, which was a way for the insights of Marxism to be applied to the **built environment**, that is, to the planning, buildings, and infrastructure of cities themselves (Keil 2009). As we will discuss more later, scholars like Harvey and Lefebvre understood the city to be the material result of class struggle, and the built environment to be both the site of struggle and the archive of that struggle. Adding nuance and intersectional framings of oppression into this larger framework, in the 1990s, Laws (1994) wrote:

> The slogan, "No Justice, No Peace", chanted in marches, spray painted across gutted buildings and broadcast into millions of homes during the 1992 Los Angeles riots, made the issue of social justice and injustice a little more visible, and possibly more threatening. But injustice is not only contested in mass violence of the sort witnessed during urban riots. Women, for example, who argue against the injustice of an urban system which prevents them from walking city streets at night for fear of violent attach, demand better street lighting and escort services. Similarly, gay men who risk attack in a society that promotes compulsory heterosexism work to promote a tolerance of diverse sexual orientations.

Let us consider different ways of thinking about a city and then use these lenses to explore some particular cases.

Built environment as an archive of history

Think for a moment about the city or town that you know best. Imagine its streets and buildings and the people flowing through it. How does the physical environment – the mountains, lakes, and rivers, the ocean, or the other aspects of the topography shape what is and is not possible in the city? What about the climate? Is it a city built for cold weather, or warm? And history? Was it built before the car or after? Did it begin to develop thousands of years ago, like Damascus, Beirut, Madurai, Kathmandu, Beijing, or Paris? And is this history evident in the built environment, or are the structures that make up the city of more recent provenance, like the intentional modernism of Chandigarh or Brasilia? How have cultural practices and preferences or historical events affected the built environment? When you imagine the site 20 years ago, or 100 years ago, how was it different? How were the people similar or different to those who are there today? Urban sites are always in flux – we can think of them as a contested archive that tells the stories about who has lived there and how they have lived, but also conceals and obscures those stories. The built environment is a record of the values of a place – what is preserved and what is easily accessible or protected all tell us a little bit about what the inhabitants have valued over time, but the absences are just as revealing. Statues and names on buildings indicate important figures in the life of the city or the country within which it is located – but they also omit the ordinary people who have lived in the city but not had the wherewithal to construct sturdy structures that will last generations or bear their names. You will remember from the introduction the way that building names and statues on a university campus signal broader global processes at work. Along similar lines, Derek Alderman and Reuben Rose-Redwood have written extensively on the complex politics of naming streets, considering for instance, the renaming of streets after Dr. Martin Luther King Jr. (Alderman 2000; Rose-Redwood, Alderman, and Azaryahu 2010, 2008). Like all archives, then, cities are sites of struggle: as they change over time, arguments about zoning and planning change: what should be preserved as heritage? Where should the landfill go? Which neighborhoods should be connected by public transportation?

The city as an archive is not one that is interpreted the same by all. Some rooms or street corners in the city can be unmarked archives not made by the powerful like a monument or a named building, but may be meaningful all the same. Some may be memories significant to an individual: this is where I had my first kiss, this is where I was the victim of a hate crime, this is the street corner I avoid because of the group of men who call out to me when I pass. This archive is personal and invisible, and may be known to no one or only a handful of friends. Others may be part of shared networks of conversation – which is the best taco truck, is there a rush hour short cut? Either way, these archives are deeply political in their capacity to affect our individual and shared politics: is the city safe? Does the local administration care for my safety? Or is it protecting someone else? Is the condition of the city a sign of things going well, a metanarrative of future success?

In his ongoing book project, *A Queer New York*, Jack Gieseking is inspired by asking, "How do LGBTQ+ people – namely lesbians and queers among them – produce space? And, in pursuing that question, how do we record the historical geographies of a group most often referred to as 'invisible'?" (Gieseking, interviewed in Moore 2018). In developing a mapping of the queer city, Gieseking veers away from only the expected bars or community centers to also seek out everyday spaces and intentionally attends to the ways that intersectional (Crenshaw 1991) experiences of identity shape our situated knowledge (Haraway 1991) of the city. That is, in Kimberlé Crenshaw's and other formulations (e.g., Combahee River Collective 1977), aspects of our identity such as gender and how we are racialized *intersect*, such that, for instance, a Black woman faces different and overlapping forms of discrimination from either a white woman or a Black man – facing, in the original case for intersectionality made by Crenshaw, both racial discrimination and gender-based discrimination. These experiences then shape a person's situated knowledge of the urban environment: their knowledge of the city is related to their position. Consider as one example that due to threat of sexual assault, women may have a different mental map of a city that helps them protect themselves, while women who are Muslim in places where there have been anti-Muslim hate crimes may additionally have a sense of where they may be targeted for their religious identity (Kwan [2002] has used GIS to create maps of these dynamics). A person with limited mobility who uses a wheelchair might know how to traverse spaces and also not be able to access some spaces. Apart from issues of access and equity, consider that children map landscapes for the possibilities of play, skateboarders for places to do tricks, real estate agents and developers for investment opportunities: that is, our experiences and expertise shape what we see and do not see in the city.

Gieseking notes that even as some commentators declare a "post-gay" era, in which lesbian and gay people assimilate into society, marry, adopt children, and see their sexual orientation as not central to their identity, this may be contingent on being cisgendered, able-bodied, wealthy, and white (in the context of the United States). Through nuanced accounts of a single city, he suggests doubt that "many working class, poor people, people of color, gender minorities, people with disabilities feel like things couldn't improve, especially in terms of the spaces they inhabit" (quoted in Moore 2018; see also Gieseking 2015). Gieseking's work provides us a complicated lens on the meaning of archive.

From our ideas of heritage, we might think of a place like the Stonewall Inn, a bar in New York's Greenwich Village that in the 1960s was home to a lively social scene inclusive of gay, lesbian, genderqueer, transgender, and other folks with marginalized sexual orientations or gender identities, across the economic spectrum. Early in the morning of Saturday, June 28, 1969, police began a raid on the bar, but were met with unexpected resistance as the police searched patrons and collected alcohol (Carter 2005). Patrons, now out on the street, as well as bystanders, began mocking and heckling the police and rumors of police violence began to spread.

Oral histories of the night describe a spontaneous outpouring of built up anger. Sylvia Rivera explained, "You've been treating us like shit all these years? Uh-uh. Now it's our turn! … It was one of the greatest moments in my life" (Deitcher 1995, p.67), and another person present explained, "We all had a collective feeling like we'd had enough of this kind of shit" (Carter 2005, p.160; See also Teal 1971). Police detained and beat patrons with batons, trying to arrest them, the crowd fought back and threw bottles and debris, and a fire started in the bar. The next day, rioting began again. The events of the riots and their aftermath inspired increased advocacy and action on the part of gay and lesbian groups in the city, as well as alliances between queer activists and other leftist social movements. On June 28, 1970, the eve of the anniversary of the riot was celebrated as Christopher Street Liberation Day, and in Chicago and Los Angeles, the event was also recognized, with the first Pride parades. The Stonewall Inn has ever since been part of the archive of New York City, and the building was designated part of a National Historic Landmark in 1999, and in June of 2016 it was designated the Stonewall National Monument by President Barack Obama (the moment being perhaps more poignant because of the Orlando, Florida nightclub shooting that same month, in which nearly 50 people were killed, many of them young queer people of color). As part of the archive, it has been not only a site of pilgrimage but also celebration – for instance after the legalization of same-sex marriage.

Gieseking's project, however, seeks to understand the city not only through the visible archive, but also through less visible spaces. In an interview, he says:

> Every time I give a talk and ask my audience where they would look for a gay person if tasked with finding one, they reply, straight and queer alike: cities, gay neighborhoods, and gay bars. This city-neighborhood-bar triumvirate that defines the public's geographical imagination of queer life needs to be upended – or queered, really – on the basis of gender, race, class, and disability. I hope my work contributes to that sort of broader thinking by showing the complicated, varied, and often more partial and peripheral sorts of spaces that queers depend upon to survive and thrive. (Moore 2018)

As this interview suggests, Gieseking observes that queerness is never in isolation, but is related to other factors shaping the city and how we inhabit it.

The city as the material of class and race struggle

Let us return to an idea hinted at earlier: that the city is the material reflection of social class struggles.

Lefebvre's theories of the production of space have profoundly influenced urban geography. He argues that space is a product of social and economic relations. In the simplest terms, let us think of the production of spaces of capitalism. Because capitalist firms rely on economies of scale (high volume of production), this lends itself to uniformity and efficiency. Because they require not a steady rate of profit but rather an increase, capitalist firms also have motivation to expand into new markets and to increase their sales, whether they are selling cappuccinos or drywall. How might this mode of production shape a city? It might mean that franchises such as Starbucks or Pret a Manger are instantly recognizable. It might mean that cities become spaces of consumption with very few truly public spaces. Along with Lefebvre, in the 1970s and 1980s, geographers David Harvey and Neil Smith (Harvey's student) brought Marxist approaches into geography and theories of urban space by elucidating processes of gentrification and the staking out of claims to justice by staking out a claim to the city. Though these approaches now form a foundation from which other arguments are made, they were revolutionary at the time.

Neil Smith (1979, 2005), David Harvey (1973, 2008), and Geraldine Pratt (1982), demonstrated that flows of capital profoundly shape urban spaces in ways that then lead to political conflicts. We can think of capital – money to invest – as water that flows into spaces of potential and reshapes city structures in ways that have been analyzed through key concepts of the **rent gap** and **gentrification**. As urban neighborhoods fall into disrepair because infrastructure development is limited by taxes and city planning policy, or as other cultural, political, and economic processes lead to wealthy residents moving away from city centers and rooting themselves in suburbs on the outskirts of town, property prices can fall. This creates a rent gap, that is, a gap between the potential value of property and the value of the property in its current space. This is where we think of capital as water that seeks to flow into gaps and fissures. When developers see property reach a large enough gap, the ease of turning that gap into profit by reinvesting in it such that it reaches the upper bounds of what people will pay for that space leads to investment. These processes are related to the spatial fix of capitalism – in which capitalism evades or temporarily resolves crisis by moving from one form of profit to another, such as from one form of physical infrastructure or the built environment to a different mode or space (Harvey 1999).

These processes have now been intensified by **financialization.** Financialization refers to the increasing portion of the global economy tied into *not* making things, trading them, or resource exploitation, but rather the making of profits in the world of finance (e.g., lending, investment, hedge funds). This has had profound effects on housing markets, making them risky and more vulnerable and has been linked to the recent US housing crisis (Aalbers 2016; Mawdsley 2018; Ward 2017).

Let us return, then, to this broad idea: that cities are both the material reflection of social processes and the terrain through which struggle plays out. If we return to the cases of Mumbai and Phnom Penh, the class relations between elites, here often more tied into global flows of capital and resources, are made visible and material in the dispossession of land from the evicted, and in the ways that those who arrive in the city landless or who are displaced then struggle for a right to exist in the city.

In Sapana Doshi's (2013) research on redevelopment in Mumbai, she complicates narratives of urban displacement by finding that class politics and the politics of the poor are more complicated that a simple binary between slum dwellers and the wealthy – there is not one experience that all slum dwellers face, and the politics of the city are a complex network of state bureaucrats, developers, non-governmental organizations (NGOs), banks, and residents. When slums are cleared to make way for fancy high-rise apartment complexes, some residents are relocated through advocacy by NGOs, but they are relocated to distant low-value land, while other residents are not relocated at all. Only a few are relocated near their residences. These differences are heightened by local politics of ethnic and religious difference, which means that ethno-religious minority neighborhoods face additional challenges as they are not seen to have a right to the city at all.

The territorialized city

Not everything is captured by the class relations described above. In conversation with them, we can understand the city as both producing and being produced by political practices of gender, race, ethnicity, and religion, as well as through specifically class-based cultural practices. Here we might think back to Nayak's (2010) discussions of white nationalists in the United Kingdom. Building on our understanding of the city as territory we might ask: Are women safe in the city? Is their safety further compromised if they women who are transgender? What if they are CIS-gendered but gender non-conforming? Can visibly-identifiable Muslims traverse the city without harassment? Did the locally run corner store that catered to folks buying ingredients to cook the foods they remember from back home close down? And has it been replaced by a cute little place with cold brew coffee in mason jars? These are political questions. They are driven by capitalist processes but cannot be understood without attention to other political theories. Think for instance of, "ethnic" neighborhoods: Chinatowns, Little Vietnams, or London's Brick Lane. Here, constructions of race and ethnic identity, as well as racial capitalism (Robinson 1983), are manifest in, complicated by, and produce racial categories and global histories (Anderson 1987). We can think of these as the territorialization of the city in complex ways, and also keep in mind that this is happening as cities become "spaces of enclosure," through the entrenchment of capitalist interests and the reduction of public spaces for spaces of capital (Vasudevan, McFarlane, and Jeffrey 2008). Let us consider this through three examples.

We begin with an excerpt from Nefertiti Tadiar (2016, p.58) on traveling Philippine roads:

All my life I have plied the 270-km route between San Fernando, the provincial capital of La Union, and Manila, the nation's capital. For decades, from my family's hometown in the north, we took the two-lane MacArthur highway, which was laid down by the US colonial government in 1928 following the earlier established route of the now defunct Manila Railroad, and which ran through every town along the north western coast of Luzon and through the provincial towns across its central plains. After the trains stopped running, it was the only way by land to reach the city.

In those years the broad, modern, multi-lane approach to Manila was always dramatic in its contrast with the never quite straight and winding narrow road that connected town to town with a rhythm of clutter and expanse as our car or bus would alternately crawl through the thickets of town centers with their familiar array of plaza, municipal hall, market, school, and the traffic of pedestrians, street and market vendors, hawkers, bus touters, commuters, school-children, police, cars, jeepneys, tricycles, horse-drawn carriages, and stray dogs, which milled and moved around them and slowed our travel, and speed through the suddenly spacious but never empty stretches of country road that opened up between the towns. When I began driving this route myself, I learned how to feel and move with this rhythm, to become part of and one with it. I learned how to bide and accelerate my speed, not simply to passively conform to the changes in density and velocity of traffic and vibrant life spilling within and between towns, but also to make time in the fleeting openings in the opposite lane …

Today, the route from Manila to San Fernando bypasses almost all the towns. We are on one of the connecting elevated expressways redeveloped and newly built over the last 10 years – NLEX (Northern Luzon Expressway), SCTEX (Subic-Clark Tarlac Expressway), TPLEX (Tarlac-Pangasinan-La Union Expressway) – which in sections has steadily cut across the rice fields on the outskirts of populated centers, in places parallel to the MacArthur Highway, and the drive is smooth, steady, with no dips or surges of speed or sudden swerves. No rhythm of bide and accelerate, this virtually hands-free, no clutch, autopilot drive. Just that tranquilizing hum of the tires on leveled asphalt. And no people or animals to be seen, much less encountered, on the road except a sprinkle here and there at a distance in what has become, for a whole new urban social stratum, scenery.

From this moving perch, which hovers just so slightly above the ground, the cultivated plains of Central Luzon are no longer the rural areas one found at the end of the road from the city or that one could glimpse from the road between provincial towns, a place that took effort to reach. Now these quilted fields of small plots of rice and sugar cane, interspersed with tracts of mango orchards and timberland, are merely the scenic backdrop for one's passage through urban corridors, the continuous highways that President Arroyo proposed in 2006 to connect all the "super regions" of the country.

In these few short paragraphs, Tadiar demonstrates the ways that the infrastructure connecting urban centers is the product of capitalist investments (the smooth roads built to facilitate "uber-urbanization") is also entangled in imperialism (the MacArthur highway of her youth, named for an American general), and the fragmentation of space, as rural spaces become the backdrop to the city. Here, connections between urban centers facilitate the detachment of rural people from the urban world.

On the other side of the globe, in Chicago, Rashad Shabazz (2015) traces the ways that policing, surveillance, and architectures of confinement, often promulgated in the name of improving the city and uplifting low income residents had the result of "spatializing Blackness." That is, over the course of the twentieth century, city planners, police, and developers shaping the city and residents' mobility, sought to contain crime and manage interracial "vice." They did so through policing spaces where Black and white people danced and drank together, by creating housing developments like tiny "kitchenettes," that forced large families into close quarters, and by generating prison-like spaces that in turn placed limits on the expression of Black masculinity. In Shabazz's terms, parts of Chicago's South Side were confronted with daily forms of prison or carceral power that effectively *prisonized the landscape*" (Shabazz 2015, p.2). For Shabazz (2015, p.3), that leads us to ask, "What happens when people are raised in environments built to contain them? How does it affect their sense of mobility and inform their conditions of possibility? What role does this play in how they perform gender?"

But bodies themselves can be a kind of moving territory, and the city can be read in other ways. Thus, Jack Gieseking's (2015) research in New York City reads the city as linked urban territories, which are traversed by lesbians and queer women in reference to their own lives and the territorial practices that relate to their sexual orientation. In maps and conversations, these women tell Jack where they can and cannot hold hands or kiss their girlfriends (Figure 6.2). Which neighborhoods are safe territory? How does this change over time? For some, the West Village (location of the Stonewall events above) is a "queer boulevard," signaling safety – but this is complicated by class and race, and occasional experiences of homophobic violence *even* in the Village. Mixed-race and working-middle class, one woman's primary memory on arrival is one of invisibility. Other women wrestle with moving through spaces where their Blackness is welcome to a space where their queerness is accepted – thus their hyphenated identities (Fine 1994) of race, ethnic identity, gender identity and expression and sexual orientation cannot be reconciled in one territory (recalling intersectionality). Poignantly, two of Jack's interlocutors, "Bailey, who identified as femme, and Tre, who

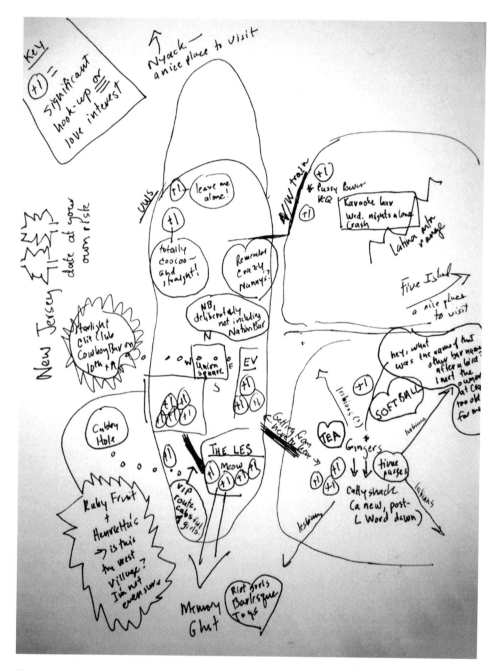

Figure 6.2   A mental map of important lesbian-queer spaces in New York City, created by Sally, '96 (year of coming out). Reproduced with permission of Jack Gieseking.

possessed a more masculine gender presentation and identity," describe Grand Army Plaza as a crossing point.

> Tre liked to "fuck with" sexual norms in specific publics by embracing her masculine gender presentation to claim more rights to such a space. Tre later added she told her girlfriend to "wait till we get to Grand Army Plaza [to touch]." Then all the white people get on the train and [at this point]: "Motherfucker, I have privilege." She went on to explain that she uses the White privilege of Park Slope as a form of protection against Caribbean and West Indian expectations of heteronormative gender presentations and male–female relationships. While Tre does not feel welcome in Park Slope because of her Blackness, she uses parts of Park Slope as the territory beyond the border for where she can be publicly gay and masculine. (Gieseking 2015, p.267)

Situated knowledge of the city

The cities described so far – fragmented by economic class, territorialized by race and money – are of course more complex than I have represented them here. A city can be the material through which class struggle plays out, and the site of racial capitalism that makes it toxic for Black and brown people's neighborhoods. At the same time, it can be the place where someone met their girlfriend, developed a political perspective, started a social movement, or learned a new language, and all of these things could be inflected by the racialized and class fragmentation discussed earlier. You might take your partner to a city so they could better understand who you are and the place that made you. Mehta (2009) describes the city thus as an organ in your body, that is, the city has fundamentally become part of who you are, such that you would not be that person without the experience of that place. Walking through the city, you forge your own path, not necessarily moving the ways intended by urban planners and sometimes breaching territorialized spaces. De Certeau (1984) distinguishes between **strategies**, which are the grand plans that structure the city, and **tactics**, which are the everyday means through which ordinary people make the city work for them. Tactics could be homeless residents who find ways to survive despite anti-homeless planning features (e.g., park benches made impossible to sleep on), or teenagers who loiter and skateboard in areas meant for transit. Tactics are the ways that we navigate a city that may have been set up to thwart our desires. Strategies emerge from a grand and panoramic view of the city, we develop tactics from the sidewalk, trying to catch the last bus home from a party, make ourselves seem like locals, or avoid tourist areas. It is the everyday but also transformative experience of the city.

Think again of a city that you love and know well. If you were to bring a close friend to meet the city, you might take them to your favorite restaurants, the little park few people visit, the bar you love but reminds you of a romantic breakup or any other number of places known to you. But your experience of that place will be mediated by your economic class, your ability to get around in it, your language, your gender, and your appearance, as well as so many other things. Visiting the city of Mumbai for the first time, I was thinking of the ways it is depicted in fiction and film. I wanted to go to the movies, I wanted to eat bhelpuri (a snack with puffed rice, tamarind sauce, and other add-ins) on Chowpatty beach and soak in the city. As a tourist with a limited budget but there for leisure, I could manage to create these experiences but insulate myself from other kinds of experiences one might have in

Mumbai, even though I knew the city also as a microcosm of wealth disparity and ethnic and religious divides. My husband, traveling with me, was more skeptical about the pleasures of the city. His experience as an ethnic minority in India meant he was thinking of the potential for discrimination and noticing different aspects of the city that were easy for me to brush aside or overlook. This meant he learned different things. For example, he would ask every taxi driver or rickshaw driver what village they were from and how much they made, as well as whether they owned the taxi we were in. He found the experience of the city more unsettling than I did. A friend who was traveling with us on her first trip to India, was having an entirely different experience, adapting to language, food, and traffic patterns (but also noticing and pointing out to us things that we failed to see because we had become used to urban India).

So who experienced the "truth" of the city? Of course, this is a silly question, each of us did and none of us did. The "truth," is that we cannot really know a city outside of ourselves and our own situated relationship to it: as outsider or insider or insider but with a minority background, as a woman or man, as a wealthy resident or as a recently arrived migrant. The Mumbai of Mukesh Ambani, whose 27-story home in the city center is one of the world's most expensive, is not the Mumbai of the backpacker or the Mumbai of the rickshaw driver. This has implications for how we study cities, as well as for how cities are planned.

Until this point in the chapter, we have considered *ways* of understanding a city. In the remainder of the chapter, let us think through urban politics from two different frames: first, as a specific site of geopolitics, and then by questioning where (and if) the urban world ends.

War Cities

Stephen Graham (2004b, p.165) writes, "War and the city have intimately shaped each other throughout urban and military history." From the urban fortifications scattered from North Africa to Central Asia, we learn that cities have been built with warfare in mind since cities were built at all. As war has developed with cities in mind, so cities have developed with war as threat. Developing Hewitt's (1983) concept of place annihilation, Graham pushes us to think about **urban geopolitics**, "the telescoping connections between transnational geopolitical transformations and very local acts of violence against urban sites" (Graham 2004a, p.191; Fregonese 2012). Escalations in urban violence and theorized shifts in security trends from a state-centric focus to cities as geopolitical sites (Agnew 2003; Dalby 2010) have led to an "urban geopolitical turn" (Rokem et al. 2017; Fregonese 2009; Graham 2004b).

But how do we proceed in studying urban geopolitics? Sara Fregonese (2012) asks, "So how to adopt the urban geopolitics approach without creating new geopolitical truisms and without reducing cities to rescaled battlegrounds, unavoidable stages for the unfolding of new geopolitical codes?" For her, it is crucial that we move beyond a simple conception of urban geopolitics as a post-cold war progression of warfare intensified under the state of exception occasioned by terrorism, and instead engage in empirical work. Moving away from scalar approaches that simply assert that post-cold war the site of conflict shifts from state to city, she seeks to understand urban geopolitics through questions of sovereignty.

Urban geopolitics gives us a different insight into the "right to the city," as refugees and ethnic minorities are targeted through strikes and planning interventions intended to homogenize cities. Thus, both state-sanctioned demolitions and violence often, "demonize those spaces and victimize their dwellers precisely because of their material presence amidst or besides the town" (Fregonese 2012, p.295; see also Perry 2012 on urban Brazil; Ramadan 2009 on refugee camps in Lebanon; Graham 2005 on Fallujah). Sara Fregonese and Adam Ramadan (Fregonese 2009; Ramadan 2009) explore everyday and infrastructural forms of violence, which could include **urbicide** – the deliberate killing of cities, or more targeted violence in camps or neighborhoods, and even the specific and important roles that urban hotels play as conduits for war and conflict (Fregonese and Ramadan 2015). Through this approach, we can understand the city itself as a terrain of geopolitical violence through its infrastructure. This is distinct from (but related to) approaches to urban geopolitics that work through the city as a specific site of militarization and securitized urban imaginaries.

In the 1975-1976 years of the Lebanese civil war, Beirut became a crucial symbolic and material terrain of conflict that could be read as a form of urbicide (Fregonese 2009). Across the terrain of the city, layered on top of tensions between Christian and Muslim residents, two rival militias struggled to gain control of the city: the Lebanese or Isolationist Front, and the National Movement, which supported Pan-Arab nationalism and was sympathetic to the Palestinian cause. This set of conflicts was entangled in Lebanon's legacy as part of the French Mandate, as well as in sectarian conflict within the army. Fregonese uses the concept of urbicide to understand the city in this time period, but she also points to the need to think about urbicide as contextually grounded. In the context of regional and global Cold War superpower discourses of the Middle East, the city of Beirut became one of many "'hollow spaces' of chaos," part of the representation of "Lebanon and Beirut as unruly and Orientalized spaces," which, "led some to see their partition and destruction as paradoxically inexplicable and yet quasi-inevitable" (Fregonese 2009, p.310). Closer attention to the fabric of the city itself reveals a different story.

Urbicide helps us to think about the ways that the destruction of a city might be a military strategy, a method of generating instability, or harming the values that the city stands for. Yet, Fregonese's grounded reading complicates both the idea of (parochial) rural and (extroverted, cosmopolitan) urban in opposition and adds nuance to the idea of urbicide itself, both by tracing the complicated movement of violence through the city, and by suggesting that representations of urbicide as signal of "new wars," is too easy. As one example, she hones in on the Beirut Holiday Inn. One of a row of aspirational modernist buildings along the coast, the Holiday Inn, part of the "Battle of the Hotels" that became the focus of conflict in October 1975. Here, the landscape of the city itself shapes what occurs, as hotels' purpose: leisure, profit, are transformed, as the high-rise structures intended for tourism become ideal for warfare. The building figured in militia propaganda, thus becoming part of "complex urban spatialities" that hold symbolic significance *and* also are the terrain of war, both targeted by and used for attacks. In an image of the building made by the al Mourabitun militia the destruction of the site is called into territorial narratives of responsibility and strength. The writing reads, "on 21 March 1976, the Mourabitun crashed the symbol of fascist treachery, and swore that they will continue the fight whatever the price is."

In Fregonese's (2009, p.317) analysis, the tracking of violence and meaning through the city is not chaotic but organized and strategic for the players involved, who are "engaged … in complex material and epistemological battles for the affirmation of different ideas about the Lebanese nation and territory." Sites like the Holiday Inn are both tactical and discursive for territorial struggles in the city. At a longer-term and different scale, the destruction of cities like Beirut, and their representations in the media, and a Western-inflected reading of these cities as "chaotic spaces and breeding grounds for terrorism," might have enacted a city-focused kind of warfare resulting in the urbicide of Falluja and Baghdad (Fregonese 2009; citing Graham 2006).

Rokem (2016; Rokem et al. 2017) suggests that we ought to attend to the fabric of the city itself as a site of ordinary and mundane geopolitics through segregation and mobility, and through ways that the domestic site of the home itself is made in relation to conflict: "How does urban conflict interact with everyday interior domestic spaces, how do people reshape them and reassign functions during conflict?" (Fregonese in Rokem et al. 2017, p.256).

Urban Planet?

Where do cities end? Or perhaps, do cities end? Neil Brenner and Christian Schmid (2014) and Andrew Merrifield (2013) ask us to leave behind "methodological cityism," and think of processes of urbanization as extending across and through the planet. This has ignited a series of debates and led to questions about how we define "urban," and why. Brenner and Schmid (2014, p.750) argue that "[there is] no longer any outside to the urban world," that is, that through the demands placed on the planet by urbanization, we can no longer find a bit of land, ice, water, or sky, that is not implicated in urbanization. Two main ideas center this work. First, the idea that we should take care in how we abstract and define the urban: what are the limits of the idea of the urban? How do we define it? Is it too simple to define the urban as a city over a certain size or density? Secondly, this work seeks to trouble the separation between rural and urban, by arguing that today these categories are inseparable. Let us consider the history and implications of this idea.

Brenner, Schmid, Merrifield, and other proponents of planetary urbanization build on the work of Henri Lefebvre, discussed earlier in the chapter. In *The Urban Revolution*, Lefebvre (2003, p.1) opens with a striking hypothesis: "Society has become completely urbanized," and goes on in the book to argue that the development of capitalism is insepara- ble from the concurrent urbanization of the world. Here he means that it is the concentration of people in cities that has underwritten capitalist accumulation. As Merrifield (2013, p.911) explains, "Urban fabric does not narrowly define the built environment of cities, but, says Lefebvre, indicates all manifestations of the dominance of the city over the countryside." For Linda Peake (Ruddick et al. 2018, p.3), Lefebvre describes "a new global imaginary of the urban as a fabric that has thickened and extended its borders." We can think here across time and space, of the workers pouring into cities during the industrial revolution in Europe, the need for inexpensive labor reshaping the rural surroundings and need for cheap raw materi- als transforming the colonies, today, the need for inexpensive meat and grain to feed urban dwellers reshaping rural agricultural areas from Iowa to the Punjab. This intensification and expansion of capitalism requires urban processes, from the consolidation of bourgeoisie power to the foundation of industrial growth and economies of scale. To focus then on the city as a specific form becomes then confusing and distracting – it makes us focus on a spe- cific object when we ought to be looking at urban processes unfolding all around us. Lefebvre suggests then we should think about urban processes instead of cities per se.

Referring to 2006 as the tipping point when the world became more urban than rural, and the continued progression since then, Merrifield describes the urban as "shapeless, formless and apparently boundless, riven with new contradictions and tensions that make it hard to tell where borders reside and what's inside and what's outside." Merrifield connects Lefebvre's theorization to Marx's assertions of an ascendant and inevitable world market that would come from endless capitalist expansion: "the tendency to create the world market is directly given in the concept of capital itself. Every limit appears as a barrier to be overcome," (Marx 1990, p.20; Merrifield 2013). While Marx's world market and Lefebvre's concept of the urban are real enough, vital necessities for the reproduction of capitalism on an expanded scale; both are embodied in nameable people, in living agents and actual economic practices, in institutions and organizations; both are a vast web of exchange relations based around money, capital, and culture. Yet, at the same time, both should be conceived as fluid processes circulating around the globe; both flow as non-observable phenomena, too (Merrifield 2013, p.913).

The urban is a "single, indivisible substance whose attributes – the build environment, transport infrastructure, population densities, topographical features, social mixes, political governance – are all the formal expressions of what pervades it ontologically," (Merrifield 2013, p.913). Simultaneously, the urban is a site of encounter: "the sheer proximity of people to other people, the sheer simultaneity of activities, of events and chance meetings is the very definition of the urban itself" (Merrifield, 2013, p.916). Bayat (2009), in the chapter following this one, will describe this as the politics of the street – that is, the ways in which these chance encounters and observations, slowly tilt and shift politics, so that societies may transform through incremental adjustments. To rethink what the limits of the city are also means to rethink what the *right* to the city is. If the city has no limits, what is the right to the city? It is not the same as the claims made to take over consolidated places in the city.

This is all very compelling, but in what direction does it compel us? And in what circles do these ideas travel and transform? As many scholars have been quick to point out, within the rather insular world of planetary urbanization literature there is an almost incomprehensible lack of engagement with parallel developments in feminist urban studies, postcolonial theory, and critical race theory (e.g., among many others Roy 2016; Ruddick et al. 2018; Buckley and Strauss 2016; Derickson 2017). Some, like Roy (2016), fear that planetary urbanization may become a newly universalizing theory, others point to earlier interventions by feminist theorists that had already troubled borders between urban and rural (Buckley and Strauss 2016; Derickson 2017).

What Have We Learned and Where Do We Go From Here?

In this chapter, we have considered the ways that the city can variously be a site of class struggle, a personal and collective archive, and a site of organizing. In the chapter that follows, we will continue tracing the threads of organizing, to understand when and how people develop strategies for political change.

Keywords

Built environment   The physical structure of a place, that is, the planning, buildings, and infrastructure of places and spaces.

Creative destruction   Old ways of life and economic systems destroyed in order to make room for new ones.

Domicide   Destruction of home, which also entails cultural, attachment, and memory loss.

Financialization   Financialization refers to the increasing portion of the global economy tied into *not* making things, trading them, or resource exploitation, but rather the making of profits in the world of finance (e.g., lending, investment, hedge funds).

Gentrification   The process in which investors, developers, and private citizens buy up inexpensive land or take up inexpensive rents and create higher-priced businesses and housing in the city, displacing previous residents.

Rent gap   The gap between the potential value of property and the value of the property in its current space.

Strategies   The planning of cities engendered and manifest by state and city power structures, agencies, and officials.

Subaltern cosmopolitanism   The practice of ordinary, dominated classes creating new ways of life and cultural practices through encounter. Defined in relationship to cosmopolitanism which is often associated with wealthy and transnational cities and classes of people.

Tactics   Everyday means through which ordinary people make the city work for them.

Urban geopolitics   Connections between transnational geopolitics and localized urban violence.

Urbicide   The deliberate killing of cities.

Further Reading

Gentrification and dispossession

Casolo, J. and Doshi, S. 2013. Domesticated Dispossessions? Towards a Transnational Feminist Geopolitics of Development. *Geopolitics* 18(4): 800–834.

Derickson, K.D. 2015. Urban Geography I Locating Urban Theory in the "Urban Age." *Progress in Human Geography* 39(5): 647–657.

Derickson, K.D. 2016. Urban Geography II Urban Geography in the Age of Ferguson. *Progress in Human Geography* 41(2): 230–244.

Doshi, S. 2013. The Politics of the Evicted: Redevelopment, Subjectivity, and Difference in Mumbai's Slum Frontier. *Antipode* 45(4): 844–865.

Ranganathan, M. 2015. Storm Drains as Assemblages: The Political Ecology of Flood Risk in Post-colonial Bangalore. *Antipode* 47(5): 1300–1320.

Shabazz, R. 2015. *Spatializing Blackness: Architectures of Confinement and Black Masculinity in Chicago*. Chicago: University of Illinois Press.

Smith, N. 2005. *The New Urban Frontier: Gentrification and the Revanchist City*. London: Routledge.

Planetary urbanization

Brenner, N. (ed). 2014. *Implosions/Explosions: Towards a Study of Planetary Urbanization*. Berlin: Jovis.

Buckley, M. and Strauss, K. 2016. With, Against, and Beyond Lefebvre: Planetary Urbanization and Epistemic Plurality. *Environment and Planning D: Society and Space* 34(4): 617–636.

Derickson, K.D. 2017. Masters of the Universe. *Environment and Planning D: Society and Space* 36(3): 556–562.

Merrifield, A. 2013. The Urban Question under Planetary Urbanization. *International Journal of Urban and Regional Research* 37(3): 909–922.

Ruddick, S., Peake, L., Tanyildiz, G. and Patrick, D. 2018. Planetary Urbanization: An Urban Theory for Our Time? *Environment and Planning D: Society and Space* 35(3): 387–404.

Postcolonial, subaltern, and Other cities

Datta, A. 2012. "Mongrel City": Cosmopolitan Neighbourliness in a Delhi Squatter Settlement. *Antipode* 44(3): 745–763.

Ghertner, A. 2015. *Rule by Aesthetics. World-Class City Making in Delhi*. New York: Oxford University Press.

Gidwani, V.K. 2006. Subaltern Cosmopolitanism as Politics. *Antipode* 38(1): 7–21.

Mayaram, S. (ed.) 2009. *The Other Global City*. New York: Routledge.

Negi, R., Thakur, K., and Ali, S.S. 2016. Contoured Urbanism: People, Property and Infrastructures in the Indian Himalayas. *Urbanisation* 1(2): 134–148.

Phadke, S., Khan, S., and Ranade, S. 2011. *Why Loiter?: Women and Risk on Mumbai Streets*. New Delhi: Penguin Books.

Robinson, J. 2006. *Ordinary Cities: Between Modernity and Development*. London: Routledge.

Robinson, J. 2016. Thinking Cities through Elsewhere: Comparative Tactics for a More Global Urban Studies. *Progress in Human Geography* 40(1): 3–29.

Roy, A. 2003. *City Requiem, Calcutta: Gender and the Politics of Poverty*. Minneapolis: University of Minnesota Press.

Roy, A. 2011. Slumdog Cities: Rethinking Subaltern Urbanism. *International Journal of Urban and Regional Research* 35(2): 223–238.

Roy, A. and Ong, A. 2011. *Worlding Cities: Asian Experiments and the Art of Being Global*. Chichester: John Wiley and Sons.

Simone, A.M. and Pieterse, E. 2017. *New Urban Worlds: Inhabiting Dissonant Times*. Cambridge: Polity Press.

Urban geopolitics

Fregonese, S. 2012. Urban Geopolitics 8 Years On. Hybrid Sovereignties, the Everyday, and Geographies of Peace. *Geography Compass* 6: 290–303.

Graham, S. (ed). 2008. *Cities, War, and Terrorism: Towards an Urban Geopolitics*. Malden, MA: Blackwell.

Ramadan, A. 2009. Destroying Nahr El-Bared: Sovereignty and Urbicide in the Space of Exception. *Political Geography* 28(3): 153–163.

Rokem, J., Fregonese, S., Ramadan, A. et al. 2017. Interventions in Urban Geopolitics. *Political Geography* 61: 253–262.

Chapter 7

Social Movements

On a November morning, a group of 13 kayakers push off from the shore of Henoko village in Okinawa to confront the combined power of the US and Japanese states … As occurs most mornings, the kayakers set out to test the Japanese Coast Guard's ability to dictate that this seaspace … is the property of the USA and a suitable site for the building of a new air base. As the kayakers approach a floating barrier that marks the boundary of the proposed construction area, a circling Coast Guard boat begins to crisscross in front of the kayakers to harass and impede them … Eventually, one kayaker paddles across the barrier with a Coast Guard boat in pursuit. Then, other kayakers move through the unguarded opening and soon the Coast Guard boats back off – defeated but still monitoring – while the 13 kayakers affirm, for at least another day, that the bay belongs to them. (Davis, S. 2017, p.110)

In the opening excerpt, Sasha Davis begins an exploration of the ways that Okinawan activists work to delay the construction of a military base in Oura Bay, Japan. There are several points that Davis helpfully draws out of this case. First, that the struggle to keep the base out of Henoko is not an international struggle between governments, but rather a challenge to the state from a social movement questioning state rights to mediate local people's relationship to a foreign power (Davis, 2017). Secondly, this is not a relationship only between these two parties. Rather, the Okinawa protesters are connected to global networks of anti-militarization activists working to close military bases and to block future construction (Davis, S. 2015). These connections are embodied experiences. Okinawan activists have been to other militarized sites across the Asian-Pacific region from Puerto Rico to the Philippines and activists from these sites have been to Okinawa. In the process, activists have learned, "how to cut fences, how to steer kayaks through rough seas, how to safely chain oneself to scaffolding in the sea with scuba gear on and how to deal with different police responses," and they are also creating new solidarities through "putting their bodies in shared emotional and visceral states" (Davis 2017, p.114).

Social-movement-driven direct actions across the world have included wide-ranging and creative approaches to social issues. In 1977, the mothers of children who disappeared during Argentina's suppression of activists came together in the Plaza de Mayo in Buenos Aires, wearing white scarves, protesting the military dictatorship by demanding an answer for their missing children through their presence. In 2014, the deaths of Black men and acquittals of the police officers that killed them inspired events such as staged die-ins and drew mainstream attention to the Movement for Black Lives, which begun by Alicia Garza, Patrisse Cullors, and Opal Tometi in July 2013 after the acquittal of Trayvon Martin's vigilante killer in the US state of Florida. In 2015, women college students in Delhi began a set of actions that became *Pinjra Tod*, "Break the cage," a group demanding freedom from gendered policing and greater accountability for issues such as sexual harassment and hostel fees at universities. In each of these cases, people came together in reference to a specific social problem and worked to create a new space of political engagement (rather than the existing avenues, such as voting). Revisiting the formal/informal politics discussion from earlier in the book, this chapter opens up activist spaces for political intervention.

How do we change the world? Should you write letters to your elected representatives? Start a hashtag on twitter? Take to the street with placards and slogans? Meet with your neighbors and family members, collect information, organize and begin to see your common points of oppression? Should you create an alternative set of strategies so that you rely less on the state? Or should you try to dismantle, change, or otherwise influence the state itself? This book has introduced a number of difficult social and political problems, but for each problem that we encounter, whether it is sexual harassment in Hollywood or in public transportation in Mumbai, you will find active and engaged people working to change their world. What strategies do they use? This chapter explores social movements, and what Bayat (2009) has designated "nonmovements" to understand how people have worked to change the world.

Social Movements and "Identity Politics"

A **social movement** is a group of individuals or loose coalition of smaller groups seeking to create societal or political change, sometimes through seeking to change government structures, other times through working to create *different* forms of governance (or even abolish governance), or still other times working to change society. To create this change, they use strategies such as the occupation of public space or place and tactics such as **direct action** apart from only focusing on electoral politics and existing systems. Direct action refers to tactics that are not mediated through state actors, that is, a strike or an occupation of public space, rather than an appeal to a legislator for attention to an existing problem. Over the course of history, social movements have transformed our world: think of the civil rights movement, labor movement, and movements for the rights of women and the rights of LGBTQ+ people. Today, you will think immediately of #NODAPL, young people rallying

Figure 7.1   Protestors at COP21 try to force action on climate change. Signs read, "What are we going to do about the United States/Must pay climate reparations," and "Reduce US Greenhouse gasses by 50% of 1990s levels by 2025 starting now." Reproduced with permission of Erika Wise.

for action on climate change (Figure 7.1), the #metoo movement begun by Tarana Burke. All of these have had profound effects both through creating changes in discourse and understanding of these issues for individuals and families, and through influencing the laws and political discourse social movements have direct impacts and also shift mainstream conversations.

Social movements could be built around a particular identity (though we will complicate this later) or around a specific concern (the environment, climate change, police violence) (McCarthy 2009). Social movements are not political initiatives led by one organization or institution, but are shifting and changing networks of people and groups (Nicholls 2007), in fact, they may be full of disagreement, contradictions, or only broadly allied forces. We can think for instance, of social movements for the rights of LGBTQ+ people. For some folks or organizations in this movement, their chief concern might be the intersectional experiences of trans people of color, and their right to safety and security, while for others their concern might be lobbying the government for queer people's right to marry and adopt children. At times these different constituencies might overlap and come together to push for change on one or more issues, but their priorities may also be quite distinct (Puar 2007).

An additional characteristic of social movements is that they are often tied to a shared identity, *but*, that is not to say that a shared identity marker (such as race) determines one's political orientation or desire to join a social movement. It is rather that becoming part of a social movement involves creating a sense of shared identity. We will return to this idea. Social movements have recently been given sustained attention in political geography; however, this is a new development, which Koopman (2017) suggests is at least in part due to the contributions of feminist theorists, who have pushed for less state-centric approaches to the study of political geography.

The concept of the social movement implies a tripartite distinction between market, state, and **civil society** (McCarthy 2009), in which civil society includes the associations and other groups of people reproducing and changing societal norms and engaging in political processes. For Marx and Engels, as we discussed in earlier chapters, the labor movement would be a natural consequence of the un-managed and escalating exploitation of labor in the service of profit. Since the 1960s, however, theorists have discussed the rise of different forms of social movements, which may be (though we should take care not to assume homogeneity), more closely focused on one issue, might cut across class lines and go beyond specific and tangible goals to include broader questions, and also may avoid more traditional political parties or procedures.

So, are social movements another name for **identity politics**? Let us take care when using this frame and consider what it means. Painter and Jeffrey (2009, p.126) define identity politics as "when group identity difference is a source of conflict or becomes the focus of efforts to bring about social change." Thus, if people with disabilities organize "around a shared sense of identity as disabled people and expressing the concern that discrimination was based on (possibly unconscious) prejudice against disabled people" we could call this identity politics (Painter and Jeffrey (2009, p.126). Painter and Jeffrey (2009) also highlight one of the foundational examples of identity politics as social movement: the US Civil Rights Movement (Figure 7.2). Think for a moment of Rosa Parks refusing to sit in the back of the bus: this iconic moment signals a strategy of civil disobedience that was explicitly spatial, rooted in identity, and also targeted both state systems and the need for broader societal change. And yet, being Black during the era of the Civil Rights Movement did not determine Black people's actions: one could be a Black person during that era and *not* join a social movement, and people who were racialized as white also signed on and supported this movement in smaller numbers. Furthermore, Parks's action was not an impulsive moment, but one that came out of organizing and conversations. Similarly, not all women identify with and participate in feminist movements, and not all who term themselves feminists share the same goals.

This reminds us that our inherited or inscribed characteristics do not determine our politics, but rather, as stated above, our sense of identity may be shaped *through* political engagement. What it means to be a Black woman, what it means to be an Indigenous man, what it means to be a person with a disability, or a person who is attracted to people who are the same gender – these are aspects of identity that are shaped by and intersect with other aspects of who we are. These do *not* drive involvement in social movements, *however* our interpretation of what it means to hold these identities may be changed by participating in a social movement or participation in a social movement may enable us to see our identities in a different way. Our interpretations of our own identity may be formed through conversations, shared practices, and political engagement with other people who might share some of our experiences or have life experience quite distinct from our own.

The term "identity politics," can also be used in a trivializing manner. This can detract from the very real concerns at stake. This also makes invisible the ways that social

Figure 7.2   Leffler, Warren K, photographer. *Civil rights march on Washington, D.C. / WKL.* Washington, DC, 1963. Photograph. https://www.loc.gov/item/2003654393/.

movements grounded in some form of politics tied to identity have fundamentally changed the world as in the example of the civil rights movement, as well as, for instance, in decolonial struggles across the globe.

As one case study of the trivialization of identity politics, consider, for instance, a spate of headlines in the United States recently: "Time to give up on identity politics," (Shivani 2017), "Tax, Class, and the limits of identity politics," (Schultz 2017). Summing up some versions of this conversation, a letter to the *New York Times* in December 2016 (Williams 2016) reads:

> In the 1960s we were admonished to look past skin color or ethnicity so that we could see a person's true identity, and we took that to heart. Now, people identify themselves and others according to the racial, ethnic or gender group into which they were born. This used to be considered the very foundation of racism. What has happened to our ability to treat one another as individual human beings rather than as stereotypes of one interest group or another? Identity politics has turned into walls between people; it makes serious conversation about justice, jobs and opportunity impossible. We need to break down those walls.

In other terms, political scientist Mark Lilla (2016) writes that the urge to "become aware of and 'celebrate' our differences," "is a splendid principle of moral pedagogy – but disastrous as a foundation for democratic politics." He goes on to say, "the fixation on diversity in our schools and in the press has produced a generation of liberals and progressives narcissistically unaware of conditions outside their self-defined groups, and indifferent to the task of reaching out to Americans in every walk of life." This is a paradoxical statement: it suggests that focus on difference is a problem, but also accuses those who discuss difference are "indifferent," to "Americans in every walk of life," thus implying that these "Americans in every walk of life," do not value diversity, nor *are* they "diverse." It further suggests that those people who *cannot* disregard or discard their own difference are an obstacle to progressive politics. Let us explore the complexity of what identity might mean for a social movement by considering understandings of identity as developed in feminist thought.

Feminism and Intersectionality

If Black women were free, it would mean that everyone else would have to be free since our freedom would necessitate the destruction of all the systems of oppression. (Combahee River Collective 1977)

If we think about other critical approaches we have encountered in this book, we might ask: can identity be a side interest or something that can be swept out of the way or put off for later? What if your identity makes your survival contingent? When your existence as a transgender person puts you at risk for gender-based violence, or your gender increases your likelihood of experiencing violence in the home, or your existence as a Black person subjects you to excessive policing, racial stress, and health risks, then you may be differently oriented toward the idea of an identity-based politics. We can in fact understand social movements, including those that are tied to specific racial, ethnic, or other identities, as creative and forward-oriented mechanisms of survival that recognize the contingency of survival in relationship to historical structures that have rendered a close and tight connection between things like class, gender, race, and survival outcomes. In fact, many social movements have been expressly structured around survival: from Indigenous movements in North America like Idle No More and #NODAPL to struggles for food sovereignty by the Zapatistas, the Black Panthers, the Republic of New Afrika and others. It is also the case that social movements, like feminism, have been integral to scholarly development in the discipline of geography (Eaves 2019).

Before we go on, let us return to a crucial framework for understanding identity: **intersectionality.** Here, it is important to also acknowledge the complications of our position in society, and *not* to think of identity as something internal, as a flavor, a characteristic, or something that just makes us different from other people. This idea was taking shape through the work of Black feminists in the 1980s, with contributions from bell hooks (1981) and Patricia Hill Collins (1990), who described a "matrix of oppression." In 1980, Audre Lorde wrote, "As a forty-nine-year-old Black lesbian feminist socialist mother of two, including one boy, and a member of an interracial couple, I usually find myself a part of some group defined as other, deviant, inferior, or just plain wrong" (Lorde 1984, p.114). Kimberlé Crenshaw's (Crenshaw 1989; 1991) naming and theorization of intersectionality demonstrates the way that *intersecting* systems of oppression mean that people from marginalized groups may face obstacles to having their discrimination understood and acted on in legal systems. Consider for instance, that mechanisms to report and manage discrimination may be fundamentally flawed if they understand only (for instance) white women's experience of discrimination due to gender or Black men's experiences of discrimination due to race. An analysis focused only on gendered discrimination or racial discrimination cannot understand the ways that oppression operates for Black women, as these mechanisms of discrimination intersect in their lives. Furthermore, in the case of advocacy work, an understanding of these kinds of marginalization as distinct may fail to be effective, or may even lead to antagonism between activist groups. Crenshaw writes:

> In mapping the intersections of race and gender, [intersectionality] does engage dominant assumptions that race and gender are essentially separate categories. By tracing the categories to their intersections, I hope to suggest a methodology that will ultimately disrupt the tendencies to see race and gender as exclusive or separable ... the concept can and should be expanded by factoring in issues such as class, sexual orientation, age, and color. (Crenshaw 1991, p.1244)

In addition to helping us understand the centrality of structural racism and gender-based discrimination, and the ways that work to draw attention to them cannot easily be dismissed as "identity politics." Crenshaw outlines the challenges faced by social movements if they do not attend to intersectionality in their political organizing, because without attention to overlapping forms of oppression, analysis of political issues are limited: "women of color experience racism in ways not always the same as those experienced by men of color and sexism in ways not always parallel to the experiences of white women, [so] antiracism and feminism are limited, even on their own terms" (Crenshaw 1991, p.1252).

Crenshaw's work on intersectionality can be drawn on to address other forms of structural oppression (ableism, homophobia), but it is important to acknowledge its roots in Black feminism and its emphasis on *structural* forces, not on identity as a freewheeling concept or a way in which we are "all different." It is also part of a larger conversation about the limits of **white feminism** or **imperial feminism**, which illuminates some of the challenges faced by social movements. *White* feminism does not necessarily imply the feminism practiced by all white women, but rather a mode of feminism. White feminism centers *white* or "colorblind" experiences of gender, and is not attentive to issues of race (and perhaps also economic class). In particular, since the 1970s and 1980s, scholars and scholar-activists like Angela Davis, bell hooks, Audre Lorde, and activist groups, like the Combahee River Collective, have pointed to issues and events in which white feminism (even when well intentioned) has failed Black women. White women have often framed reproductive health as a struggle to access birth control and to obtain the right to safe abortions in order to have bodily autonomy. This is an important cause, but Black women (and in the US context, Indigenous women as well) have often been faced with forced sterilization, eugenics programs, and structural forces that have limited their ability to raise healthy children (Davis, A.Y. 2011; Collins 1999). Maternal mortality and infant mortality remain consistently and strikingly higher for Black women in the United States. Fighting for the right to an abortion without also fighting for the rights of Black women to have access to prenatal care, safe deliveries, and adequate care for their infants limits the scope of feminist sisterhood. Similarly pointing to the limitations of white feminism, bell hooks writes to problematize white-supremacist-capitalist-patriarchy so that issues of both race and class can be central to feminism. bell hooks's (1981) book, *Ain't I a Woman*, was titled with a reference to the famous off the cuff speech given by Sojourner Truth and published in 1864. Truth gave the speech 25 years after she escaped slavery with her daughter and went to court to free her son from the man who enslaved him. Truth's speech is a reflection on the different meanings of womanhood for herself as a person who had been enslaved:

> That man over there says that women need to be helped into carriages, and lifted over ditches, and to have the best place everywhere. Nobody ever helps me into carriages, or over mud-puddles, or gives me any best place! And ar'n't I a woman? Look at me! Look at my arm! I have ploughed and planted, and gathered into barns, and no man could head me! And ar'n't I a woman? I could work as much and eat as much as a man – when I could get it – and bear the lash as well! And ain't I a woman? I have borne thirteen children, and seen most all sold to slavery, and when I cried out with my mother's grief, none but Jesus heard me! And ain't I a woman?

hooks goes back to Truth's observations in order to point out that Black women during this era had different experiences, needs, and goals, than Black men, and that their struggles were also not part of the feminism of white women at the time – many of whom had either advocated for prioritizing women's right to vote before the enfranchisement of Black men, or framed the issue in terms that drew on anti-Black racism. In hooks's words, then, "Black women were placed in a double bind; to support women's suffrage would imply that they were allying themselves with white women activists who had publicly revealed their racism, but to support only black male suffrage was to endorse a patriarchal social order that would grant them no political voice" (hooks 1981, p.3).

hooks's observations, made in the 1980s, also resonate with the analysis of Frederick Douglass, the Black abolitionist who worked with and supported white suffragettes like Elizabeth Cady Stanton in their quest for voting rights. Douglass's support for the predominantly white suffragette movement, and his own speeches connecting the struggles of Black men and women and white women demonstrate that shared sense of identity is created through movement organizing, and also the need for an intersectional approach to analysis. Douglass vocally and consistently supported voting rights for women, but when the 15th amendment was put forward to guarantee voting rights for Black men, Stanton not only opposed it but also relied on racial tropes to do so. In 1869, clarifying that he supported women's right to vote, he observed in response to Stanton's rhetoric:

> When women, *because they are women* are hunted down through the cities of New York and New Orleans; when they are dragged from their houses and hung upon lampposts; when their children are torn from their arms and their brains dashed out upon the pavement; when they are objects of insult and outrage at every turn; when they are in danger of having their homes burnt down over their heads; when their children are not allowed to enter schools; then they will have an urgency to obtain the ballot equal to our own. (quoted in Staples 2018)

White feminism is thus feminism that is driven by a worldview that centers whiteness *or* assumes a universal undifferentiated subject, as we discussed in the chapter on power and will return to in the chapter on decolonizing political geography. This kind of feminism can be not only exclusionary for women of color, but even run in direct opposition to some of their interests. In relation to this (and in a context and era in which racialization in the United States has often been framed as a Black/white binary, although this has never captured the complexity of how people are racialized in the United States), US-based **Black**

feminism (though also encompassing a range of theories and positions that necessarily are heterogeneous and dynamic!) has been framed as a specific approach to feminism that draws on Black women's lived experiences, and incorporates analyses of race and class (as well as other positions, such as sexual orientation) into *both* understandings of oppression *and* understandings of how to proceed. It is thus informed on the one hand by Black women's own experiences of discrimination, but also their experiences of working for a different world, whether that meant working for women's rights or being a part of other political movements, such as the Black Panthers, the Civil Rights movements, or other Black political organizing (such as Black Nationalism, which we will return to later in the chapter).

Some strands of Black feminism are also deeply intertwined with Marxism, for example, Patricia Hill Collins (1990; see also Harding 1986; Smith, D.E. 1974) elaborates on the idea of **Black feminist epistemology** (a more specific designation than **feminist standpoint epistemology**, but sharing a premise valuing lived experience as expertise). This is in relation to Engels and Marx's vision of the world in which workers' views of the world are informed by their situated position. A factory worker, for example, may understand the world differently because of their experience on the shop floor: they *feel* the labor extracted from their body in repetitive movements, they witness the class differences between white collar employees' lives and their own lives, and see the products of their labor sold for more than the cost of raw materials and their wages. Meanwhile, factory owners naturalize private property and ownership. Collins, in conversation with other feminists, suggests that Black women's specific experiences provide them with insight into the world that is grounded in their position in it – that is, their epistemology – their ways of knowing the world – are informed by their experience of racism and sexism. You will recognize that this is a complex argument! After all, across the globe, or, in the context of the United States, across the nation, each individual woman's experience is as unique as her own life, even across the spectrum of economic class – what is her favorite song or piece of literature? Is her top political priority climate change? Her political opinions, her own internal world of delight and sorrow, her dreams and her aspirations, *cannot* be essentialized into racialized or gendered categories – which we already know to be socially constructed and changing. The life experience of someone like Oprah, Michelle Obama, Serena Williams, or Beyoncé, for instance, cannot be generalized (though one notes that even their tremendous class privilege has not exempted them from racism). Collins of course is well aware of this, but simultaneously argues that due to the structural forces of racism and sexism, there may still be a specific epistemology and in particular a heightened clarity and insight into how things work that many Black women may recognize.

In addition to the work that Black feminists have done to unravel the universalism and exclusions of white feminism, there is a parallel and overlapping critique of what has been labeled **imperial feminism** (see, e.g., Amos and Parmar 1984; Fluri 2011b; Legg 2010; McClintock 1995; Mohanty 1991) to distinguish it from oppositional or independent forms of feminism that implicitly or explicitly critique Eurocentric feminist visions. These could include transnational feminism, third world feminism, Indigenous feminism, Muslim feminism (e.g., among many others Mohanty 2003; Sangtin Writers Collective and Nagar 2006; Abu-Lughod 2002; Mahmood 2011). Chandra Talpade Mohanty (1991) laid out the risks of imperial feminism in clear and forceful terms in her landmark article, "Under Western Eyes," in which she points to ways that the image of the "third world woman," as victim in need of a Western savior locates agency (the ability to enact your own will in the world) in the West, and homogenizes women in the Global South to represent them as the real victims of patriarchy. This kind of imperial feminism is a "feminist" update of colonial tropes in which, "white men [save] brown women from brown men" (Spivak 1988).

Social Movements in Space

We have begun this chapter by considering the ways that social movements emerge from and forge particular forms of shared experience. Now we turn to more explicitly spatial questions.

How might geographers study social movements differently from, say, sociologists and anthropologists? For one thing, they might pay attention to how space is a key tactic for social movements, and how we might understand them through spatial theories, such as scale, territory, or place (Koopman 2017, p.342). Are social movements tied to specific kinds of places or social structures? Are they formed because of urban labor markets? That is, do the specific labor questions in a city create place-based worker movements (Castells 1983)? For Castells (1996), this could lead to localized struggles of non-elites that are separate from global networks of capital and powerful decision makers; however, for geographers like Massey (2004) or Amin (2004), this imaginary of place detracts from the complexity of places and how they are formed.

Social movements might emerge from a specific historical conjuncture that shapes ideology or strategy and roots that struggle to a particular place. History is also rich with examples of how "counter-topographical" lines connect struggles across space (Katz 2001): in the 1940s, Bhimrao Ramji Ambedkar, a champion of Dalit rights in India, corresponded with Black sociologist W.E.B. Du Bois for advice and for a copy of the appeal that Du Bois had drafted to the United Nations expounding the injustices faced by Black citizens in the United States – a strategy that was picked up again decades later by the National Campaign on Dalit Human Rights (Cháirez-Garza 2014; Krishna 2014; Kapoor 2003). In the 1950s, Martin Luther King Jr.'s strategies of civil disobedience were famously influenced by Mohandas Karamchand Gandhi's tactics of anti-colonial mobilization. We find then, even in these two cases, that social movements seek resonance and connection across sites where forms of oppression they face are historically and contextually grounded, and also that social movements may learn from one another and deploy creative spatial tactics to achieve their ends (such as the civil disobedience tactics of sit-ins and marches). The study of social movements is about how people create new identities and come together to change the world, with an emphasis on the ways that alternate forms of connection and cosmopolitan citizenship are created and the ways that such mobilizing works across national borders, intersects with technologies such as social media, and challenges the supremacy of the nation-state. Beaumont, Miller and Nicholls (2016, p.2) observe that geographers often pick up a particular spatiality for analysis when we might be better served by considering the ways that these spatialities are relational, such that "place, space, scale, territory, networks, mobility, play distinctive yet interlocking roles in shaping the structures, strategies, dynamics and power of social movements." These interlocking but distinct ways of understanding social movements come together in examples discussed later. For instance, the close-knittedness of being rooted in a particular place and working for a goal may create the conditions in which people are able to build trust necessary to foment political action. The cultural importance of a place may generate political action as well, such that we could consider a mountain or the spirits that inhabit it as political actors (Gergan 2015; 2017). This approach would not be in opposition to also understanding the same social movement that relies on trust and builds from a sense of place to also draw on territorializing strategies or to be understood as a contingent assemblage (defined later). Social movement participants also creatively "shift scales," by deploying different messages for local, national, and global audiences to draw different kinds of support (Nicholls, 2013). As we proceed to consider a range of social movements, keep the relationality of spatial analysis and strategy in mind and think about the ways that our understanding of each movement might be enriched by alternate approaches.

Movements as Assemblage

The kayakers from the beginning of this chapter are not alone in the sea – these 13 people are part of something larger. For Davis and others, it is helpful to use the terminologies of **apparatus** and **assemblage** (defined later) to think through how these sets of connection come into being, transforming and shifting the spatial relations between places and people in the process.

The kayakers introduced by Davis are participating in direct action. As you will remember, direct action is distinct from conventional political outlets that are designated by the state (e.g., voting), and can involve a spectrum from nonviolent resistance (such as sit-ins) to sabotage, or a more diverse set of tactics that could include violence. The kayakers' action in the bay can be understood to be an innovative form of re-territorialization, or an attempt to assert different forms of governance in this place. Through temporary occupation, translocal assemblages work to create territory and new forms of governance in opposition to state governance goals.

An **apparatus**, developed from Foucault's (2007) idea of the *dispositif*, a set of state regulatory principles, informs logic and regimes of governance, ideals which are enacted through the governance of a population. While these logics are associated with the state, Deleuze (1988) and Legg (2011) stress that we ought not to see these logics and practices as originating in the state, but rather, the state is an outcome of the consolidation of these practices. For Davis, we understand this social movement better if we think of it as a form of translocal **assemblage**. The concept of assemblage gained traction in geography in the early 2000s, borrowing on the work of French theorists Gilles Deleuze and Félix Guattari (1987), who used the term constellation to refer to transient and contingent comings together of ideas that come to take on a life of their own. Assemblage thinking, in the terms of Anderson et al. enables us to understand sometimes fleeting and sometimes more long-lasting entities that consist of people, objects, places, and non-human actors, enabling "an openness about spatial form," and an experimental approach to thinking about politics (Anderson et al. 2012, 173; see also Dittmer 2014). Arun Saldanha (2007), for instance, has used these qualities of assemblage thinking to great effect in an analysis of race, specifically whiteness, and the ways it emerges among tourists in Goa, India, through a coming together of trance music, psychedelics, sunlight, and time. For Davis, understanding the kayaking activists as a translocal assemblage helps to incorporate the place-based nature of their work with the transnational experiential ties that they have with other activists. As with the goals of broader anti-militarization activism, which Davis identifies as a combination of environmental protection, peaceful conflict reservation, decolonization, and privileging the safety, health, and security of people, with attention to gender and other differences: a shift on "who security is for – from the state to individuals – as well as a shift in the scale of concern from the national/global to the local/body" (Davis, S. 2017, p.115 see also; Hyndman 2004; Loyd 2012).

Davis's theorization of anti-militarism activism as assemblage reminds us to think carefully about the relationships between movements in distant places. For one thing, we need to take care not to essentialize place by relying on nationalist or localist portrayals (Massey 2004). This is an important idea but one that we must consider in relationship to political objectives and context (e.g., Indigenous struggles for sovereignty may rely on ideas of place that have some characteristics of this kind of representation, but also contain openings for solidarity and justice). We also need to take care not to create neat binaries of local vs. global, place vs. space: such neat oppositions "project fixed interests and identities on the actors we study, with certain actors being essentially 'local', 'global', or bound to particularistic territories" (Beaumont, Miller, and Nicholls 2016, 11; Featherstone 2003). Davis's vision of anti-militarist activism as an assemblage complements Massey and Featherstone's relational approach to place.

Social Movements and the State: Zapatismo and Autonomy

How do social movements work for social change against/within state space? Since the 1994 uprising in Mexico, geographers have been drawn to understanding the Zapatista movement and what it teaches us about sovereignty, social movements, autonomy, and Indigenous rights (though Reyes and Kaufman and others might consider the use of rights terminology bowing to the language of the liberal state). Geographers like Chatterton (Chatterton 2010; Pickerill and Chatterton 2006) have traveled to Zapatista territory to learn how to enact autonomous practices in other spaces. Pickerill and Chatterton (2006, p.731) call for **autonomous geographies**, or geographies inspired by Zapatismo, which enable a "vocabulary of urgency, hope and inspiration, a call to action that we can dismantle wage labor, the oil economy, or representative democracy, and [demonstrate] that thousands of capable and workable micro-examples exist."

Latin America has been at the heart of a recent wave of decolonial struggles that have led to new ideas about what social movements mean and what they can do. In particular, the Zapatista movement for autonomy is groundbreaking in its conceptions of the relationship between formal politics and the state and social change, and in the work that members of the movement have done to understand **autonomy**, or independence from state systems (Reyes 2015; Reyes and Kaufman 2011). In Naylor's (2017, p.24) terms, "The struggle for autonomy for *campesinos/as* (peasants, as they self-identify) is not simply a rejection of state governance and neoliberal market structures, it is a process of creating self-reliant and secure livelihoods … Autonomy is all at once intimate, individual, and communal." In the context of the literature on autonomy, Naylor is arguing for more rooted and embodied ways of understanding what autonomy means to individual peasants as they work to untangle their lives from the reach of state forces through growing corn and coffee for sustenance. Let us dwell a little on the possibilities entangled in the idea of autonomy.

Reyes and Kaufman (2011) center the Zapatistas in current present and forward-looking imaginaries of radical social change due to their ideal of *mandar-obedeciendo*: rule by obeying. As discussed in the state-formation chapter, Reyes and Kaufman argue that this is not an attempt to create a state or a state alternative, thus, it is distinct from those prior and contemporary decolonial nationalisms (e.g., the independence movements that surged across Asia and Africa in the mid-twentieth centuries) that sought to maintain a state form but to remove colonizers from power and replace them with Indigenous rule. *Mandar-obedeciendo* enables the Zapatistas to move toward the practical and material unmaking of sovereignty, because their analysis is that sovereignty itself is "intimately tied to the history of conquest as well as to the regime of social control proffered by contemporary global capitalism" (Reyes and Kaufman 2011, p.506). How do you unmake sovereignty? Sovereignty is a concept that is foundational to the modern state system, and one that is also foundational to its violence, having developed in tandem with colonialism and imperialism. For Zapatistas, it is only by tearing down the foundations of the state system *or* simply building something new that we can survive. Possibility thus presents itself through the creation of autonomy, which is not only crucial for Indigenous people's survival, but "also … an antidote to the dispersed form of global 'paracoloniality' that accompanies the appearance of what the Zapatistas have called 'the Empire of money'" (Reyes and Kaufman 2011, p.506).

This marks an important distinction among various social movements. Some may be pushing for incremental (but not insignificant change), for fundamental legal changes, or for more radical outcomes within society and within the state, but along this spectrum, to some extent, the idea of domination or subalternity is rooted in exclusion from "the site of the effective exercise of sovereignty" (Reyes and Kaufman 2011, p.507). For the Zapatistas, "their aim is freedom and not simply … a reversal of positions within domination," so the replacement of one sovereign with another is not their goal; in fact, modern sovereignty creates a double-bind. If they are excluded from the structures of rule, they must demand inclusion to achieve humanity on the terms set out for them. But to be included would mean accepting the terms of governance formed through practices of domination, or to accept a "surreptitious call for the self-annihilation of these subaltern subjects and their particular historical differences … the only trajectory afforded them on the road to freedom is to … leave behind their historical existence against which the concept of sovereignty has already been defined" (Reyes and Kaufman 2011, p.512). You might recall now our earlier discussion of Indigenous refusal in the citizenship chapter.

After a short-lived conflict, a series of negotiations continued over several years, ending with reforms that were agreed upon by Mexico's three major political parties. However, the EZLN and the National Indigenous Congress rejected them. Rather than further negotiate and thus legitimize the power of the Mexican state, the Zapatistas chose to implement their own autonomous practices. We must clarify that this was not posed as autonomous power against the state, or a separate sovereign state, or that it was a return to pre-existing Indigenous structures. Rather, it was a new form of living together conceived of as functioning differently from state forms through the idea of *mandar-obedeciendo* that diffuse power through "mutual obligations, shared responsibilities, and the accountability and revocability of delegates," (Reyes and Kaufman 2011, p.516). These (non)governance practices drew on existing Indigenous practices but also sought to intensify their potential.

Mandar-obedeciendo takes place through autonomous self-government councils: Councils of Good Government are created with the intention of carrying out the will of the people, formalized in 2003. These ways of managing life are founded in the idea that our social worlds contain radical tendencies and that "autonomy is the daily struggle to act within *mandar-obedeciendo* over and against sovereign power and its derivative in governance" (Reyes and Kaufman 2011, p.517). For Naylor (2017), the spatial frames of analysis that one uses to understand autonomy are crucial to whether or not it is visible. We might seek to understand campesinos/as through lenses of organized resistance, occupation of territory, or power-sharing with the state, but all of these would be to make the lived experience of autonomy invisible. Instead, understanding how "campesinos/as experience autonomy as the living, breathing, embodiment of Indigenous resistance in the highlands multiplies our understandings of autonomy" (Naylor 2017, p.25). Naylor thus calls for an attention to the micro-practices of farmers that decenter the state and state-centered analyses, picking up an approach that we will return to as feminist geopolitics in later chapters. We can also see echoes of the starting points of this chapter, as campesinos/as do not represent all farmers, but rather Zapatista practices and identity is created intentionally from shared struggles and commitments that emerge from but transform individual lived experience. In the next section, we turn to movements for land and life in both urban and rural Brazil.

The Land is Ours Now! Movements for Land and Justice in Brazil

How do imaginaries and analyses of space and place inform social movements? In this section we consider this question through distinct cases of people claiming land and livelihoods in Brazil.

> On April 17, 1997, more than 50,000 people marched through the streets of Brasília in a historic demonstration of support for what had become the largest grassroots social movement in Brazilian history—O Movimento Dos Trabalhadores Rurais Sem Terra (the Movement of Rural Landless Workers, or the MST). Created officially in 1984, in the wake of a repressive military dictatorship, MST members aggressively occupied "unproductive" land as a way of pressuring the newly elected government for rights to the property. Over the next 19 years, the Brazilian government responded to the MST's actions with an erratic combination of violence and diplomacy that generated a frightening list of rural victims ([Comissão Pastoral da Terra] CPT 2000), but also led to the redistribution of over 1,000 rural properties. Today, [in 2004] the MST represents approximately 1 million people on land reform settlements and in temporary squatter camps throughout Brazil. (Wolford 2004, p.409)

Wolford (2004) argues against what she labels as the "Official Genesis Story" of the MST: that it was a natural outcome of political opportunity, religious mobilization, and ongoing agricultural restructuring. If this was the case, Wolford (2004, p.409) asks: "There were many poor people in rural Brazil who were affected by agricultural modernization, political opening, and religious organization, and most of them did not join the movement. So what distinguished those who did join from those who did not?" This speaks to a point made earlier in the chapter: people's situated identities do not determine their politics. Wolford argues that attention to geography, in particular the spatial imaginaries of differently situated groups of people, can help us to have a more nuanced and productive understanding of these political dynamics. Thus, she compares two groups: former plantation workers from the Northeastern State of Pernambuco and small family farmers from the southern state of Santa Catarina. What she finds is that while members of both groups do join the MST, they do not necessarily have the same spatial imaginaries.

As we might expect, this question is a deeply contextual one. As a developed and urban economy, part of the "BRIC" (Brazil, Russia, India, and China) block that is understood to be a major player on the world stage, why is Brazil fraught with rural unrest? This is tied to histories of empire and land tenure going back to the Portuguese arrival in 1500 that led to the development of a politically powerful agrarian elite, which managed to maintain hegemony through political transitions. When Brazil began to experience rapid economic growth in the late 1960s, leading into the 1980s, rapid urbanization and economic change was accompanied by increasingly concentrated land ownership: by 1985, 80% of the land was in the hands of only 10% of landowners. In 1978, land occupations began in the South, and in 1985, MST "established a short-term goal of securing 'land for those who work it' and a long-term goal of creating a just, socialist society." By 2004, 230,000 occupations had been carried out, leading to 1,000 land settlements (Wolford 2004, p.412). While the Brazilian Constitution was progressive, in practice, the hand of the state had to be forced to consider land reform, and the struggle for land and survival in Brazil is ongoing, particularly given a recent sharp turn to the right. We now turn to claims to land in urban Brazil.

In the opening to her book on Black women's grassroots organizing in Brazil, Keisha-Khan Perry describes a compelling scene in the Palestina Black neighborhood on the edges of Salvador, in Brazil's coastal state of Bahia. Military and police have accompanied a bulldozer and moving truck who have arrived to demolish the homes of Telma Sueli dos Santos Sena and Ana Cécilia Gomes Conceição, two women who had been asserting their right to the land in courts and with the backing of the local neighborhood association. The arrival of the bulldozer led to outrage and a crowd gathered outside the homes. In the escalating tension, with Telma Sueli dos Santos weeping and demanding justice, family and neighbors stepped up to affirm her right to the land. Amilton dos Santos, the driver of the bulldozer, refused to demolish the home, insisting that he was sick. Perry observes that the newspaper article covering the events foregrounds dos Santos as a heroic figure, fighting the urban-renewal driven land grabs occurring across the city, but his heroism should not detract from the long-term and often unreported work of Black women in Salvador and across Brazil to fight forced displacement and defend the life and livelihood of their communities (Perry 2013; see also the work of Vaz 2018 on solidarity economies in Rio de Janeiro). Perry (2013), Kia Caldwell (2007), and Christen Smith (2015), among others, have argued that Black women's theorization and enactment of political strategies for liberation and survival have been missing from many accounts of urban land struggles in Brazil.

Perry uses the story of the bulldozer driver to illustrate how media attention may focus on men's actions, such that in her words, "a decade later, in popular memory the incident remains a story about Senhor Amilton, not about the courageous homeowner who defied the police, Dona Telma" (Perry 2013, p.13). When Perry sets out to meet land rights activists and meets Dona Telma, she finds that Telma had been long struggling to keep her home, and the actions of the day that the bulldozers arrived at her home were not spontaneous. In fact, Telma had been observing coverage of these kinds of home clearances and had organized in advance – while media coverage suggested the crowd outside her door formed spontaneously, a women-led activist group had been preparing for this inevitable day. At a meeting when Dona Telma told her story, Ana Christina, another activist exhorted the people assembled to stand up for their rights: "What kind of city do we live in that prepares architects and engineers to demolish homes and expel local populations in order to implement their urban development projects … The land belongs to the people" (Perry 2013, p.14). Following on from our earlier discussions of intersectionality and epistemology, Perry's argument about the centrality of Black women in Brazil to struggles for land is premised on their social and political positioning. She observes that they "have both collective memory of residence and, in some cases, legal documentation of ownership of ancestral land. They also serve as the primary mediators of familial and social relations within their communities, influencing political decisions and how important resources such as land are distributed. Historically, in Brazil, land has been perceived as *o lugar da mulher*," that is, "the women's place" (Perry, 2013, p.15). Perry argues that this positioning leads Black women to be at the forefront of understanding how race, gender, and class come together in urban development policy. Along with other scholars, Perry observes that Blackness in Brazil is framed as a cultural legacy, however, Black activists incorporate culture into political analysis and strategy, while nationalist appropriation of Black culture seeks to excavate political intention and quest for autonomy from Black cultural practices (Bledsoe 2016; Caldwell, 2018; Perry 2013; Vaz 2018).

As a Black woman from the United States, with close ties to Black Brazilians, Perry faces great challenges in her research in Brazil, including not only committing to work in solidarity alongside the women she focuses on, but also at times to face physical danger (experiences she documents with great insight in Perry 2012). As a transnational scholar moving between Brazil and the United States, Perry is also able to see both resonance with anti-Black violence in the United States and ways that urban politics are contextually-specific, for instance, due to Brazil's particular history of racial democracy, colonial ties, and a history of *quilombola* (community-building by formerly enslaved people). Along similar lines, Caldwell (2018) observes a recent surge of Black women entering politics in relation to the intersectional axes of patriarchal and racialized oppression experienced both in Brazil and the United States. One of our tasks as we seek to understand the geography of social movements, then, is to understand the ways that patterns of marginalization, visibility/invisibility, and political strategy and action may both resonate and diverge, here across distinct contexts in Brazil and the United States. Each holds its own historical contexts for organizing and for oppression, while also being tied together by what Paul Gilroy has termed the Black Atlantic (1993).

Christen Smith, like Perry, centers the work done by Black women's movements to cultivate theories for liberation, and in doing so she reveals the ways that their activism creates new spatial theories of the world. Smith (2016, p.73) writes that:

> Black women across the Americas exist in a state of precarity. We are always standing on the precipice of the social world; teetering on the edge of invisibility, dis-ease and insanity, triply affected by gender/sexuality, race, and class. As a result, our contributions to society typically go unremarked.

Working against this current, Smith seeks to recover theorizations of the trans-Atlantic Black experience through scholar activist Beatriz Nascimento's research and documentary filmmaking on quilombos, and through her life as part of Brazil's Black Movement. Nascimento was part of activist movements both inside and outside the university, seeking to create space for Black people in both contexts. Quilombos are not only a material and historical entity – the spaces where enslaved people created their own territories and communities, but, in Smith's (2016, p.78) terms, through the Black Radical Tradition in Brazil, quilombos are also

> the practice of finding refuge from the total condition of slavery—including those conditions that extend beyond the temporal boundaries of physical bondage, like racism and the erasure of Black history. Quilombos are not only physical and cultural spaces that are materially tangible historically and today but also trans-temporal, trans-spatial spaces of Black liberation that Black people in Brazil have articulated in response to the conditions of subjugation.

Nascimento theorizes the quilombo as a practice of liberation, "as the process of Black liberation self-determination and organization," as "Black autonomy and escape," (Smith 2016, p.78). Smith (2016, p.80) writes that:

> Nascimento engages with an age-old question for African Diaspora scholars: in what ways does the body become the primary territorial homeland for dislocated "Atlantic" African peoples in the Americas, and how can the spirit then complicate this territoriality through ontological transcendence? Embedded in her interpretation was the notion of the Black body as a seamless extension of the land—the subject of Black migration, escape, and liberation. Her conceptualization of quilombo is uniquely gendered because she privileges the body as a political site. Moreover, her theoretical engagement with the politics of trance and spirituality locate her in dialogue with Black feminist discussions of the body as spiritual-political portal, specifically, the work of Jacqui Alexander (2005).

Thus, her theorization is that "we are the land, the land is us" (Smith 2016, p.80), and through her research she maps connections between Angola and Brazil, between quilombos and favelas. Citing Katherine McKittrick (2006), Smith points to how Black women create oppositional geographies of humanness, in which embodied life becomes an expression of memory and assertion of humanity. This way of being in the world teaches us about the ways that identity is *made* part of political movements through theorization and action – here through the ways that Nascimento conceives of the quilombo as transcendent of its materiality and as a way to structure political action.

Along parallel registers, Adam Bledsoe (2017) traces these ties through considering the history of marronage and *quilombola* across the Americas. Bledsoe (2017, p.31) defines maroon settlements as "settlements established by runaway slaves, who sought to escape their condition as fungible, accumulated property," and argues that such settlements, like the Gullah-Geechee community in the United States, or the Gamboa de Baixo quilombo in Brazil, help us to understand and analyze ongoing Black liberation struggles. Bledsoe (2019) also points to ways that Afro-Brazilian communities in the Bay of Aratu create subjectivities in relation to the environment that enable them to resist the extraction of natural resources.

Movements, Nonmovements, and the Politics
of Refusal and Fun

What are we to make of the relationship between social movements, described earlier, and other forms of resistance, rebellion, or social transformation? They are sometimes related and sometimes begin and remain quite distinct. Asef Bayat (2009) has made a compelling case for attention to what he calls **social nonmovements**. A nonmovement is the gradual shift of societal and political norms over time through small changes that occur simply as a result of people trying to live their lives, but they can have profound impacts when people's small changes build, even if this is not part of a large and defined social movement. Bayat's argument is centered in his reading of Middle East politics, which he observed to be wildly misread by Euroamerican academics and policy-makers. As he notes, in the media, orientalist imaginaries continue to be influential, with, for instance, the "Arab street" being understood as a scene of potential chaos and violence, *or,* paradoxically, the Middle East being read as unchanging and apathetic. These representations cannot explain the transformation that has occurred in many Middle Eastern countries over the last decades, which are due in fact to small and incremental changes in daily life that add up to profound societal differences.

Iran has seen a quiet transformation in the roles that women play in society, and while European and American representations focus on the need for improved women's rights, it has also seen a rise in feminism. In Bayat's reading, this is perhaps partly due to women's intentional organizing, but also derives simply from women going about their daily life in the ways that they choose. For some women, this might mean an interpretation of their religious identity that requires veiling and seclusion. For others, they might have different interpretations of religion that do not call for veiling at all or perhaps call for more symbolic use of the headscarf rather than a very strict wrapping of the headscarf that does not allow for any hair to be visible. What does this have to do with a nonmovement? Bayat argues that simply by one or two women in a neighborhood going out in the street with a casual headscarf showing an inch of hair, an individual woman might feel she can be a little lax, or in his terms, a little more "bad hijabi" when out in public. Similarly, as family friends and neighbors begin to send their daughters to go not only to college but on to receive higher degrees like MDs or PhDs, without much conscious struggle, this becomes a new norm.

What Have We Learned and Where Do We Go From Here?

In this chapter we have considered the ways that people try to change the world, and how this may or may not be related to questions of identity. The next chapter builds on this one, by working through some of the many ways that scholars and others have worked to implement changes inside the discipline of geography itself, as well as in academic life more broadly.

Geographer at Work: Willie Wright

Willie Wright is an assistant professor of geography at Rutgers. He received his PhD in Geography from the University of North Carolina at Chapel Hill in 2017.

Provisional Government of the Republic of New Afrika

The Republic of New Afrika (RNA) was formed March 31, 1968 in Detroit, Michigan. The Black revolutionary nationalist government emerged out of a two-day Black government conference organized by Gaidi and Imari Obadele. Believing that New Afrikans (e.g. Blacks in America) are a nation of people never given the chance to express their national character in the form of a government and territorial sovereignty, the PGRNA called for the creation of a Black-led nation-state within the borders of what is currently known as the United States of America. New Afrikans have claimed five southern states (LA, MS, GA, AL, SC) as New Afrikan territory and seek to obtain it through political and embodied means. One way the PGRNA has sought to legitimate its claims and formalize its provisional government is via a plebiscite. A plebiscite is a referendum by which citizens (e.g. New Afrikans) vote on an issue of national interest (e.g. whether to pledge allegiance to the RNA or the USA).

In the course of this study, I conducted 12 months of fieldwork, 6 months in Detroit and 6 months in Jackson. I was following the political and spatial trajectory of RNA citizens, a number of whom originated in Detroit and migrated to Jackson, Mississippi to manifest a New Afrikan nation. In addition to following the paths laid by New Afrikans, I was hoping to challenge research on social movements, much of which has attributed political organizations' growth to a finite timeline and have focused heavily on the Civil Rights Movement as a model for activism and justice for Blacks in America. However significant, this work obscures the political ideas, practices, and outcomes of more radical Black movements and organizations, such as the RNA. While in Detroit I conducted archival research on the city's history of labor organizing and the impact of de-industrialization on its people and infrastructure.

My research in Jackson developed into personas as well as professional practice. I engrained myself with local cooperatives – Cooperation Jackson and the Cooperative Community of New West Jackson – seeking to impact the city's political economy through cooperatively owned businesses and building eco-villages. Whereas in Detroit I lived alone, in Jackson I stayed with a family, all of whom were interlocutors in my study. Thus, the static lines that define "objective" research were blurred as my study became intimate and embodied in the space of the home. In addition to interviewing and observing my participants, I became an active supporter and sustainer of their organizations. Believing that a key limitation of research on social movements is not only a scholar's focus on the Civil Rights Movement, but also a lack of engagement with organizations that requires intellectual *and* physical labor, in Jackson I deliberately merged my personal, political, and professional interests. I attended meetings, made suggestions regarding organizational structure and strategy, and participated in farm work with members of Cooperation Jackson and the Cooperative Community of New West Jackson. Moreover, I actively campaigned for Chokwe Antar Lumumba, the current mayor of Jackson, Mississippi. Instead of simply observing the political and spatial legacies of the RNA, I actively worked to bring them about.

Though the RNA is not recognized as having official sovereignty over its proposed five-state nation, the spatial and political aspirations of this social movement organization have taken root. In Detroit, the RNA's legacy has been spatialized in the form of a street named after Chokwe Lumumba, a native Detroiter, human rights attorney, and former citizen of the RNA. In Jackson, Mississippi the RNA's political legacy became embodied in the mayoral election of Chokwe Lumumba in 2013 and the 2017 election of his son, Chokwe Antar Lumumba. Moreover, the existence of political and communal organizations like the Malcolm X Grassroots Movement, the Cooperative Community of New West Jackson, and Cooperation Jackson are testament to the RNA's enduring impact in either city. Collectively, Detroit and Jackson's political and spatial expressions indicate that, despite daunting obstacles, social movements can generate significant long-term outcomes, at times, beyond the scope of its activists.

Keywords

Apparatus   A set of state regulatory principles, informs logic and regimes of governance, ideals that are enacted through the governance of a population.

Assemblage   Transient and contingent comings together of ideas, materials, and people that come to take on a life of their own.

Autonomous geographies   Geographies inspired by Zapatismo, which seek to create independent spaces from state systems that also do not recreate state forms of hierarchical power and violence.

Black feminism   Has been framed as a specific approach to feminism that draws on Black women's lived experiences, and incorporates analyses of race and class (as well as other positions, such as sexual orientation) into *both* understandings of oppression *and* understandings of how to achieve liberation.

Black feminist epistemology and **feminist standpoint epistemology**   Signals the situated position from which a Black woman or (for feminist standpoint epistemology) any woman, experiences and creates her own knowledge about the world. Builds on Marxist understanding of epistemology in which workers have a clearer view of how the world works because of their social position. For Black feminist epistemology we can understand that Black women may have a more sophisticated understanding of racism because of the way they are racialized in society, in addition to their gendered understanding of patriarchy.

Civil society   Associations and other groups of people reproducing and changing societal norms and engaging in political processes outside formal political organizations.

Direct action   Actions by activists that do not only focus on electoral politics and existing systems. For instance, destroying military equipment or oil pipelines, staging sit-ins or die-ins in public places, squatting (the occupy movement).

Identity politics   Politics in relation to identity differences such as race or gender.

Imperial feminism   Imperial feminism seeks to protect and promote women's rights, in ways that may reinforce or strengthen empire and further racial hierarchies.

Intersectionality   How intersecting systems of oppression mean that people from marginalized groups may face obstacles to having their discrimination understood and acted on in legal systems.

Social movement   A group of individuals or loose coalition of smaller groups seeking to create societal or political change, sometimes through seeking to change government structures, other times through working to create *different* forms of governance (or even abolish governance), or still other times working to change society.

Social nonmovements A nonmovement is the gradual shift of societal and political norms over time through small changes that occur simply as a result of people trying to live their lives.

White feminism White feminism centers *white* or "colorblind" experiences of gender, and is not attentive to issues of race (and perhaps also economic class).

Further Reading

Anti-militarism

Loyd, J.M. 2012. Geographies of Peace and Antiviolence. *Geography Compass* 6(8): 477–489.

Lutz, C. and Enloe, C. 2009. *The Bases of Empire: The Global Struggle against US Military Posts*. New York: New York University Press.

McCaffrey, K.T. 2002. *Military Power and Popular Protest: The US Navy in Vieques, Puerto Rico*. New Brunswick, NJ: Rutgers University Press.

Feminism and geographies of feminism

Arvin, M., Tuck, E., and Morrill, A. 2013. Decolonizing Feminism: Challenging Connections between Settler Colonialism and Heteropatriarchy. *Feminist Formations* 25(1): 8–34.

Collins, P.H. 1990. *Black Feminist Thought: Knowledge, Consciousness, and the Politics of Empowerment*. New York: Routledge.

Combahee River Collective. 1977. *A Black Feminist Statement*. https://americanstudies.yale.edu/sites/default/files/files/Keyword%20Coalition_Readings.pdf.

Crenshaw, K. 1989. Demarginalizing the Intersection of Race and Sex: A Black Feminist Critique of Antidiscrimination Doctrine, Feminist Theory and Antiracist Politics. *University of Chicago Legal Forum* 1: 139–167.

Crenshaw, K. 1991. Mapping the Margins: Intersectionality, Identity Politics, and Violence against Women of Color. *Stanford Law Review*, 43(6) 1241–1299.

Davis, A.Y. 2011. *Women, Race, & Class*. New York: Vintage.

Dixon, D.P. and Jones, J.P., III. 2006. *Feminist Geographies of Difference, Relation, and Construction*. London: Sage.

Eaves, L.E. 2019. The Imperative of Struggle: Feminist and Gender Geographies in the United States. *Gender, Place & Culture* 26(7–9): 1314–1321.

hooks, b. 1981. *Ain't I a Woman: Black Women and Feminism*. London: South End Press.

Lorde, A. 1984. *Sister Outsider: Essays and Speeches*. Fredom, CA: Crossing Press.

Lugones, M. 2010. Toward a Decolonial Feminism. *Hypatia* 25(4): 742–759.

Mahmood, S. 2011. *Politics of Piety: The Islamic Revival and the Feminist Subject*. Princeton, NJ: Princeton University Press.

Mohanty, C.T. 2003. *Feminism without Borders: Decolonizing Theory, Practicing Solidarity*. Durham, NC: Duke University Press.

Mollett, S. and Faria, C. 2018. The Spatialities of Intersectional Thinking: Fashioning Feminist Geographic Futures. *Gender, Place & Culture* 25(4): 565–577.

Nagar, R. 2014. *Muddying the Waters: Coauthoring Feminisms across Scholarship and Activism*. Champaign: University of Illinois Press.

Oberhauser, A.M., Fluri, J.L., Whitson, R. et al. 2017. *Feminist Spaces*. London: Taylor & Francis.

Pratt, G. and Rosner, V. 2012. *The Global and the Intimate: Feminism in Our Time*. New York: Columbia University Press.

Rose, G. 1993. *Feminism and Geography: The Limits of Geographical Knowledge*. Cambridge: Polity.

Staeheli, L., Kofman, E., and Peake, L. 2004. *Mapping Women, Making Politics: Feminist Perspectives on Political Geography*. New York: Psychology Press.

Taylor, K.-Y. 2017. *How We Get Free: Black Feminism and the Combahee River Collective*. Chicago: Haymarket Books.

Todd, Z. 2016. An Indigenous Feminist's Take on the Ontological Turn: "Ontology" Is Just Another Word for Colonialism. *Journal of Historical Sociology* 29(1): 4–22.

Emotional, Assemblage, and Visceral Politics

Bondi, L. 2016. *Emotional Geographies*. New York: Routledge.

Dittmer, J. 2014. Geopolitical Assemblages and Complexity. *Progress in Human Geography* 38(3): 385–401.

Hayes-Conroy, J. and Hayes-Conroy, A. 2013. Veggies and Visceralities: A Political Ecology of Food and Feeling. *Emotion, Space and Society* 6: 81–90.

Nayak, A. 2011. Geography, Race and Emotions: Social and Cultural Intersections. *Social & Cultural Geography* 12(6): 548–562.

Pain, R. 2009. Globalized Fear? Towards an Emotional Geopolitics. *Progress in Human Geography* 33(4): 466–486.

Tolia-Kelly, D.P. 2006. Affect – An Ethnocentric Encounter? Exploring the 'Universalist' Imperative of Emotional/Affectual Geographies. *Area* 38(2): 213–217.

Sharp, J. 2009. Geography and Gender: What Belongs to Feminist Geography? Emotion, Power and Change. *Progress in Human Geography* 33(1): 74–80.

Sultana, F. 2011. Suffering For Water, Suffering From Water: Emotional Geographies of Resource Access, Control and Conflict. *Geoforum* 42(2): 163–172.

Space and social movements

Beaumont, J., Miller, B., and Nicholls, W. 2016. Introduction: Conceptualizing the Spatialities of Social Movements. In *Spaces of Contention*. New York: Routledge, pp.11–34.

Castells, M. 1983. *The City and the Grassroots: A Cross-Cultural Theory of Urban Social Movements*. Berkeley, CA: University of California Press.

Featherstone, D. 2003. Spatialities of Transnational Resistance to Globalization: The Maps of Grievance of the Inter-Continental Caravan. *Transactions of the Institute of British Geographers* 28(4): 404–421.

Naylor, L. 2019. *Fair Trade Rebels: Coffee Production and Struggles for Autonomy in Chiapas*. Minneapolis, MN: University of Minnesota Press.

Nicholls, W., Miller, B., and Beaumont, J. 2016. *Spaces of Contention: Spatialities and Social Movements*. New York: Routledge.

Nicholls, W.J. 2007. The Geographies of Social Movements. *Geography Compass* 1(3): 607–622.

Pickerill, J. and Chatterton, P. 2006. Notes towards Autonomous Geographies: Creation, Resistance and Self-Management as Survival Tactics. *Progress in Human Geography* 30(6): 730–746.

Routledge, P. 1993. *Terrains of Resistance: Nonviolent Social Movements and the Contestation of Place in India*. Westport, CT: Praeger.

Tyner, J. 2013. *The Geography of Malcolm X: Black Radicalism and the Remaking of American Space*. New York: Routledge.

Vasudevan, A. 2015. *Metropolitan Preoccupations: The Spatial Politics of Squatting in Berlin*. Chichester: John Wiley & Sons.

Chapter 8

Decolonizing Political Geography?

> Decolonization is a recognition that "a ghost is alive so to speak. We are in relation to it and it has designs on us such that we must reckon with graciously."
> (Ramírez, in Naylor et al. 2018, p.6; citing Tuck and Ree 2013; and Gordon 2008)

> Decolonization brings about the repatriation of Indigenous land and life; it is not a metaphor for other things we want to do to improve our societies and schools. The metaphorization of decolonization makes possible a set of evasions, or "settler moves to innocence", that problematically attempt to reconcile settler guilt and complicity, and rescue settler futurity.
> (Tuck and Yang 2012, p.1)

On the night of November 20, 2016, the US North Dakota Police used water cannons, tear-gas, and rubber bullets against Indigenous and allied protestors at one of the encampments near the Standing Rock Sioux reservation (Wong 2016). Several camps had been in operation since the summer of 2016, with citizens of more than 300 Native nations as well as other non-Native allies holding this space in order to preserve Native sovereignty and defend the land against the potential environmental impacts of the Dakota Access Pipeline (Estes 2017). On the icy night that the water cannons were used, at least 300 people were injured, many by hypothermia, and 26 water defenders were hospitalized, with injuries including bone fractures and compromised vision due to rubber bullets (Wong 2016).

In the wake of the incident, the American Civil Liberties Union repeated its call for investigation by the Department of Justice; reporting on the event, journalists and scholars placed this night in a historical trajectory. Julia Wong (2016) drew historical connections:

Political Geography: A Critical Introduction, First Edition. Sara Smith.
© 2020 John Wiley & Sons Ltd. Published 2020 by John Wiley & Sons Ltd.

"The use of water cannons against protesters invokes images of African Americans being bombarded with fire hoses during the civil rights movement, but the crowd control tactic was developed in Germany in the 1930s, according to the ACLU." Diné scholar Andrew Curley wrote on the Standing Rock Movement:

> Like the civil rights protests of the 1960s, the major media paid attention when police repression reached dangerous levels. As Dene scholar Glen Coulthard said in 2012 during Idle No More, "If history has shown us anything, it is this: if you want those in power to respond swiftly to Indigenous peoples' political efforts, start by placing Native bodies (with a few logs and tires thrown in for good measure) between settlers and their money, which in colonial contexts is generated by the ongoing theft and exploitation of our land and resource base." This is what community members at Standing Rock did and the response from those in power was tear gas, rubber bullets, dogs, and water cannons.

Indigenous activists and scholars put this movement into a longer historical trajectory: one in which **decolonization** is an active and ongoing process of struggling for sovereignty, rights, and land, under ongoing conditions of settler colonialism (Curley 2016; Dhillon and Estes 2016; Estes 2017; Whyte 2017). This chapter seeks to understand both how political geographers might learn from ongoing struggles to decolonize the world, *as well as* how we might turn these lenses toward the discipline of geography itself. We will consider both the material ways that colonial processes or colonial ruination are ongoing, here in the denial of sovereignty to Indigenous nations to facilitate capitalist resource extraction, *and* the ways that conceptual frameworks, categories, and discourses enable these processes. We will also grapple with Tuck and Yang's challenge *not* to use the term as a metaphor but to consider what it means to keep to their clarification that decolonization means in the strictest sense "the repatriation of Indigenous land and life."

Within the discipline of geography, Patricia Noxolo (2017a, p.342) begins a recent reflection on decolonial theory from her own positionality, that is, from her own relationship to the topic at hand. She writes: "I am, if you like, a classic postcolonial tenured scholar: daughter of Commonwealth migrants to the formerly colonizing country, writing about the legacies of colonialism both in the formerly colonizing and in the formerly colonized countries." This article is part of a rich, difficult, and productive set of conversations emerging in our discipline, asking how, as geographers, we might take the imperative to decolonize our discipline. When scholars like Noxolo incorporate their own relationship to colonial history into their storytelling or analysis, they not only make these historical processes and their results more "real," they also demand that we take Tuck and Yang's (2012) reminder seriously. Noxolo's own life story tells us: "decolonization is not a metaphor." That is, if we want aspire to create a world that is decolonized, we must *both* explore the colonial roots of concepts that we deploy, *and* we must consider our own and our institution's relationship to Indigenous land, imperial wealth, and continued imperial violence. That means asking questions about geography's relationship to colonial institutions, asking who inhabits institutional and disciplinary spaces, whether those institutions fund further colonial incursions (for instance, through military collaboration), and whether or how we and our institutions can push for the acknowledgment and repatriation of Indigenous land and for reparations. It can also mean beginning the difficult processes of reevaluating who writes and teaches in our field, whose texts are assigned, and to whom researchers are accountable.

To decolonize is to ask who makes knowledge and under what conditions, but it is also to ask: to what end do we make new knowledge about the world? Does our knowledge production aid in the repatriation of native land? Reparations for those whose ancestors were enslaved to build other people's wealthy nations? The return of wealth and treasure stolen from colonized lands? If not, who are we writing and reading for, and what is our moral justification for those choices?

Let us return to the first pages of this book, in which I established the setting in which I write: a building on a US university campus named for a leader of the Ku Klux Klan (KKK), a white supremacist organization. This was an intentional beginning, because it grounds us in the unsettling ways in which we as academics are entangled in the production of knowledge and history that is tied to colonizing processes. In fact, this institution that I work for has in the past made money from the sale of people who were enslaved (McGee 2019). The ways that we are entangled are not uniform or homogenous – for instance, in some cases to be an Indigenous person or to be an immigrant from a previously colonized place is to carry a different set of experiences, and different orientations to the past and the future. This is a little tricky to think through because we do not want to essentialize difference (e.g., to assume that all Indigenous people have one set of political orientations, experiences, or beliefs) – but at the same time, we do not want to ignore differences and proceed as though being a settler in a settler colonial state or of white British heritage in the United Kingdom, or being of a majority religious, ethnic, or racial background in other places is the norm or the default position.

Thus, let us make this a little less abstract through a return to the stately building whose complex history has given it three names: Saunders, its original name, Carolina, the university's new given name, and Hurston, the name given to it by activists and retained in student and faculty imaginaries. As political geographers, we consider the landscape and its uses to both reveal power and politics and to extend or disrupt existing power geometries. So then, let us recall that this brick building in which I sit has ties to chattel slavery, and underneath the new stone sign that names the building Carolina Hall the name Saunders haunts the building like a ghost – a ghost recalling the early-twentieth century when ordinary white people upheld white supremacy as a cultural value by having the name of a KKK leader engraved in stone above the main entrance to the building. This history has been named and is the topic of vigorous debate. But of course, this is not the complete story of this land. Indigenous people have lived here for thousands of years, and remain here now. Oral traditions, historical records, and archaeologists, all inform us that prior to the founding of the university, this state was home to the Lumbee, the Eastern Band of Cherokee Indians, Haliwa Saponi, Coharie, Sappony, Waccamaw Siouan, Meherrin, and the Occaneechi Band of the Saponi Nation, and I am grateful to UNC historian Malinda Lowery, a member of the Lumbee Tribe of North Carolina, for this important context. The campus itself is on land that was taken from local tribes through treaties and wars. Local archaeologists have excavated Occaneechi and Shakori villages in nearby Hillsborough and Sissipahaw, and can document the histories of these people to the sixteenth century, though of course that history precedes this record (Hudson 2017; Jeffries 2015). That in the research for this book it was impossible to find more information about the people who lived here is a sign of the problems with which this chapter struggles. That my impulse is to point to evidence and archival sources to document the authentic relationship between Native people and this land is a sign of the ways that both you and I have been inculcated in a particular way of understanding both land and knowledge. We might do well then to think back to Daigle's reconceptualization of belonging from our discussion on the nation. That our university still hires and retains very few Native faculty, that our Native student population is similarly small, and that Native people, like the Lumbee Tribe, in our state are having to struggle to prevent the Atlantic Coast Pipeline that would compromise their sovereignty and threaten their environment likewise illustrates the multifaceted nature of the ongoing settler colonialism we face today and its complications (Emanuel 2017; 2018).

  Postcolonial and decolonial scholars ask us to consider that this history is not a footnote, but rather that the context for this book is fundamental to how knowledge is made and to how people like us learn how the world works. How is it, for instance, that the university I work with began to consider and visibly mark and contextualize its relationship to slavery and Jim Crow racism only in 2015, and has taken only small steps thus far? And further, that 2017 was the year that the institution began considering how to publically mark and document its relationship to the people who lived on this land centuries before it was founded (Hudson 2017)? Perhaps part of the answer to these questions lies in the demographic makeup of the university itself.

  If you never considered who has taught you over the course of your lifetime, who writes the books for your syllabi or your bookshelf, take a moment to do so, and to ask where most of this faculty are educated and books are published, and how these flows of knowledge, to you, matter. This has been a strand of thought woven through this book, so the intent of this chapter is not to introduce entirely new ideas, but to put together the pieces of a map that have been scattered across the chapters, in hopes that this book can be not only a way to look backward at where our discipline has been, but also to consider where these paths can take us.

  We will start with a broad-brush overview of the links between material conditions, knowledge, and embodied life, that is: what happened, how it shapes what we know, and how what happened and what we know shapes our lives. After this overview, we will consider first the ways that theorists and scholars have worked to understand colonialism as an ongoing global system, then the ways that colonialism is related to knowledge, and finally, the various ways that political geographers propose to create new ways of knowing and being in the world. This chapter draws on postcolonial, decolonial, and decolonizing scholarship. There are disjunctures, disagreements, tensions, and shared worlds in these bodies of literature as well – and we will return to these in the closing sections of this chapter.

Power/Knowledge and Imperial Ruination

Postcolonial, decolonial, and decolonizing theory are premised on the fundamental idea that imperial and colonial encounters have altered relationships between people and places, affecting the political, economic, environmental, and cultural structures of the world. This has occurred, broadly, through the death and destruction that accompanied imperial exploration and the settler colonies or imperial encounters that followed. Ann Laura Stoler (2013) has referred to the ongoing effects of colonialism and empire as **imperial ruination**, which signals that after the formal end to empire the consequences of that encounter continued to unfold, whether in the economic processes of development that have unevenly benefited specific segments of society in formerly colonized places, or the continued environmental effects, or the perpetuation of ethnic and racial divisions that originated in or were reconfigured and strengthened during the time of European colonization.

Before we turn to theorizations of the structuring effects of the colonial era, it is useful to consider frameworks and ideas that are foundational or implicit to much of this work. There is a vast literature on these ideas, but as a starting point, three inter-related ideas are crucial to carry forward into this chapter. First is the idea that knowledge production was central to the functioning of colonialism and empire, both by serving practical ends, and by creating elaborate justifications for empire (Said 1979). Second is the observation that this knowledge production was necessary to create, maintain, and uphold the colonizer/colonized divide. This divide was in fact quite fragile and colonizers and settlers worked hard to uphold it, meaning, the difference between the white people who colonized and the Black and Brown people who were colonized was not natural, but was *made* through colonialism (Stoler 1995). Third, that the forms of racial thinking that emerged during colonization were premised on a hierarchy of humanity that is written into much subsequent thinking, and today we travel in its wake (Sharpe 2016; Hartman 1997).

Edward Said's transformative scholarship on Orientalism is a cornerstone of postcolonial thinking, initiating a rich literature on the ways that knowledge production – from maps and ethnographies to travelogues and fiction – was crucial to imperialism. The title of Said's landmark 1978 book, *Orientalism*, is a reference to orientalists, that is, scholars of the Orient, or the "East." Said argues that scholars of the Orient were not writing to accurately describe "the East," at all, but rather to do political work by creating a mythical East in order to develop a coherent narrative about the West: "as much as the West itself, the Orient is an idea that has a history and a tradition of thought, imagery, and vocabulary that have given it reality and presence in and for the West" (Said 1979, pp.4, 5).

Let us begin by just thinking of what it means to designate "the East." This already depicts Near East, Middle East, and Far East, in relation to Europe, telling us immediately that the person using these terms imagines themselves in Europe. These writers depict the Orient as a place that is timeless and changeless, a place that is feminized, and a place that is passive. Its rulers are portrayed as despots devoid of logic or strategy, and holding the region back in its timeless inertia. This representation of the Orient as a passive woman, in need of rescue from despotic leaders, sets the stage for a heroic rescue. In opposition to the East as a timeless, exotic, and mysterious woman, whom one might desire but never understand, we have the representation of the West – depicted as strong, rational, masculine, and forward thinking. These roles and their variations underwrite much imperial rationale: for instance in the discourse that British colonizers could "save" local women from patriarchal abuse through law and civilization – a pattern of thought that replicates during the "War on Terror," through the trope of "saving Muslim women" (Mohanty 1991; Spivak 1988; L. Abu-Lughod 2013). I suspect if you spend some time thinking about these roles, you might find examples of how these same stereotypes and imagined geographies continue to haunt representations of Asia, even in seemingly trivial pop culture representations that nonetheless shape global imaginaries. Consider some of the representations, originating in Hollywood, that continue to dominate global cultural productions. Why is it that Hollywood continues to cast white men as leading characters in films set in East Asia? Why are women of East Asian origin cast as girlfriends, rather than protagonists? Why do so few films from Hollywood have men of Asian origin as romantic or action-hero leads while so many have Middle Eastern villains?

From this analysis of the content of orientalist literature, Said brings us to two parts of a framework for understanding its effects. Our initial impulse on considering the ways that the Orient has been represented might be to correct inaccuracies. Well, we can say, "archival documents point to several ways in which these stereotypes were wrong." Said takes this one step further: he argues that attempting to verify or discredit these fantasies is irrelevant, because the portrayals were never even about the Orient at all, but rather were a heroic story about the West itself. By describing the "East," as a place awaiting domination, the story was actually centered in the narrative of the "West," as modern, rational, masculine, and heroic. Consider then that *writing about the world writes the world*. It is through the construction of these fantasies that British, French, Italian, Portuguese, and Dutch colonizers were able to concoct narratives that justified colonialism and made it a logical response to the world they had created. The theft of labor and resources from newly colonized places required an elaborate discursive framework in order to make sense of the violence that it entailed.

Let us turn to the second main idea in our overview. Said provides us one way into the colonial logics that enabled this system to operate, though we must also keep in mind that it was never a seamless system of domination but always fraught with internal incoherence, crises, internal and external resistance, and desperately in need of shoring up. The *feeling* of empire: as both violent and fragile, is summed up vividly in the writings of George Orwell, the author of works like *1984* and *Animal Farm*, who grew up as the child of a British Imperial officer and later was himself a police officer in Burma. In the short story, "Shooting an Elephant," he writes:

> At that time I had already made up my mind that imperialism was an evil thing and the sooner I chucked up my job and got out of it the better. Theoretically – and secretly, of course – I was all for the Burmese and all against their oppressors, the British. As for the job I was doing, I hated it more bitterly than I can perhaps make clear. In a job like that you see the dirty work of Empire at close quarters. The wretched prisoners huddling in the stinking cages of the lock-ups, the grey, cowed faces of the long-term convicts, the scarred buttocks of the men who had been flogged with bamboos – all these oppressed me with an intolerable sense of guilt. But I could get nothing into perspective. I was young and ill-educated and I had had to think out my problems in the utter silence that is imposed on every Englishman in the East.

In "Shooting an Elephant," and in *Burmese Days*, Orwell gives life to the sweaty, florid life of the British Empire in ways that demonstrate both its venality and its fragility – in his fiction, British officers strain to maintain their appearance of power, masculinity, and vigor, in the face of resentful subjects and their own personal weaknesses. Drawing on archival records, advertisements, and other fragments of empire, Stoler (2002; 1995) and McClintock (1995) teach us that the work of maintaining divisions between colonizer and colonized was in fact detailed and strenuous, involving care to bring up children who maintained their whiteness despite their love for their colonized nannies, the separation or management of intimate relationships between colonizers and colonized, and elaborate discourses of cleanliness and purity. This was the work of trying to make race science make sense. Further complicating an easy divide between these categories are the imperial citizens who fought against empire *and* the imperial subjects who were complicit in or profited from participation in it – though neither of these groups undo or outweigh the overarching logics and violence of colonialism (Gandhi 2005; Burton 1994; Sinha 2000).

We will also discuss the ongoing conversation about how to live and thrive "in the wake," of colonial violence (Sharpe 2016). For the sake of simplicity, I provide here two paths into thinking about what Ann Laura Stoler has referred to as "imperial ruination." We then turn to possible ways forward, which point to an always-incomplete decolonization. There is much cross-pollination between these approaches, and they also bear the stamp of the era in which each originated, but it is worth thinking through each of these for what they reveal about not only the colonial era, but about the ways we continue to live with its effects.

With this overview in mind, let us turn to two linked strands of thinking around the colonial encounter. These are separated out here for clarity, but it is important to note that there is cross-pollination between these two strands – they are not in opposition, but rather complement each other. The first centers on development and the relationship between colonialism and our current economic and political state. The second centers on how colonialism has affected scholarship. After this we will turn to how political geographers can pick up these analyses moving forward.

World-as-System, Radical Dependency Theory, and Critical Development Studies

Europe is literally the creation of the Third World. The riches which are choking it are those plundered from the underdeveloped peoples. (Fanon 1963, p.58)

In 1867, Dadabhai Naoroji, the first Indian to become a Professor of Mathematics and Natural Philosophy at an Indian institution, articulated the relationship between England and India as a profound drain of wealth and resources that would affect generations of Indians to come. Calculating the financial exchanges between India and England, and taking into account the investment in infrastructure, Naoroji (1887) articulated the ways that England simultaneously enriched itself and its future prospects while hampering India's future. In 1871, he built this argument, stating, "The natives call the British system, 'Sakar ki Churi,' the knife of sugar … it is all smooth and sweet, but it is the knife notwithstanding." Demanding the return of a greater portion of India's wealth, he spoke to the British: "if you cannot feel yourself actuated by the high and noble ambition of the amelioration of 200,000,000 of human beings, let your self-interest suggest to you to take care of the bird that gives the golden egg of 12,000,000 pounds a year to your nation, and provisions to thousands of your people of all classes."

When famine struck British India in the late nineteenth century, the famous British railroads were not used to move food from points of plenty to points of starvation – rather, poor men, women, and children were allowed to die or conscripted to labor in order to receive rations that were the equivalent of the number of calories given out at Buchenwald concentration camp (Davis 2002). Despite internal dissent at this inhumanity both by white British subjects back home and in official imperial roles and by imperial Indian subjects, this was not only allowed but was justified as a moral good that would curb laziness and overpopulation. By the turn of the century, the injustice measured by Naoroji had become part of strategies of protest and freedom, as first the economic boycott of British goods to protest the partition of the state of Bengal in 1905 and later forms of protest such as the Salt March in 1930.

The specificity of the Indian case rests in its centrality to British Empire and the drain of wealth which simultaneously fed the industrial revolution in Britain, thus introducing a deepening and intensifying inequality that transformed the British colonial state of Bengal from an "inexhaustible source of riches" to a country with one of the lowest median incomes in the world. It is also indicative of a larger pattern, and in the 1960s this was articulated as World-Systems Theory and Dependency Theory by Immanuel Wallerstein (1974), Samir Amin, and Andre Gunder Frank. These theories were in part a response to popular ideas of the day, which presented history as a timeline in which all countries marched toward progress, following the examples of Europe and the United States. A prototypical example would be Walter Rostow's (1990) "stages of growth." His stages, from "traditional society" to "transition" to "drive to maturity," and a later addition, "high mass consumption," imagined the world as an undifferentiated slate in which each country could move through the same series of stages. For more critically-minded scholars like Wallerstein, Amin, and Frank, this was a profound misunderstanding of how the world worked. Wallerstein built on Marx's ideas of division of labor to observe that capitalism not only required a division of labor but one that was *transnational* in nature, and that global inequality was not a quirk or accident of the system, but was rather foundational to how capitalism operates. Before we proceed, let us consider this more carefully.

Think about the industrial revolution that occurred in Europe beginning in the nineteenth century. This revolution set Europe on a path to accelerated technological development and economic growth, however, it did so at a cost. In addition to the writings of Karl Marx and Friedrich Engels, one might think of the works of Charles Dickens, which brought to light the laboring classes who suffered through poor working conditions, child labor, and slum living conditions that led to illness and debility in Europe's major cities. For someone like Wallerstein, who had spent years studying anti-colonial movements in India and Africa, Rostow's theory of economic development simply did not make sense. How could a place like India or Rhodesia (which was to become Zimbabwe) follow the steps outlined in Rostow's model of development? England's rise in the developing capitalist system had been premised not only on advancing technologies, but also on the expansion into new markets, and the extraction of profit from inexpensive or coerced labor. Capitalist firms do not succeed by maintaining a steady rate of profit, but rather by finding ways to increase the rate of profit. During the industrial revolution, for instance, Indians found themselves purchasing cloth from British mills and supplying raw materials like cotton and jute that were likewise fueling British development. Thus, Wallerstein argued it was more practical to think of the world as a system rather than to understand countries independently. Wallerstein argued that the capitalist system had developed as a global division of labor, in which an "economic core," drew raw materials from a recently-independent semi-periphery and still-colonized periphery, as well as exploiting and extracting labor. Andre Gunder Frank suggested we think of this through the lens of dependency: that the core then was dependent on this extraction model, but also that the economies of the peripheral countries were developed so as to make them profoundly dependent on the participation of the core. This meant that even after independence, formerly colonized places struggled to develop their own economies in order to provide the social services and infrastructure that had not been developed during the colonial era. Samir Amin (1974) referred to this as "accumulation on a world scale."

Wallerstein (2003), Gregory, and countless anti-colonial activists and thinkers have argued that present-day imperialism, particularly the role of the United States in the Middle East, is not new but is an extension of this world system. The fundamental ideas in this work are picked up in the writing of geographers and others and has fueled critical understandings of international development.

Decolonization Begins With Thought – On Being Ethnographically Detained

> As soon as the native begins to pull on his moorings, and to cause anxiety to the settler, he is handed over to well-meaning souls who in cultural congresses point out to him the specificity and wealth of Western values. But every time Western values are mentioned they produce in the native a sort of stiffening or muscular lockjaw. During the period of decolonization, the native's reason is appealed to ... But it so happens that when the native hears a speech about Western culture he pulls out his knife – or at least he makes sure it is within reach. The violence with which the supremacy of white values is affirmed and the aggressiveness which has permeated the victory of these values over the ways of life and of thought of the native mean that, in revenge, the native laughs in mockery when Western values are mentioned in front of him. In the colonial context the settler only ends his work of breaking in the native when the latter admits loudly and intelligibly the supremacy of the white man's values. (Fanon 1963, p.42)

As the previous section suggests, the colonial encounter has been a devastatingly material and economic one, in which the enslavement of people from West Africa, the prying open of Chinese borders to admit British opium grown in colonized India, the plunder of resources from Africa, the creation of labor-intensive and environmentally destructive rubber and other plantations in Southeast Asia, and the attempted and actualized genocide of Indigenous populations in the Americas all fueled the economic growth of Europe. However, as we recognize from Said's ideas of Orientalism, these violent economic processes not only move resources and people from one part of the world to another, they are tied up in how we think about the world itself.

Maori scholar Linda Tuhiwai Smith brings together Robert Young (2004), Janet Abu-Lughod (1989), and others to make a set of assertions about history, challenging, in particular, the tendency to create a universal history or history as a totalizing history and rely on an idea of progress. Rather we might ground our understandings of history in Indigenous and other frameworks that have been erased through colonizers' historical narratives, or described as variations on a European past. How can we avoid telling *all* histories, whether they be the history of Nigeria or the history of France, as part of the story of Europe: through European categories that already lead us to insistently compare the history of that place with the history of the place we are writing about. What if we could cultivate theories that did not normalize the entire world into categories of thought that originate in Europe? What if we could be more specific and draw on local theoretical frameworks for understanding the world instead, and also always locate theories that do come from Europe as deeply embedded in that context, and *not* as universal? And yet, this is not how knowledge is made at this time. When students from colonized places attend university and seek to become scholars, they must learn to be comfortable with an extensive body of thought (and usually language) that originated in Europe in order to become an expert on their own place of birth, their own Indigenous group, or their own community.

Now, let us move cautiously to think about the invention of race and the ways that it is formed into something solid and real-seeming during the colonial moment. In his landmark book, *Habeus Viscus*, Alexander Weheliye centers the work of Sylvia Wynter and Hortense Spillers to build an independent but resonant argument to decenter universal theory. Weheliye engages with two theories we discuss in this book – Foucault's theory of biopolitics and Agamben's theory of the state of exception. For Weheliye, these theories do not do as much as they intend because they imagine that there is a universal subject free from race or gender, and by doing so, they imply white male subject. Why does this matter? Weheliye argues that the repeated implication of a raceless genderless universal subject does two things. First, it sidesteps the ways that that power operates through racialization and gendering – and here he points out the ways that both Agamben and Foucault use examples that are fundamentally about race while referencing the possibility of a universal subject. This is a very powerful and well-argued set of ideas that cannot be wedged into this chapter, but to which I heartily refer you. To cite Weheliye (2014, p.63) citing Kanye West, "that shit cray." Weheliye's second point crucial for our discussion of the decolonization of thought is that the repeated and unquestioned centering of a universal subject means that others, such as Black feminist theorists, have their work "ethnographically detained."

The phrase "ethnographically detained," packs centuries of history into two words, speaking directly and eloquently to the themes of this chapter. Weheliye asks us to consider, why can Michel Foucault theorize for all of us, but Sylvia Wynter cannot? To put it another way, Ramírez (in Naylor et al. 2018, p.7, see also Mott and Cockayne 2017) writes, "We all theorize from our experience, and yet it is only those who make their experience visible in their theorizing that are accused of 'identity politics,' while whiteness and masculinity remain unmarked and unquestioned voices of authority."

As a way forward, Sofia Zaragocin (in Naylor 2018, p.5) argues for a **decolonial feminist geopolitics**, that is, a geopolitics that "considers the coloniality of gender and sexuality of imperialist-racialized spatial resistances related to auto-determination or competing notions of sovereignty (Indigenous and others)." In this, she wishes us to understand the relationship between global territorial conflicts and the ways that colonial encounters shaped gender and sexuality.

The considerations we have encountered thus far have been taken up (incompletely) by political geography. Here, we turn to a more meta approach and consider what are the imperatives for our own scholarly praxis – that is, how do these ideas and theories not only tell us about the topics we study, but also inform who studies what, and how?

Geographer at Work: Deondre Smiles

Deondre Smiles is a PhD candidate in geography at The Ohio State University.

Niwiidosemaa Aanikoobijiganag-Walking with Ancestors: Anishinaabe bodies in the settler colonial state

Native American bodies keep turning up. In recent years, more and more examples of Native remains and burial grounds being dug up and disturbed through various means have made their way into the American public consciousness. However, while these events are certainly troubling and ghastly to any observer, they largely appear unremarkable and non-urgent. Much as the Indigenous bodies found during these projects are understood as dead and lifeless, any controversy or insights surrounding these bodies also is taken to be inactive. If anything, white citizens have publicly expressed their annoyance with the inconveniences associated with finding Native bodies, such as delayed construction timeframes or traffic congestion, rather than with the act of discovering the bodies themselves (Stojevich 2017).

In my ongoing research, I argue that treatment of the bodies of Indigenous dead offer a powerful intervention into the ways that Indigenous people resist destructive and disruptive aspects of settler colonialism. Minnesota has played host to several events in this relationship. It is known that Minnesota's famed Mayo Clinic was founded by a doctor whose practice and medical teaching was built on the disinterment and display of Indigenous remains. How widespread was that practice in the nineteenth century, and to what degree does it endure in the use of Native American cadavers in medical education? Why and how are Native American dead autopsied against the consent of family members? A road construction project in northeastern Minnesota sparked controversy when it disturbed a well-documented tribal burial ground that has been disturbed by construction projects several times before. Why did this occur? In all of these cases, what roles did individual members of settler society play, alongside the role of the state? A closer look at these historic and ongoing processes reveals the extent to which settler colonial society goes to remarkable lengths to establish control over Indigenous spaces, and will seek to "know," "register" and "assimilate" the Indigenous dead into settler knowledge about science, medicine, and anthropology. This begs the question: What exactly can Indigenous people do in the face of this treatment and modes of remembrance of their deceased?

In fact, there exist many possibilities as to what Indigenous people can, and often do. In prior work, I have described how members of my own tribe, the Ojibwe, mobilized effective resistance to the autopsy of two tribal members by a county medical examiner in Minnesota (Smiles 2018). I am working extend that analysis to more deeply investigate the ways in which Ojibwe practices and attitudes concerning death and burial – very different from Western forms of recognizing and honoring death – enable and animate particular forms of resistance to settler colonial structures.

I seek to explore the ways that the treatment of Ojibwe bodies in death and Ojibwe ontologies surrounding death, burial, and sacred spaces, can offer provocative insights into the historical and ongoing production of settler–Indigenous relations, and prospects for "everyday" resistance. I am interested in exploring the ways that these ontologies, which are expressed in both traditional and modern ways, come into conflict with Western ideas of the proper treatment of bodies after death, especially in pursuit of scientific/medical knowledge, and the construction of infrastructure. I am interested in the ways that Ojibwe tribal governments are reversing a long legacy of settler colonial scientific racism by invoking data sovereignty through their usage of death statistics collected by the state. I also am interested in exploring the unique and surprising ways in which segments of settler society openly ally themselves with Indigenous people in support of Indigenous sovereignty.

My work centers on my home state of Minnesota, where I collaborate with my fellow Ojibwe people and their tribal governments.

What Now? How Do We Decolonize?

This chapter has brought together major critiques of political geography and the academic production of knowledge. If you do not intend to go into academia, perhaps this seems of marginal importance to your life. But consider that a college or university degree is now considered a requirement for getting ahead in life, and that our politicians, media figures, and bureaucrats, as well as those who write the books we read or make the movies we watch – all of these people are picking up pieces of knowledge produced in academic settings and using them to make truth about the world. It is then important for all of us to think about how knowledge is made. Though this is not a text on research methods, attention to the *how* of research informs the ways that we understand all the writing that we consume. How can we pick up these lessons, which cross academic and activist circles, and carry them forward to make a different world? Here we consider propositions from geographers and others.

Decolonizing methodologies

What does all this mean for academics, researchers, and those who aspire to produce knowledge in and about the world? **Methodologies** are the systematic set of methods that are used to create knowledge. Whether stated or implicit, every piece of academic writing that you read has a methodological approach – that is, it is based on assumptions about how we can learn about the world and transmit knowledge. This includes decisions based on how the researcher sees the world: for instance, can we discover the "truth" of the world? Or are there many truths? How might we know this truth or truths – through quantitative assessment of large data sets? Through slow ethnographic work with small groups of people? Can we be objective in research and is this our goal? Indigenous scholars (and many others) have called for a profound reconceptualization of the research process. Outside of the discipline of geography, Linda Tuhiwai Smith (2012) has written a compelling and accessible treatise on *Decolonizing Methodologies*. Speaking from her own experience as a Maori researcher writing for other Indigenous researchers, Smith writes with pain and skepticism that research can be decolonized at all. Her audience is Indigenous people working with Indigenous people in order to make knowledge that is in solidarity with their struggles rather than in the **extractive model of research** – in which you extract knowledge from a place for use elsewhere. Working collaboratively may mean partnering with local organizations in your research and aligning your research with their goals, choosing different research methods, studying "up," or researching sites of power rather than marginalized people, or a range of other strategies that disrupt the history of our discipline's Eurocentric past. Whether researchers can work across historic inheritances of oppression and whether they can work across power differentials is an open question. Some researchers from Indigenous communities, such as Audra Simpson (2007), who you will recall from the opening to the citizenship chapter, call for "ethnographic refusal," or a refusal to be known and pinned down by academic sciences, particularly when that knowledge may be created in the service of erasure and elimination.

Within geography, Richa Nagar, beginning from a collaboration with seven women designating themselves the Sangtin Collective, has modeled new and creative ways to work through different situated positions and relationships to academic knowledge. In *Playing with fire* (Sangtin Writers Collective and Nagar 2006), the collective chronicles how they came to work together and to openly write, argue, and discuss their own internal differences of caste, class, and other forms of privilege and subjugation that shape not only their relation to external power structures but also to one another. Nagar (2014) has cogently and compellingly argued for cultivating forms of "radical vulnerability," through which people can work together and build political alliances and relationships of trust across difference.

This kind of work benefits from Haraway's (1991) starting point: that all knowledge is situated knowledge, or rooted in the researcher's position to it. Haraway wants us to take care not to do the **God-Trick** of assuming we can operate from the skies, seeing everything and writing a single truth about the world. Instead, beginning from a framework of situated knowledge means we must start research with awareness of our own positionality, or assessment of the ways that who we are affects what we see and what we know. For instance, if I undertake research, it is important to recognize that my whiteness, my gender, my age, my current class position and past class background, my political beliefs all may affect (among other things!):

1. Who talks to me and what they reveal
2. What research questions I choose to investigate, as well as what kinds of questions I generate in interview questionnaires
3. What I notice or pursue when reading and coding interviews,
4. Which findings I choose to write about and who I imagine my audience to be, and
5. How audiences pick up and read my work (if they do), and what political uses it enables or forecloses.

These are only a starting point – you can imagine other considerations.

Decolonizing methodologies means working not to extract knowledge from ethnic minorities, marginalized people or places, Indigenous people, or formerly colonized places. Rather, it means finding ways to shape our work such that it can support their projects of decolonization, and, when necessary, realizing that some knowledge may be "off limits" for incorporation into academic ways of knowing.

Naylor (2018, p.1) asks: "how [might] the colonial difference … provide better understandings of entanglements across space?" But, remember that "to decolonize is to reconnect and re-embody the relationship to land" (Ramirez in Naylor et al. 2018, p.7), or in Daigle's (in Naylor et al. 2018, p.3) terms, a decolonizing approach to geography requires geographers "not only to think about but embody the relational accountability that is tied to living and working on one's own Indigenous territory, or as a(n) (uninvited) visitor on stolen and occupied Indigenous lands." This does not mean theorizing upon the survival or suffering of Indigenous people (that is, writing about them), but must mean decolonizing how knowledge is made and how colonial forms of knowledge remain and are imbedded in our academic institutions (Naylor et al. 2018; Noxolo 2017b; Smith 2012). *Beyond* this, it means searching for ways that our work can contribute to the material return of stolen lands, the refusal to appropriate and profit from Indigenous, Black, or formerly colonized people's ideas, theories, and pain (Tuck and Yang 2012; Todd 2016; Sharpe 2016; McKittrick 2017; Jazeel 2017; Esson et al. 2017).

Daigle (in Naylor et al. 2018, 3) points to discrepancies in how decolonization is approached (or avoided) in different places. In particular, she suggests that settler colonial nations, such as Canada, the United States, Australia, and New Zealand, have not had substantial conversations on decolonization, so that scholars in these places may ascribe to postcolonial or even decolonial approaches without paying attention to "ongoing dispossession of Indigenous lands, bodies, and nationhood in settler colonial contexts," or to what Indigenous people are requiring of scholars working in that area. Instead of working with this near-at-hand set of issues, "geographers have mostly grappled with responsibilities to spatially distant neighbors, and spatially proximate strangers along the lines of class" (Naylor et al. 2018, p.3; Noxolo, Raghuram, and Madge 2012).

Decolonizing the academy

Many of the reflections and decisions discussed in this chapter take place within a university institution and a disciplinary framework, which also influence these choices as well as how what we write will be received. Knowledge is shaped as much, for instance, by those who are *discouraged* from producing it as it is by challenging or hostile work environments, that is, the absences that remain in our departments or the scholars whose work is hampered or slowed down by these challenges (Tolia-Kelly 2017).

What this means in concrete terms is that professors, researchers, and students, ought to be aware of how their daily work and activity may be upholding these structures or working to dismantle them (Jazeel 2017; Naylor et al. 2018; Noxolo, Raghuram, and Madge 2012). Where and how do you do research? What authors appear on syllabi? Who is hired the next time there is a job search? How are graduate students and professors evaluated? It is crucial here to take care that the project of decolonization or postcolonial scholarship does not simply become the latest trend (Jazeel 2017).

While questions of how to be a geographer in the wake of colonialism have been ongoing since the mid-twentieth century, when independence movements across Asia and Africa profoundly influenced academic thought more broadly, these discussions have taken different forms, from anti-imperialism to postcolonialism. Today there is a convergence of interest around decolonization. Decolonization, which is also the framing for this chapter, builds on earlier work and ideas from postcolonial theory and in some cases subaltern studies, as well as those thinkers who animated and theorized independence movements in the twentieth century – such as Frantz Fanon – but it understands this work to be always ongoing, never one moment in time. As Naylor (Naylor et al. 2018, 1; citing Mignolo 2002) writes in a recent set of interventions, "The colonial difference is the site of othering whereby systems of knowledge are hierarchized. To think from colonial difference then is to not only acknowledge centuries of imperialism and contemporary 'othering,' but also to recognize and speak from the underside." What might we ask or say from the underside? Daigle (in Naylor et al. 2018, p.5), writes:

> As geographers center and learn from Indigenous movements and everyday acts of decolonization, the larger needs and demands of the decolonial should become immediately apparent. The ostensible boundary between academics' professional and personal lives quickly crumbles away as Indigenous peoples demand the dismantling of structural and intimate colonial political

geographies, and advocate for the rebuilding of new ones that are accountable to the legal and lawful caretakers of Indigenous lands and waters. Without embodying such radical and transformative accountabilities – as necessarily unsettling, potentially discomforting and contentious as they are – geographers risk reproducing a prevalent trope and buzzword in academia, and the very structures of settler colonialism and white supremacy that we claim to dismantle in our calls for decolonization.

How Do We Decolonize? Abya Yala and Standing Rock

Mapping another world: Abya Yala

Sofia Zaragocin (in Naylor et al. 2018) calls for us to conceive of place-rooted politics and embodied ontologies as a means to a decolonial feminist geopolitics. She offers the framework of Abya Yala as one example. Abya Yala is an Indigenous geography of Latin America, "a utopic territory," a "counter-geography," and a "geopolitics of the past and present within counter-hegemonic positions" (Zaragocin in Naylor et al. 2018, p.6 citing ; Castaño 2007; González 2012; Miñoso, Correal, and Muñoz 2014). Zaragocin (Naylor et al. 2018, p.6) defines Abya Yala as

> a geopolitics that reaffirms pre-conquest territory and a desired futurity of decolonized space in which Indigenous and Afro-descendent women's politics are encouraged and created. Abya Yala space serves as an imagined counter-geography defined from a plurality of feminist positions that seek metaphorical and material politics of decolonization.

When scholars and activists refer to "Latin America" as Abya Yala, they make a claim to belong to a place that existed before it was colonized, and they demand that place continue to exist even into the future as a space for both Indigenous women and for the Afro-descendant women whose ancestors arrived on the continent through slavery. To say Abya Yala is to work to build a different future through epistemology (ways of knowing) but *also* through action, that is, by fighting to protect the land and Indigenous and Afro-descendent women's sovereignty and bodily security.

Zaragocin and others develop new terms that work for the practice of decolonization. One epistemology emerging parallel to the embrace of Abya Yala is *cuerpo-territorio* (Body-Territory), a concept that is central to Latin American feminist theory. "*Cuerpo-Territorio* places the community and territory as a single subject of political agency that resists and identifies violations against women's bodies and territories as part of the same process" (Naylor et al. 2018, p.6 citing Cabnal 2012; Miradas Criticas del territorio desde el Feminismo 2017). If centered in political geography, this concept builds on decolonizing calls for alternative epistemologies that can contend with the ongoing political work of Indigenous elimination (Wolfe 2006), the role of colonial gender and sexuality in contributing to gender-based violence (María Lugones 2010), and the **indigenization** of settlers, "whereby settlers appear as naturally belonging to Indigenous land through legal, cultural or violent processes of forced territorial dispossession" (citing Morgensen 2012; Naylor et al. 2018, p.6; Veracini 2010; 2011; see also Leroux 2018; Reardon and TallBear 2012). In her reading, we cannot separate out racialized sexuality and gender from settler colonialism, as they are at its heart (Zaragocin in Naylor et al. 2018; Morgensen 2012). This idea is also expanded on by scholars like Maria Lugones (2010).

For Zaragocin, the work of building Abya Yala is in language, but is also material. Zaragocin works in Ecuador with feminist collectives documenting and working against **femicide**, or the killing of women based on their gender. Her analysis posits this death in relation to colonialism, and thus through intentional and collective work based in decolonial feminism, she seeks to create new ways of being in the world in relation to territory (Zaragocin 2012; in press).

Native sovereignty: Standing Rock

Mni waconi. Water is life. And life for Indigenous peoples is about our right to control our lands and preserve our resources for future generations (Curley 2016).

We must remember we are part of a larger story. We are still here. We are still fighting for our lives, 153 years after my great-great-grandmother Mary watched as our people were senselessly murdered. We should not have to fight so hard to survive in our own lands. (LaDonna Brave Bull Allard 2016; cited in Whyte 2017, p.154)

As LaDonna Brave Bull Allard reminds us, we do well to consider that the struggle against the Dakota Access Pipeline began long before there was a Dakota Access Pipeline (DAPL), before there was the Energy Transfer Partners backing the project and before there was a US Army Corps of Engineers, the agency which permits the routing of the pipeline. Oceti Sakowin (a term including the Lakota, Dakota, and Nakota speaking people) resistance to the DAPL had begun in earnest in 2014, when the Corps changed the route of the pipeline to avoid Bismarck and move it closer to their lands (Estes 2017). Nick Estes, a scholar who is part of the Kul Wicasa, of the Lower Brule Sioux Tribe and active in the Standing Rock movement places the current struggle as the latest in a long history of incursions into Native territory:

In 1803 the *wasicu* – the fat-takers, the settlers, the capitalists – claimed this stretch of the river as part of what became the largest real estate transaction in world history … the Louisiana Purchase … None of the Native nations west of the Mississippi consented to the sale of their lands to a sovereign they neither recognized nor viewed as superior … Thus began one of the longest and most hotly contested struggles in the history of the world. (Estes 2017, p.116)

In the years after the Louisiana Purchase, the United States led armies against the original residents of the plains, resulting in 1851 and 1868 Fort Laramie Treaties that defined a 25-million-acre territory to be the Great Sioux Reservation, while unceded territory exceeded that, stretching from the Missouri River to the Bighorn Mountains. Estes writes:

Four decades of intense warfare, however, took their toll. More than ten million buffalo were slaughtered to starve us out. Settler hordes invaded and pillaged our Black Hills for its gold. Our vast land base diminished, and the treaties were nullified when Congress passed the Indian Appropriations Act of 1876, which abolished treaty making with Native nations, and the Black Hills Act of 1877, which illegally ceded the Black Hills and created the present-day reservation system. (Estes 2017, p.116)

Alongside the analysis of Wynter and Fanon above, Estes (2017, p.116) also points to the settler state's denial of the humanity of Native people: "Every act on our part to recover and reclaim our lives and land and to resist elimination is an attempt to recuperate that lost humanity – a humanity this settler state refuses and denies even to its own." This denial of humanity was manifest in the nineteenth century in the massacre of 300 Native people at Wounded Knee, the breaking up of Great Sioux Reservation lands, and the dismantling of Native water rights for dams and agricultures. In the mid-twentieth century, against the 1908 Winters Doctrine that had granted water rights to original treaty territories, the Pick-Sloan Plan allowed the Army Corps and Bureau of Reclamation to build dams that flooded Oceti Sakowin lands, leading to the loss of 309,584 acres, and the forced relocation of Native families (Estes 2017).

Resistance to these incursions of settler colonialism has been ongoing, and Standing Rock has been an important place for this struggle. The American Indian Movement of the 1970s occupied the site of the Wounded Knee massacre, in the Pine Ridge Indian Reservation, and a year later thousands of members of Native nations met at Standing Rock to begin work that would result in the 2007 Declaration on the Rights of Indigenous Peoples. Spectacular forms of violence in quashing activism, mundane forms of violence in heightened police stops, and ongoing slow violence of environmental racism have been continuous but have failed to halt Indigenous claims to sovereignty. The revoking of the Keystone XL pipeline in 2015 marked a victory that built strength to work against DAPL, and carried forward alliances between Native and non-Native activists as well as the use of direct action (Estes 2017). The #NODAPL movement also demonstrated practices of countersovereignty through the work done at the encampments to create intersectional forms of solidarity (Dhillon and Estes 2016; Mays 2016).

In December, 2016, the Obama administration delayed the permits for DAPL until a fuller environmental impact statement review was conducted, but the camp was forcefully evicted in February 2017, and the Trump administration pushed instead for the project to go forward.

Reflecting on what geographers should take from the Standing Rock movement, Curley calls in theorizations of settler colonialism (Dunbar-Ortiz 2014; Wolfe 2006), environmental racism and racial capitalism (Pulido 2017), and Indigenous refusal (Simpson 2014). He asks that we, "identify and expose the unequal social and political arrangements of power over lands and resources that limits our sovereignty and contributes to ongoing environmental racism," because, "Fundamentally, colonization is about the dispossession of Indigenous lands and resources through makeshift and sophisticated mechanisms, from blunt racialization to the more elusive practices of transnational corporations" (Curley 2016). To reiterate the starting point of this section, geographers would do well to work harder to understand Indigenous conceptions of space and territory, so that questions of environmental impact, for instance, are not separated from questions of tribal sovereignty. Estes (2017, p.120) likewise urges for an understanding of the colonial state as an instrument of illegitimate corporate access to Native land, and takes the view that "treaty rights, and by default Native sovereignty, protect everyone's rights."

The case of the Standing Rock movement gives us a vivid and current case of the imperative to understand political geography in relation to decolonization. As Whyte (2017, p.159) states, "Settlers create moralizing narratives about why it is (or was) necessary to destroy other peoples (e.g., military or cultural inferiority) or they take great pains to forget or cover up the inevitable violence of settlement." Indigenous people fighting for land and livelihood insist we must both understand the epistemologies and ontologies that enable settler violence and appropriation *and* the material effects and processes of this violence and the resistance to it.

What Have We Learned and Where Do We Go From Here?

In October 2015 I travelled to South Africa for the first time, visiting Witwatersrand University (Johannesburg), University of Cape Town (UCT) and Rhodes University in Grahamstown. Rhodes was my first stop, and I knew relatively little about an institution I would soon find out had been renamed by students The University Currently Called Rhodes.

As we pulled up, my eyes were drawn to the grand, whitewashed archway over the entrance to the university's campus. On it, in thick, dark spray-paint, stood the words Black Power. Like many universities across the country, Rhodes students occupied campus buildings, marched on management meetings and struggled in solidarity with university staff. Earlier that year, RhodesMustFall [Figure 8.1], a UCT campaign against a statue of the British colonialist, turned into a movement against the imperialism he represented. For the first time since the anti-apartheid movement, South African students were grabbing international headlines, as they struggled for universal access to an education that does not reproduce the imperial logic their parents' generation fought to dismantle. As geographers, particularly those based in the old centre of Empire, how can our work be used to dismantle colonialism and its legacies? (Elliott-Cooper 2018)

Do the struggles and theoretical frames of this chapter seem abstract to you? Or do they seem very close to your own and your families' experience of surviving or thriving in this world? Whatever your answer to this question, as people participating in academic life and knowledge production or consuming its products, we are all caught up in the questions broached in this chapter. As you will remember from the introduction, the universities where academic knowledge is produced are themselves caught up in the lived, historical, and embodied experiences of empire, political discourses, class dynamics, and in both colonial processes and resistance to imperial ruination (Dimpfl and Smith 2018). Beginning from the reflection above, Adam Elliott-Cooper (2018, p.332) suggests that we might look to the #RhodesMustFall and #FeesMustFall campaigns for justice in education in South Africa to understand how the history of the discipline has shaped it and what we might want for the future. He writes:

The demands being made in this struggle call for the intellectual and moral contributions of Black people to be added to this land and labor, as the enabling components of the academy … We can either attempt to ignore and implicitly reproduce, the imperial logics that have influenced the shape of British Geography since its inception or actively rethink and dismantle imperialism's afterlife by unlearning the unjust global hierarchies of knowledge production on which much of the Empire's legitimacy was based. (Elliott-Cooper 2018, p.3)

This is true of all academic institutions, though it perhaps becomes more apparent during moments of crisis, such as the fraught conversations over the confederate landscapes that opened this book or in the resonant events in South Africa described earlier and to which we will return in the final chapter of this book.

Figure 8.1   Louis Botha statue in Cape Town with paint during the #RhodesMustFall campaign. Reproduced with permission of HelenSTB. https://www.flickr.com/photos/104328095@N04/ 17105110632

Keywords

Decolonization   An active and ongoing process of struggling for sovereignty, rights, and land, under ongoing conditions of settler colonialism and imperialism.

Decolonial feminist geopolitics   A geopolitics that incorporates analysis of coloniality into its understanding of geopolitics and sovereignty.

Extractive model of research   Research that extracts knowledge from a place for use elsewhere.

Femicide   Killing of women based on their gender.

God-Trick   The pretense of objectivity and omniscience in research.

Imperial ruination   Term indicating that after the formal end to empire the consequences of that encounter continued to unfold, whether in the economic processes of development that have unevenly benefited specific segments of society in formerly colonized places, or the continued environmental effects, or the perpetuation of ethnic and racial divisions that originated in or were reconfigured and strengthened during the time of European colonization.

Indigenization   Process through which settlers work to seem to themselves and others as the natural and rightful occupants of a place they have settled through violence and dispossession.

Methodologies   The set of methods and accompanying logics that are used to create knowledge.

Further Reading

Colonialism and racialization
Fanon, F. 1963. *The Wretched of the Earth*. New York: Grove Press.

Fanon, F. 2008. *Black Skin, White Masks*. New York: Grove Press.

Leroux, D. 2018. "We've Been Here for 2,000 Years": White Settlers, Native American DNA and the Phenomenon of Indigenization. *Social Studies of Science* 48(1): 80–100.

Lowery, M.M. 2010. *Lumbee Indians in the Jim Crow South: Race, Identity, and the Making of a Nation*. Chapel Hill: University of North Carolina Press.

McClintock, A. 1995. *Imperial Leather: Race, Gender and Sexuality in the Colonial Contest*. New York: Routledge.

Simpson, A. 2009. Captivating Eunice: Membership, Colonialism, and Gendered Citizenships of Grief. *Wicazo Sa Review* 24(2): 105–129.

Stoler, A.L. 1995. *Race and the Education of Desire: Foucault's History of Sexuality and the Colonial Order of Things*. Durham, NC: Duke University Press.

Stoler, A.L. 2002. *Carnal Knowledge and Imperial Power: Race and the Intimate in Colonial Rule*. Berkeley, CA: University of California Press.

TallBear, K. 2013. *Native American DNA: Tribal Belonging and the False Promise of Genetic Science*. Minneapolis, MN: University of Minnesota Press.

Education, decolonization, and racial justice
Bhambra, G.K., Nisancioglu, K., and Gebrial, D. 2018. *Decolonizing the University*. London: Pluto Press.

Daigle, M. and Sundberg, J. 2017. From Where We Stand: Unsettling Geographical Knowledges in the Classroom. *Transactions of the Institute of British Geographers* 42(3): 338–341.

Elliott-Cooper, A. 2018. "Free, Decolonised Education" – A Lesson from the South African Student Struggle. In J. Arday and H.S. Mirza (eds), *Dismantling Race in Higher Education: Whiteness and Decolonising the Academy*. Cham: Springer, pp.289–296.

Johnson, A., Joseph-Salisbury, R., and Kamunge, B. eds. 2019. *The Fire Now: Anti-Racist Scholarship in Times of Explicit Racial Violence*. London: Zed.

Joseph-Salisbury, R. 2019. Institutionalised Whiteness, Racial Microaggressions and Black Bodies out of Place in Higher Education. *Whiteness and Education* 4(1): 1–17.

Laliberté, N., Catungal, J.P., Castleden, H. et al. 2015. Teaching the Geographies of Canada: Reflections on Pedagogy, Curriculum, and the Politics of Teaching and Learning. *The Canadian Geographer/Le Géographe Canadien* 59(4): 519–531.

paperson, l. 2018. *A Third University Is Possible*. Minneapolis, MN: University of Minnesota Press.

Smith, L.T., Tuck, E., and Yang, K.W. 2018. *Indigenous and Decolonizing Studies in Education: Mapping the Long View*. New York: Routledge.

Indigenous sovereignty

Byrd, J.A. 2011. *The Transit of Empire: Indigenous Critiques of Colonialism*. Minneapolis, MN: University of Minnesota Press.

Coombes, B., Johnson, J.T., and Howitt, R. 2012. Indigenous Geographies I: Mere Resource Conflicts? The Complexities in Indigenous Land and Environmental Claims. *Progress in Human Geography* 36(6): 810–821.

Coulthard, G.S. 2014. *Red Skin, White Masks: Rejecting the Colonial Politics of Recognition*. Minneapolis: University of Minnesota Press.

Curley, A. 2018. A Failed Green Future: Navajo Green Jobs and Energy "Transition" in the Navajo Nation. *Geoforum* 88: 57–65.

Curley, A. 2019. Unsettling Indian Water Settlements: The Little Colorado River, the San Juan River, and Colonial Enclosures. *Antipode*. doi: 10.1111/anti.12535.

Daigle, M. 2016. Awawanenitakik: The Spatial Politics of Recognition and Relational Geographies of Indigenous Self-determination. *The Canadian Geographer/Le Géographe Canadien* 60(2): 259–269.

Daigle, M. 2019. The Spectacle of Reconciliation: On (the) Unsettling Responsibilities to Indigenous Peoples in the Academy. *Environment and Planning D: Society and Space* 37(4): 703–721.

Daigle, M. and Ramírez, M.M. 2019. Decolonial Geographies. In N. Theodore, T. Jazeel, A. Kent et al. (eds), *Keywords in Radical Geography: Antipode at 50*. London: Wiley, pp.1–13.

De Leeuw, S. 2016. Tender Grounds: Intimate Visceral Violence and British Columbia's Colonial Geographies. *Political Geography* 52: 14–23.

De Leeuw, S. and Hunt, S. 2018. Unsettling Decolonizing Geographies. *Geography Compass* 12(7).

Dhillon, J. 2017. *Prairie Rising: Indigenous Youth, Decolonization, and the Politics of Intervention*. Toronto: University of Toronto Press.

Estes, N. 2019. *Our History Is the Future: Standing Rock versus the Dakota Access Pipeline, and the Long Tradition of Indigenous Resistance*. New York: Penguin Random House.

Estes, N. and Dhillon, J., eds. 2019. *Standing with Standing Rock Voices from the #NoDAPL Movement*. Minneapolis, MN: University of Minnesota Press.

Holmes, C., Hunt, S., and Piedalue, A. 2015. Violence, Colonialism and Space: Towards a Decolonizing Dialogue. *ACME: An International Journal for Critical Geographies* 14(2): 539–570.

Naylor, L., Daigle, M., Zaragocin, S. et al. 2018. Interventions: Bringing the Decolonial to Political Geography. *Political Geography* 66: 199–209.

Radcliffe, S.A. 2017. Geography and Indigeneity I: Indigeneity, Coloniality and Knowledge. *Progress in Human Geography* 41(2): 220–229.

Simpson, A. 2014. *Mohawk Interruptus: Political Life across the Borders of Settler States*. Durham, NC: Duke University Press.

Simpson, L. 2011. *Dancing on Our Turtle's Back: Stories of Nishnaabeg Re-Creation, Resurgence and a New Emergence*. Winnipeg: Arbeiter Ring.

Knowledge production

Catungal, J.P. 2017. Feeling Bodies of Knowledge: Situating Knowledge Production through Felt Embeddedness. *Tijdschrift Voor Economische En Sociale Geografie* 108(3): 289–301.

Esson, J., Noxolo, P., Baxter, R. et al. 2017. The 2017 RGS-IBG Chair's Theme: Decolonising Geographical Knowledges, or Reproducing Coloniality? *Area* 49(3): 384–388.

Haraway, D.J. 1991. Situated Knowledges: The Science Question in Feminism and the Privilege of Partial Knowledge. In *Simians, Cyborgs, and Women*. London: Routledge, pp.183–202.

Jazeel, T. 2017. Mainstreaming Geography's Decolonial Imperative. *Transactions of the Institute of British Geographers* 42(3): 334–337.

Kobayashi, A. and Peake, L. 2000. Racism out of Place: Thoughts on Whiteness and an Antiracist Geography in the New Millennium. *Annals of the Association of American Geographers* 90(2): 392–403.

Lugones, M. 2010. Toward a Decolonial Feminism. *Hypatia* 25(4): 742–759.

Macharia, K. 2016. On Being Area-Studied: A Litany of Complaint. *GLQ: A Journal of Lesbian and Gay Studies* 22(2): 183–190.

Mahtani, M. 2014. Toxic Geographies: Absences in Critical Race Thought and Practice in Social and Cultural Geography. *Social & Cultural Geography* 15(4): 359–367.

Mignolo, W.D. 2002. *Local Histories/Global Designs: Coloniality, Subaltern Knowledges, and Border Thinking*. Princeton, NJ: Princeton University Press.

Mohanty, C.T. 1991. Under Western Eyes: Feminist Scholarship and Colonial Discourses. In C.T. Mohanty, A. Russo, and L.M. Torres (eds), *Third World Women and the Politics of Feminism*. Bloomington, IN: Indiana University Press, 51–80.

Nagar, R. 2014. *Muddying the Waters: Coauthoring Feminisms across Scholarship and Activism*. Champaign: University of Illinois Press.

Naylor, L., Daigle, M., Zaragocin, S. et al. 2018. Interventions: Bringing the Decolonial to Political Geography. *Political Geography* 66: 199–209.

Noxolo, P. 2017. Decolonial Theory in a Time of the Re-colonisation of UK Research. *Transactions of the Institute of British Geographers* 42(3): 342–344.

Noxolo, P., Raghuram, P., and Madge, C. 2012. Unsettling Responsibility: Postcolonial Interventions. *Transactions of the Institute of British Geographers* 37(3): 418–429.

Pulido, L. 2002. Reflections on a White Discipline. *The Professional Geographer* 54(1): 42–49.

Sharp, J. 2008. *Geographies of Postcolonialism*. London: Sage.

Sinha, M. 2000. Mapping the Imperial Social Formation: A Modest Proposal for Feminist History. *Signs: Journal of Women in Culture and Society* 25(4): 1077–1082.

Smith, L.T. 2012. *Decolonizing Methodologies: Research and Indigenous Peoples*. 2nd ed. New York: Zed Books.

Spivak, G.C. 1988. Can the Subaltern Speak? Speculations on Widow Sacrifice. In C. Nelson and L. Grossberg (eds), *Marxism and the Interpretation of Culture*. London: Macmillan, pp.271–313.

Stoler, A. 2002. *Carnal Knowledge and Imperial Power: Race and the Intimate in Colonial Rule*. Berkeley, CA: University of California Press.

Todd, Z. 2016. An Indigenous Feminist's Take on the Ontological Turn: "Ontology" Is Just Another Word for Colonialism. *Journal of Historical Sociology* 29(1): 4–22.

Tolia-Kelly, D.P. 2017. A Day in the Life of a Geographer: "Lone", Black, Female. *Area* 49(3): 324–328.

Tuck, E. and Yang, KW. 2012. "'Decolonization Is Not a Metaphor'". *Decolonization: Indigeneity, Education & Society* 1(1). 1-40.

Weheliye, A. 2014. *Habeas Viscus: Racializing Assemblages, Biopolitics, and Black Feminist Theories of the Human.* Durham, NC: Duke University Press.

World systems theory, dependency theory, and critical geographies of development

Amin, S. 1974. Accumulation and Development: A Theoretical Model. *Review of African Political Economy* 1(1): 9–26.

Andolina, R., Laurie, N., and Radcliffe, S.A.. 2009. *Indigenous Development in the Andes: Culture, Power, and Transnationalism.* Durham , NC: Duke University Press.

Davis, M. 2002. *Late Victorian Holocausts: El Niño Famines and the Making of the Third World.* London: Verso.

Fluri, J.L. and Lehr, R. 2017. *The Carpetbaggers of Kabul and Other American-Afghan Entanglements: Intimate Development, Geopolitics, and the Currency of Gender and Grief.* Athens, GA: University of Georgia Press.

Pulido, L. 2017. Geographies of Race and Ethnicity II: Environmental Racism, Racial Capitalism and State-Sanctioned Violence. *Progress in Human Geography* 41(4): 524–533.

Sultana, F. and Loftus, A. 2013. *The Right to Water.* London: Routledge.

Wainwright, J. 2008. *Decolonizing Development: Colonial Power and the Maya.* Malden, MA: Blackwell Publishing.

Wallerstein, I. 1974. *The Modern World-System I: Capitalist Agriculture and the Origins of the European World-Economy in the Sixteenth Century.* Vol. 1. Berkeley: University of California Press.

Wright, M. 2006. *Disposable Women and Other Myths of Global Capitalism.* New York: Routledge.

Chapter 9

Geopolitics

Steadfastly looking at the camera, residents of the Pakistan-Afghanistan border region hold a banner, asking: "Terrorist? CIA or Taliban? Ask the victims of drone attacks!" The subscript states that they are from the Foundation for Fundamental Rights (Shaw and Akhter 2014). In asking who is categorized a terrorist and connecting this categorization to drone strikes, these men are raising questions at the very heart of contemporary scholarship on critical geopolitics. How does technology transform warfare? How does the categorization of people and places produce military strategy? What are the ethics of geopolitical strategy, and how is it entangled in global history? There is also a larger question embedded in their plea: what does the Westphalian sovereignty we learned about in Chapter 5 mean when you live under drones? As we learned from Elden (2009), the sovereignty of some is used as a means to unravel the sovereignty of others.

In a 2012 report titled "Living under Drones: Death, Injury, and Trauma to Civilians from US Drone Practices in Pakistan" (Cavallaro, Sonnenberg, and Knuckey 2012), researchers presented evidence that the portrayal of drones as precise is profoundly misleading. Instead, they argue that civilians are deeply affected by drones. Drone strikes not only kill civilians, these casualties are underestimated by the ways that "civilian" is defined in relation to age and gender. If military-age men are killed, the impetus is placed on families of the deceased to clear their names: they are assumed to be militants (Figure 9.1).

In their detailing of the bureaucracy of drone warfare, Shaw and Akhter reveal a compelling and complex set of questions that emerge from the increased use of drones, particularly by the US military in Pakistan, Yemen, and Somalia. How does the categorization of places

Political Geography: A Critical Introduction, First Edition. Sara Smith.
© 2020 John Wiley & Sons Ltd. Published 2020 by John Wiley & Sons Ltd.

Figure 9.1 "Drones protest at General Atomics in San Diego" by Steve Rhodes is licensed under CC BY-NC-ND 2.0.

on Earth – particular the "AfPak" region comprising both sides of the border between Afghanistan and Pakistan and the Federally Administered Tribal Area of Northern Pakistan – enable forms of warfare such as drone strikes? This should recall Said's (1979) idea of orientalism as a way that Europeans represented the "East" in order to colonize it, Gregory's (2004) insistence that we live in the "Colonial Present," and Stoler's (2013) idea of imperial ruination. Shaw and Akhter also ask: how does technology itself begin to shape warfare and violence, making it more bureaucratic, transforming the ethical questions it entails, and having different and lasting effects both on soldiers and civilians? Finally, how does the use of drone warfare change what is considered possible?

Shaw and Akhter (2012) argue that the contemporary designation of Federally Administered Tribal Area of Pakistan as a zone of exception is rooted in the colonial description of that region as troublesome and hard to govern, and, further, that this zone of exception designation lays the ground for drone strikes against citizens who then have very little recourse to justice. We can recall other examples of the ways that categorization of places into zones of threat or zones of protection has bolstered political action: doctrines of *terra nullius* or manifest destiny imagined some places to be empty or uncivilized, providing justification for their colonization or other imperial tactics (for instance in settler colonial societies such as the United States or Australia, or under imperialism in the "Scramble for Africa"). During the Cold War, communism and capitalism were imagined and represented in a biological manner – as models of economic government that could spread from one country to another as a virus or invasive species. As people rose up against colonialism, the representation of colonized people as passive or dangerous people in need of paternalistic care, as the subject of justified violence, grew, and false theories of biological race proliferated.

This chapter will explore the emergence of geopolitics as an academic discipline and then trace the interventions in thinking that have radically transformed this field of study. We will encounter men and a few women who were very much rooted in their time, place, and personal interests (the survival and thriving of Europe and the United States as empires), and who imagined the world on these terms: as countries striving in a competitive zero-sum struggle for dominance. We will also encounter critically-minded scholars who suggest that it is by creating these maps of the world that we *make* the world, and that even things such as our choice of television or movies might be subtly shaping what seems possible and impossible in world politics.

Classical Geopolitics

Lineages of geopolitics often begin with Friedrich Ratzel, also a figure who influenced the development of the field of geography more broadly defined. In 1897, he published *Politische Geographie*, the first book with such a title. Drawing on a distorted interpretation of Charles Darwin's and Herbert Spencer's theories of evolution, Ratzel theorized the state as an organism, a living being, which needed to expand and grow in order to maintain itself. His concept of *lebensraum* or "living space," theorized the state as organism. In this framework, state territory was conceptualized as the base of existence, and assuming that to grow in strength and population states had to expand their territory to feed this organism.

Before we continue with this discussion of geopolitics as a subdiscipline and describe its radical transformation over the twentieth century, let us return to one of the core takeaways I hope you will remember from this book: words, concepts, categories, and concepts have meaning and power beyond the page or voice that speaks them – at times they might enable violence and at times they prevent it. When you encounter powerful ideas – such as the idea that a state is a living organism that can and must compete against other states – recall the suggestion from the introduction that ideas and concepts enable specific forms of politics. What does the idea of the state as organism enable? Keep this thought in mind as we continue the chapter.

Just as Ratzel's ideas could be put to use in justifying the expansion of Germany, the theorizing of Halford Mackinder and Alfred Mahon are profoundly tied to their own geographical contexts in Britain and the United States. Their exchange in the first years of the twentieth century is an often-used and revealing example of **classical geopolitics**. Halford Mackinder, sometimes described as one of the major architects of the discipline of geography, was Oxford University's first Professor of Geography. Mackinder sought to strengthen the position of the nascent discipline by proving its worth. Simultaneously, he was firmly embedded in the British context and invested in Britain's imperial success (Toal 1996). Across the Atlantic, in the United States, Alfred Mahon, a retired naval officer, wrote on military strategy and physical geography, arguing that sea power is the determining force in world history. This set the stage for Mackinder's famous 1904 paper, "The Geographical Pivot of History" in which he laid out an ambitious vision of the world telling a sweeping story of the world in three stages based on military strategy. In the first, pre-Columbian, era, land power, that is, the capacity to travel overland on horses, for instance, had been the most important form of military might. After Columbus,

Mackinder argued, there had been an era in which sea power became the most crucial. However, he argued, in his vision of the present and future, the post-Columbian era would mark a shift in which landpower – or the power to travel overland – would return to being the most important strategic tactic. Thus, Central Asia and Russia, the large expanses of land connecting Europe with Asia, would become the "Pivot Area," or "heartland," due to its complete inaccessibility by sea but great potential once connected by railroads (so that its resources could be extracted).

Mackinder presented his ideas as universal: as though they were neutral, objective, and applicable to all times and places. Yet, we understand his analyses better if we interpret them as provincial: situated within his own time, place, and national interest. While Mackinder understood the future to be determined by the fate of Central Asia, his interests were in how Britain could maintain its imperial might. At the turn of the century, India, the "Jewel in the Crown," was increasingly restless, and Europe was engaged in the "Scramble for Africa." Mackinder was looking to the future, and understood the world at the level of the nation states of Europe and the rising United States. His visions of the world were thoroughly embedded in the interests of the nations of Europe in competing with one another to extract resources and further develop their own economic and military might. Thus, in 1919, he wrote, "Who rules East Europe commands the Heartland; Who rules the Heartland commands the world-island (Europe and Asia); Who rules the World-Island commands the world" (Mackinder 1919, p.150). Mackinder and other scholars of what would later be called geopolitics blurred the boundaries between academic life and political life: Mackinder served in government positions, and advocated for Britain to take a strong position as a bulwark against a possible Russian-German alliance. Mackinder had what Painter and Jeffrey (2009, p.202) describe as a "geopolitical gaze," that is, "the self-confidence to assert a particular model of interstate relations on a global scale." In this geopolitical gaze, the world is conceived of at the scale of nation-states, in terms of competition for environmental resources, and a "desire to construct a grand narrative of human potential based on geographical factors" (Painter and Jeffrey 2009, p.202).

Back across the Atlantic, geographers and geography-oriented political scientists in the United States had similarly context-bound perspectives on the world. Isaiah Bowman, like Mackinder, moved between academic and policy-oriented circles, advising US President Woodrow Wilson and later the US State Department, but also serving as Director of the American Geographical Society and President of Johns Hopkins University. Nicholas Spykman, political scientist at Yale during this period, also perceived Central Asia as a pivot point, but contrary to Mackinder, Spykman believed in the continued importance of sea power (Jones et al. 2015). To understand the genre of classical geopolitics, let us consider the similarities between visions of these thinkers.

- Their conceptions are conceived from a particular point of view (that of a state, seeking to survive), and this position shapes how the world is represented, *but this position remains unrecognized.* That is, ideas emerging from one context are presented as universal.
- They assume a natural connection between the environment, territory, and power, often in a formulation in which power demands control over the environment and expansion of territory.
- The unit of geopolitical analysis is the state.

As we have found by this point, this is one way to view the world, but not the only way! It is quite different from the anti-state thinking of the autonomous social movements that we encountered with the Zapatistas, from Cree ontologies of land, from anarchist approaches (Springer 2012), and from the idea of the *cuerpo-territorio*. Many of the social movements we encountered in fact work to destabilize the state-focused politics that we find in these early geopolitical thinkers. There is also an undercurrent to the work above that we might even think of as potentially dangerous, though as presented above this danger may not be clear. To explore this, let us think about logics embedded in the classical geopolitics explored earlier.

In the United States, some of Ratzel's ideas were expounded upon by one of the most well-known early woman geographers, Ellen Churchill Semple, who traveled to Germany to study with Ratzel. Semple embraced and elaborated upon the strands of **environmental determinism** embedded in Ratzel's work. Environmental determinism is the idea that the landscape shapes much about a population's characteristics. The links between environmental determinism and scientific racism, which we discussed previously, should be quite clear. Semple's observations began with her writing on Appalachia, where Semple suggested that the rugged nature of the environment had led to a slowing of social and cultural development. Semple (1911, p.1) wrote, "Man is a product of the earth's surface … Nature has been so silent in her persistent influence over man, that the geographic factor in the equation of human development has been overlooked."

In Semple's thinking, you will recognize connections to ideas we have earlier encountered and critiqued: essentialism, which assumes that a population can be understood through one or two essential characteristics, which all members share, and a connection to the place in which people reside. Semple's worldview is thus quite compatible with the orientalism that Edward Said revealed in European writings that imagine the "East" as a place of homogenous people all similar in their shared characteristics as opposed to people of European origin. This kind of thinking lends itself to **Social Darwinism**, the "survival of the fittest" idea that those who rule are by nature superior, and to the Eugenicist thinking of Thomas Malthus, who believed that overpopulation was one of the world's greatest dangers, and that poor people were naturally inferior and incapable of stemming their own reproduction. In the early twentieth century, these strands of thinking were widespread in Europe and the United States. In the United States, for instance, there were not only wide-spread miscegenation laws that sought to prevent supposedly superior people of European origin from having children with people of African origin, but also immigration by quota. Environmental determinism was a widespread theory in early twentieth century. Today, critically minded geographers understand it to be tied to the kinds of racialization that upheld imperialism, though Jared Diamond has marketed variations on these ideas to popular audiences (for a discussion, see Blaut 1999).

The dangerous potential of this kind of eugenicist thinking of course was to come to dark fruition in World War II Germany. Here, ideas of another of Ratzel's students, Karl Haushofer, became influential in German strategy (though some have argued that his influence has been overstated – see Agnew and Muscarà 2002; Toal 1996). Economic struggles in Germany in the 1920s enabled political scapegoating at first, and then the final solution: genocide. What was to become the Nazi philosophy of ethnic cleansing began with eugenic laws targeting those with genetic illness, children of miscegenation, and other supposedly undesirable characteristics were to be sterilized, and then came to focus on Germany's Jewish population. The German study of *geopolitik* "sought to center ideas of progress and civilization upon the notion of an expanded German homeland" (Jones et al. 2015, p.197); it intensified after Germany's World War I defeat. As German nationalism began to portray Germany as under threat from outside, Haushofer began to expand on Ratzel's ideas to argue that Germany had a right to imperial expansion in its quest for *lebensraum*. It was also at this time that Carl Schmitt, a law professor in Berlin, expounded pragmatic theories of realpolitik, particularly in relation to sovereignty. Schmitt was focused on the role of the ruler, or sovereign, as decision maker, and in the ways that sovereignty was manifest in the right of the ruler to, at times, defy the law (this is a starting point for Agamben's state of exception). Schmitt supported Hitler's suspension of the constitution though this logic, stating, "The leader defends the law," (Schmitt 1996; Jones et al. 2015, p.198). For Schmitt, the prevention of conflict justified that the ruler might deviate from the law.

The horror of World War II, both the violent white nationalism of the Holocaust, and massacre of six million Jews, as well as the darkly transformative turn in understandings of progress after the use of nuclear bombs and devastation of Hiroshima and Nagasaki, led to profound changes and shifts in how scholars theorized the world. Immediately following the war, geopolitical scholarship lay dormant as the extensions of geopolitical logic to their most extreme versions led to reluctance to continue to engage in such theorization (Toal 1996; Painter and Jeffrey 2009). In the United States, geopolitical thinking along these lines fell out of favor in mainstream political circles until the 1970s, when very similar geo-graph-ing to that of Mackinder and Bowman began to emerge and thrive in the cold war mapping of the world into mutually-antagonistic spheres of US and Soviet interests. The intentional disengagement of the non-aligned movement of previously colonized states enabled politi-cians and citizens to imagine a world divided into "us" and "them." A quite different and revitalized geopolitics emerges in the 1990s as critical geopolitics. Before we turn to critical approaches to geopolitics, let us consider some alternatives to the history I have presented to you here.

Is the History of Geopolitics the History of the West?

When considering the ideas that have shaped [International Relations] thinking, why do we make so much of Thucydides, Machiavelli, Hobbes, Lock, and Kant, but not Ashoka, Kautilya, Sun Tzu, Ibn Khaldun, Jawaharlal Nehru, Raul Prebisch, Frantz Fanon, and many others from the developing world? (Acharya 2014, p.648; see also Acharya and Buzan 2009 and Salama 2011)

The theories of geopolitics described earlier are necessarily included in every political geog-raphy textbook – and I include them here as well. In fact, had I *not* included them, readers would have noted and pointed out this omission. But before we turn to the proliferation of critical and radical approaches to geopolitics, let us note that the above theories are grounded in a quite Eurocentric vision. Political geography has developed as a largely Eurocentric and Anglophone discipline, and thus classical geopolitics as a discipline has been defined by European thinkers. Even critical geopolitics, itself intended as a critique of knowledge-production, has often been unintentionally oriented toward the West – not due to the failings of its practitioners, but perhaps more to the structures of the academy itself, which make it quite challenging at times to diverge from this default path (Sharp 2013).

It is important to remember that this is an artifact of some of the processes we have read about throughout the book, in particular how academic knowledge has been premised on using theories from Europe to explain the rest of the world as the object of knowledge (Chakrabarty 2008; Smith 2012). Geopolitical theorizing has been conducted by rulers and their subjects across the globe, but this has not been woven into most histories of the discipline. Consider just two examples. Kautilya, also known as Chanakya, was an advisor to kings in the Maurya dynasty in the fourth century BCE, in what is today India. In the *Arthashastra*, Kautilya wrote a comprehensive theorization on how to rule an empire that contains explicitly geopolitical elements – for example, the shorthand, "the enemy of my enemy is my friend," may derive from Kautilya's spatial mapping of this: "The king who is situated anywhere immediately on the circumference of the conqueror's territory is termed the enemy. The king who is likewise situated close to the enemy, but separated from the conqueror only by the enemy, is termed the friend (of the conqueror)" (Boesche 2002; Kautilya 1915). As Acharya (2014) suggests, we could also turn to Ibn Khaldun, Sun Tzu, or others. At this point you should be recalling Weheliye's (2014) analysis of the ways that Black feminists have been "ethnographically detained," and Linda Tuhiwai Smith's (Smith 2012; see also Macharia 2016) points out that the Global South is marked as a repository of data, while Europe is marked as the source of theorization and ideas.

This example is just meant to signal that though geographers have often focused on a key set of ideas and imaginaries of the world that emerged in Europe, others have emerged elsewhere and in turn have shaped these imaginaries. Around the turn of the twentieth century, when Mackinder and Ratzel were writing, across what we now designate as the "Global South," counter-geopolitical visions were also welling up among colonized people. If we ignore these counter-visions because they were not labeled as "geopolitics," we are missing half of the story, as well as the ways that these ideas informed European theorizations of the world.

You will recall that in the mid-nineteenth century in colonized India, Dadabhai Naoroji was arguing that the drain of material resources and the education of Indians abroad was leading to the long-term draining and stagnation of the subcontinent. He wrote: "All [Europeans] do is eat the substance of India, material and moral, while living there, and when they go, they carry away all they have acquired …" (cited in Metcalf and Metcalf 2006, p. 124). One task that Naoroji set himself was to estimate the amount of wealth drained from India. In 2018, economist Utsa Patnaik compiled data on tax and trade and came to the conclusion that Britain was responsible for the drain of almost $45 trillion between 1765 (the first year that the East India Company began collecting taxes in a tract in Bengal) and 1938 (Chakrabarti and Patnaik 2018; Hickel 2018). By the turn of the twentieth century, legions of leaders in India (which included present day Pakistan and Bangladesh), including Bal Tilak and Mohandas Gandhi, were theorizing the relationship between their home and the imperial government of England. They were also considering the best strategic means to free themselves from the empire, from *swaraj* and *swadesh* theories of economic independence and sovereignty to transnational solidarity movements, such as the support of the khilafat movement to restore power to the Ottoman caliphate.

Over the course of the twentieth century imaginative reconsiderations at the global scale included ideas such as **negritude** – a philosophy of Blackness seeking to create new political and cultural sensibilities based in global Black experience (Césaire 2000). Other conceptions of the world were grounded in understandings of the world in relation to whiteness, Black consciousness, and colonial violence that were ontological in nature, that is, they understood these conflicts and violence to be at the heart of how the world is structured and works (Fanon 1963; 2008). Decolonial and anti-colonial movements were likewise tied fundamentally to theorizations of geopolitics – such as the non-aligned movement (Young 2016; Prashad 2008), the Pan-African movement (Sharp 2013), and others.

Though focused in Europe and the United States, a parallel story on the "others" of geopolitics could be told through the work of Deborah Dixon (2015), who has traced how geopolitics appear in unexpected sites, spaces, and minds. Similarly to the intimate geopolitics of the chapter following this one, Dixon explores how geopolitics manifests in "lines of inquiry that set flesh, bone, abhorrence and touch at the forefront," through strange stories of the Tsar of Russia purchasing monstrous baby skeletons as a symbol of scientific progress and the complicated politics of a conservative Texas governor using stem cells for a medical treatment. Dixon's approach allows her to find voices not signaled in traditional accounts of geopolitical thinking, such as the geopolitics that emerge in the context of seventeenth-century women-led salon culture in France.

Critical Geopolitics and the Popular Geopolitics of War

In the 1990s, a cluster of scholars revived academic approaches to geopolitics in a very different form from the classical geopolitics of the earlier-twentieth century. Scholars like Sharp (1998; 2000), Toal (1996) Toal et al. (1998), and Dodds and Sidaway (1994), took the field in a radical new direction. Instead of taking the environment and geography for granted and then creating strategy and analysis based on state power in relation to geography, these scholars brought frames of postcolonial and critical scholarship to bear on the topic, asking instead how geographic categories and constructs themselves *wrote* the world. For instance, what representations of the Soviet Union were necessary to bolster American support for the Cold War? While US media represented the Soviet Union in specific ways to bolster its message – as Ronald Regan's comments on it as an "Evil Empire," media in the Soviet Union represented the United States as hypocritical to its values, for instance with imagery of the lynching of Black men in the US South (Roman 2012). How did the Cold War framework for understanding the world linger on after its supposed end? How might we bring Said's framework of orientalism to bear on questions of geopolitics and foreign policy?

These scholars asked how political logics required and produced imaginaries of the world that then justify state action and develop popular support for state strategy. In the aftermath of the September 11, 2001 attacks in the United States, political geographers built an insightful and important set of literature to provide historical and spatial context for the subsequent war on terror. In particular, they demonstrated how imperialism and orientalism undergird reactions to terrorism, and provide a cogent analysis of the tactics and strategies of these governments in reacting to terrorist attacks using the tactics we have discussed as states of exception and also using the concepts of sovereignty in paradoxical ways.

Subaltern Popular Geopolitics and the Audience

Sharp (2011; 2013) proposes that we take care to understand how even our critical and productive discursive analyses of geopolitics are themselves often deeply rooted in Western and Eurocentric positions that reiterate rather than interrogate some of the ways that the world has been written. Sharp is in conversation with Ayoob's (2002) concept of subaltern realism, asking how focusing on "great powers" produces a distorted view of the world. Following Enloe (1989, p.1) "if we employ only the conventional, ungendered compass to chart international politics, we are likely to end up mapping a landscape peopled only by men, mostly elite men." Sharp proposes the idea of **subaltern geopolitics**, a practice of understanding how the world is written from the perspective of the dominated (the subaltern). From this view, discourses we have encountered above, such as the "War on Terror," appear much different.

As we know from the previous chapter, much academic literature is still either quite Eurocentric or Anglo-Eurocentric, and often elaborates on theoretical concepts with European heritage, *or* it can be quite siloed. For instance, the flourishing literature on decoloniality and territory emerging from Latin America in Spanish and Portuguese remains not as widely read beyond that context as one might expect. As An and Zhu (2018) observe, there is a need for a "pluri-centric geopolitics conducted by non-Western scholars." An and Zhu in particular point out that the rise of the BRICS countries (Brazil, Russia, India, China and South Africa) has not yet resulted in a similarly seismic shift in how our world is written into political life. That is, even as critical scholars write about how imaginative geographies shape our thinking and enact particular forms of politics, our categories remain embedded in these geographies.

We will return to Sharp's own use of subaltern geopolitics in Chapter 10, on security, but here let us consider a few cases in which her concept has been taken up.

In the Philippines, as elsewhere, the global rhetoric of the "War on Terror," is read through the local context and filtered through situated understandings of Filipino political actors' use of global narratives for their local goals. Woon (2014) picks up subaltern geopolitics and popular geopolitics to unravel the ways that the island of Mindanao becomes a key and Othered geopolitical imaginary in national media. **Popular geopolitics** is the study of how media from journalism to film to fiction, as well as public-facing political actions intersect with, shape, and are shaped by political discourse and practices. How, for instance, do popular representations of places as "war-torn," normalize and naturalize military intervention?

Media portrayals of Mindanao portray the southern island as conflict and terrorism-prone, in ways that perpetuate violence. Mindanao has a higher percentage of Muslim residents than other regions in the Philippines, and is both economically poor and resource-rich. Scholars suggest that separatist struggles in Mindanao, like many of those that we have encountered thus far in this book, are tied to marginalization of the region, specifically its Muslim residents, and to the Spanish (1565–1898) and US (1898–1946) colonial period. While the Aquino administration of the 1980s also tried to develop a less antagonistic relationship with residents of Mindanao, the US "war on terror" marked a turn toward militarization, as both the United States' and Philippines' governments see Southeast Asia as a new base of operations for Al-Qaeda. This has led to a counter-insurgency program running alongside peace negotiations.

Much of the rich and important work in geopolitics has focused on how wars are justified in order to be made legitimate, and much of this literature focuses on the US-led war on terror. Woon, however, turns instead to *internal* war against the Philippines's "own 'dissident' citizenry." He argues that the media heightens the drama of events in Mindanao by focusing on corpses and bodies that connote "a sense of excessive deaths and devastation and indicat[e] a situation spinning out of control" (2014, p.666). With coverage of violent events crowding out other representations, the island is transformed into "an undifferentiated, monolithic entity, one that is besieged by potent threats of terrorism," that are specifically tied to Muslim rebel groups and also shape a binary between supposedly antagonistic Muslims and peace-loving Christians (Gaerlan Jr 2013).

How do we know whether media accounts really have such an impact on people? Much of popular geopolitics is focused on discourses present in the text themselves. It can actually be quite difficult to figure out just how much these texts may be influencing people and in what direction: people might interpret media they read or watch quite differently from one another, and they also consume media widely and from a variety of sources. In a given day, you may have seen CNN or the BBC in a waiting room, watched YouTube or scrolled through Twitter or Facebook on your phone, watched a movie on your computer or in the theatre, or had a cringe-worthy meme forwarded to you by that one aunt or uncle. You may have consumed the comic takes on a politician's gaffe before you hear the soundbite itself, and you will likely never listen to the speech in full. In this environment, in which we are saturated with media consumption, it may be difficult to pinpoint specific pieces of pop culture that have shaped us. We will, *however,* doubtless be exposed to cohesive and contradictory discourses that travel across these different forms. This fact of mediated social life still makes research on audiences quite difficult. To explore how media consumption works in the case of portrayals of Mindanao, Woon (2014) draws on what Dittmer and Gray (2010, p.1673) call "Popular Geopolitics 2.0," in which scholars use qualitative methods to pay attention to "the everyday intersections of the human body with places, environments, objects and discourses linked to geopolitics." As we will see in the case of the analysis of Chinese films below, this approach shares much in common with feminist approaches to geopolitics.

Woon (2014, p.663) turns to a survey of 3000 media consumers in the Philippines and 87 interviews drawn from the survey respondents. With this research, he explored how readers of a common newspaper, *The Philippines Daily Inquirer* (*PDI*), thought Mindanao was portrayed. This included how their own backgrounds (for instance, gender and religion) shaped their perceptions, as well as how "new geographies of Mindanao produced through *PDI* became memories and resources for readers to draw on in their future interpretations and reactions toward geopolitical events in the Southern Philippines." From the interviews and survey, audiences are understood as part of an assemblage – creating geopolitical spaces and identities through interactions between people and the media. What does this mean in practical terms?

Woon's (2014, p.669) respondents described Mindanao as dangerous, saying, "We read about violence in Mindanao almost everyday in *PDI*. I still remember this picture in *PDI* that showed some Abu Sayyaf rebels holding the chopped-off heads of victims … That picture scarred me for life." Most respondents had never been to Mindanao, and felt that it was too dangerous to visit, but were confident that they knew it as a place through the voyeurism provided by *PDI*. They fear violence will spread to their own regions: "bodies emanating from Mindanao are conceptualized as vectors of threat whereby their enhanced mobilities over time will potentially allow issues of violence and (in)security to spin out of control" (Woon 2014, p.671). For Christian media consumers, their descriptions of this possibility deploy the US Bush administration's rhetoric of "Why do they hate us?" Muslim respondents took a different approach by drawing lines between authentic and inauthentic versions of Islam.

In interviews, those with whom Woon spoke described residents of Mindanao as potentially threatening bodies emanating from the region, and contrasted this with security challenges in which governments could tighten international border security. Respondents evoke a scary future to suggest changes are urgently needed. This is an **anticipatory geopolitics** (Anderson 2010), which emerges in quotes like this one "If we are not careful in future, terrorists can move internally from Mindanao to Manila quite easily and live amongst us" (Woon 2014, p.671). Anticipatory geopolitics is the framing of the future such that it enables or seems to require geopolitical steps to be taken in the present.

Movies that Make Us Geopolitical Subjects

Reading a national newspaper helps us to understand how geopolitical imaginations are written into existence or how representations of a place reinforce stereotypes. But a different way to understand how we see the world and make sense of it is through popular culture such as film. In their immersive world-making experience, films can even seem hyper-real, and can come to be our story of historical events.

Critically engaging with geopolitical representations is something that you can begin today. That is not to downplay the expertise needed to analyze a film, place it within its historical and geographic context, and unweave the lessons that the film projects into the world! However, as someone interested in political geography you can experiment with these techniques and ideas immediately. Choose a specific film and start with straightforward questions. Who is the audience for this film and where are they located? What is it depicting? Where was it made and by whom? These are starting points that are recommended for beginning visual geographies or popular culture analyses (Rose 2016; Dittmer 2010). Building on these, who are you asked to root for? Who is the enemy? What needs to be true for the premise of the film to work? Are scientists villains or heroes? Are the residents of the places where the film takes place mainly "backdrop," for foreign and/or white protagonists? Where does the story start: with a place that is marked by unexplained and naturalized conflict (e.g., *Blood Diamond*), or is the history of that place globally contextualized (e.g., the fictional Wakanda in *Black Panther*)? In what direction and to what effect is humor deployed and who is expected to laugh? Are you included in an unspoken "we," meant to laugh at or fear those who are different from you and root for those who share your values, your background, your appearance?

But before the "how," let us begin with the "why." Films are made to be affective and emotional, that is, to engage not only your mind, but also your senses and feelings. Though there is debate and overlap between the concepts, in the dark of the theater, loud sounds seem louder, quiet moments make you listen, and the intent is *never* to bore. Instead, you are meant to be "on the edge of your seat," to laugh, or to cry, depending on the genre of film: thriller, tearjerker, comedy, romance, war movie, or some combination of all three. Movies do this by engaging in tropes and trends of the day, as well as through plotting, acting, pacing, and lighting. Portraying masculine leads as superheroes, suave and efficient soldiers or spies, from Captain America to James Bond, for instance, sends an emotional or even affective call to the viewer to identify themselves with (or be attracted to, or both) this protagonist (Dittmer 2012; Sharp 2002). Characters often stand in for national ideals, or are a proxy for a villainous nation's evils. The stories that we see in movies are appealing because they make sense to us – or because the ways they surprise are compelling. We can think of this as narrative coherence – the idea that a narrative that rings true to us is appealing, and makes sense, and we interpret it as the truth (Dittmer 2010).

Thus, when current events, or allegories that seem to speak to current events, are retold through cinema, there is the chance we might change our mind, *or* that our existing ideas might be reinforced. A film like Jordan Peele's *Get Out* relies on and reverses prominent tropes of Black men as dangerous and criminal. Peele recasts Black men in the US as vulnerable and in need of rescue, and an upper middle class white family as villains in a horror movie. This might disrupt your belief in white innocence, *or* it might give voice to previous experiences of whiteness and provide a new vocabulary for you to express something you have felt all your life. You might think it is a clever analysis, or you might find you wake up that night replaying it in your mind, unable to stop thinking about how your white roommate joked about some of the lines and did not understand why the way she did so felt somehow, surprisingly, dangerous. A person might leave the theater uncomfortable with their emotional reaction to the film, laugh with recognition at interior moments they had felt and not expressed, now witnessed on the screen, or find themselves needing to talk and process the film with friends who might understand their point of view. Such a film could lead to arguments even between close friends or to things clicking into place in ways that change your understanding of daily life. Or it might be consumed as one among many pieces of entertainment. In any of these cases, the way the film makes sense to you is related to how the writer and director, Jordan Peele, calls you into a certain story, and asks you to take a specific place within the narrated world.

Dittmer (2010) gives us more specific tools to think about the work that narratives do, by specifying **metanarratives** (stories about how the world works), **ontological narratives** (stories about who we are), and **collective narratives** (stories about our people, community, or nation). These different kinds of narratives might shape the possibilities that we imagine in the world, and sometimes can even hide what is right in front of our faces. A metanarrative could be as simple as "progress," that is, a belief that over time, we are progressing in terms of human development, modernity, technology, and so forth: that our [collective] children will have better lives, healthier lives, and more choices than we do. You might believe that in the natural course of things, for instance, people who are transgender, who are religious or ethnic minorities, or who are differently-abled, will be more included in society and face fewer barriers in the future. As an alternative, your metanarrative might well be, "everything is going to hell." With this view, you might look back to a rosy past, in which people were stronger, worked harder, walked to school, did not have mobile phones, and did not care about avocado toast or likes on Instagram. When you were young, you might say, people had conversations face to face, men were men, and women were women … OK, I have made these into two rather stark caricatures, and yet, we recognize pieces of these ideas in ourselves or people that we know. These metanarratives structure how we interpret the world around us. When we see someone acting in a particular way, whether in our local coffee shop or on a screen, we might interpret their actions through these frames – but they might also inform how we vote and whom in our community we feel deserves welfare.

Metanarratives are about the fundamental ways that the world works. But ontological narratives appeal to our personal sense of self and identity. When we see someone make an awkward blunder in a sitcom, or a funny face at an awards show, we might think "#relatable!" Or even post the moment as a gif on our twitter, shouting out to all the fellow awkward people in the world. By doing so, we feel seen and recognized, that we are part of a narrative out there in the world. But this also orients us toward others (Ahmed 2004). If we want to be James Bond, then we want to defeat his enemies. During the height of the US war on terror, both American and global audiences watched *24*, a show in which a white male protagonist, Jack Bauer, works to foil terror plots, often through the use of violent tactics such as torture. If emotions work through us to create a sense of belonging or repulsion, to orient our bodies toward some and away from others, what might consistent ticking-time-bomb scenarios do for US audiences tuned in to watch Bauer use torture to extract information from enemies usually portrayed as brown, Muslim, and fundamentally other? Following Ahmed's description of the ways that emotional politics orient bodies toward or away from one another, this kind of depiction asks the viewer to identify with and root for Bauer, thus to understand and condone his use of violence as rational and necessary. For those audiences at home in the United States who already feared terror and ascribed to this kind of nationalism, the series provided them a heroic protagonist, and a set of hypothetical but perhaps plausible storylines.

We might be inclined to dismiss these shows as "just for entertainment," but it is notable that *24* was watched by politicians and policy-makers, and famously cited by the US Supreme Court Judge Antonin Scalia (Grayson, Davies, and Philpott 2009; Dodds 2010b). One of the lawyers who was fundamental to the development of the Bush administration's interrogation techniques also used the TV show as a rhetorical device in his 2006 book, asking "What if, as the popular Fox television program *24* recently portrayed, a high-level terrorist leader is caught who knows the location of a nuclear weapon in an American city. Should it be illegal for the president to use harsh interrogation short of torture to elicit this information?" (Yoo 2006; cited in Stelter 2010).

This is where there are connections between the narratives from Dittmer (2010) that we saw earlier. In *24,* the viewer is asked to identify with the Jack Bauer character, played by Keifer Sutherland, just as in *Get Out*, Peele sets up the film so that we root for Chris, played by Daniel Kaluuya. This is what Dittmer refers to as an ontological narrative, in which we connect ourselves with a character or protagonist. But he also identifies *collective* narratives, narratives about who "we" are as a collective. I use the scare quotes to indicate that there are always exclusions in a collective "we." In *24*, the collective narrative is one of the United States being a nation under threat – we are meant to want this nation to survive and be protective, even if that requires violence. *Get Out* disassembles this national narrative, asking the viewer to root not for the United States as a nation, but for collective Black survival, incorporating haunting echoes of the enslavement of African people through imagery such as the auction and through small details such as Chris using cotton, an important part of the economy of enslavement, to save himself by plugging his ears. *Get Out* entreats the theater audience to root for Black survival, to view a young white woman eating froot loops on her bed as terrifying, not innocent. Collective narratives ask you to identify with a group of people, often a nation-state, though this may be unstated. We see the use of collective narratives below in films made about the Nanjing Massacre.

The Flowers of War: Gender, War, and Popular Geopolitics

In *The Flowers of War*, a 2011 film based Yan Geling's 2007 feminist novel *13 Flowers of Nanjing*, a group of 13 sex workers (the flowers) band together to sacrifice themselves and gain the freedom of 13 schoolgirls during the Nanjing Massacre. When Japanese soldiers demand the schoolgirls act as "geishas," the sex workers volunteer to take their place. In the film adaptation, their rescue is aided by a white foreigner, played by Christian Bale. An, Liu, and Zhu (2016) analyze not only the film itself, but also its emotional pulls to nationalism through comments left on a popular social media site devoted to films. An, Lui, and Zhu ask why we do not think more about gender when we talk about popular geopolitics, even though when we lightly scratch the surface, we find geopolitical films are gendered in ways so predictable they lend themselves to parody (think, for instance, of "Bond girls," and the comically infallible masculinity of so many action heroes). In their analysis of *The Flowers of War*, these scholars bring together two new practices for popular geopolitics: attention to gender and qualitative research on audience reactions to the film, rather than only analysis of the discourses in the films themselves. In addition, they offer a feminist geopolitical analysis that attends to the importance of the body from a self-described "non-Western perspective."

The Nanjing Massacre refers to Japanese occupation of Nanjing during the Second Sino-Japanese War from 1937 to 1945. From December 1937 to February 1938, approximately 300,000 Chinese were killed during this occupation, and the events have been woven into contemporary forms of Chinese nationalism (An, Liu, and Zhu 2016). During the first decade of the 2000s, tensions arose between Japan and China due to territorial disputes and the symbolic visits of Japanese prime ministers to the Yasukuni Shrine to war dead, leading to anti-Japanese demonstrations in urban China. It is in this context that several films were made on the Nanjing Massacre. These representations rely on gendered narratives, particularly a focus on women as victims of sexual violence, and as righteous heroes, to foment specific gendered forms of nationalism. Chinese viewers comment on these films (e.g., the quality of the acting), but also substantially on politics. For instance, writing on *Flowers of War*, one viewer opines, "I loved the women, and hated the Japanese soldiers who humiliated our nation and us," thus engaging in a clear us/them narrative. Commenting on another film, *City of Life and Death*, one viewer writes, "The only thing I know is hatred: I hate Japan and Japanese people; I hate that I am not living at that time and cannot fight against the Japanese devils," while others chime in to agree and strengthen these comments (An, Liu, and Zhu 2016, p.795).

Back at home after a movie, in bed on their phones, or with their laptops on a kitchen table, or perhaps immediately after viewing *Flowers* on their home computer, the audience is processing and reliving the film, especially the violence against women graphically portrayed on the screen. They do not do this alone: they reach out to others through social media. In this moment their connection is not only to those who made the film or to the historical moment, but to other people who've seen it, and through this, the social media site becomes a place itself where an emotional geography is produced, one which strengthens an emotional and affective Chinese nationalism. "Individual emotions of hatred, anger, mercy, and love are evoked; at the same time, such emotions are employed to establish the binary identity of the Chinese 'us' and the Japanese 'other' in both reel-life and real life" (An, Liu, and Zhu 2016, p.795).

What Did We Learn and Where Do We Go From Here?

As a subdiscipline within political geography, **critical geopolitics** and related fields, like popular geopolitics, are flourishing and give us many tools to make sense of political geography. From its early roots as an academic endeavor adjacent to and inseparable from state power, today's scholars of geopolitics often have a critical angle that asks how our representations of the world shape our political engagement, even though there is still a contingent of political geographers endeavoring to use geopolitical theory to strengthen imperial and military might. From critical scholars of geopolitics, we can take away with us a few central ideas.

Our representations of the world are *deeply* political: the categorization of places and people have material consequences. Representations of the Middle East as chaotic and unstable lend themselves to military intervention. The use of gendered representations, and embodiment of women as proxies for the nation can be a tool for developing and deepening "us or them" forms of nationalism, and this can work through popular culture just as effectively (if not more so) through the mechanisms of formal geopolitics encapsulated in policy documents and politicians' speeches.

We take away that representations of the world are often, if not always, tied to situated positions: from Mackinder's pivot of history that honed in on Britain's need to maintain its military might to the *PDI*'s portrayal of Mindanao as a potential site of contagious chaos, to *24*'s vision of a world in which American use of force is justified, these "graphings" of the world always represent not a neutral and disembodied "god trick" view from nowhere (Haraway 1991), but rather a view located within a specific context and set of concerns.

How can you use these ideas? You might use them to study policy documents, political platforms, or politicians' rhetoric. *How* do they use language and ideas to persuade people that their vision of the world is one that people should support? How has the recent turn to the right, from the United States and Brexit to the Philippines and India, to Turkey, relied on specific representations of people and places as dangerous? How do people create a heightened sense of threat or a vision of a scary future to marshal votes or a sense of cohesive nationalism?

In the next chapter, we will move beyond how geopolitics are represented to us in popular culture to how they are *felt, embodied, and experienced.*

Keywords

Anticipatory geopolitics The framing of the future such that it enables or seems to require geopolitical steps to be taken in the present.
Collective narratives Stories about our people, community, or nation.

Classical geopolitics   Geopolitics as an approach seeking to understand how states can maintain power and military might through spatial and environmental analysis.

Critical geopolitics   The study of geopolitics which asks how geographic categories and constructs themselves *write* the world.

Metanarratives   Stories and assumptions about how the world works.

Negritude   A philosophy of Blackness seeking to create new political and cultural sensibilities based in global Black experience.

Ontological narratives   Stories about who we are as individuals.

Popular geopolitics   The study of how media from journalism to film to fiction, as well as public-facing political actions intersect with, shape, and are shaped by political discourse and practices. How, for instance, do popular representations of places as "wartorn," normalize and naturalize military intervention?

Subaltern geopolitics   Understanding how the world is written from the perspective of the dominated (the subaltern).

Further Reading

Critical approaches to geopolitics

Acharya, A. and Buzan, B. 2009. *Non-Western International Relations Theory: Perspectives on and Beyond Asia*. Abingdon: Routledge.

Ayoob, M. 2002. Inequality and Theorizing in International Relations: The Case for Subaltern Realism. *International Studies Review* 4(3): 27–48.

Agnew, J. and Muscarà, L. 2002. *Making Political Geography*. Lanham, MD: Rowan & Littlefield.

Dalby, S. 1991. Critical Geopolitics: Discourse, Difference and Dissent. *Environment and Planning D: Society and Space* 9: 261–283.

Dodds, K.-J. and Sidaway, J.D. 1994. Locating Critical Geopolitics. *Environment and Planning D: Society and Space* 12(5): 515–524.

Elden, S. 2009. *Terror and Territory: The Spatial Extent of Sovereignty*. Minneapolis: University of Minnesota Press.

Enloe, C. 1989. *Bananas, Beaches and Bases: Making Feminist Sense of International Politics*. London: Pandora Books.

Flint, C. and Falah, G-W. 2004. How the United States Justified Its War on Terrorism: Prime Morality and the Construction of a "Just War." *Third World Quarterly* 25(8): 1379–1399.

Kirsch, S. and Flint, C. (eds) 2011. *Reconstructing Conflict: Integrating War and Post-war Geographies*. Farnham: Ashgate.

Müller, M. 2008. Reconsidering the Concept of Discourse for the Field of Critical Geopolitics: Towards Discourse as Language and Practice. *Political Geography* 27(3): 322–338.

Painter, J. and Jeffrey, A. 2009. *Political Geography*. Thousand Oaks, CA: Sage.

Prashad, V. 2008. *The Darker Nations: A People's History of the Third World*. New York: The New Press.

Sparke, M. 2000. Graphing the Geo in Geo-Political: Critical Geopolitics and the Re-Visioning of Responsibility. *Political Geography* 19: 373–380.

Toal, G. 1996. *Critical Geopolitics: The Politics of Writing Global Space*. Minneapolis: University of Minnesota Press.

Toal, G. and Dalby, S. 1998. *Rethinking Geopolitics*. London: Routledge.

Toal, G. Dalby, S. and Routledge, P. 1998. *The Geopolitics Reader*. New York: Routledge.

Drones

Akhter, M. 2019. The Proliferation of Peripheries: Militarized Drones and the Reconfiguration of Global Space. *Progress in Human Geography* 43(1): 64–80.

Shaw, I. 2016. *Predator Empire: Drone Warfare and Full Spectrum Dominance*. Minneapolis: University of Minnesota Press.

Shaw, I. and Akhter, M. 2012. The Unbearable Humanness of Drone Warfare in FATA, Pakistan. *Antipode* 44(4): 1490–1509.

Shaw, I. and Akhter, M. 2014. The Dronification of State Violence. *Critical Asian Studies* 46(2): 211–234.

Environmental determinism, population, and geography

Bandarage, A. 1997. *Women, Population, and Global Crisis: A Political-Economic Analysis*. London: Zed.

Bashford, A. 2014. *Global Population: History, Geopolitics, and Life on Earth*. New York: Columbia University Press.

Blaut, J.M. 1999. Environmentalism and Eurocentrism. *Geographical Review* 89(3): 391–408.

Hartmann, B. 1995. *Reproductive Rights and Wrongs: The Global Politics of Population Control*. Boston, MA: South End Press.

Robbins, P. 1998. Population and Pedagogy: The Geography Classroom after Malthus. *Journal of Geography* 97: 241–252.

Robbins, P. and Smith, S. 2017. Baby Bust: Towards Political Demography. *Progress in Human Geography* 41(2): 199–219.

Popular geopolitics

Dalby, S. 2008. Warrior Geopolitics: Gladiator, Black Hawk Down and the Kingdom of Heaven. *Political Geography* 27(4): 439–455.

Dittmer, J. 2005. Captain America's Empire: Reflections on Identity, Popular Culture, and Post-9/11 Geopolitics. *Annals of the Association of American Geographers* 95(3): 626–643.

Dittmer, J. 2010. *Popular Culture, Geopolitics, and Identity*. Lanham, MD: Rowman & Littlefield Publishers.

Dittmer, J. and Gray, N. 2010. Popular Geopolitics 2.0: Towards New Methodologies of the Everyday. *Geography Compass* 4(11): 1664–1677.

Dodds, K. 2008. Hollywood and the Popular Geopolitics of the War on Terror. *Third World Quarterly* 29(8): 1621–1637.

Dodds, K. 2010. Jason Bourne: Gender, Geopolitics, and Contemporary Representations of National Security. *Journal of Popular Film & Television* 38(1): 21–33.

Sharp, J.P. 2000. *Condensing the Cold War: Reader's Digest and American Identity*. Minneapolis: University of Minnesota Press.

Sharp, J.P. 2002. *Patriotism, Masculinity, and Geopolitics in Post-Cold War American Movies*. London: Taylor & Francis.

Sparke, M. 1994. Writing on Patriarchal Missiles: The Chauvinism of the Gulf War and the Limits of Critique. *Environment and Planning A* 26: 1061–1089.

Chapter 10

Security

> What happens when people are raised in environments built to contain them? How does it affect their sense of mobility and inform their conditions of possibility?
>
> (Shabazz 2015, p.3).

We begin this chapter with an 18-year-old Afghan man who is trying to get to Europe. This man is represented in European security discourse as a threat. In fact, the images of the "security state," and "Fortress Europe" are arranged around protection from potential threats, such that their confinement and containment is part of political campaigns. As we discussed in the previous chapter, if people fitting this age and gender profile (military-age men) are killed in a drone strike, they are considered to be enemy combatants unless their families can prove the contrary. Militarization, heightened security, and the enclosure of borders around bodies themselves ironically compromise the security of this young man and others like him. In this chapter, I will encourage you not to take security for granted, but to think carefully about how the idea of security is produced and what kinds of political work it does. The young man tells his story as follows:

> From Afghanistan I went to Pakistan; from Pakistan, to Iran; from Iran, to Turkey, Greece, and then Italy. Part by car, part on foot, part on a rubber dinghy, at sea … Then, inside a truck … I was arrested [in Greece] because I was illegal … I had just called my mother reassuring her that I was in Greece. I thought that was part of Europe, too, so I/ I didn't expect what they did to me. If Greek police catch you … they'll give you a good thrashing. I called my mom, I said I am arrived, so don't worry now we'll see what we can do from here. As soon as I hang up – it was a telephone booth – I get out, and two steps ahead I'm caught by the police … They took

Political Geography: A Critical Introduction, First Edition. Sara Smith.
© 2020 John Wiley & Sons Ltd. Published 2020 by John Wiley & Sons Ltd.

us to prison. I did a month inside. More than a month inside. There was no hope, I didn't even have the guts to call my mother … I had called her some time before, telling her that I was in Greece, didn't I? (Young adult male migrant, Sicily, July 2011, quoted in Mountz 2017, p.77)

The young Afghan, interviewed as part of Alison Mountz's multi-sited ethnography of detention, speaks to the paradoxical securitization of migration – the way that people's movement across borders is treated as fundamentally a problem of (state) security. As borders are viewed through the lens of security, there is a proliferation of technologies and ideas about how to "secure" these borders. This securitization reshapes how borders operate in the world. Rather than signaling enclosures around territory, current developments in security discourses and practices enclose people through the use of biometric data, online tracking, and other technological developments. Securitization also creates *insecurity*, fear, and trauma for the migrants themselves, and heightens the anxiety for communities with incoming migration. The complexities of security discourse for asylum seekers are particularly fraught. In Mountz's (2015, p.184) words, "The border, once conceived of as a line on a map, is changing spatially into a form more akin to an archipelago: it is transnational, fragmented, biometric, intimate, and contracted out with proliferating spaces of confinement."

In this chapter we will engage with and complicate the meanings of security, a concept driving a wide range of political-geographic practices, from militarization of borders to incarceration. We will cut through simplistic understandings of security occurring both at the level of individual bodies – the young man above, his fears, and his relations with his mother – and simultaneously being part of global patterns and discourses. First, we will follow Mountz and her collaborators' lines of inquiry to understand carceral archipelagos. Then we will trace the conceptions of risk and fear that are the other side and driving force of securitization, and transition to a more global view of security through a subaltern geopolitics perspective from Tanzania. We will close the chapter by considering the argument that we can achieve security not by building walls and prisons but by tearing them down.

The 1951 UN Convention Relating to the Status of Refugees defines **asylum seekers** as migrants crossing international borders to request protection from a demonstrated fear of persecution. The process of seeking asylum has been made more difficult in the last decades as global security regimes have shifted and become more rigid, such that "spaces of securitization are blocking paths to asylum and instead resources are invested in proliferating forms of confinement" (Mountz 2017, p.75). Asylum seekers are figured both as those fleeing danger *and* as a sign or warning of danger. They are among the world's most vulnerable populations, and yet in political campaigns and policy documents they often appear as threats that justify a state of exception (Hall et al. 2013), a supposedly temporary time of heightened risk and danger, in which civil liberties and other rights may be curtailed due to immanent threat. Think, for instance, of those detained at Guantanamo Bay, a US military prison where people deemed enemy combatants were held without charges, and some subjected to torture, due to the "war on terror" (Reid-Henry 2007), such human rights abuses were enabled by the rhetoric of the state of exception. We will return to this idea later in the chapter. But for now consider Mountz's work on island detention and broader work on **border securitization** or **border militarization**, that is, the increasing intensity of security processes and military presence at the border. We can witness border securitization both as the ways that migrants are framed as threat and, as Mountz explores it, through the novel spatial arrangements produced by securitization.

In particular, and recalling the chapter on borders, securitization in recent decades has led to approaches that target the body of the migrant rather than or in addition to the physical border itself.

This securitization process has a very distinctive geography, and Mountz's work has highlighted this through attention to islands as special sites of **carcerality**: the practices and discourses associated with incarceration. Why islands? Islands are often sites of landing – for instance, refugees fleeing Libya or Tunisia may land on the Italian island of Lampedusa. In other cases, they are designated security spaces, as in the case of Australian detention centers (Figure 10.1) on Nauru, Manus, and Christmas Island (which closed in 2018). In her words, "Detention centers function as islands within islands, as if to accentuate and parody the desire to contain and isolate … detainees (and islanders themselves) are often subjected to proliferating mechanisms of isolation: separating detainees from islanders, men from women, new arrivals from those already detained" (Mountz 2017, p.75). This research derives from her years of work on migrant detention in sites including Lampedusa, an Italian island off the coast of Tunisia, and Christmas Island – Australian Overseas Territory that was colonized by the British and subsequently administered by Japan, Singapore, and (today) Australia, as well as Guam, a US territory. For Mountz (2015), borders are becoming archipelagos. Mountz conceives of detention and enforcement as both material archipelagos – in that asylum-seekers and other migrants are quite often detained on islands or in other island-like liminal spaces – and as a more conceptual archipelago

Figure 10.1 Australian Detention Center. Reproduced with permission of David Stanley. https://www.flickr.com/photos/79721788@N00/25427566270

form. She visualizes carceral, detention, and enforcement spaces along the lines of Foucault's (1978a) invocation of a carceral archipelago. You will recall from our earlier encounters with his work that Foucault's focus is on the ways that institutions like the prison are the result of logics of power that infuse our daily life. The prison thus creates prison practices and prison spaces throughout our ordinary lives. The **enforcement archipelago** is thus, "the ever-more dispersed infrastructures, practices, policies, people, sites, and tactics that exclude migrants from entering the sovereign territory of states to work or seek protection" (Mountz 2015, p.185).

If this is initially confusing, imagine if you will, that borders are manifest *not* only at the border between two sovereign states (where we might expect them!). The border is *also* in, for instance, the site of the Embassy in the distant locale – itself a militarized or protected space where aspiring tourists, students, or aspiring migrants may wear their best clothes, speak in their most careful ways, and present themselves as *deserving* and *harmless* migrants or tourists. It is also the liminal space of containment, where "enemy combatants" are kept in a non-space.

Detention of asylum-seekers can lead to trauma and self-harm. Mountz recounts field-notes made by Kate Coddington after an interview with Pradeep (a pseudonym), who had been detained on Christmas Island and then in Melbourne.

> Pradeep, a Tamil man from Sri Lanka, said that he'd had such destructive thoughts the past couple weeks – heard voices telling him to hang himself from the fan, from the fence, decided that a hunger strike was the least destructive thing he could do. First in 2.5 years of detention. He was so depressed that he didn't see other options. (Fieldnotes, Melbourne, 2011, in Mountz 2017, p.78)

For Pradeep, the process of seeking asylum and being detained, rather than leading to security from conflict in his homeland of Sri Lanka, in fact brings him to the brink of self-harm. The securitization of migration has in fact led him to not be safe from himself.

Foucault (1978) argued that the prison was not only a space of confinement for prisoners themselves, but was rather that the presence of prisons in the world spreads confinement beyond institutional spaces. Prison is evident in the self-discipline that we discussed in the power chapter, and the figure of the criminal is in our minds as much as in the streets. Rashad Shabazz, for instance, quoted at the opening of this chapter, draws this idea out into the spaces of the city of Chicago, making the argument that low income neighborhoods and housing developments were built to "spatialize Blackness," and to contain it ... that is, that the city was planned as a pre-carceral space (Shabazz 2015). The existence of the prison thus disciplines society.

Whether detained migrants are visible or invisible is not an accident. The securitization of life is highly visible, as it is a means for the state to demonstrate its strength and its role as protector, but on the other hand, migrants are sometimes invisibilized. The prison contains even those outside: the invisibilization of migrants is a comfort to those who see them as a threat, but makes their situation more precarious. Simultaneously, their securitization may be made spectacular as a way to showcase the protective work of the state or a particular political party. Mountz then explores what it means to have thousands of migrants detained, ostensibly for security purposes. What kinds of new publics are created by those who witness this detention? What New Geographies?

Imaginaries of uncontained migration are often spoken as the transgression of racialized others who are understood to be out of place. These imaginaries enable political campaigns that rely on fear that in turn requires security measures (Smith, Swanson, and Gökarıksel 2016; Squire 2016). The question of security-driven detention is crucial for our times, and relates not only to asylum-seekers but to others as well. In 2013, in the United States alone, 441,000 migrants were detained in 200 immigration jails at a cost of around \$2 billion (Detention Watch Network 2017). It is important to remember that the vast majority of these detainees have not committed any crimes beyond the absence of paperwork, and that this includes a great number of families in detention (Martin 2011).

In Chapter 5's discussion of state formation, we considered the ways that the ideal of the state requires recognized and defended borders. Elections are won or lost on the basis of campaigns focused on security, but what does security mean? How do we know it when we see it? Is security signaled by guns and walls along a border? Or is it signaled by a lack of border demarcation at all? And how might we consider security when we think of all the words to which we append it – food security, border security, information security, climate security, economic security? In this chapter we consider how we might define security as well as how the idea of security is used in political action.

This chapter works to cast a different light on the idea of security through a few distinct lines of thought. First, that the process of making places secure is about more than security, but is also part of a broader form of performative politics that suggests by default that we are in a position of risk and fear. Risk, fear, and security are ideas that do political work. They prop up "strongman" politics (here I am keeping the masculinist and gendered term intentionally), in which a politician portrays themselves as the only person capable of protecting their country. Fear politics also are woven into justifications for a state of exception, in which our values and liberties may need to be curtailed in order to protect us during a security emergency, and they are wrapped into justifications for military imperialism. Second, this chapter works to help us think through the relationship between people's security and the security of the nation-state, and to consider how these two may at times be distinct, uneven, and sometimes at odds. We will engage with these ideas through the work of people seeking to abolish prisons and borders. Finally, we will also consider the current political era, which remains shaped by the ways that terrorism and discourses around terrorism have created new global imaginaries of security and securitization.

Security and Violence, Risk, and Fear

> Fear is on the up. It is the denouement of books diagnosing the ills of western society; the bread and butter of self-help manuals designed to effect a cure. Fear is written on the world, in lurid orange embossed letters, in sedate newspaper headers, embedded in memos, emblazoned on YouTube; it is written on the bodies that police dark corners, hide underground, that avoid, evade and evacuate multiple landscapes of risk. As the twenty-first century gathers momentum, fear is a motif for the human condition. (Pain and Smith 2008, 1)

Calls for security are driven by fear as a crucial geopolitical force, and while security measures – from interventions at airports to the securitization of children – are driven by fears both globally oriented and intensely, intimately local, they also can ramp up rather than tamp down fear (Amoore and Hall 2009; Pain and Smith 2008). Consider the feeling you might have on entering a place guarded by soldiers with guns drawn. Though the soldiers are there for security, on entering you may feel your body tense, your eyes scan the perimeter for the threat. Of course, if you are a soldier or have received military training, these same affective reactions (that is, reactions that are *felt* in the body before you put them into words) might be muted or intensified as the scene may seem more mundane to you, or remind you of the sensations of danger and watchfulness that you yourself experienced on duty. Pain and Smith point to ways that fear is marketized, in products and objects meant to generate a sense of security, and also politically expedient. As they argue, messages about danger both cultivate and assuage the fears of what Isin (2004) has called "the neurotic citizen."

One of the promising ways of studying fear is then not to *assume* fear as pre-existing, but to understand the means through which fear is generated, or, in Pain and Smith's (2008, p.2) terms, "Fear does not pop out of the heavens and hover in the ether before blanketing itself across huge segments of cities and societies; it has to be lived and made." This living and making occurs through both local and global scales, but is always embodied. Pain and Smith's intervention in our understanding of fear is to consider scholarship on fear as having two distinct lineages. In one lineage, fear is understood at the micro-scale, and often centered on difference as a mediating factor for how fear is experienced in daily life (for instance, due to race or gender-related vulnerability), and in one, geopolitical scenarios drive fear that is represented as disembodied and global. What if global fears are constantly being materialized in daily life and everyday life is not necessarily centered on abstract global fears? Pain and Smith ask us to carefully *embody* geopolitics, by working to understand how bodies feature in geopolitical storytelling. Security is paradoxical. By saying we need security, by taking action to make places, people, and states more secure, the result is often that people feel *more* insecure. Katz, Pain and Smith, and others suggest that *fear* is made in part *through* security.

A second, and separate lesson we will pick up is that security means quite different things depending on your relationship to the state. The current "War on Terror" has created a state of "globalized fear," as well as a great interest in fear on the part of academics and the media, though sometimes this interest requires greater attention to the way that fear operates on the ground, through emotional and political practices (Pain 2009). For instance, in elections in 2016-2017 in Europe and the United States that heralded a turn to the right, (and 2018, in Brazil) were decisions at the ballot box made due to personally felt and experienced fear and anxiety?

Katz (2008) warns us that security practices change the fabric of our everyday life. Writing in New York after the attacks of September 11, 2001, Katz suggests that the **discourse** of security and securitization has become banal, or normal. Buying a few things at a neighborhood bodega, she sees a small kit enticing parents to collect information about their child to have on hand in case of abduction or disappearance. Marketed with friendly stick-figures signaling it as something for kids, the kit entices the parent or guardian to think about the worst case scenario, and to prepare for it by cutting a lock of their child's hair and keeping it with their other biometric data. In conjunction with "nanny cams," or security cameras hidden inside stuffed animals, there is a wealth of relatively inexpensive technology to keep children protected from horrible outcomes – but as she points out, by purchasing these security-related items, we may be participating in a spiraling sense of living in a frightening and unpredictable world. For Katz, this is inseparable from national security discourses. She argues that the **performance of security** stages and foregrounds fear and risk in ways that then prepare us to accept other forms of security – so then **performing** security at home may lead to acceptance of security regimes more broadly. Katz describes this as an "**ontological insecurity**" tied to a general sense of insecure futures that blends economic insecurity, security threats from terrorism, and other forms of fear. Katz (2008, p.70) argues that appeals to security must be justice-oriented:

> it is time to refuse the bait of fear and its erosive consequences at all scales … insecurities help make people receptive to the promises of security in whatever precious or bunkered form it is offered, but they can only be countered by returning to notions of security rooted in social justice and focused on the broadest concerns of social reproduction and restoration of the social wage. Everything else is indefensible.

A pervasive sense of insecurity can take different forms across contexts and across situated positions, as research on young people in Scotland express in relation to the politics of Scottish independence. Taking up this notion of ontological insecurity, Botterill et al. (2016; Botterill, Hopkins, and Sanghera 2018) describe how young people in Scotland navigate a complex terrain of multicultural national discourses and everyday racism. Working with minoritized young people, they find a foundational ontological insecurity:

> We argue that the impacts of racism, Islamophobia and economic insecurity on young people has the potential to produce ontological insecurity – the anxious "being in the world" – because of the effects of racism on personhood. Racism and Islamophobia do not only influence a feeling of not belonging, they are a threat to a sense of being – to the core of personhood and validation that one belongs in a particular place, and can function equally. (Botterill et al. 2016, p.126)

Some scholars suggest that our time is one in which both fear and **risk** (potential proximity to harm or danger), have taken on new importance and new meanings. In 1986, the world reeled from the Chernobyl catastrophe, in which a steam-blast and subsequent release of radioactive material at a nuclear facility in Pripyat, Ukraine (then part of the Soviet Union) led to immediate and subsequently long-lasting health and environmental consequences for the Ukraine and surrounding region. It is in this context that Ulrich Beck authored *Risk Society* (1992; see also Giddens 1990; 1991). Beck argues that people's understanding of risk was shifting from an understanding of risk as an unintended side effect of processes of modernization to being understood as a central and unavoidable product of modern life. That is, populations move from the quite hopeful idea that our modern life involves a certain degree of risk (let us say, using a car is very convenient and worth the very clear dangers of automobile travel) to the idea that risk is a central and unavoidable feature of our time, and that it is everywhere, and that, even worse, experts cannot handle the degree of risk to which we are exposed (for example: we know all the apps on our phone could be hacked, or our data sold to the highest bidder, but then again, it seems pointless to figure out which ones so we give up entirely and click yes to terms of agreements without trying to assess risk). In Beck's view, science and experimentation has escaped the lab and now takes place on a global scale, exposing us to a "risk society," in which we are exposed not only to the risks of "natural" disasters like hurricanes, floods, and earthquakes, but rather come to fear human-originated disasters more.

> By risks, I mean all radioactivity which completely evades human perceptual abilities, but also toxins and pollutants in the air, in the water and foodstuffs, together with the accompanying short- and long-term effects on plants, animals and people. They induce systematic and often irreversible harm and generally remain invisible. (Beck 1992, p.22)

This risk is insidious in part because it is imperceptible and in part, because it is accompanied by doubt regarding the role of experts and their **technocratic** regime (in which rule by those with technological expertise is primary). A **technocracy** is a regime of governance in which experts are required in hope that they can engineer technological fixes to the risks paradoxically created by advances in technology.

Beck's view of risk, which he developed primarily in regard to environmental risks, is not incompatible with Pain and Smith's understandings of the geopolitics of fear. In both cases, the proliferation of fear and risk is accompanied by a parallel proliferation of discourses and solutions that tend to reinforce the very thing that they promise to protect against. As you might also expect, fear and risk cannot be extracted from their social, cultural, and political contexts, thus, they are tied to race, ethnic identity, and gender in ways that multiply and proliferate, but also converge – such that, for instance, Kumarini Silva (2016) demonstrates that fear of labor migration and fear of terrorism become blurred into a fear of "Brown Threat," against which other insecurities are staged (see also Fojas 2017; Shah 2012; Puar 2007).

Gendered and Embodied National Securities

Ideas of national security have demonstrable political impacts. Security displacement is a key form through which the US "war on terror," is maintained and justified (Fluri 2014). For US citizens, state actors and political discourses, attached to a slew of disarticulated entities from private security contractors to military technology companies to policy makers to journalists, work to create the impression of war held at bay: a war that is simultaneously "everywhere" and "elsewhere." This logic of the elsewhere war is represented in the media, through bodies both real and imagined, and as such, it is gendered.

As you will recall from earlier in this book, the nation is often represented in gendered terms – for instance as a woman in need of protection – while simultaneously women's beauty can be held to or judged according to national standards of idealized beauty (with all the racial and gendered elements that you might expect). This gendered nationalism defines whose bodies are to be secured and whose are a security threat. "Machines of state security necessarily focus on the body as a site to 'protect' or as a potential agent of 'insecurity'" (Fluri 2014, p.797).

What might we do with this idea: that representations of particular bodies and spaces are fundamental to how people understand who is to be protected or secured and whose body becomes a security threat? Writing this during the height of the Trump presidency in the United States, it is difficult not to immediately think of the national rhetoric of immigration and policing. In Fluri's language, some bodies are represented as in need of protection: these are the "Real Americans," to be protected from those crossing the border without papers – famously represented by Trump as "bad hombres," and "rapists." Similarly, the US debate over police violence and the framing of "Black Lives Matter" as an assertion that Black people's bodies *should be* valued and protected *but are not* speak to how representations of bodies and spaces come to matter. Why are Black people in the United States, minding their own business, consistently represented as threats? Even Black children, like Tamir Rice, age 1, shot by police in front of his sister in a Cleveland Park in the US Midwest, was perceived as or at least represented as a threat, rather than a child in need of protection. Ahmed and others have written of these forms of epic reversal, in which violence is justified through affective and narrative reversal of vulnerability (Ahmed 2004; DiAngelo 2011; Gergan, Smith, and Vasudevan 2020; Gökarıksel and Smith 2016; Smith and Vasudevan 2017).

Security, Sovereignty, and Subaltern Geopolitics

As we have seen in this chapter, there is a tight and complex relationship between security and sovereignty. On the one hand, security threats have been marshaled as a reason for the breaching of sovereignty, for instance, in the use of drone warfare in the AfPak and Yemen, or in the example of the US Patriot Act (Amoore 2006).

As we have already learned, geopolitical visions are fraught not only with colonial legacies and injustice, but also one that is profoundly narrow and inaccurate. Let us now tilt this vision a bit and rely on what Sharp refers to as subaltern geopolitics. Sharp draws on Mohammed Ayoob's (2002) concept of "subaltern realism" for this project. You'll remember from earlier chapters that subaltern is a term developed by Antonio Gramsci and later further elaborated by Marxist and postcolonial scholars to refer to the relationship between the dominated and dominant classes. This generated a wealth of scholarship, including the field of subaltern studies that emerged in India as a way to develop history from the point of the view of the dominated or peasant class. Ayoob (2002, p.40) urges us to consider geopolitics not from the perspective of the dominant states, but rather to draw "upon the experience of subalterns in the international system." Following on the work of critical geopolitics, with which we have just engaged, Sharp (2011) builds an understanding of subaltern geopolitics that brings together state perspectives with the imagined geographies of popular geopolitics.

What does it mean to conceive of geopolitics from the perspective of global subalterns? Let us first remember that all such schema require attention to the risks of essentialism, splintering urbanism, and class allegiances that transcend national boundaries. Those caveats aside, what can we learn from situating ourselves within the media context of places marked as subaltern? As Sharp argues, and as we discussed in the chapter on critical geopolitics, the binary geopolitical metanarratives of the Cold War have recently been rearticulated as a new geopolitical vision driven by the powerful – that of civilization and freedom versus terror and chaos (e.g., Tuathail 2003; Bellamy et al. 2007). Sharp points out that the "cartoon world" (Tuathail 2003) of freedom versus terror is disassembled by views from other places, though she cautions us *not* to mistake her reading of Tanzanian discourses on security as a universal "African" vision of geopolitics.

In the early days of its independence from Britain in the 1960s, the Tanzanian leader Julius Nyerere sought a "third way," as part of the larger non-aligned movement that was full of potential at the time and which left a lasting intellectual and material legacy. Thus, Nyerere sought to create an African socialism that looked to pre-colonial societal frameworks and structures, but in the nationalism of the Tanganyika-Zanzibar unification in 1964, also may have sought to remain out of the Cold War. This was a violent nation-building process for Zanzibaris and other Tanzanians, and subsequently, Zanzibaris continue to advocate for greater equity and autonomy. After the 1980s and 1990s, Tanzania moved into a free market and then multi-party democratic system. Tanzania was primed to be part of later narratives of the War on Terror by the August 1998 bombing of US Embassies in Dar es Salaam and Nairobi, Kenya, setting off a Clinton-ordered bombing of sites in Sudan and Afghanistan to target Osama bin Laden's bases – in what was "perhaps the first overt geopolitical recognition of the networked nature of post-Cold War geopolitics" (Sharp 2011, p.299). Local consequences included intensified debate on religious difference, which includes a regional dimension as Zanzibar is majority-Muslim.

To build a case for understanding our world through subaltern geopolitics, Sharp performs a media analysis of an English-language newspaper, *The African*, focusing on the issues immediately after the attacks of September 11, 2001, and through the 2003 editions to include coverage of the invasion of Iraq. Sharp observes that while *The African* cannot fund independent journalists for international coverage and must rely on picking up international reports, the editors curate an intentionally radical international vision through article selection, editing, choice of left-of-center commentators, and use of images of refugee camps and vulnerable families during the "War on Terror." Sharp *does not* suggest that her reading enables us to have a "Tanzanian view," but rather that this analysis gives us a glimpse of "geopolitical imaginations in the Tanzanian media through which geopolitical representations and practices of identity formation are played out" (Sharp 2011, p.301). What do we learn about security from these geopolitical visions?

Sharp makes several key observations. First, the initial reactions to the attacks of September 11 are that of empathy and connection – drawing parallels to the 1998 attacks in Dar es Salaam. This in itself is not surprising as famously, despite the long history of US imperialism, globally the reaction to the attacks was largely one of empathy. I was in the Leh, Ladakh during the attacks and was not surprised but was certainly moved by the reactions of acquaintances – the first person to offer kind words to me, as a US citizen abroad, was a Kashmiri Muslim man who I knew to be sharply critical of US foreign policy. What is notable in this case (and also illustrative perhaps of global trends), is that this empathy quickly became something more complex. Soon articles emerged noting "America regarded its own victims of terror as more important than others, that somehow terrorism against Americans should be considered as more important than elsewhere," and, as Sharp notes, that this attack was not surprising (Sharp 2011, p.301). The immediate reaction included a simultaneous rejection of "Osama bin Ladenism," and a critique of American foreign policy, e.g.:

> Is America humble enough to admit that it has been wrong in its dealings with the rest of the world and that it must change in the interests of lasting peace? The fact is that the war did not start with Tuesday's murderous strike on American soil. It simply changed the rules, the

battlefield, the ugly scorecard and the balance of evil power in a contest that has been raging for a long time. To many observers, it is America's smug, arrogant isolationism that has begotten this disaster. (*The African* September 19, 2001, cited in Sharp 2011, p.301)

As will be immediately clear, this is a quite different positioning of security than that presupposed by the United States and its allies in the war on terror. While US security discourses are predicated on locating and stamping out terrorist organizations and individuals, the view in this editorializing commentary is that security has been breached by its own foreign policy, described here as "smug, arrogant isolationism." This arrogance is described in relation to: climate change, US race relations and international diplomacy, refusal to deeply engage with the UN, military politics, and the "belief that US foreign policy privileged the 'white nations'" (*The African*, September 14, 2001, cited in Sharp 2011, p.301). In a broader perspective, the articles as a whole reveal a geopolitical vision of US dominance in which *The African* "present[s] its views as coming from … a 'postcolonial optic,' where the perspective from below allowed it to see the effects of US policy better than the Americans" (Sharp 2011, p.302). This was paired with security concerns expressed in relation to the Global South, in particular, fears of revenge: 10% of editorials expressed this fear, for instance, begging Bush "to restrain his anger and act in a reasonable manner to save the world from this impending bloodbath" (*The African* September 25, 2001, cited in Sharp 2011, p.302). These visions, notably, are not represented as state-specific, but rather portray a collective victimhood across the Global South. Sharp's call for subaltern geopolitics includes both an affirmation of some of the ways that US imperialism is portrayed in the pages of *The African*, as well as the point that there is more to the story as well: that in an order to destabilize one hegemonic worldview of security another should not be put in its place. As she observes, in *The African* a different set of politically expedient discourses also emerges, essentializing Tanzanian identity and downplaying fractures and challenges internal to Tanzania and East Africa.

Security as Abolition

We continue to find that the prison is itself a border. This analysis has come from prisoners, who name the distinction between the "free world" and the space behind the walls of the prison. (Dent, quoted in Davis and Dent 2001, p.1236)

For every body that is washed ashore at the EU border, there is a family living with ambiguity, not knowing if their loved one is dead or alive. For such families their loved ones are missing, having left home and never having been heard from since. In the absence of information about the fate of loved ones, families cannot start the mourning process and live forever with uncertainty. (Kovras and Robins 2016, p.41)

Some of us are taught as children that it is police and armies, borders and prisons that make us safe, that cages to contain people are an unavoidable but necessary evil. Another school of thought suggests quite the opposite: that the abolition of prisons is what will secure all peoples' freedom, and that the abolition of borders will protect us all. The title of this section reflects the complications of security when we think about how it is entangled in difference and insecurity. Loyd, Mitchelson, and Burridge (2013) describe resonances between "borders and prisons – walls and cages." They frame these two pairs – border/walls, prison/cages – as parts of two regimes of power: **global apartheid** and **policing and prison regimes**. For Loyd, Mitchelson, and Burridge (2013, p.1), "*Global apartheid* … is a condition in which the wealthiest regions of the world erect physical and bureaucratic barriers against the movement of people from poorer regions of the world," and while migration is fundamental to human history, "nation-state sovereignty continues to be invoked to deny this freedom and to rationalize the fatalities that these sovereign practices create." Parallel to this condition – which limits mobility through border/walls, they point to policing and prison regimes as "a condition in which the state is built and society is governed through crime legislation," and rule of law "obscures the oppression that is produced through the enforcement of criminal legislation" (Loyd, Mitchelson, and Burridge 2013, p.1).

You may (or may not!) find the idea of the abolition of borders and prisons, walls and cages, to be a radical, even preposterous idea. If you *do* find it to be too much, remember that we understand a category, phenomenon, or process better by exploring its edges, limits, and failures.

Prison abolition

Critical Resistance is an organization among many that is seeking to reduce the role of what they define as the Prison Industrial Complex (PIC). In their mission statement, they write that their goals are to:

> build an international movement to end the Prison Industrial Complex by challenging the belief that caging and controlling people makes us safe. We believe that basic necessities such as food, shelter, and freedom are what really make our communities secure. As such, our work is part of global struggles against inequality and powerlessness. The success of the movement requires that it reflect communities most affected by the PIC. Because we seek to abolish the PIC, we cannot support any work that extends its life or scope. (http://criticalresistance.org/about/)

Scholars and activists Angela Davis and Ruth Wilson Gilmore have argued forcefully for this move toward **abolition**, or the end of the prison system and a turn toward restorative or transformative justice. Both draw on the contested and compelling idea of the **Prison Industrial Complex**, "the set of institutions, practices, and ideologies responsible for creating and maintaining a condition of mass incarceration" (Loyd, Mitchelson, and Burridge 2013, p.5). It is important to note that this is distinct from work to *reform* prisons. Work focused on reforming prisons suggests that there can be a just prison system. **Abolitionists** (and some other critics of incarceration) tie the history of the prison to slavery and colonialism, argue that its existence makes human security impossible, and attend to the ways that criminality itself is made in relation to the prison system. Thus, the word abolition has intentional resonance with the abolitionists who sought to end slavery.

Wacquant (2002, p.41), describes mass incarceration as one of a series of "peculiar institutions," that have "operated to define, confine, and control African-Americans in the history of the United States," including chattel slavery, the Jim Crow system of discrimination and segregation, the *de facto* segregation of the "ghetto," and, finally, what he refers to as the "remnants of the dark ghetto and the carceral apparatus with which it has become joined."

Angela Davis, a longtime activist, scholar, and now Professor Emerita at the University of California, Santa Cruz, who has herself been incarcerated, has been one of the most vocal and persistent advocates of prison abolition. Davis (1998) has brought Foucault's (1978a) *Discipline and Punish*, as well as his earlier reflections on a visit to the Attica Prison (Foucault and Simon 1991) into conversation with critical theories of racialization, pointing to a genealogy of systems of incarceration in the United States, including the reservation system of settler colonialism, the mission system, the World War II Internment camps, and slavery, and attending to the intersections of race and gender that characterize these state interventions into individual and community life.

Davis argues that punishment and incarceration has always been informed by, mediated by, and implicated in how race is invented and re-invented (1998). She argues that in the context of the United States, under slavery, the imprisonment of white people meant to reform them, such that even imprisonment affirmed white humanity, slavery was already a form of incarceration founded on the denial of humanity (1998, p.99). Geographer Ruth Gilmore, in an interview with Jenna Loyd clarifies:

> I don't think once upon a time prisons and jails were used judiciously and then just got out of control recently. That is *not* what I think. But what I do know is that the use of prisons and jails as all-purpose solutions for all different kinds of social, political, and economic problems and challenges *is* different than what it was in the past … What has happened over the last twenty years is that different kinds of people have found themselves confronted with suddenly having to prove or assert innocence or non-guilt in the face of criminalizing machinery, including legislation and the ideologically produced representation of all different kinds of people as already criminals. (Loyd and Gilmore 2012, p.42)

The idea of prison abolition can be disorienting because of how naturalized prisons are as a form of security. Abolitionists seek to build a world that *does not need* prisons. Their conception of prison is that of a site full of, in Gilmore's words, "modestly educated women and men in the prime of their lives," who "otherwise would be making, moving, growing, and caring for things," but who "instead are in cages" (Loyd and Gilmore 2012, p.46). This caging is due to structural economic conditions and racialized processes that destabilized their labor markets at the same time as "get tough on crime," bills led to new forms of criminalization (Loyd and Gilmore 2012, p.46; see also Gilmore 2007; Anderson 2016; Alexander 2012). Thus, "abolition is utopian in the sense that it's looking forward to a world in which prisons are not necessary because not only are the political-economic motives behind mass incarceration gone, but also the instances in which people might harm each other are minimized" (Loyd and Gilmore 2012, p.52). Across the United States (perhaps unsurprisingly as it has one of the highest rates of incarceration in the world), social movements have advocated for prison abolition and the reduction of harm from imprisonment, drawing on the concept of "**transformative justice**," an idea developed by collaboration among abolitionists and others. Abolitionist Mariame Kaba draws on Generation Five's definitions to explain transformative justice as a means that seeks to develop **community accountability** without alienation or imprisonment. Community accountability is a theorization of ways to create a community of people and groups that are accountable to one another through the development of values, safety and support systems, and behavior that does not require reliance on the police or imprisonment. Community accountability was developed by the

Incite! Women of Color Against Violence campaign (see Kaba 2012 to learn more). Abolition in practice looks like working to free specific prisoners (e.g., the #FreeBresha campaign), to help young and adult people navigate legal systems, organizing work around bail as a system that keeps people imprisoned over minor offenses (see for instance, the Black Love Bail Out, and the Mamas' Bail Out day actions: https://nomoremoneybail.org/), as well as work around education and community development.

Against borders: Migration as a human right

Alongside the prison abolition argument (and even entangled in it) is a parallel argument for abolishing borders (e.g., Nevins 2013; Jones 2016; Loyd and Gilmore 2012). As Gilmore and others argue, border and prison abolition are both theoretically and practically linked, as changing economic landscapes result in increasing rates of incarceration *and* migrant incarceration or detention. Joining already existing calls of activists, scholars have begun calling for the right to migrate to be understood as a human right (e.g., among others, Casas-Cortes, Cobarrubias, and Pickles 2015; Jones 2016; Loyd, Mitchelson, and Burridge 2013), and for a fundamental understanding of borders *not* as a site of security, but as a site that generates violence, as we discussed in more detail in Chapter 5.

Countless activists, relief workers, and scholars have been working for immediate relief for those whose insecurity is heightened by the violence of borders. These actions include a range of explicitly spatial approaches, such as sanctuary cities (Darling 2017; Kocher 2017; Ridgley 2008), as well as work through the court system to intervene in individual cases of deportation. Rebecca Torres has not only written on the intimate geopolitics of border bureaucracy (Torres 2018), but has done this alongside collaborative policy and advocacy work with refugee and migrant children. Megan Ybarra has written on the ways that deportation compromises family security and has cascading effects of trauma (Ybarra and Peña 2017), and on the ways that the racialization of migrants is mobilized by the United States and Mexico, for instance to differentiate between Central American and Mexican migrants, shoring up security discourses but intensifying vulnerability and violence directed at migrants (Ybarra 2018). In tandem with this, Ybarra has collaborated with activists working to close detention facilities, and created a short documentary film in English and Spanish (available at www. hungerstrikershandbook.org). Jeremy Slack (Slack 2016; Slack and Whiteford 2011) has not only written on the violence of the border, but has also served as an expert witness, written policy reports, and otherwise worked to protect the safety of migrants. Geographers and other scholars have called for border abolition and for consideration of migration as a human right. Reece Jones (2016, p.1) begins his book *Violent Borders: Refugees and the Right to Move* with a reflection on visiting Morocco with a group of young US students on a study abroad trip:

> As soon as our bus, with its EU license plates, arrived at the lot, fifteen or twenty Moroccan youths, roughly the same age as the American students, surrounded the vehicle, peering underneath it … For the study-abroad students, safely seated inside taking cell-phone videos, this was just part of the adventure.

Drawing on his long-term research on violence at the India-Bangladesh border (e.g., Jones 2009; 2012), but pulling this detailed ethnographic work into a global appraisal of the violence wrought by borders, Jones makes the case for the human right to migrate. Jones theoretically ties borders to regimes of private property and the multitude ways that wealth is understood to belong to citizens, and access to territory and survival is denied to those who exist as refugees or are subject to other forms of forced migration. Jones approaches borders not as a natural phenomenon at the border protecting citizens from violence, but as entities that *create* violence.

Jones's meta-approach to bordering and bounding echoes what Loyd, Mitchelson, and Burridge argued in *Beyond Walls and Cages*: that walls and cages, borders and prisons must be approached together. Their analysis focuses on criminalization itself, which affects both migrants and prisoners. They write,

> The imperative of freedom now necessarily means finding a way out of the dead end of organizing around exclusions, such as those captured vividly in the common statements "We're not criminals" and "We're innocent; those are the real criminals." (Loyd, Mitchelson, and Burridge 2013, p.7)

In their view, "claims of virtuous innocence" (the exceptional migrant),

> effectively [erase] the history and legacy of slavery and ... are doubly pernicious considering the central role that anti-Black conceptions of Black people's inherent violence and criminality have had in restricting Black people's freedom, justifying police violence against them, and fueling mass imprisonment as a generalized institution of surveillance, capture, and discipline.

Against this frame, the activist slogan "No One Is Illegal," which emerged from sanctuary movements of the 1980s and 1990s, encompasses both forms of criminalization. It also expertly flips on its head the securitization of individuals that we have discussed previously.

> For Rose Braz, a California-based, anti-prison organizer, "abolition means a world where we do not use prisons, policing, and the larger system of the prison-industrial complex as an "answer" to what are social, political, and economic problems" (Critical Resistance 2008). While contemporary prison abolition is explicitly rooted in continuing the work of ending slavery in all its forms, this radical vision of freedom also recognizes the non-freedom of forced and restricted mobility. Paul Robeson (1988, 67), the great artist and Black political leader, made this clear: "From the days of chattel slavery until today, the concept of travel has been inseparably linked in the minds of our people with the concept of freedom." Further, abolition's clear challenge to legalized means of subjection enables a questioning of the use of national citizenship (or other arbitrary exclusionary boundaries) to categorically frame power relations. (Loyd, Mitchelson, and Burridge 2013, p.8)

You will recall that one strand of our chapter on citizenship focused on the possibility that citizenship fails us, that is, fails to protect all human beings' rights, fails to protect the most vulnerable. Here, Loyd, Mitchelson, and Burridge tie that possibility to the abolition of prisons and borders.

Geographer at Work: Edgar Sandoval

Edgar Sandoval is a PhD candidate in Geography at the University of Washington.

Miguel hoists his weathered backpack onto his shoulders, heavy with supplies for the first day of the school year. As with the four previous ones, his first day of fourth grade in an all-English classroom was further weighed down by his mother's words. Standing in front of him, she reminds him in Spanish: "Don't forget. If you tell anyone that your parents are undocumented, they will send all of us to Mexico." Miguel's mother understood that school offered them opportunities, but it also operated as a site of violence that could jeopardize the mixed-status family's safety through deportation. My research analyzes how this ambivalent relationship to school might resonate in projects of economic revitalization in post-industrial US suburbs where city leaders seek to explicitly collaborate with federal authorities, such as Immigration and Customs Enforcement (ICE), to deport undocumented residents, even as immigrant communities imagine their future.

My research focuses on how immigrants and mixed-status families differently navigate the relationship between immigration policing and economic development. It explores how anti-immigrant conditions in the suburbs reflect local imaginaries of race, nation, and place, and manifest at the municipal level. My research is situated in Waukegan, Illinois, one of Chicago's multiethnic towns where Latinxs emerged as the demographic majority following the economic disinvestment that accompanied the departure of manufacturing industries in the region. Reacting to this demographic change, Waukegan elites enacted xenophobic local ordinances under the umbrella of economic revitalization to displace marginalized communities and thus attract more affluent people to settle in the suburb. The previous mayor made comments that an automatic towing ordinance for those driving without a license was an effort to produce economic precarity for undocumented migrants who he claimed brought crime to the suburb. Efforts to reconstruct a place to become desirable to white, middle-class professionals often work through measures that exclude those who are considered undesirable, such as immigrants, people of color, and peoples who are impoverished. I engage with the local politics of economics and immigration to better understand how these complex processes transform the landscape, and the effects that this transformation has on residents. I study how "racialized speculation" (Bahng 2018) functions through projects of economic revitalization to read undocumented residents, immigrants, and their families out of the suburban landscape and out of a future.

I grew up in the suburban town of Waukegan, Illinois, where my relationships with family and friends were profoundly and intimately structured by the local state's enactment of xenophobic ordinances and practices. My family and I felt the transformation that occurred in Waukegan's landscape, and this exclusion became embedded in our consciousness and in how we came to navigate the suburb. As a mixed-status family, we came to understand that violence, beyond bodily harm, is not tied to the status of being legal or illegal but to the complex arrangement of laws that govern through languages of citizenship and legality. While it is crucial to understand the extension of the spatiality of immigration governance from the southwest border toward the interior United States – and its use in projects of economic revitalization throughout suburbia – equally important are the ways that immigrants and mixed-status families alter their everyday placemaking practices within landscapes of violence.

They must differently navigate how white elites exert control over desirable spaces through racialized projects of economic revitalization that disavow undesirable populations through the carefully state-controlled securitization of municipalities. Undocumented residents would rather drive around – rather than through – Waukegan to avoid the traffic checkpoints and carry out their daily tasks, avoiding local shopping areas in favor of those outside the suburb. My use of navigation builds on the "mobilities turn" (Cresswell 2006) to also consider, in addition to spatial movements, discursive strategies, such as when residents speak Spanish outside a room to discuss how to maneuver a city council meeting in English. For those of us who do not identify as heterosexual or cisgender, the effects of these policies on our livelihoods and in relation to our families become particularly violent. My research draws on the embodied experiences of residents caught at the crossroads of these policies to rethink navigation and violence, and the relationship between the two, more expansively.

In my research, I bring geography into conversation with "queer of color" theorizing to propose that the everyday can help scholars and activists tell more vibrant and complex stories about migrant communities. By centering the insights offered by migrant communities, my research builds upon scholarship that takes navigation practices as forms of resistance against different forms of power around citizenship, race, class, and gender. I draw inspiration from undocumented artists' calls to shift representations of migrants' lives from one of trauma, pain, and suffering to one that includes complexity, hope, and wisdom (Sandoval 2019). Because although Miguel and his family – and many others through the United States and the world – feel the violent effects of immigration enforcement, many continue to find ways to produce more livable lives in their everyday practice.

What Have We Learned and Where Do We Go From Here?

In this chapter, we have considered the ways that security moves like a projection across bodies and borders. The militarization of borders may help some people feel more secure while increasing the vulnerability of others. The rhetoric of security may in fact generate the fear that it seeks to assuage. In this next chapter we bring together the focus on embodied life and the previous chapter's consideration of geopolitics to consider when and how geopolitics are intimate.

Keywords

Abolition   Work to make human security possible without prisons or policing.

Asylum seekers   Migrants crossing international borders to request protection from a demonstrated fear of persecution.

Carcerality   Practices and discourses associated with incarceration.

Enforcement archipelago   Dispersed means of policing and security (infrastructure, places, people) that keep migrants from moving.

Global apartheid   Analysis of the world as a site in which wealthy regions create barriers to prevent poor people from moving.

Ontological insecurity   General sense of insecure futures that blends economic insecurity, security threats from terrorism, and other forms of fear. Ontological security sometimes creates a sense of existential insecurity

Performance of security/security theater   Security-centered actions that dramatically stage security but may lead to feelings of risk and danger and normalize the militarization of daily life.

Policing and prison regimes   Regimes in which the state is heavily dependent upon and experienced as crime legislation and its enforcement.

Prison Industrial Complex   Modeled on the "military industrial complex" this refers to the institutions and ideas that enable mass incarceration (for instance, for profit prisons, the criminalization of relatively minor offensives such as small amounts of drug possession).

Risk   Potential proximity to harm or danger.

Technocracy   A regime of governance in which experts are required in hope that they can engineer technological fixes to the risks paradoxically created by advances in technology.

Further Reading

Abolition

Alexander, M. 2012. *The New Jim Crow: Mass Incarceration in the Age of Colorblindness.* New York: The New Press.

Critical Resistance. 2008. *Abolition Now! Ten Years of Strategy and Struggle against the Prison Industrial Complex.* Oakland, CA: AK Press.

Davis, A. and Dent, G. 2001. Prison as a Border: A Conversation on Gender, Globalization, and Punishment. *Signs: Journal of Women in Culture and Society* 26(4): 1235–1241.

Davis, A.Y. 1998. Racialized Punishment and Prison Abolition. In J. James (ed.), *The Angela Y. Davis Reader.* Malden, MA: Wiley Blackwell, pp.96–107.

Gilmore, R.W. 2007. *Golden Gulag: Prisons, Surplus, Crisis, and Opposition in Globalizing California.* Berkeley, CA: University of California Press.

Jones, R. 2016. *Violent Borders: Refugees and the Right to Move.* London: Verso Books.

Kaba, M. 2012. Prison Culture: Transformative Justice. *Prison Culture* (blog). http://www.usprisonculture.com/blog/transformative-justice/.

Loyd, J.M. and Gilmore, R.W. 2012. Race, Capitalist Crisis, and Abolitionist Organizing. In J.M. Loyd, M. Mitchelson, and A. Burridge (eds), *Beyond Walls and Cages: Prisons, Borders, and Global Crisis.* Athens, GA: University of Georgia Press, pp.42–54.

Loyd, J.M., Mitchelson M., and Burridge, A. 2013. Introduction: Borders, Prisons, and Abolitionist Visions. In J.M. Loyd, M. Mitchelson, and A. Burridge (eds), *Beyond Walls and Cages: Prisons, Borders, and Global Crisis.* Athens, GA: University of Georgia Press, pp.1–15.

Asylum and refugees

Bahng, A. 2018. *Migrant Futures: Decolonizing Speculation in Financial Times.* Durham: Duke University Press.

Bettini, G. 2013. Climate Barbarians at the Gate? A Critique of Apocalyptic Narratives on "Climate Refugees." *Geoforum* 45: 63–72.

Bialasiewicz, L. 2012. Off-Shoring and out-Sourcing the Borders of Europe: Libya and EU Border Work in the Mediterranean. *Geopolitics* 17(4): 843–866.

Bose, P.S. 2014. Refugees in Vermont: Mobility and Acculturation in a New Immigrant Destination. *Journal of Transport Geography* 36: 151–159.

Bose, P.S. 2018. Welcome and Hope, Fear, and Loathing: The Politics of Refugee Resettlement in Vermont. *Peace and Conflict: Journal of Peace Psychology* 24(3): 320–329.

Coddington, K. 2018. Landscapes of Refugee Protection. *Transactions of the Institute of British Geographers* 43(3): 326–340.

Davies, T., Isakjee, A., and Dhesi, S. 2017. Violent Inaction: The Necropolitical Experience of Refugees in Europe. *Antipode* 49(5): 1263–1284.

Daley, P. 2013. Refugees, IDPS and Citizenship Rights: The Perils of Humanitarianism in the African Great Lakes Region. *Third World Quarterly* 34(5): 893–912.

Ehrkamp, P. 2017. Geographies of Migration I: Refugees. *Progress in Human Geography* 41(6): 813–822.

Farbotko, C. and Lazrus, H. 2012. The First Climate Refugees? Contesting Global Narratives of Climate Change in Tuvalu. *Global Environmental Change* 22(2): 382–390.

Gorman, C.S. 2017. Redefining Refugees: Interpretive Control and the Bordering Work of Legal Categorization in US Asylum Law. *Political Geography* 58: 36–45.

Loyd, J.M., Ehrkamp, P., and Secor, A.J. 2018. A Geopolitics of Trauma: Refugee Administration and Protracted Uncertainty in Turkey. *Transactions of the Institute of British Geographers* 43(3): 377–389.

Martin, D. 2015. From Spaces of Exception to "Campscapes": Palestinian Refugee Camps and Informal Settlements in Beirut. *Political Geography* 44: 9–18.

Mould, O. 2018. The Not-so-Concrete Jungle: Material Precarity in the Calais Refugee Camp. *Cultural Geographies* 25(3): 393–409.

Hyndman, J. and Mountz, A. 2007. Refuge or Refusal: The Geography of Exclusion. In D. Gregory and A. Pred (eds), *Violent Geographies: Fear, Terror, and Political Violence*. New York: Routledge, pp.77–92.

Mountz, A. 2010. *Seeking Asylum: Human Smuggling and Bureaucracy at the Border*. Minneapolis: University of Minnesota Press.

Mountz, A. and Hiemstra, N. 2014. Chaos and Crisis: Dissecting the Spatiotemporal Logics of Contemporary Migrations and State Practices. *Annals of the Association of American Geographers* 104(2): 382–390.

Ramadan, A. 2013. Spatialising the Refugee Camp. *Transactions of the Institute of British Geographers* 38(1): 65–77.

Seitz, D.K. 2017. Limbo Life in Canada's Waiting Room: Asylum-Seeker as Queer Subject. *Environment and Planning D: Society and Space* 35(3): 438–456.

Tyner, J.A. 2013. Population Geography I: Surplus Populations. *Progress in Human Geography* 37(5): 701–711.

Borders and security

Bigo, D. 2002. Security and Immigration: Toward a Critique of the Governmentality of Unease. *Alternatives* 27: 63–92.

Casas-Cortes, M., Cobarrubias, S., and Pickles, J. 2015. Changing Borders, Rethinking Sovereignty: Towards a Right to Migrate. *REMHU: Revista Interdisciplinar Da Mobilidade Humana* 23(44): 47–60.

Coleman, M. and Stuesse, A. 2014. Policing Borders, Policing Bodies: The Territorial and Biopolitical Roots of US Immigration Control. In R. Jones and C. Johnson (eds), *Placing the Border in Everyday Life*. Burlington, VT: Ashgate, pp.33–63.

Fojas, C. 2017. *Zombies, Migrants, and Queers: Race and Crisis Capitalism in Pop Culture*. Urbana, IL: University of Illinois Press.

Ibrahim, M. 2005. The Securitization of Migration: A Racial Discourse. *International Migration* 43(5): 163–187.

Kovras, I. and Robins, S. 2016. Death as the Border: Managing Missing Migrants and Unidentified Bodies at the EU's Mediterranean Frontier. *Political Geography* 55: 40–49.

Loyd, J.M., Mitchelson, M., and Burridge, A. 2013. *Beyond Walls and Cages: Prisons, Borders, and Global Crisis*. Athens, GA: University of Georgia Press.

Loyd, J.M. and Mountz, A. 2018. *Boats, Borders, and Bases: Race, the Cold War, and the Rise of Migration Detention in the United States*. Berkeley, CA: University of California Press.

Nevins, J. 2001. *Operation Gatekeeper: The Rise of the "Illegal Alien" and the Remaking of the US–Mexico Boundary*. London: Routledge.

Silva, K. 2016. *Brown Threat: Identification in the Security State*. Minneapolis, MN: University of Minnesota Press.

Torres, R.M. 2018. A Crisis of Rights and Responsibility: Feminist Geopolitical Perspectives on Latin American Refugees and Migrants. *Gender, Place & Culture* 25(1): 13–36.

Williams, J.M. 2015. From Humanitarian Exceptionalism to Contingent Care: Care and Enforcement at the Humanitarian Border. *Political Geography* 47: 11–20.

Williams, J.M. 2016. The Safety/Security Nexus and the Humanitarianisation of Border Enforcement. *The Geographical Journal* 182(1): 27–37.

Chapter 11

Intimate Geopolitics

Back in 2004, I set out to do my MA research in the high altitude region of Ladakh, in India's Jammu and Kashmir State. Jumping into my first research project, I noticed a trend I had not anticipated. I was asking questions about politics, but the answers revolved around holidays, dinner parties, love affairs, and marriages. Why were politics so quickly channeled into these intimate revelations, before I had even thought to ask such questions? By 2015, however, I was not surprised when a group of Buddhist activists sent India's Prime Minister, Narendra Modi, a letter complaining that Muslims in the region were waging "Love Jihad," that is, attempting to convert Buddhists to Islam by making them fall in love with and marry Muslims. By the time this letter came out, I had long been thinking of my own research agenda as being focused on intimate geopolitics: the ways that geopolitical struggle is entangled in and comprised through our day to day intimate interactions with one another. In 2015, the activists demanded intervention in the region. More recently, in the summer of 2017, a similar situation arose when Stanzin Saldon, who also goes by Shifah, married a Muslim man, Syed Murtaza Agah. Born into a Buddhist family, she had converted to Islam and then married a close friend. The Ladakh Buddhist Association (LBA) demanded that she be returned to her family. Shifah wrote her own opinion on the topic, which was published in *Indian Express* (Saldon 2017). Saldon writes:

> While communal passions were fueled against the entire Muslim community, which had noth-
> ing to do with my personal decision, no one wanted to check the facts. Nobody asked me my
> view as if I don't matter in this game of misogyny played in my name. Because the choices that
> I have made are used to mischievously target my lawfully wedded husband and the entire

Political Geography: A Critical Introduction, First Edition. Sara Smith.
© 2020 John Wiley & Sons Ltd. Published 2020 by John Wiley & Sons Ltd.

Muslim community, I have decided to stand up and speak for myself. The LBA's statement is not only false and concocted, it is a brazen attempt to suppress and threaten a woman who has shown the courage to follow her heart.

How might love affairs become a topic of national political conversation? I started to understand this question and the ways that it was tied to South Asia's colonial encounter with the British through research with people about their love lives and personal decisions. What I learned was that while individuals sometimes felt compelled to defy family, religious nationalism, and state institutions that proved inextricable from these forces, they rarely succeed. A Buddhist man, Paljor (these are pseudonyms), who had married a Shia woman, told me that their marriage was politically problematic from the point of view of Shia Muslims, because it would result in children who would take the religion of their father, and thus, "from [Fatima], there will be three or four Buddhists." When he told me that, I began to see how the Buddhist majority and Muslim minority were conventionally understood to be creating a future political population through their choices about marriage and family planning. This is why, as the 19-year-old daughter of a Buddhist mother and Muslim father told me, such marriages are impossible today. I myself had come to Ladakh from the United States, married into a Ladakhi Buddhist family, and been accepted (although my partner's family would certainly have preferred him to marry another Ladakhi). Why was I accepted, even though I am white, my Ladakhi is clumsy, and my family background is not Buddhist? This taught me that it was *not* simply a case of "difference" as a problem, but rather that these political issues were tied to territory itself, as well as to the colonial history of the region.

On the eve of independence, the British had drawn borders according to demographic divides to create the new nations of India, East Pakistan (today's Bangladesh) and West Pakistan. This cartography is entangled in a **reprosexual** understanding of desire, that is, an assumption that marriage, love, and/or sex, will result in having children or have reproduction as a goal (Friedman 2000; Warner 1991) layered onto a history in which religious identity has become inescapably political. Every person's body is then counted and written into religious-political and heterosexed nationhood – a nation understood in relation to heterosexuality (Nast 1998). This means that the meeting of differently marked bodies is now forbidden, and desultory teatime chatter chances on the topic of bodily rates of multiplication. Births and love affairs: read through the lens of territorial sovereignty and an uncertain future, they cannot be untangled from geopolitical strategy. In Ladakh, sovereignty can feel particularly fraught, as Ladakhis are ethnic, linguistic, and religious minorities. Many also belong to the Scheduled Tribes, that is, a recognized Indigenous category, and live in a fragile mountain environment that is inaccessible by roads most of the year.

Wedged between the conflicted borders of Pakistan and China, Jammu and Kashmir State (J&K) has been subject to territorial dispute since its inclusion in independent India in 1947. J&K consists of three regions: Kashmir valley with a Sunni Muslim majority, Jammu with a Hindu majority, and Ladakh, split between Tibetan Buddhists and (mainly Shia) Muslims. Upon India's independence, J&K was a Muslim-majority region with a Hindu ruler. Kashmir's status was complex during partition, and has been contested ever since, with the region being claimed by both India and Pakistan, its borders "lines of control" subject to a militant separatist movement since the 1990s, intensified by military and police human rights abuses. But this story is about Ladakh, which you have likely not heard of! And this formulaic description is itself a symptom of the territorialization of religion.

In Ladakh's Buddhist majority Leh district, political struggles have increasingly been voiced in the language of religious identity, culminating in the 1989 "agitation," in which the Ladakh Buddhist Association (LBA) imposed a social boycott on Ladakhi Muslims in order to get the attention of the national government (Aggarwal 2004; van Beek 2000). Buddhists were forbidden from social and economic interaction with Muslims under threat of physical coercion or monetary penalties (despite kinship and marital ties across the Buddhist–Muslim line). This action was part of an ongoing political movement in Leh district demanding independence from J&K (but not from India). In 2019, as this book is in copyedits, Ladakh has been slated to become its own Union Territory – to receive a further degree of independence from the state, in a move that is related to the national government's desire to integrate Kashmir into India (Bhan, Duschinski, and Osuri 2019; Varma 2019).

The January 2015 letter to Modi accused local Muslims of waging "love jihad": a campaign of religious conversion through marriage, in the words of the LBA secretary Sonam Dawa, "luring Buddhist girls" and converting them to Islam (Ashiq 2015; Ul-Qamrain 2015). The phrase "Love Jihad," deployed for the first time in the public record in Ladakh in 2015, has been used across India since at least 2009 to denote a supposed campaign of demographic aggression on the part of India's Muslims: conversion through inter-religious love marriages accompanied by conversion to Islam (Gupta 2009; Mohan 2011). Here, tensions over territory foster an intimate geopolitics in which the body's capacity to desire and reproduce is marshaled for the purposes of commanding and defending territory through population numbers. Buddhist–Muslim intermarriage, once unremarkable, is now forcefully prevented and Buddhist leaders claim that marriages of Buddhist women to Muslim men are part of a strategy of deliberate demographic aggression. Widely adopted in the late 1980s, many Buddhists now describe birth control as a sin, a disruption of the cycle of reincarnation, and a capitulation to the perceived threatening growth of the Muslim population. This is a struggle to manage birth, the body, and desire. The idea of a love jihad links up with a larger set of Hindu nationalist discourses of demographic decline and territorial loss going back decades (Hendre 1971), echoing partition's logic of bodies conflated with territory. Of course, it is crucial to note that these beliefs are *political*, not tied to religious doctrine for ordinary people who are Hindus! Just as with other religions such as Christianity or Judaism, people interpret their religious identity as Hindus differently, not in a uniform manner, and, naturally, many Hindus oppose this nationalist discourse.

The birth of a child contributes to territorial projects: the number of future voters, soldiers, and the demographic distribution of citizens populating and constituting state territory are determined by this complicated decision. Ethnic and religious boundaries are enforced or blurred by decisions about whom one can love or marry, and with whom one can bear children, and babies become one way to speak about the geopolitical. In other contexts, these logics have resulted in catastrophic sexual and other forms of violence. Over the course of my research, I began to understand that reproductive bodies and potential babies are caught up in geopolitical projects, as entities that can not only *be* territory, but can also *make* territory. How are political and territorial aspirations enacted and confound bodily practices? How is the geopolitical known through the body? Ladakh's pro-natal campaign and ban on inter-religious marriage exposes both the territorializing potential of bodies and the force of the body's corporeality: that is, the way that bodies *feel* has an effect on geopolitical outcomes. My research in Ladakh contributes to **feminist geopolitics**, described in the next section.

Feminist Geopolitics

Since the turn of the millennium, building on critical geopolitics scholarship, there have been calls for a wide array of approaches to geopolitics. These have included calls for anti-geopolitics or alter-geopolitics attendant to resistance and "geopolitics from below" (Koopman 2009; Routledge 2003), as well as subaltern geopolitics (Sharp 2011) rooted in the Global South. There have also been calls for emotional geopolitics (Pain and Smith 2008). In this chapter, we take up calls for feminist geopolitics (Dowler and Sharp 2001; Hyndman 2001), and attention to the global intimate (Mountz and Hyndman 2006; Pratt and Rosner 2012). This movement builds on the critical geopolitics turn of the 1990s, by treating geopolitical understandings of the world as produced knowledge/power, taking seriously the everyday lives of geopolitical practice, and questioning the lines between war and peace.

How did I arrive at this approach – one in which I asked men and women questions about their love lives and how many children they had in order to find out about questions of territory and politics? Feminist geopolitics, came to seem like the only possible approach to me when I began talking with people and learning that the ways they understood political change was often located at the level of intimate inter-personal relations. I should stress here that this is *not* a peculiarity of Ladakh! Think of how your friends and family talk about political issues – do they reference heated holiday dinners? Do they use the examples of how political changes or economic issues have impacted them personally? Have your parents or friends migrated from one place to another in search of political freedom, or survival? Have you, your parents, or your grandparents seen war or persecution? Does this shape their experience of day-to-day life? When your grandparents or perhaps even your parents were born, it is likely that there were restrictions on who they might partner with – could they or their peers easily marry someone of the same gender? Could they marry a person of a different race? Does your own sexual orientation, gender identity, or ethnicity mean that you have to navigate your daily life differently from your fellow students? Does your appearance mean you are more likely to be pulled over driving to school? Or detained for extra questions at an airport? These daily experiences are tied up in global geopolitical questions – but daily intimate experiences of violence, joy, struggle, or boredom are missing from many political theories and accounts. Why? How can we account for these?

Chapter 9 traced the ways that "classical" and strategic geopolitics both continued to play out through military strategy and practical actions by commanders and politicians while a quite different strand of critical geopolitics developed out of the impulse of scholars like Jo Sharp and Gerard O'Toal to study and unravel what kinds of world imaginaries lie underneath and uphold the state-centered world views that enable particular political strategies. You will recall the ways that these scholars argue that geopolitics is based in a kind of world-making that orders the world for action – for instance into spheres such as the "first world," or "third world," or elusive imaginaries of the Middle East – that writing about the world writes the world.

In addition to building on critical geopolitics, feminist geopolitics engages in work on embodied nationalism and bodies as a conflict space. In Luiza Bialasiewicz's (2006) compelling examination of civilizational rhetoric in the United States and Europe, she observes parallel tropes: an emergent moral geography in which immigrants are portrayed as a "demographic-reproductive menace." This narrative makes women's bodies a primary site of cultural defense. Although not necessarily relying on the language of territory, work on **embodied nationalism** touches on links between state formation, bodies treated as though they were territory, and the political use of women's reproductive bodies in particular. Research on the partition of India and Pakistan has been especially important, as scholars have painstakingly documented the logics and practices that render women's bodies a territory in dispute and put their symbolic protection ahead of their own desires (Butalia 2000; Das 1995). Post-partition, "cartographic anxiety" and patriarchal nationalism are reiterated and reinscribed in maps, landscapes, and territories that are read and made through gendered and sexualized fears and desires in South Asia and among the diaspora (Bacchetta 2000; Das 2007; Krishna 1994; Nagar 1998; Oza 2007).

Feminist Geopolitics and Scale

When you encounter **scale** in a geography text, it is often first in relation to cartography. The scale of a map of course indicates the relationship between the map you see before you and the world itself – thus one inch may be the equivalent of 500 miles or one centimeter may refer to 50 kilometers. This gives us a way to interpret the map and orient ourselves to what the map represents in the "real" world. But we also use scale to refer to the local scale, the national scale, the global scale. We do this with a sense that we know what we are referring to … but where is the global scale located? Where does it actually exist? In a landmark paper, geographer Sallie Marston (2002) argued that scale is in fact socially constructed – that it exists in our minds and in our conversations, in language that we use – and that this existence does a particular kind of work in the world. So local comes to seem small and particular, while the global scale is bigger and important. But what if we begin from a departure here and suggest that there is no global scale – *everything* happens in a particular place, which cannot be folded into a scalar umbrella. Later scholarship calls for abandoning or reconfiguring hierarchical scale in favor of understanding **relational ontologies** – a difficult phrase meaning simply the relationship of each place to all other places in a non-hierarchical way (Marston, Jones III, and Woodward 2005).

This may seem abstract! But consider for a moment that we sometimes refer to things happening on the "national stage," or "in the global arena." Now consider what we mean when we say that. Perhaps it means that the things that occurred (the signing of a treaty, a peace agreement between two countries) were broadcast around the world via television, over the internet, or through other means. Perhaps we mean that they have global importance (for instance, if world leaders agree to take stronger action to stave off the most severe impacts of global climate change). However, even if all these things are true, the events themselves are located in a particular site and embodied in not only the world leaders, but in the network of people who feed them information, take care of their health, or who gave birth to them. Even the most "global," of events is profoundly grounded and embodied. Merje Kuus (2015a; 2015b) has explored this through the diplomats and bureaucrats' style and technologies. Fiona McConnell and Elaine Ho (Ho and McConnell 2017; McConnell 2017) have traced how diasporic subjects and liminal political actors in diplomatic spaces embodied by "non-state" or non-governmental organization (NGO) actors, such as the Unrepresented Nations and Peoples Organization – a collection of stakeholders without legal state recognition or status who nonetheless take action within the UN. Let us also remember that conversations and decisions that will influence the shape of the city, where poor people live in the city, and how many police are in which neighborhoods, do not occur on a different plane of existence – they also occur in specific places (boardrooms, government offices, TV news studios) that are influenced by intimate geopolitics as well: who is in the room? Who is heard? Do the answers to these questions comprise disruption or maintenance of existing systems?

On the other end of the power spectrum, national and global policies do not take place in an abstract place known as "the global"; they are grounded in the minutia of everyday life: families detained together or children separated from their parents, people who cannot bring their life partners to live in their country of origin because of homophobic marriage and citizenship laws, farmers who can no longer farm corn because their small holdings in Mexico cannot compete with US-government-subsidized agriculture in Iowa. Let us consider two quick case studies of feminist geopolitical analysis at work before turning to a longer reflection on feminist geopolitics and corporeal modernity in Afghanistan and Honduras.

In her work in the US city of Philadelphia, Vanessa Massaro turns to the geopoliticization of intimate spaces. After spending two years doing fieldwork in the "inner city" Gray's Ferry neighborhood, a designated "Front Line" in the war on drugs, Massaro shows us how ordinary porches and corner stores are not only drug war front lines (already a military language is familiar to us). "They are also the intimate spaces of daily life in the inner city, and, while intersecting with the drug economy's reproduction, serve a far wider range of purposes" (Massaro 2015, p.370). For Massaro, paying attention to these spaces, which are both treated as "front lines" in the war on drugs, and ordinary spaces of care and relationships within the city, allows us to see the drug war differently – and teaches us that the drug war is more complicated. She argues that, "without such attention, the drug war is read as a top-down process of victimization [which is] only one piece of a much more complicated story of resistance and reworking in lived practice" (p.371). Massaro observes that residents symbolically maintain intimate public spaces as "drug corners," as part of ongoing resistance to how the drug war destroys their social networks, their means of survival, and their physical spaces.

Just as the stories of a broken marriage and policed bodies above have indicated, **feminist geopolitics** breaks down the ways we have thought of **scale.** Massaro (2015, p.371) writes that, "The city is produced in relation to multiscalar conflict, fear, and security." Politicians running for national office (the office of president, the role of Congressperson in the US context), or for seats on the city council or in the mayor's office may run campaigns saying they will be "tough on crime." City planners may envision the city as a secure space, a space of surveillance, or as a space of community and green parks. In this way, conflicts between people involved in the drug trade, their families, and their neighborhoods, are entangled in, influence, and are influenced by events in many other sites and places.

Rebecca Torres (2018) traces how US immigration policy has deepened its impacts on the intimate lives of refugees and migrants from Latin America over the course of the Barack Obama and Donald Trump eras. You will recall from our chapter on critical geopolitics, the ways that representations of space come to write space. As Alison Mountz and Nancy Hiemstra (2014) have observed, representations of the border as chaotic and migrants as a crisis have enabled security rhetoric such as we saw in the previous chapter on security. Here, too, Torres describes a border zone that has infused everyday life in the United States for migrants, who, now subject to expedited removal, are not able to access due process. As Torres notes, this expansion of deportation and subsequent reduction in access of migrants to rights that began under Obama occurred during a drastic decline and negative migration from Mexico. In particular, a "surge" of Central American and Mexican unaccompanied children in 2014 was deployed as a state of exception (Agamben 2005), enabling the expansion of homeland security state migration control.

To understand the intimately geopolitical lives of this policy for those affected, Torres volunteered with a legal aid group to interview unaccompanied Central American youth and women and children in an immigrant family detention center. Torres found that it was common for young people or children to have experienced threats and coercion; consider this story from 11-year-old Maria, who was accused of lying about her aunt's identity:

> They took us with the police and they said: tell the truth, "is she your aunt or isn't she your aunt?" Because if not, I am going to take you and put you in a dark room and I'm not going to give you anything [to eat or drink]. (Torres 2018, p.22)

Of the youth that Torres surveyed, 18% had experienced threats from Border Patrol. On the other hand, 62% had not been asked key questions that could have enabled them to pursue asylum rather than face deportation. Torres found that Mexican children in particular were not granted the care that they needed or provided the legal aid and services that might allow them to escape dangerous circumstances. Torres interviewed José, who had been conscripted into working for a crime boss in Mexico. Arriving at a migrant shelter injured in bloody clothes, under law, José should have been asked if he feared return to Mexico, and his safety should be assessed. But as Torres's research reveals, these steps are regularly not taken, so that boys like José may be returned to Mexico and be targeted by the same smugglers or bosses for violence, rather than be accepted as asylum-seekers.

As with the children, women who have faced domestic violence are also viewed with suspicion. Under the law, people who have experienced domestic violence, sexual trafficking, or sexual violence can seek residency in the United States through the Violence against Women Act, in practice, this is not always extended. Torres gives the example of Leticia, from El Salvador, fleeing domestic violence. Leticia faced a barrage of questions from the judge about her clothing and hairstyle, and was accused of lying about her injuries. Torres (2018, p.31) approaches this series of interactions through the lens of feminist geopolitics, observing;

> The issue of credibility goes beyond the ability to recount factual details, but it also involves the ability to perform – to recount experiences of trauma in a manner which a judge finds believable. Judges are not impartial blank slates. They are gendered, racialized, political, and shaped by their own life experiences. There is a corporeal dimension to credibility in legal spaces: one must embody credibility and deservingness of protection as perceived by the judge. Several attorneys, for example, mention the challenges of children and youth physically maturing during the long waits for court dates – transforming from an innocent looking young child to a more menacing adult-like teenager.

In Torres's accounting, feminist geopolitics enables us to ground our understandings of the border in the intimate nature of not only migrant experiences in courtrooms, detention centers, and at apprehension, but also allows us to see how mundane ways that officials at the border heighten everyday forms of restriction and border tightening. Her attention to the ways that those with legal standing to claim asylum are denied the right to do so and children in need of protection are made more vulnerable leads her to argue that through the actions of border officials, the state suspends refugee rights by "withholding of protection, coercion and deception, micro-aggressions, and seemingly arbitrary decision-making – actions that can have life or death ramifications," thus "Rather than protecting those most vulnerable to violence (women and children refugee/immigrants), the asylum-detention regime is producing migrant illegality" (Torres 2018, p.32). Building on Torres's use of feminist geopolitics, in the next section we turn to the ways that feminist geopolitics illuminates political processes through a focus on the body.

Feminist Geopolitics and Corporeal Modernity

In her groundbreaking work on politics in Afghanistan, Jennifer Fluri introduces the idea of **corporeal modernity.** This idea allows us to see how intimate and embodied experiences are tied to ideas about the nation and to what it means to be modern, and that, furthermore, these links have geopolitical effects. Through her analysis, we see that conversations about women's clothing are also conversations about modernity and empire, and that gender plays a role in geopolitics.

   In 1978, the People's Democratic Party of Afghanistan took over the government and began to form a communist state. This was followed by the 1979 Soviet invasion of Afghanistan, and the relatively "hot" cold war, which lasted from 1979 to 1989. During this time aid was politicized, and the Soviet Union, as they had in other satellite states, such as Mongolia, worked to centralize authority and to "nationalize" Afghan women. In the meantime, the United States, Pakistan, and Saudi Arabia were supporting Mujahidin resistance, which also involved a rhetoric of defending "homeland and women." After the fall of the Soviets in 1991 and the fall of the Najibullah regime in 1992, a civil war lasted until the Taliban takeover in 1996. This led to a new era of aid intended to influence Taliban restrictions on women. During the Taliban era, Afghanistan became a region of transnational feminist concern, with women such as Oprah Winfrey and Eve Ensler drawing attention to women's concerns. After 2001, interventions also focused on women, and the situation of Afghan women was folded into the stories that were scripted about the region (see also Abu-Lughod 2013).

   In approaching geopolitics in this region, Fluri (2011a, p.521) makes the central point that the "corporeal has represented, and continues to represent, a key site onto which, and through which, conceptualizations of 'modernity' and 'tradition' are enacted." What does she mean when she refers to "the corporeal"? Here, Fluri is referring to the body, and in particular, the ways that how women dress and behave, and the spaces that they have access to or do not have access to – the way their bodies move through and inhabit space – come to stand in for much more than individual choices and behaviors. Rather, they come to be symbolic of and stand in for something about the nation as a whole. Thus, specific political actors (for instance, after 2001, US President George W. Bush, his wife Laura Bush,

Afghanistan's President Hamid Karzai) speak to women's bodies or their burqas to say something about the country as a whole, and to place it in history. Afghan women wearing burqas come to stand in for "tradition," while women wearing other forms of dress (a business suit, a bikini, military fatigues) come to stand in for modernity. A few things are crucially at stake here.

First, these concepts – "tradition," and "modernity," ought to be carefully interrogated when we come across them. There is no place or group of people on earth that lives today as they did 100 or 500 or 1000 years ago. All cultural practices – be they language, food, clothing, or religion, change over time. So when something is described as "traditional," the first question is: which tradition? When was this tradition? Why is this time period being referenced as tradition? Whom does this benefit? These same questions can be asked when things are described as being modern, or when some places are being described as less modern than others. We are all living on the same planet and with the same timeline as a backdrop. In political action, media coverage, and certain forms of feminist intervention, women's veiling or the burqa is represented as though it is an artifact of a different era, rather than a different way of being in the world today.

Fluri's research in Afghanistan takes on these issues and draws our attention to imperial feminism – feminism that approaches from outside, that imposes a unitary idea of women's rights that is decontextualized, and has a history of supporting imperial intervention (this idea was introduced in Chapter 8). Laura Bush's support of intervention into Afghanistan is an example of this, as it uses women's issues to make an imperial argument for intervention, while also imposing an external idea of what women's liberation looks like. Beyond the way these concepts are deployed in political speeches and policy documents, for her research, Fluri travels to Kabul as part of a longer project, and observes how international men and women from Europe and North America position themselves in relation to local Afghan men and women and also to sex workers from China. In Fluri's (2011a, p.519) words, "The diversity of international workers and their complex and often paradoxical experiences situate the corporeal as a central site from which to symbolize, modify, or oppose prevailing expectations of gender geopolitics." Thus, some women who are aid workers in Afghanistan seek to "set an example" for Afghan women by refusing to cover their heads or dress in accordance with local norms, while other women working in the aid industry thought such attitudes are laughable. Compare and contrast the attitudes represented by three international women (all from Fluri 2011a, p.523):

I do not wear a headscarf because it will be harder for the women here to take theirs off if I agree to wear one. (Female aid worker, age 29, 2007)

There are two excuses for not covering. One, 'I don't want to fuss with it [headscarf], and two I must teach Afghans that not all people wear scarves.' Like Afghans don't know that. Why is this seen as an important step toward modernity while there is so much need for education and a crumbling infrastructure here? (Female aid worker, age 42, 2006)

I place an emphasis on gender not women! The life expectancy of men is 42½. It is about the same for women. It is rare to find post-menopausal women here and one in eight pregnant women will die. – Who has rights here? Women? Men? No one has rights here! (Female health worker, age 55, 2008)

Of course, it is not only women's comportment and behavior that is entangled in geopolitical scripts. International women also comment on the behavior of international men and point to both their difficulty expressing public vulnerability in a conflict setting, but also the ways that conflict and chaos excuse sexual violence against international women *and* the paradoxical setting up of brothels staffed by Chinese sex workers, adding another complex geopolitical layer. As Fluri's work shows us, an embodied and gendered reshaping of modernity and tradition is also geopolitical in its relationship to conflict zones and identity politics. International organizations in Afghanistan seek to define progress and freedom, and, "competitive and contested ideologies and identities mapped onto the corporeal situate the body as the morphological substance of gender geopolitics at multiple scales" (2011a, p.532).

More recently, Oliver Belcher (2018) uses feminist approaches to political geography to theorize why and how US counterinsurgency forces center interventions on family, home, and kinship relations, in order to "secure the intimate," in Kandahar. As Belcher describes it, military strategy revolves around and intensifies representations of local Pashtuns as "irreparably tribal," "outsiders vis-à-vis the central Afghan state," in ways that justify shows of force and the reconfiguration of the village in intimate and violent ways (Belcher 2018, p.97). Through this process:

> boundaries collapse, or are erected again in malicious ways, political power resides not merely in the relationship between governing institutions and the population. Rather, modalities of violence and power are instantiated in the material arrangements (re)established in the (re) built environments, (Belcher 2018, p.98)

Perversely, even as military interventions are signaled as masculine, national, and global in scope, they rely on renderings, readings, and strategies targeting and highlighting the intimate and familial spaces of family and kinship, and here dissolving or reconfiguring boundaries between public and private.

Fashion Politics

Let us pick up the concept of bodily politics and consider it in a quite different context and in relation to religious, economic, and political concerns. Banu Gökarıksel and Anna Secor (e.g., Gökarıksel and Secor 2010; 2012) have examined veiling-fashion in relation to body politics and **subjectivity**, or sense of self, by centering the veil and associated fashion as a lens. Gökarıksel (2012) has explored the work that the headscarf does in the urban space of Istanbul, Turkey, arguing that while it is often read as a sign of Islamism, its meanings are actually more complex and shift as a headscarf-wearing woman moves through the space of the city or is represented on a movie screen. As she writes, Muslim women's dress and the headscarf "is increasingly bound up with question of the (geo)political, regardless of its specific scripting as a sign of national culture, Islamic identity, resistance, faith, or alternatively, of an exotic or threatening 'Other'" (Gökarıksel 2012, p.1).

But, you might ask, how is the headscarf *geopolitical*? Consider a woman in front of a mirror in the morning, choosing a scarf to match her outfit, wishing the color did not clash with her handbag. Another woman in the same town, adjusting the fabric to better contain her hair, reflecting on the way the scarf has transformed her sense of self. A third woman, in a rush to make her bus, getting ready in a hurry, putting it on without thinking. Are these women engaging in geopolitical acts? How? What are the implications? Your response might be that these are personal choices, nothing to do with politics, but you might simultaneously recall that the headscarf has become part of an 'iconography of fear,' and that the *burqa* (the head-to-toe covering hijab variant of veiling practice) was deployed in media and politician portrayals of Afghanistan in the lead up to the US invasion (Abu-Lughod 2002; Gökarıksel 2012; Hirschkind and Mahmood 2002; Saktanber 2006).

In the context of Turkey, as one might expect, the meaning of the veil has taken turns and twists over the course of the twentieth and twenty-first centuries. In the early twentieth century with the birth of Turkey as a republic in 1923, veiling was associated with tradition, and the removal of the headscarf considered a move toward secular modernity, to the point that it was banned in some spaces. Following a coup in 1980, attendant political turmoil and then a rise to power of Islamically oriented political parties after 1994, contention around women's fashion shifted. Headscarf bans were more strictly enforced in certain spaces like university campuses, but new forms and styles of veiling fashion rose at the same time (Gökarıksel and Secor 2012). Gökarıksel and Secor converse with ordinary women talking about the veil and how they understand it in their lives, in the cities of Istanbul and Konya. They find that women take up the veil in ways that are contextualized in the politics of veiling, while simultaneously being about class signification, constructing a sense of self, and projection of a public self through attire. These nuances are tied up in choices of fabric, brand, and putting an outfit together, as well as decisions about whether to wear a bonnet under the scarf, a pin, and how to style your hair under the scarf.

These personal stylistic choices become political in how women talk about them with one another, and in the ways that they facilitate or complicate movement through state and military spaces. At the same time, they are part of a lucrative transnational fashion industry (Gökarıksel and Secor 2010), in which the "Islamic-ness," of the veil as a commodity is like a holograph: sometimes you see it, and sometimes you do not. So veiling fashion is political, it is economic, but it is also about women's methods for fashioning a sense of their own moral and pious selves in ways that are emotional and felt through bodies that embrace or rebel against the headscarf (Gökarıksel and Secor 2012; 2014).

In the next section, let us take this consideration of body politics into different areas of study and a different global context. Work in feminist political ecology and in decolonial feminism can enrich the perspectives outlined thus far in this chapter. To close our consideration of embodied geopolitics, let us turn here to a case in Honduras, and then shift to consider both particular and broader-sweeping arguments coming out of decolonial feminism situated in Latin America (Naylor et al. 2018; Zaragocin in press).

Feminist Approaches to Political Ecology and the Coloniality of Gender

In her long-term work on feminist political ecologies of Afro-descendant and Indigenous women's role in land conflict and development, Sharlene Mollett traces the ways that Indigenous women demand land and territorial security in Honduras (e.g., Mollett 2010; 2013; 2015).

Across Latin America, Indigenous women have led social movements for territory, and in their political analyses of the intersections of race and gender in state-based violence (Mollett 2015). Displacement from the land can occur through forced eviction and denial of land rights, but also through "displacement-in-place" (Mollett 2015, p.678), in which families are not forced off the land, but rather their livelihoods are restricted or they are coerced into selling their land. In her conversations with Miskito leaders in the National Miskito Organization, MASTA, she finds that they understand the pressure to leave their land in La Mosquitia, on the eastern coast of Honduras, as the result of a territorialized racial hierarchy that has marked the region as home to "backward Indians," (Mollett 2015, p.678). Here, we already see the beginnings of a way to conceive of this question through lenses of embodied geopolitics – as the racial processes that sort people into categories here also are tied to the land. But by working to understand how patriarchal power structures and gendered scripts play out for women in the coastal Miskito communities of the Honduran Rio Platano Biosphere Reserve, Mollett's work goes much further than this.

In the reserve, social worlds, family life, and labor, are organized in part through matrilocal house groupings and land inheritance, meaning that when men and women form a partnership, the man becomes part of the woman's family, receiving land for farming and assistance to build a house and participating in the matrilocal family group. Women practice subsistence agriculture through kitchen gardens and farming land cleared by men in the family. Increasingly, Miskito families also rely on cash income that is earned by Miskito men's labor in the nearby Bay Island lobster industry. Adding to this economic and social change, ethnically *ladino colonos* (colonists) are seeking to acquire land in the region, whether because they arrive as landless poor seeking a livelihood or because they represent themselves as such as part of "narco-grabs" in which colonists pose as poor farmers but then set up ranches that are part of cocaine trafficking and drug money laundering operations (McSweeney and Pearson 2013). Alongside these forms of land acquisition, we find the rise of state tourism, and the state's use of "exception" (familiar to us from chapters on state sovereignty and security), to enable foreign land ownership, against Indigenous protest. This has enabled increasing development in Miskito people's ancestral communal territory (Mollett 2015).

The difference represented by the terms Miskito and *ladino* is specific to the history of colonization in the region, in which part of the state project of Honduras was to develop nationalist and elite racial imaginaries that saw the country as an "indo-hispanic *mestizo* nation" (Mollett 2011, p.47). The British continued to control the Mosquitia region after Honduran independence, and the Wyke-Cruz treaty that incorporated Mosquitia into Honduras promised Miskito sovereignty. However, in the late nineteenth century state logic turned to integration, which was formalized in the 1880-1930 "Civilization Program," that classified Miskito people as racially distinct and inferior to *ladino* populations, and viewed Miskito land practices as damaging and wasteful for the nation; supposed Miskito racial differences were classified "as innate obstacles to integration" and the Miskito were declared in need of "whitening" (Mollett 2011, p.48) through the invitation of foreign-born developers. These processes were intended to make the region and its people suitable for inclusion in the idealized *ladino* or *mestizo* nation.

It is in this context, in which Miskito exist as racialized outsiders within their home territory, and *colono* outposts crop up within their lands, that tensions emerge through variations in how Miskito and *colono* occupants understand the land itself – partly in that *colonos* understand settling in the reserve to be a right, but there are other differences as well. Mollet gives the following example from fieldwork and archival sources.

> *Colono* interpretations of Miskito lands as essentially empty derive from more than a mis-read of the landscape. For example, *colonos* do not simply mis-understand the Miskito customary use of fruit trees to communicate possession. Rather, *colonos* insist the 'correct' way to communicate possession is to build a fence. Indeed, fences are a ladino cultural practice codified in agrarian law and custom in hopes of protecting a farmer's agricultural fields from cattle damage. (Mollett 2011, p.53)

From Mollett's analysis, we see that Mosquitia as territory becomes a problem to nation-building, and that this is tied to the ways that Miskito people are racialized in accordance with familiar colonial tropes. But where does Mollett's approach, grounded in feminist political ecology, take us next? Through her fieldwork in Mosquitia, Mollett demonstrates the ways that both the state of Honduras, and sometimes even Miskito men, portray Miskito women as housewives, rather than as farmers – in one narrative from her fieldwork she describes a conversation with a Miskito male elder in which they walk past women farming and bringing produce from their farms home, while he simultaneously explains to her that women do not engage in agriculture. This representation of the women as housewives enables the state to view Mosquitia as undeveloped land, primed for intervention (much like the *terra nullius* concept that we have encountered in settler colonialism). Thus gendered representations of labor (men as labor in the lobster industry, women as housewives), are central to the loss of Miskito land.

Simultaneously, Miskito women view their gendered roles as mothers as key to struggles for land, and explain this to Mollett directly: "we participate in the collective struggles for land because our children depend on our work, so does the future of the community, without it, what kind of home we will leave to our sons and daughters?" (Nanci, farmer Cocobila, Mollett fieldnotes 2011).

For Miskito mothers, "mothering through farming" is political work, and when mothers work for their children, "their politics of mothering aligns with other oppressed women's struggles around the world where women teach their children to live their lives one way and simultaneously garnish the resources for them to live it a different way" (Mollett 2015, pp.681–682; citing Collins 1990). This means that to be a mother is to transmit agricultural knowledge and thus requires access to land.

We learn from Mollett that interpretations of land use and agriculture are deeply gendered, racialized, and entangled in discourses and practices that emerged during the colonial encounter. The relationship between men and women, parents and their children, is nestled into a web of connections to locally-specific matriarchal social practices, to state ambitions to national identity and economic development, and to land, tilling, and planting, practices that are very much embodied, and intimately political.

To broaden this conversation outward, let us recall some of the foundational ideas of Maria Lugones (2010) from Chapter 8. Lugones makes a broad theoretical claim that dichotomous gender frameworks are central to the colonization of Latin America, and that gender is enmeshed in this dichotomous framework (by dichotomous, here, imagine that the male/female binary as not only a firm distinction, but in opposition: that one is the opposite of the other). Lugones's argument is quite rich but I will simplify it a bit here. She recalls for us that when colonizers arrived in the Americas, they did not view Indigenous men and women or the African men and women that they had enslaved as human beings, but rather, "as species—as animals, uncontrollably sexual and wild" (Lugones 2010, p.743). In part *through* the process of colonization, then, "The European, bourgeois, colonial, modern man became a subject/agent, fit for rule, for public life and ruling, a being of civilization, heterosexual, Christian, a being of mind and reason" (Lugones 2010, p.743), and here you will recognize echoes of Said's (1979) argument about orientalism. Within this worldview, patriarchal conceptions of gender meant that the colonizing woman was not viewed as an equal counterpart to the man, but rather, "as someone who reproduced race and capital through her sexual purity, passivity, and being homebound in the service of the white, European, bourgeois man" (Lugones 2010, p.743).

What then of the relations between Europeans, who saw themselves as human and as fit to govern and be governed, and the people they encountered, whom the colonizers viewed as animals? Lugones argues that as they justified their process of colonization, which included spectacular violence of death, torture, sexual assault, and enslavement, as one of civilization and that they simultaneously gendered the people they colonized. Gender, race, and coloniality, were thus tightly bound, and the "civilizing" process was to force the colonized into (an always subservient) humanity through their gender. By her use of the term coloniality in relation to gender, Lugones, building on the work of Quijano (1992), understands "the process of active reduction of people, the dehumanization that fits them for the classification, the process of subjectification, the attempt to turn the colonized into less than human beings" (Lugones 2010, p.745).

By colonizing, the Europeans also forced the world into their own gendered categories – so for Lugones to continue to begin from these categories of man and woman is to succumb to the colonization repeatedly. Rather, she suggests beginning from terms within Indigenous language and the cosmology in which they are rooted. Consider a story that Lugones uses to illustrate these ideas. She speaks with Filomena Miranda, who lives in La Paz but has deep ties to her home village, and then works with the terms that Miranda uses: *chacha* and *warmi*, among others, to demonstrate that while they *could* be translated in ways corresponding to gender, that would evacuate their richer and more layered meanings that are both more fluid and more enmeshed in the social and political world of community ties and *suma qamaña,* or "living well." Lugones does not advocate simply ignoring the gendering that has made the categories of man and woman common, but rather

> As I mark the colonial translation from *chachawarmi* to man/woman, I am aware of the use of man and woman in everyday life in Bolivian communities, including in interracial discourse. The success of the complex gender norming introduced with colonization that goes into the constitution of the coloniality of gender has turned this colonial translation into an everyday affair, but resistance to the coloniality of gender is also lived linguistically in the tension of the colonial wound. (Lugones 2010, p.750)

Lugones, in conversation with Mignolo's (2002) framing of colonial difference, and Anzaldúa's (1987) concept of the borderlands, proposes that we embrace a feminist border thinking. In this thinking, "the liminality of the border is a ground, a space, a borderlands, to use Gloria Anzaldúa's term, not just a split, not an infinite repetition of dichotomous hierarchies among de-souled specters of the human" (2010, p.753). As a response to the conditions of coloniality, Lugones asks us to participate in a proliferation of coalition building across and among multiplicitous and proliferating difference.

What Did We Learn and Where Do We Go From Here?

In this chapter, we have considered the ways that the embodied and intimate aspects of our lives – who we love, how we understand our gender identity, the degree to which we can protect ourselves and our children, and the clothes we wear – are entangled in geopolitical forces. Our choices and decisions enable or foreclose geopolitical worlds, but our own futures are also conditioned by the geopolitical world. In the next chapter, we will deepen this discussion through a discussion of security.

Geographer at Work: Pavithra Vasudevan

Intimacies of Race and Waste in an Aluminum Town

Pavithra Vasudevan is an assistant professor in African and African Diaspora Studies at the University of Texas-Austin. She received her PhD in Geography from the University of North Carolina at Chapel Hill in 2018.

Aluminum is everywhere in modern life – the computer I'm writing on, the building I'm sitting in, the car I drive, and my soda can are all made of aluminum. So ubiquitous is aluminum that sociologist Mimi Sheller (2014) calls it "the material of modernity." Aluminum transformed everyday life in the twentieth century, making it possible to create infrastructures and objects that were both lightweight and strong. Aluminum is the most abundant metal on the earth's surface, but it is always found mixed with other substances as bauxite ore. In the late 1800s, the development of a technology known as the Hall–Héroult process suddenly made it possible to manufacture aluminum on a large scale. However, manufacturing aluminum requires vast quantities of hydropower energy, as well as intensive physical labor that exposes workers to dangerous toxins. Who does this work? How are their lives affected by working in aluminum production?

My research focuses on people working in and living near an aluminum smelting factory. In doing so, I aim to explore how global geopolitics shape and are shaped by the everyday lives of those who make aluminum. In particular, I study "environmental racism" (Taylor 2014; see also Bullard 2008) to understand how Black communities are exposed to toxicity in places where they live and work. In the small town of Badin, North Carolina, Alcoa, Inc. (formerly the Aluminum Company of America) smelted aluminum from bauxite ore from 1916 to 2007. Established in the early 1900s for workers at the aluminum plant, Badin reflects the social and spatial dynamics of the "Jim Crow" US South, where rigid laws enforced racial segregation and allowed for the mistreatment of Black people. Reflecting this past, Highway 740 splits the town into two sections. East Badin, mostly populated by white residents, is where the town hall, library, museum and golf course are located, while West Badin, where Black residents live, has broken roads, no streetlights, and has not had Black-owned businesses for several decades. Racism is fundamentally about geopolitics: Black enclaves like West Badin are abandoned by the US state, set apart as a "sacrifice zone" (Lerner 2010) where Black people can be exploited and literally dumped on, without enforcement of laws and regulations that are supposed to protect all citizens.

Working in the US South, I found that the aluminum company used racism against Black people, or anti-Black racism, to avoid dealing with the negative externalities, or toxic waste by-products, of aluminum smelting. Until integration was legally enforced in the late 1960s, Black workers were forced to work in the most hazardous jobs in the plant. Interviewing former workers and their family members in their homes in West Badin, I learned about the "bull gang," the nickname for the job that most Black men were assigned to work: standing over the intense heat of large steel "pots" where aluminum was melted, using heavy sledgehammers to break the crust that developed over time, sweeping dust out from under the pots where fires burned, all the while breathing in toxic fumes as they labored day after day, for over ten hours without masks or protective equipment in the extreme heat, noise, and danger of the furnace of aluminum smelting.

Geopolitics in Badin was an intimate and gendered affair. Racism layered toxic waste into the bodies of Black men through their work, and traveled home with them on their clothes, to be washed by their wives with the family laundry. Former workers, many of whom are suffering from illnesses due to the decades spent working in dangerous conditions, are struggling with guilt and shame, wondering if they exposed their wives and children to lethal toxins. I realized through fieldwork that there was no clear separation of people's "private" lives, the realm of intimacy, from their public lives in the town and the company. Despite the history of government neglect and exploitation by the company, many West Badin residents are unable to speak out against Alcoa. Alcoa was a paternalistic company; they provided funding for churches, organized community picnics, and provided local high schools with basketball uniforms, claiming to care for their workers. People whose families worked for Alcoa for multiple generations feel conflicted by the loyalty they feel to the company, even though they are now more aware of how they have been negatively impacted by toxic exposure and racial discrimination.

However, intimacy has also allowed the Black community of West Badin to survive racial violence and maintain a sense of their own collective memory, absent in conventional histories and Alcoa's celebratory narratives of aluminum as a marvel of modernity. People realized that their health was being impacted as they began noticing how many family members were dying of cancers. Women who cared for male family members dying from toxicity have been speaking out and calling on others to break the silence. To support these organizing efforts and catalyze more conversation, I wrote a play, titled "Race and Waste in an Aluminum Town," based on oral history interviews and observations of community meetings. I staged the play in Badin with professional actors, as a way of validating the injustice people had experienced. In the community dialogue that followed the play, many more people spoke openly about their health concerns and how doctors did not take them seriously, how the company had hired their own environmental and health professionals to obscure the situation, and how the town council continued to ignore West Badin in support of the company. One of the most profound insights from this dialogue was learning about how West Badin's female elders had kept scrapbooks, collecting obituaries of workers who had died too young, as a way of preserving their memory and valuing those who had been forgotten in the story of aluminum. Efforts like these speak to how ordinary people make sense of geopolitics in their everyday lives and find ways to fight back.

Keywords

Corporeal modernity This idea allows us to see how intimate and embodied experiences are tied to ideas about the nation and to what it means to be modern, and that, furthermore, these links have geopolitical effects. Through her analysis, we see that conversations about women's clothing are also conversations about modernity and empire, and that gender plays a role in geopolitics.

Feminist geopolitics Feminist geopolitics builds on critical geopolitics by seeking critical analysis of how ideas and discourses create the world rather than taking them as natural, however, feminist geopolitics begins from day-to-day embodied life and attention to those who are often excluded from the study of geopolitics.

Relational ontologies The relationship of each place to all other places understood in a non-hierarchical or scalar way.

Reprosexual Understanding of sexual desire as always and naturally in relation to reproduction.

Subjectivity Sense of self created through social and political processes.

Further Reading

Feminist geopolitics
Dixon, D.P. 2015. *Feminist Geopolitics: Material States*. Farnham: Ashgate Publishing.
Dowler, L. and Sharp, J.P. 2001. A Feminist Geopolitics? *Space & Polity* 5: 165–176.
Fluri, J. 2011. Armored Peacocks and Proxy Bodies: Gender Geopolitics in Aid/Development Spaces of Afghanistan. *Gender, Place & Culture* 18(4): 519–536.
Gökarıksel, B. 2012. The Intimate Politics of Secularism and the Headscarf: The Mall, the Neighborhood, and the Public Square in Istanbul. *Gender, Place & Culture* 19(1): 1–20.
Gökarıksel, B. and Secor, A. 2010. Islamic-Ness in the Life of a Commodity: Veiling-Fashion in Turkey. *Transactions of the Institute of British Geographers* 35: 313–333.
Hyndman, J. 2001. Towards a Feminist Geopolitics. *The Canadian Geographer* 45: 210–222.
Hyndman, J. 2007. Feminist Geopolitics Revisited: Body Counts in Iraq. *The Professional Geographer* 59: 35–66.

Mountz, A. and Hyndman, J. 2006. Feminist Approaches to the Global Intimate. *Women's Studies Quarterly* 34(1/2): 446–463.

Pain, R. 2015. Intimate War. *Political Geography* 44: 64–73.

Pain, R. and Smith, S.J. 2008. Fear: Critical Geopolitics and Everyday Life. In S.J. Smith and R. Pain (eds), *Fear: Critical Geopolitics and Everyday Life*. Burlington, VT: Ashgate, pp.1–19.

Secor, A.J. 2001. Toward a Feminist Counter-Geopolitics: Gender, Space and Islamist Politics in Istanbul. *Space & Polity* 5: 191–211.

Staeheli, L.A. 2001. Of Possibilities, Probabilities and Political Geography. *Space & Polity* 5: 177–189.

Torres, R.M. 2018. A Crisis of Rights and Responsibility: Feminist Geopolitical Perspectives on Latin American Refugees and Migrants. *Gender, Place & Culture* 25(1): 13–36.

Tyner, J. and Henkin, S. 2015. Feminist Geopolitics, Everyday Death, and the Emotional Geographies of Dang Thuy Tram. *Gender, Place & Culture* 22(2): 288–303.

Feminist political ecology

Buechler, S. and Hanson, A.-M. (eds) 2015. *A Political Ecology of Women, Water and Global Environmental Change*, New York: Routledge.

Doshi, S. 2017. Embodied Urban Political Ecology: Five Propositions. *Area* 49(1): 125–128.

Elmhirst, R. 2011. Introducing New Feminist Political Ecologies. *Geoforum* 42(2): 129–132.

Mollett, S. and Faria, C. 2013. Messing with Gender in Feminist Political Ecology. *Geoforum* 45: 116–125.

Rocheleau, D., Thomas-Slayter, B., and Wangari, E. 2013. *Feminist Political Ecology: Global Issues and Local Experience*. New York: Routledge.

Sultana, F. 2011. Suffering for Water, Suffering from Water: Emotional Geographies of Resource Access, Control and Conflict. *Geoforum* 42(2): 163–172.

Sultana, F. 2015. Emotional Political Ecology. In *The International Handbook of Political Ecology*. Northampton, MA: Edward Elgar.

Sundberg, J. 2016. Feminist Political Ecology. *International Encyclopedia of Geography: People, the Earth, Environment and Technology: People, the Earth, Environment and Technology*, Chichester: John Wiley & Sons, pp.1–12.

Gendered violence and nationalism

Bacchetta, P. 2000. Sacred Space in Conflict in India: The Babri Masjid Affair. *Growth and Change* 31: 255–284.

Butalia, U. 2000. *The Other Side of Silence: Voices from the Partition of India*. Durham, NC: Duke University Press.

Chatterji, R. and Mehta, D. 2007. *Living With Violence: An Anthropology of Events and Everyday Life*. Delhi: Routledge.

Das, R. 2004. Encountering (Cultural) Nationalism, Islam and Gender in the Body Politic of India. *Social Identities* 10: 369–398.

Das, V. 1995. *Critical Events: An Anthropological Perspective on Contemporary India*. New Delhi: Oxford University Press.

Das, V. 2007. *Life and Words: Violence and the Descent into the Ordinary*. Berkeley: University of California Press.

Fluri, J. 2011. Bodies, Bombs and Barricades: Geographies of Conflict and Civilian (in) Security. *Transactions of the Institute of British Geographers* 36(2): 280–296.

Hyndman, J. and Giles, W. (eds.) 2004. *Sites of Violence: Gender and Conflict Zones.* Berkeley: University of California Press.

Jayawardena, K. and de Alwis, M. 1996. *Embodied Violence: Communalising Women's Sexuality in South Asia.* New Delhi: Kali for Women.

Krishna, S. 1994. Cartographic Anxiety: Mapping the Body Politic in India. *Alternatives: Social Transformation and Humane Governance* 19: 507–521.

Mayer, T. 2000. *Gender Ironies of Nationalism: Sexing the Nation.* New York: Psychology Press.

Nagar, R. 1998. Communal Discourses, Marriage, and the Politics of Gendered Social Boundaries among South Asian Immigrants in Tanzania. *Gender, Place and Culture: A Journal of Feminist Geography* 5: 117–139.

Nast, H. 2000. Mapping the "Unconscious": Racism and the Oedipal Family. *Annals of the Association of American Geographers* 90: 215–255.

Oza, R. 2007. The Geography of Hindu Right-Wing Violence in India. In D. Gregory and A. Pred (eds), *Violent Geographies: Fear, Terror, and Political Violence.* New York: Routledge, pp.153–174.

Roberts, D. 2014. *Killing the Black Body: Race, Reproduction, and the Meaning of Liberty.* New York: Vintage.

Sundberg, J. and Kaserman, B. 2007. Cactus Carvings and Desert Defecations: Embodying Representations of Border Crossings in Protected Areas on the Mexico-US Border. *Environment and Planning D* 25 (4): 727.

Tyner, J.A. 2009. *War, Violence, and Population.* New York: Guilford Press.

Williams, J. and Boyce, G.A. 2013. Fear, Loathing and the Everyday Geopolitics of Encounter in the Arizona Borderlands. *Geopolitics* 18(4): 895–916.

Yuval-Davis, N. 1989. National Reproduction and the Demographic Race in Israel. In N.Y. Yuval-Davis and F. Anthias (eds), *Women-Nation-State*, London: Macmillan, pp.92–109.

Chapter 12

Biopolitics and Life Itself

Have you ever made a New Year's Resolution? This is a Euro-American tradition of making a list of things to change about oneself in the coming year. As students call things out, I write on the board: "lose weight!" "Exercise more!" "Save money!" "Find a girlfriend!" I ask who has never made a resolution in their life, but these cases are rare. One year a self-described slacker in a black t-shirt covered with shiba inu dogs (from that year's "doge" meme) raised his hand: "Why should I try to change? I like myself how I am!" The class laughed, as have subsequent classes when I tell the story after everyone has called out their aspirations. Why is his disavowal of the quest for perfection consistently funny? Why have so many of these young people, most of them ages 18 to 22, resolved to transform themselves into someone with a specific body mass index, money in the bank, polite, and engaged in a (sometimes additionally heteronormatively framed) romantic relationship? But let us now pivot from personal to public governance.

Did monarchs have public health plans? Did they seek to get young people to exercise in schools? What was the point at which governance shifted from defending a defined and bounded territory through the threat of death to the management of population, with the attendant data-collection and calls into the state that this requires? What are the relationships between the ways that we are disciplined into being docile subjects and the ways that we seek to better ourselves along the lines that have been laid out for us – to be thin, fit, and

---

Political Geography: A Critical Introduction, First Edition. Sara Smith.
© 2020 John Wiley & Sons Ltd. Published 2020 by John Wiley & Sons Ltd.

successful? Some of these questions have been derived from the writings of Michel Foucault on **biopolitics** and **governmentality**. It is difficult to overstate the degree to which these related concepts have influenced the discipline of political geography, though, as we will discuss later in this chapter, there are other scholars we might turn to as well.

If governance is about the management of populations, then it also requires intense and specific forms of knowledge – both intensive (about individuals) and extensive (about populations). Bodies must be known in order to be managed, and thus they must be enmeshed in a set of disciplinary technologies of knowledge: their vital statistics, places of residence, levels of education all managed in databases in which they are both known and abstracted as individuals and as collectives. And it is of course not only the state that is engaged in these practices, but the technological mechanisms that follow us from store to store and from website to website. In class, to delight and amusement, we put on the screen the Claritas MyBestSegments website (https://segmentationsolutions.nielsen.com/mybestsegments). This website targets companies and advertisers, enabling them to look up postal codes in the United States and learn about the demographics and preferences of the populations. In class, students shout out the postal codes of their families and friends to find out how their neighborhoods are read by marketers and companies. This reveals "segments" such as "Upward Bound: Upper Mid Younger Family Mix," or "Striving Selfies: Low income middle age mostly Without Kids." Nutshell descriptions of each segment include tidbits like, "Owns a Nissan, Eats at Burger King, Shops at GameStop…" These glimpses of managed populations, like the slacker in the dog shirt, *always* generate conversation and the laughter of nervous and ironic recognition. We may laugh at the ability of a data company to "know" us through our fast food choices, but Safia Noble's (2018) book, *Algorithms of Oppression*, reminds us that simple things like Google searches recreate the biases that we have observed in day-to-day life in other spaces. Racism and sexism may be reinforced through the ways that search engines function and private interests operate. Analyzing the results that emerge for searches like "Black girls," Noble suggests that the internet does not provide us with the equal playing field that we might hope for – even as it also offers the possibility of transnational solidarity, global communication, and the flow of information.

We might also consider the ways that biopolitical ideals are caught up in the ways that people who are differently abled experience the political and cultural world. Ability/disability is called into moral judgments that are entangled in value judgments about who is deserving in society in ways that build on what we have already learned about intersectional experiences. Political geography has only recently and inadequately grappled with these questions (e.g., Mowl and Fuller 2014; Parr and Butler 1999).

In this chapter, we will consider the possibility that things like our internet searches, our New Year's resolutions, and our diets are related to the forms of self-governance that Foucault referred to as biopolitics. Beyond that, we will take a critical approach to understanding what is invested in the idea of "humanity" itself, and consider molecular and non-human geographies.

Biopolitics as a Theoretical Framework

Biopolitics refers to the set of technologies described by Michel Foucault in a series of lectures at the College of France between 1975 and 1976, now published as *Society Must Be Defended* (Foucault 2003). At the heart of Foucault's argument is a shift away from monarchical power. The will of the sovereign can be capricious, violent, and explicitly focused on the maintenance of order through defense of territory, but Foucault documents a historical shift to **biopower**. Biopower is a subtle and extensive range of technologies that operate through governmentality and the "conduct of conduct." That is, when you set your alarm early, bathe and brush your teeth, and seek to get to school or work on time to get ahead in life in the ways that are available to you, it is *not* that you do so because a police officer or soldier is at your door requiring you to comply. Rather, you yourself take pleasure in the compliance, or feel otherwise compelled to do so in order to care for yourself and your loved ones within our neoliberal society, which emphasizes personal responsibility, or you see it as a means to an end that you desire. In the words of Nicolas Rose (1996, p.41) "under conditions of advanced liberalism," the state "does not seek to govern through 'society' but through the regulated choices of individual citizens, now construed as subjects of choices and aspirations to self-actualization and fulfillment." Through this "politics of life itself," we even may care for our cells: eating superfoods, applying sunscreen, feeling guilty when we do not. In this way, we simultaneously create a sense of a future self, reduce our burden on the state, and absorb a neoliberal mindset that we are responsible for our own care: that we as individuals succeed or fail through our own willpower and discipline or lack thereof.

Foucault describes a shift occurring in Europe in the seventeenth century, in which "the ancient right to take life or let live was replaced by **biopower** power to foster life or disallow it to the point of death" (Foucault 2003, p.138). This is a new technique of power focused on bodies and population in the collective, rather than only territory, thus, power means power over life. Foucault is one of many who have examined political and economic changes during Europe's agricultural and industrial revolutions, and the resulting new ways of living, often in towns and cities Legg (2005, p.139). Disciplinary institutions – prisons, asylums, but also schools – separated out deviants, but also *created* categories of people that then belonged in these institutions. Alongside this **disciplinary power**, was the "conduct of conduct," through forms of governmentality, in which the state regulates its populations through tactics that "can range from calculations at the level of the state down to hints and guides as to how an individual should act" (Legg 2005, p.139). This form of power required an understanding of populations at the macro level – through birth rates, infant mortality, and the like (but we could think of the populations discussed earlier, who "own a Nissan," "Eat at Burger King"). "Modern European states sought to create the self-regulating subject who would vote conscientiously, invest responsibly and work diligently [Figure 12.1], while moving about and maintaining the modern city with suitable civic pride though these dream-citizens are of course always also resisting and reconfiguring these governmental webs" (Legg 2005, pp.139–140). Through statistical surveillance and regulatory mechanisms of hygiene, urban planning, and education, governments now manage populations conceived of *as* populations. This requires "statistical citizenship" (Hannah 2001), and also calls citizens into a heteronormative and reprosexual frame that is implicit in the modern census (Brown 2005; Warner 1991); that is, it normalizes heterosexual families as the center of population and governance, and assumes that through the heteronormative nuclear family, reproduction is at the heart of sexuality.

Foucault argues that population itself becomes the focus of governance: "the improvement of its condition, the increase of its wealth, longevity, health, and so on," and thus it is the population upon which government acts, directly or indirectly to encourage the birth

Figure 12.1   1929 US poster encourages hard work and industrial productivity. Reproduced with permission of Library of Congress. https://www.loc.gov/item/2010650613

rates of some and shape flows of populations into specific regions or activities (Foucault 1991; Legg 2005). This incorporates forms of disciplinary power, "anatamo-politics," in which institutional settings such as prisons teach us to be docile bodies. But biopolitical power also includes more affirmative subjectivities. We create our sense of identity and self through our actions, and work to improve ourselves (as in the New Year's resolutions), but these do not occur in a vacuum and simultaneously make us more governable.

Contemporary states include sovereign territory, and individuals both disciplined into and aspiring and working toward becoming citizens – each of us variously immersed within and reproducing these processes of power. The geographers' task is to understand the spatial processes through which this occurs – sometimes as microtechnologies but also as techniques that allow for the management of population, a scaling up.

Biopolitical Geographies

Geographers have taken up Foucault's contributions in thoughtful ways and in a wide array of contexts. In a careful and insightful historical geography of India between the two world wars, Stephen Legg (2014) shows us how the British worked to protect the vitality of British soldiers and officers by regulating prostitution – sometimes confining sex workers to certain portions of the city, sometimes regulating the bodies of the prostitutes themselves. His book, *Prostitution and the Ends of Empire*, begins with an unnamed 13-year-old girl thrown out of a window in 1930 Burma. Who was she and what became of her? Legg asks: what can we parse from her story recorded in a League of Nations report, as it is told through colonial tropes of vulnerability, rescue, and danger? Legg takes such events or the legislation meant to prevent them, and reveals how they result from a nest of networked processes including colonial governmentality, the evolving science of sex and disease, gender, and morality. As Legg demonstrates, "the national, the imperial, and the international are always experienced at the level of the body, the encounter, and the local. But this does not, for a second, diminish the power of distant geographies" (p.viii). Legg describes the **civil abandonment** of women working as prostitutes in Delhi, as well as the networked spread across British India of a series of provincial laws meant to suppress prostitution. What he means by civil abandonment is that while the British worked to protect their own soldiers, prostitutes were the population that was "let die" in Foucault's equation. The shift from the segregation of brothels to their suppression is a window into how sex and hygiene were understood by British administrators, social workers, and Indian nationalists. Legg suggests that Foucault's methodologies allow us to de-reify the relationship between sites that we might assume to be at distinct scales, that is, not to think of distinctions between empire, nation, and the body as natural, and thus to understand some of the tropes held up by colonial powers (the moral framework of empire, rule of law, the power of civil society) as they unfolded through complex and sometimes contradictory networked impulses. Legg thus both draws from Foucault but also critiques Foucault's lack of acknowledgment of empire's fundamental violence – a theme we will return to in the close of this chapter.

By pushing sex workers out of the public eye, municipal officials intended to preserve the morality of civil society, and thus to create civil society. This exiled and abandoned the prostitutes to the margins of the city. Anti-trafficking legislation moved through the provinces as a set of improvisations and experiments, with echoing concerns of male desire, protection of women, brothels as sites of contagion. Biopolitics allows Legg to describe the segregation of prostitutes as civil abandonment and the idea that empire is as much about neglect as it is about intervention, and to move back and forth between individual embodied life and spatial practices of empire.

Working at the end of the twentieth and beginning of the twenty-first century, scholars working in urban Brazil, describe these politics of neglect. João Biehl (2013, p.4) describes **zones of abandonment** in urban Brazil, places where marginalized people are abandoned by the state and social services: he asks, "how life-enhancing mobilizations for preventing and treating AIDS could take place at the same time that the public act of allowing death proliferated." Tracing the lives of patients at a clinic, in particular one woman named Catarina, at a clinic called Vita in Porto Alegre. Catarina, suffering from a host of medical issues, describes herself as forgotten, as "dead alive, dead outside, alive inside." By co-creating an ethnographic work of her abandonment, Biehl (2013, p.8) captures the lived experience of life "disallowed to the point of death," in Foucault's terms (2003, p.138). In other contexts, but relatedly, Steve Lerner (2010) has referred to places destroyed by environmental pollution as **sacrifice zones** (a concept extended through Vasudevan's "shadow geographies," in the previous chapter): places inhabited by people who are sacrificed in the name of development, a corollary to the zones of abandonment described by Biehl.

Biopolitics, Governance, and Obesity Talk

So I feel compelled to confess the reason why I am taking this class. I have struggled with bulimia for the past 5 years. The stuff that this class is dredging up for me is difficult.

Why am I taking this class? I don't give a crap about obesity. I really don't think it, in itself, is a problem. My mom's fat, she's alive. I'm incredibly thin. What I am concerned about is the stigmatization of fatness. (Students quoted in Guthman 2009, p.1100)

Crisis is inherent to capitalism: contradictions and antagonisms between capital and labor and the need for generation of surplus and the quest for new markets results in newly emergent crises. As we have discussed in earlier chapters, capitalism requires that capital be constantly in motion – the goal is not to sell the same number of shoes that you sold last year, but to sell more, with a greater profit margin on each, and to more people, in more places! From the perspective of capitalist expansion, it is important to find spaces for profit at each step – from the financial industry that loans the capital to the ships that carry the goods to the insurance companies that sell insurance to the workers on those ships. This is one of the starting points for a key set of theories of Marxist geography – the idea of the **spatial fix** (Harvey 1982; 1989) suggests a geographic mechanism through which capital sustains itself: by turning to new geographies of accumulation. Under the neoliberal turn after the economic crisis of the 1970s, the economic crisis, felt in the United States in falling manufacturing profits and fast rates of inflation, generated a rapid turn to increasingly neoliberal forms of governance such as the withdrawal of state services and turn to globalization as the spatial fix. This meant that the standard of living in wealthy places could be sustained through the use of cheap labor that also enabled greater consumption – the "commodification of everything." But what does that have to do with the reflections on body image at the beginning of this section?

The two quotes above are taken from Julie Guthman's (2009) writing on biopolitics, obesity, and teaching. Guthman writes about teaching a small undergraduate course in the US West Coast on "The Politics of Obesity." This research is embedded in the US context, though related, but context specific, work can be found globally in sites from India (Solomon 2016) to Mexico (García-Deister and López-Beltrán 2015). Through her larger research project and experiences of teaching the course, she finds that obesity talk today is embedded in "neoliberal rationalities of self-governance, particularly those that couple bodily control and deservingness" (2009, p.1111), such that *even* very critically aware and thoughtful students struggle to untangle these ideas – that fat is a moral failure of bodily control – from their thinking. Considering how fat becomes a question of morality allows us to see that biopolitical governance extends even to the views we have of our own bodies. This conversation is part of an emergent literature in geography on fatness and food politics. Rachel Colls has developed a critical geography of fatness, encompassing both the spatial experience and materiality of fat as well as the associated governmentalities and politics. Hayes-Conroy and Hayes-Conroy (2008; 2013) have written about food and the body as a form of visceral politics. Rachel Slocum (2008), Ashanté M. Reese (2018; 2019), and others have considered food and race through corporeal feminist theory and Black Geographies.

Public health has been concerned with body weight for some time, but Guthman and DuPuis (2006, p.428), point to the rather different language emerging around the end of the twentieth century – language describing obesity as an epidemic, and then suggesting a particular and specific cause: mothers who work, fast food, television, sloth. First, Guthman and DuPuis wish us to question the kinds of work and politics that words like epidemic and crisis engender. They ask us to move from asking, "Why have US consumers come to eat endless amounts of fatty and calorie-laden food?" to asking "what is it about the contemporary period that has made obesity a social problem of such gargantuan proportions in the United States?" By doing so, they move away from the individual choice implicated in the first question, and to move toward approaches that do not seek a simple or singular cause or solution. Instead, they suggest to us that "neoliberalism both produces obesity and produces it as a problem. As a consequence the obesity debate itself creates impossible, unachievable standards for economic, biological, and political competence in today's world, privileging a few and leaving the rest to their couch-potato doom" (Guthman and DuPuis 2006, p.429). Here, Foucault's distinction between those whose lives are fostered and those who are allowed to die are replicated in the distinction between the fit and successful subject and those of us consigned to "couch-potato doom."

One way to learn about food and obesity is to do a little experiment. Give five people one US dollar (or the local equivalent) and set them on a mission to buy as many calories as they can with that dollar. Do you want to win? Buy processed fat-based foods: a giant bag of off-brand Oreo cookies from the Dollar Store, a pound of plain lard from the grocery store. So one answer here is that if we think about what it is like to be poor and need to fill your stomach for a hard day of work, your options are not likely to be healthy ones. The dollar challenge demonstrates the difficulty of eating healthfully through the exaggerated performance of the ways that the market (and in the case of the United States, farm subsidies) makes it easier and cheaper to fill up on food that isn't necessarily the healthiest. Though it is hardly health food, a hamburger on a dollar menu is a very practical and efficient use of dollars for calories. Thus, if we want to explain obesity, we might look to the (itself political) food system, which in the United States and many other places makes it cheaper to get full from Twinkies than from carrots (Pollan 2007). This of course is a supply-side explanation. Other explanations could be simply that changes in lifestyle mean that our taste for food, particularly calorie-dense food, simply is too much for the ways that we live today. That is, "Eating is pleasurable. We like food; it is yummy," (Guthman and DuPuis 2006, p.431) and our bodies are very good at storing fat – something that no longer is as necessary to extending our lives but rather can become a liability. We could also think of the ways that our fast paced and often anxious ways of living make a pack of Cheetos and a pint of ice cream a quick fix for a bad day at work, particularly when we do not have the political agency to change our working conditions.

Of course another approach, which has further developed in recent years is a cultural and feminist analysis that says it is not obesity that is the problem but rather its stigma. In this case, we might approach the politics of obesity by problematizing the idea of obesity itself – suggesting that ideal body types are not only based in objective assessments of health, that measures like Body Mass Index are misleading, that diet interventions can do more harm than good, and that thinness is premised on self-denial (Evans and Colls 2009). As they put it, here, one point of emphasis is how people come to discipline themselves by fearing fatness (Guthman and DuPuis 2006).

Guthman and DuPuis describe these three ideas as, "it's the economy, stupid," "it's only natural" and "it's the politics of exclusion." While each idea may contain a partial explanation, they also tend toward simplification: in the first, appetite is portrayed as a symptom of capitalism, and the complicated politics of the food supply are omitted. In the second, we must question what is "natural," and how that can be uniform across difference, and also how to then fight "nature" – this becomes an individual-problem, which you must overcome through stoic management of your own desire (we will return to this idea). When it comes to the politics of exclusion, Guthman and DuPuis agree to some extent with the assessment: that naming the problem of obesity is also generative of the problem (and here, they are drawing on Stoler's (1995) reading of Foucault (1978b) – the primary idea being that the repression of desire is a solicitation for desire to emerge and proliferate. That is, "proscriptions about food make us obsess about food" (Guthman and DuPuis 2006, p.436): we go on a diet and immediately crave all the food that we have just forbidden to ourselves. *And yet*, Guthman and DuPuis also bring up the idea of "revolting bodies," (LeBesco 2004) – the idea that while the fat acceptance movement is a meaningful way for many people to abandon or refuse societal expectations, it misses the political critiques of the food system and also forecloses other possibilities. That is, not only is the question of fatness relegated to the individual, but then, "in the move to absolve the individual eater of responsibility, we are faced with an untenable polarity: fat people are stripped of their subjectivity while thin people appear to at least have the possibility of exercising a choice" (Guthman and DuPuis 2006, p.435; LeBesco 2004).

What if, then, *our own bodies* have become a spatial fix for the latest crisis of capital? That is, cheap fast food is an ideal fix – involving both high profit margins and an outlet for surplus food, *and* a complementary set of commodity-based solutions that are also quite profitable. Think here of weight-loss frozen dinners, gym-memberships, and new innovations, such as "food products that do not act like food" like artificial sweeteners that pass through the body. Our bodies thus are a new geography of capital – a space for consumption both through eating and through dieting: "by thwarting the body's metabolizing functions, these products allow producers to sell much more of these products per person, ultimately speeding up the circulation of capital … This double fix of eating and dieting … has become a central piece of the US economy" (Guthman and DuPuis 2006, p.441).

What is neoliberal and biopolitical about the circulation of capital through the food system and our bodies? There are many interconnected ways this plays out on a neoliberal stage – on the one hand, the commodification of everything means the increasing reach of capital into new spaces (here, not only the body, but even our sense of self – our **subjectivity**) is implicated in capitalist processes, through our relationship to what we eat and the effect it has on our bodies. If we take Foucault's arguments about the subject seriously, in fact, our subjectivity is a residue of these above processes. The neoliberal form of political economy within which we find ourselves simultaneously is the milieu in which we engage in the **government of the self**: we cultivate our sense of ourselves as individuals in part through our participation in the market.

What then do we do with this knowledge? As Guthman (2007) says elsewhere, engaging with critiques of the food system that emphasize our incapacity to resist a troubled and inescapable consumption-based economy selling us sugar and fat may perversely leave us so frustrated that we turn to Cheetos. Guthman and DuPuis ask us to keep both the pressures of the food system and the biopolitical urge to govern ourselves as good subjects in mind, and, hence, to resist both through our own bodies and by engaging in the political system.

Let us take a turn from this review of the causes of obesity and its framing as a public health problem to the experience of managing our own bodies, and the rather more complicated set of concerns and pleasures that brings up. Also engaging with Foucault, and in a set of arguments that are premised upon his biopolitical work, Robyn Longhurst writes a first person analysis of what it is like to "become smaller" (Robyn Longhurst 2012; in conversation with Heyes 2006; Murray 2008) – her reflections move us from the sphere of the neoliberal economy of food production to the embodied experience of biopolitics. This reflection comes after a period of losing weight, and follows up on her earlier work (Longhurst 2005; 2012, p.876) in which she interviewed women in Hamilton, New Zealand who "self-identified as fat, large, big, overweight or obese." In her analysis of these interviews, Longhurst finds, and also recognizes herself in, expressions of shame, disgust, humor, and courage. Longhurst in turn writes a strikingly autobiographical reflection on her process of losing weight – which is imbued with biopolitical themes in that her own body is part of a set of subject-making power struggles, in which she "wrestle[s] with critiquing discourses around women and slimness while desiring to be slim" (Longhurst 2012, p.877).

Because of Longhurst's commitment to an autobiographical approach, she tells us (and we may well relate to) the sense of governance and bodily discipline that accompanies dieting: packing a lunch for a child and not eating a scrap of leftover cheese from a sandwich, weighing herself every day, monitoring each thing that she eats. Drawing on Heyes (2006; Longhurst 2012), she sees herself investing in her own "docile body," (Foucault 1978a). Longhurst's self-reflections also identify the kind of biopolitical willpower that Guthman attributes to Pollan – the kind of willpower that makes Guthman wish to eat Cheetos. Longhurst (2012, p.881) both enjoys the pleasures afforded by "fierce determination, bodily vigilance and will power," but also feels left out and that perhaps she has "sold out": she finds her position to be paradoxical, and likewise, paradoxically entangled in Foucault's concepts of biopolitics and **care of the self** – that is, the ethics of care directed toward our own subjectivity. In her own experience she recognizes both a sense of human possibilities in her management of her own body, asking: do we really choose our own aspirations? Or are they determined for us? Here, too, we might consider the built environment. How our cities and towns are (or are not) designed so that we can move through them without a car, how we can (or cannot) find fresh and healthy food in our neighborhood, and how we do (or do not) spend most of our time traveling from home to work, to children's schools, under considerable time pressure, and can or cannot afford a small garden or have time to travel to a community garden.

We can understand biopolitics through food consumption and the politics of fat. On the one hand, we become subjects through food – our definition of self is in part defined by what we eat – think of the supposed affinity of millennials and generation z for consuming avocados and documenting this love on Instagram. Simultaneously, neoliberalism calls for control and self-regulation: we either manage our own bodies efficiently or become targets of intervention due to our inability to do so. Think of, for instance, the idea that health insurance companies might give you discounts for stopping smoking, visiting a doctor, or losing weight. Guthman and Dupuis (2006, p.443, citing Foucault's *History of Sexuality* [Foucault 1978c]) describe the relationship this way:

> Foucault describes how biopower emerged with the industrial revolution, which required able-bodied workers. It involved the penetration of social and self-disciplinary regimes into the

most intimate domains of modern life, including the body. With the emergence of biopower, the "population" (along with the self) became a thinkable unit of regulation and intervention, as government increasingly intervened on behalf of improving biological vitality.

The measurement of success in these terms is public health statistics that measure and assess populations – but through these measurements we each as individuals also find ourselves compelled to compare ourselves. The language of the "obesity epidemic" (much like the carceral form of the prison discussed in the chapter on security) thus disciplines us all, and furthermore, "neoliberal governmentality produces contradictory impulses such that the neoliberal subject is emotionally compelled to participate in society as both out-of-control consumer and self-controlled subject. The perfect subject-citizen is able to achieve both eating and thinness, even if having it both ways entails eating nonfoods of questionable health impact (Splenda) or throwing up the food one does eat" (Guthman and DuPuis 2006, p.444). Many may also recognize here gendered resonance in the ways that women in many contexts are expected to adhere to standards of beauty and a specific body type, but simultaneously hide the labor required to achieve these targets: the no-makeup makeup look, the supermodel who loves cheeseburgers. You may also recognize a politics of difference – that thinness is now associated with wealth in many contexts, and that health interventions often reference specific racialized populations. Thinness is spreading as a global standard into places that had valued chubbiness.

Because thinness demonstrates our capacity for self-restraint in a world of cheap Twinkies, it is also a sign that we are a deserving subject. If we take these messages seriously then we must take care to pay attention to what the project of the "obesity epidemic" does to us and to others, both by paying attention to the agricultural politics and the capillary power (the ways that power comes to be not a top-down phenomenon but one that we ourselves engage in at the level of individual bodies and through interpersonal relationships).

In teaching her course, Guthman finds that the students at her institution – the University of California at Santa Cruz – are quite prepared to critique the ways that obesity is represented in shows like *The Biggest Loser* (a US TV show in which teams and individuals compete to lose weight), and yet they are frustrated in the classroom. Over the course of her class, one group of students gets increasingly angry at the suggestion that someone can be both healthy and fat, and other students are drawn into an ongoing conflict that students reflect on in their journals. Other students found it traumatic to have to talk about bodies and body size in the classroom, or expressed confusion about why thin people and the thin teaching assistants expressed support for fatness. One student writes:

> I've never been in class where people had so many opinions of the subject! It's weird but I've never realized obesity was such an emotional issues. It is so political – but not just for fat people … I mean most of the people in this that have strong viewpoints aren't themselves fat, but I get the feeling that they are anti-fat. But why do fat people make people mad? (Guthman 2009, p.1121)

What Guthman finds is that even critical, "overtly anti-corporate," students surprise her with the degree to which in the case of obesity they turn to a neoliberal narratives of personal responsibility, rather than the political economy critiques she had seen students evoke in response to other critical issues. Students embrace their own identities in ways that are entangled in successful management of their bodies. For these students, fatness seemed to be a "*choice* to disregard the rules," and it was hard for them to express empathy for people who could not succeed as thin neoliberal subjects. Let us now turn from biopolitics in relation to body size to how we might employ biopolitics to understand security.

Bombs and Microbes: Biopolitics in the Security State

The biopolitical pervades the fabric of our daily life. Lauren Martin shows us how biopolitics operates at the US airport, and suggests that contemporary biopolitical management is premised on avoiding risk and preemption: knowing who will be dangerous before they become dangerous. Martin (2010) explores the common rule against making bomb jokes in the airport security line, which makes the bomb joke itself a threat. How is the regulation of joking a biopolitical mechanism through which airline passengers are placed in relation to the mechanisms of state security, here, agents of the Transportation Security Administration? Martin tells us: "bomb jokes present two meanings simultaneously: I have three bombs/I don't have three bombs; I have anthrax/I don't have anthrax; we must be terrorists/we cannot be terrorists" (Martin 2010, p.27). Through embodied performance – that is, through how we tell these jokes (our tone of voice, our gestures, our stance) – we declare threat, or we declare innocence. When we attempt to joke about having a bomb, we are suggesting that we are the kind of person no one would believe has a bomb (Martin 2010, p.28). In this (un)thought process, we have already acknowledged that we live in a security state, that we are/are not potential terrorists, that we are neurotic citizens seeking absolution and extended national belonging. Martin's points are made in the context of a broader discussion of biopolitics and security, some of which you are already familiar with – for instance the preemptive securitization of bodies outside national borders (Adey 2009; Amoore 2006). Martin argues that while some have said new security practices are a break with earlier forms of state power (discipline, sovereignty, government), Foucault's (2007) formulation actually allows for multiple forms to be braided together through bureaucratic practices, that "make 'the living of life' the object of government. Thus, it is not that the disciplinary focus on the making of whole, discrete subjects fades entirely, but that it is recalibrated to the production of healthy species-beings" (Martin 2010, p.30).

Bridging points between the body biopolitics made by Guthman, previous section, and Martin's work on securitization, Jenna Loyd (2009) writes about how health can be militarized at the microbial level through her research on a 2007 cholera outbreak in Iraq. Formulations opposing health to violence obscures their co-articulation, and allows health to be part of geopolitical strategy and legitimate specific forms of violence (Loyd 2009; Ingram 2005). In this analysis, which runs alongside but is distinct from the framework of biopolitics, Loyd evokes **structural violence**. In naming structural violence she points to how "social forces ranging from poverty to racism become *embodied* as individual experience" (Farmer 2003, p.30), yet this violence cannot be understood at the individual level, because premature deaths due to, for instance, racism (Gilmore 2002) become visible only through analysis at the level of the population. Cholera epidemics are a signal of poverty and vulnerability, and historically appear alongside colonial wealth extraction; in Iraq, the US invasion and occupation resulted in a 2007 cholera epidemic, the invasion and occupation of course being laid upon already existing vulnerabilities created by the Hussein regime.

Loyd asks us to consider peace and violence, war and health, on spectrums and in relation to one another, both affirming and complicating the biopolitical schema of making live/ allowing death.

Before, Alongside, and Beyond Biopolitics

While Foucault's theorization provides us with a promising way to think about body politics, can we proceed from the assumptions that he lays out for us? Foucault's work assumes there is a category of humanity that is accessible to everyone. Yes, he unravels this by demonstrating the normalization of bodies, and in his other work unpacking the ways that criminals, sexual deviants, and people with differing mental capacity are enlisted in these normalizing projects. But can Foucault's biopolitics really help us understand the death-dealing differential life prospects meted out by racialization (Gilmore 2002)? The Black Lives Matter movement in the United States is fundamentally a movement against biopolitics as we know it within our currently existing racial structures. The movement began as response by Alicia Garza, Patrisse Cullors, and Opal Tometi to the July 2013 acquittal of unarmed 17-year-old Trayvon Martin's vigilante killer in Florida. In 2014, Black Lives Matter protests gained the silent "hands up, don't shoot" gesture in reference to the August 2014 fatal shooting of unarmed teenager Michael Brown in Ferguson, Missouri, by a police officer subsequently acquitted by a grand jury. That same 2014 winter, a New York City policeman was acquitted by a grand jury despite videotaped evidence of the July 2014 choking of Eric Garner, and t-shirts worn at protests and at sporting events called us to remember Garner's last words: "I can't breathe." In each case, the loss of a young black man's life was followed by a second symbolic death, in the highlighting of the victim's supposed flaws and mistakes and the subsequent failure to hold anyone accountable for the death. A growing litany of these police killings was then given intersectional nuance by #SayHerName, a recounting of Black female, queer and trans victims who had not only been subject to violence but then omitted from the public recounting. The names of Sandra Bland, Renisha McBride, Tamir Rice, Walter Scott, Freddie Gray, Philando Castile, and too many others signal particular lives valued and mourned, but also indicate a repetition and wearing down of life. In Foucault's terms, they demonstrate a profoundly racialized difference in whose life is fostered and whose life is "disallowed to the point of death" (this section is drawing from Smith and Vasudevan 2017)

In *Habeas Viscus*, Alexander Weheliye raises critical questions about the limits of biopolitics. Weheliye observes that even as Foucault describes his theories of biopolitics in relation to racism, he naturalizes race rather than consistently and critically interrogating it. Weheliye draws on Black feminists Hortense Spillers and Sylvia Wynter to argue that Foucault's theories of biopolitics do not adequately speak to "how deeply anchored racialization is in the somatic field of the human" (Weheliye 2014, p.4). You will recall that Weheliye argues that while Foucault's theory of biopolitics is picked up to analyze everything from airports in global settings to race and prison in the United States, the work of Black feminists such as Spillers and Wynter is "ethnographically detained," that is, because their knowledge emerges in part from embodied and fleshy experience, it is judged to be specific to particular populations and places, never to stand in for the knowledge of humanity itself. This is a great loss, as their work demonstrates that rather than assume the possibility of a

Political Geography: A Critical Introduction

universal category of human, the history of race demonstrates that the functioning of white racism has made a universal category of human impossible. Thus, we ought to keep the critiques presented in Chapter 8 with us when we pick up biopolitics as a frame, and consider the question we have turned to before: what does this framework enable? What does it render invisible? How can we put it in conversations with others who are interested in similar questions but from quite different perspectives?

Other Governed Bodies

Foucault's writings can be placed in conversation with others who tried to understand the workings of government through individuals. In the context of the spreading state form in British India as Indian Nationalists fought for independence, Mohandas Gandhi similarly worked to understand government as working most perfectly through self-government. Though he was envisioning this as a state of perfection, while Foucault was working from a critical angle, their renderings of population are quite similar. While Foucault envisions us as self-disciplining (but simultaneously always resisting) prisoners, always governing and surveilling ourselves, Gandhi, 50 years earlier in the 1930s envisioned an India in which "national life becomes so perfect as to become self-regulated, no representation becomes necessary … In such a state every one is his own ruler…" (Gandhi 1931, p.91). In these and other reflections, in particular in Gandhi's *Hind Swaraj* (1938), he presages the ways that Foucault's concepts of governmentality seeks to manage a population not only as "the collective mass of phenomena," but also "in its depths and its details" (Foucault 1991, p.102). Whether framed as call to progress, or critique of modernity and the British Empire, nationalist writing in South Asia in the first half of the twentieth century addressed a series of problems central to the form of the modern state. How is the relationship between the state and its citizens to be constituted? What is the role of the state in providing for the welfare of its citizens? These questions are neither spatially nor temporally limited to the early-twentieth-century South Asian context: they remain today, arising in discussions about the dismantling of the welfare state, immigration, the place of religion within the state, and the regulation of corporations after neoliberal reform. Even if it is not explicitly outlined, these writings, and the questions they engender, contain an understanding of the state as both product and producer of the human subject. For Gandhi, "a people has the government which it deserves. In other words self-government can only come through self-effort," and this self-effort is inseparable from Gandhi's values of chastity, self-control and moral development (1958, Vol. 28, p.109). Hence, "political government, that is, self-government for a large number of men and women, is no better than individual self-government or self-rule, and therefore it is to be attained by precisely the same means that are required for individual self-government or self-rule" (Gandhi 1938) (1958 Vol 32, p.294).

When Gandhi compares self-government with self-rule, he is pronouncing a judgment on India as a mass of individuals, and as a population. In 1908, he finds India to be "emasculated and cowardly," inviting British rule through their greedy materialism, which he would have them discard because "Civilization in the real sense of the term, consists not in the multiplication, but in the deliberate and voluntary reduction of wants" (Gandhi 1938, p.38). To attain both self-government and self-rule requires discipline, self-sacrifice, purity, and moral education. Gandhi describes this through writing structured as questions and answers, focusing on the cultivation of an ethical self.

Q. What is your goal in education when India obtains self-rule?
A. Character-building. I would try to develop courage, strength, virtue, the ability to forget oneself in working toward great aims. This is more important than literacy, academic learning is only a means to this greater end. (Washburne 1932, pp.104–105)

For Gandhi, we must control those boundaries through self-sacrifice and austerity. These nationalist projects dovetail with what Foucault describes as the problem of subjectivity and truth:

The procedures, which no doubt exist in every civilization, suggested or prescribed to individuals in order to determine their identity, maintain it, or transform it in terms of a certain number of ends, through relations of self-mastery or self-knowledge … What should one do with oneself? What work should be carried out on the self? How should one "govern oneself" by performing actions in which one is oneself the objective of those actions, the domain in which they are brought to bear, the instrument they employ, and the subject that acts? (Foucault 1997, p.87)

These problems are at the heart of the relationship between state and subject.

"We Are Not Animals" Dehumanization, More-than-humanness, and the Struggle to Think Beyond the Human

Since the NATO-led bombing of Libya and the fall of Muammar Gaddafi in 2011, the municipal zoo in Tripoli has been closed to public visitors and put to a different use: it is now a migrant processing center. While the capital city has twenty-two permanent processing centers, in recent years these are reported to have exceeded their capacity and each day the zoo receives on average twenty 'irregular' migrants destined for the European Union (EU), typically from Ghana, Nigeria, and Chad. (Vaughan-Williams 2015, p.1 citing; Stephen 2013)

In the theorization of Spillers, Wynter, and Weheliye earlier in the chapter and in Chapter 8, epistemic, or world-making, violence occurs historically in the definition of the human. That's quite a mouthful of a sentence, let us unpack it. These theorizations ask us to consider that certain forms of violence shape the world itself, through, for example, the creation of an idea of race that relies upon a division, or spectrum from human to non-human. You will recognize here also resonance with Fanon's (2008) ideas regarding the ways that white civilization requires the Black other, against which to define itself, and Said's (1979) conception of the Orient as an imaginative geography that creates Europe. This echoes the consideration of gender and coloniality that we encountered in the work of Lugones (2010) in Chapter 10, which demonstrates how categories of human existence were woven into the fabric of settler colonialism in Latin America. We see parallel but also complex and fraught ways that this conversation pertains to the dehumanization of undesired categories of people – the people whose life, in Foucault's terms, is not to be fostered, and thus, who are portrayed as, or treated as, less than human. This invites us to consider the definition of the human, but also, and here we run into particularly fraught and contested territory, the possibility of understanding the world differently by trying to unravel human/non-human binaries or human/non-human relationships as a naturalized hierarchy. Let us consider the work of dehumanization and think of how we can grapple with this political work when we encounter it.

A 2015 article on EU border security begins with the abrupt and instantly evocative phrase, "We are *not* animals!" (Vaughan-Williams 2015). In this research, Nick Vaughan-Williams traces how irregular migrants in spaces of detention are frequently described through the use of animalized metaphors, and that contemporary carceral spaces produces "animalized subjects." Migrants housed in a zoo, sleeping on the floor, and enduring human rights abuses, reflects on the one hand a disturbingly topsy-turvy world in which migration control has been off-shored in the ways outlined in Chapter 10 on security, and then, further, out-sourced and rendered extra-territorial (Vaughan-Williams 2015; see also Bialasiewicz 2012). Vaughn-Williams argues that this placement of human beings in a zoo is not merely a happenstance result of chaos, but rather that thousands of "irregular" migrants currently inhabit zoo-like spaces across the Mediterranean (Vaughan-Williams 2015; citing Frontieres 2013; Borderline Europe 2013).

What Did We Learn and Where Do We Go From Here?

In the last few chapters, our attention has been drawn closer and closer in to the human body. Here, we have worked to understand how the management of bodies through biopolitics constitutes a form of governance that takes a wide array of forms. Thus, our own investment in managing our own body, or our self-governance under the observation of the airport security line, become part of the broader management of populations. As we turn to the last chapter of this book, we will reverse this trajectory and consider ourselves in relation to the Earth and to the future.

Keywords

Biopower and biopolitics   Biopolitics is the subtle and extensive range of technologies that operate through governmentality and the "conduct of conduct." Biopower is the technologies to use the biological substance and inclinations of bodies.

Care of the self   Care of the self is the idea that we cultivate an ethics of care toward fostering our own subjectivity. This could be part of governmentality.

Civil abandonment, zones of abandonment   Civil abandonment is the withdrawal of care to specific segments of society. Similarly, zones of abandonment are places where marginalized people are abandoned by the state and society.

Disciplinary power   Disciplinary power refers to the "conduct of conduct," ways that the state regulates its populations through tactics.

Governmentality   Governmentality is the ways that power functions by having people self-govern, rather than through coercion.

Government of the self   Government of the self describes how we cultivate our sense of ourselves as individuals in part through our participation in the market.

Further Reading

Biopolitics and geography

Coleman, M. and Grove, K. 2009. Biopolitics, Biopower, and the Return of Sovereignty. *Environment and Planning D: Society and Space* 27(3): 489–507.

Crampton, J.W. 2007. "The Biopolitical Justification for Geosurveillance. *Geographical Review* 97(3): 389–403.

Daley, P. 2013. Rescuing African Bodies: Celebrities, Consumerism and Neoliberal Humanitarianism. *Review of African Political Economy* 40(137): 375–393.

Dillon, M. and Neal, A. 2015. *Foucault on Politics, Security and War*. Cham: Springer.

Elden, S. 2016. *Space, Knowledge and Power: Foucault and Geography*. New York: Routledge.

Foucault, M. 1991. Governmentality. In G. Burchell, P. Miller, and C. Gordon (eds) *The Foucault Effect: Studies in Governmentality*. Chicago: University of Chicago Press, pp.87–104.

Foucault, M. 2003. *"Society Must Be Defended": Lectures at the College de France 1975–1976*. Trans. D Macey. New York: Picador.

Hannah, M.G. 2000. *Governmentality and the Mastery of Territory in Nineteenth-Century America*. Cambridge: Cambridge University Press.

Legg, S. 2005. Foucault's Population Geographies: Classifications, Biopolitics and Governmental Spaces. *Population, Space and Place* 11: 137–156.

Lerner, S. 2010. *Sacrifice Zones: The Front Lines of Toxic Chemical Exposure in the United States*. Cambridge, MA: MIT Press.

Minca, C. 2015. The Biopolitical Imperative. In J.A. Agnew, V. Mamadouh, A.J. Secor et al. (eds), *The Wiley Blackwell Companion to Political Geography*. Chichester: John Wiley & Sons, p.165.

Moulton, A.A. and Popke, J. 2017. Greenhouse Governmentality: Protected Agriculture and the Changing Biopolitical Management of Agrarian Life in Jamaica. *Environment and Planning D: Society and Space* 35(4): 714–732.

Rose-Redwood, R.S. 2006. Governmentality, Geography, and the Geo-Coded World. *Progress in Human Geography* 30(4): 469–486.

Sparke, M. 2006. Political Geography: Political Geographies of Globalization (2)-Governance. *Progress in Human Geography* 30(3): 357–372.

Food geographies

Heynen, N., Kurtz, H.E., and Trauger, A. 2012. Food Justice, Hunger and the City. *Geography Compass* 6(5): 304–311.

McCutcheon, P. 2015. Food, Faith, and the Everyday Struggle for Black Urban Community. *Social & Cultural Geography* 16(4): 385–406.

McCutcheon, P. 2019. Fannie Lou Hamer's Freedom Farms and Black Agrarian Geographies. *Antipode* 51(1): 207–224.

Reese, A.M. 2018. "We Will Not Perish; We're Going to Keep Flourishing": Race, Food Access, and Geographies of Self-Reliance. *Antipode* 50(2): 407–424.

Reese, A.M. 2019. *Black Food Geographies: Race, Self-Reliance, and Food Access in Washington*. Chapel Hill: University of North Carolina Press.

Slocum, R. 2008. Thinking Race through Corporeal Feminist Theory: Divisions and Intimacies at the Minneapolis Farmers' Market. *Social & Cultural Geography* 9: 849–869.

Slocum, R. and Saldanha, A. 2016. *Geographies of Race and Food: Fields, Bodies, Markets.* London: Routledge.

Trauger, A. 2015. *Food Sovereignty in International Context: Discourse, Politics and Practice of Place.* London: Routledge.

Williams, B. 2018. "That We May Live": Pesticides, Plantations, and Environmental Racism in the United States South. *Environment and Planning E: Nature and Space* 1(1–2): 243–267.

Geographies of body size

Colls, R. 2012. Big Girls Having Fun: Reflections on a "Fat Accepting Space." *Somatechnics* 2(1): 18–37.

Colls, R. and Evans, B. 2009. Introduction: Questioning Obesity Politics. *Antipode* 41(5): 1011–1020.

Evans, B., Crookes, L., and Coaffee, J. 2012. Obesity/Fatness and the City: Critical Urban Geographies." *Geography Compass* 6(2): 100–110.

Hopkins, P. 2008. Critical Geographies of Body Size. *Geography Compass* 2(6): 2111–2126.

Hopkins, P. 2012. Everyday Politics of Fat. *Antipode* 44(4): 1227–1246.

Hopkins, P. 2019. Social Geography II: Islamophobia, Transphobia, and Sizism. *Progress in Human Geography*, 1–12

Lloyd, J. 2014. Bodies over Borders: The Sized Body and Geographies of Transnationalism. *Gender, Place & Culture* 21(1): 123–131.

Longhurst, R. 2005. Fat Bodies: Developing Geographical Research Agendas. *Progress in Human Geography* 29: 247–259.

Longhurst, R. 2012. Becoming Smaller: Autobiographical Spaces of Weight Loss. *Antipode* 44(3): 871–888.

Geographies of disability

Dyck, I. 2010. Geographies of Disability: Reflecting on New Body Knowledges. In V. Chouinard, E. Hall, and R. Wilton (eds), *Towards Enabling Geographies: "Disabled" Bodies and Minds in Society and Space.* Farnham: Ashgate, pp.253–264.

Hall, E., Chouinard, V. and Wilton, R. eds 2016. *Towards Enabling Geographies: "Disabled" Bodies and Minds in Society and Space.* London: Routledge.

Holt, L. 2010. Young People's Embodied Social Capital and Performing Disability. *Children's Geographies* 8(1): 25–37.

Mowl, G. and Fuller, D. 2014. Geographies of Disability. In R. Pain, J. Gough, G. Mowl et al. (eds), *Introducing Social Geographies.* London: Routledge, pp.164–186.

Parr, H. 2002. New Body-Geographies: The Embodied Spaces of Health and Medical Information on the Internet. *Environment and Planning D: Society and Space* 20: 73–95.

Parr, H. and Butler, R. 1999. New Geographies of Illness, Impairment and Disability. In R. Butler and H. Parr (eds), *Mind and Body Spaces: Geographies of Illness, Impairment and Disability.* London: Routledge, 1–24.

Pyer, M., Horton, J., Tucker, F. et al. 2010. *Children, Young People and "Disability": Challenging Children's Geographies?* London: Taylor & Francis.

Soldatic, K., Morgan, H., and Roulstone, A. 2014. *Disability, Spaces and Places of Policy Exclusion.* London: Routledge.

Chapter 13

Life in the Future, Among the Ruins

In artist Sammy Baloji's 2006 series, "Mémoire," and in his 2011 series, "Congo Far West: Retracing Charles Lemaire's expedition," photographs from colonial era "Belgian" Congo are superimposed and layered with contemporary photographs of mining extraction and its ruins today near the city of his birth, Lubumbashi, in what is now the Haut-Katanga Province of the Democratic Republic of the Congo. His compelling images cross the breach between a contentiously shared global geopolitical history of power and difference and today. In some images, archival photographs taken by colonial officers provide a portal through time: captured in black and white, local residents of the Congo – groups of women, imprisoned men, and miners photographed under the colonial regime stare into the lens of the camera, their gaze transported across time and space, as if willing us to reckon with them. The region's future is represented by the color photographs of desolate abandoned mining infrastructure. The subjects of these photos, through Baloji's vision and artistic labor, seem to time travel, placing their struggles into the landscape of now and reminding us that the colonial moment is with us in today's political and economic struggles. These are a visual representation of the imperial ruination described by Ann Stoler (2013). We live among the ongoing ruination of empire, which we witness through Baloji's photographs.

If we turn to another contemporary artist with an eye to imperial critique and subversion, Wangechi Mutu, now living in New York but having spent the first 17 years of her life in her native Nairobi, Kenya, beguiles us into a world that broaches similar themes, but is made unrecognizable through her manipulation of natural and human forms through collage and other techniques. In her images, empire is present in the imagery, but complicated and extended through an inextricable relationship with more than human life forms: women become trees, birds are made of elephants, snakes flourish in the hair of a bride. The tropes that are used to diminish the humanity of colonized peoples and to hyper-objectify the bodies of Black women are here accentuated. Simultaneously, the boundaries between nature and humanity are blurred, as collage allows people to be made up of not only other bits of people, but also animals, machines, and repetitive patterns reminiscent of nature that Mutu attributes to her perusal of books of tropical diseases owned by her mother (a nurse). Interviewed about the role of the Black woman's body in her work, Mutu speaks to colonialism's effects on the body:

> The black female body has been violated and revered in very specific ways by the outsider – Europeans, especially. The issues that pertain to race: pathologizing the black mind, exoticizing and fearing of the black body, objectifying the body as a specimen, or a sexual machine, or a work animal, or relating the black body to non-human species as a way to justify cruelty … Even in this state of containment and capture, our body is valued and worshipped – yet feared and reviled. (Mutu 2014)

In her art, these themes come out through questioning of the human/nature/animal divisions: she is fascinated by belief systems outside scientific rationality because, "We've – often for modernity's sake, as a race, as humans, as a colonized people, as colonizers, however you want to say it – we have disrupted those ways of thinking because it doesn't jive with the new logic, with the Enlightenment, with scientific development" (Mutu 2014, see Frazier 2016 for a discussion of Mutu's work).

Why begin a chapter about the future with art that is about grappling with the past? First, these images speak at times more carefully and evocatively than words, giving us an affective impression of empire and escape: the idea that history is with us today. Secondly, we are asked to question the nature/human boundary and echoes of the ways this binary has been used to violently confine and categorize people to the margins of humanity. These two ideas lead us to a third: how should we think about the future? In a world with a rapidly changing climate and entangled and complicated environmental effects ranging from the loss of coral reefs to warming, to unpredictable storms, scientists grapple with what some have referred to as the **Anthropocene.** The Anthropocene is a term being considered by geologists and other scientists to mark a new geologic era in which humans are an integral aspect of the earth as a system, shaping its climate, geology, and ecosystems in profound ways and leading to a break with the past. The Anthropocene is an era in which humans have fundamentally altered the Earth's systems, but in which those who have caused these alterations and those who must cope with them are often located in different, but historically linked, socioeconomic and geographic locations. When and if the Anthropocene began, and how to delineate the boundary between prior ages: these are questions with political implications, and we will return to them in a few pages. This chapter brings together the themes of this book by thinking through how political geography helps us to think about the future of our densely connected world through the *idea* of the Anthropocene, then the political geography of climate change and the Anthropocene, and finally the ways that scholars, activists, and artists are working to imagine and create a different future for all of us. This chapter is also a call to you, the reader, to think about the future in political terms. The concept of

prefigurative politics (e.g., Dyson and Jeffrey 2018) describes the ways that people work to enact in the present the kinds of social and political relationships they wish to create for the future. Here, we will consider what this might mean for us.

In her powerful book, *In the Wake: On Blackness and Being*, Christina Sharpe (2016) uses the imagery of a ship's wake to describe Black thought and life in the ongoing aftermath of slavery. Sharpe begins the book by describing the death of her sister, and then the deaths of seven other family members, and turns to center on her mother's life and her own trajectory:

> And after my father died, that precarity looked and felt like winters without heat because there was no money for oil; holes in ceilings, walls, and floors from water damage that we could not afford to repair; the fears and reality of electricity and other utilities being cut for nonpayment; fear of a lien being placed on the house because there was no, or not enough, money to pay property taxes … But through all of that and more, my mother tried to make a small path through the wake. She brought beauty into that house in every way that she could; she worked at joy, and she made livable moments, spaces, and places in the midst of all that was unlivable there, in the town we lived in; in the schools we attended; in the violence we saw and felt inside the home while my father was living and outside it in the larger white world before, during, and after his death. (Sharpe 2016, p.4)

As Sharpe (2016, p.4) looks at her mother's life, from her position as a tenured faculty member, she sees that her mother "was attuned not only to our individual circumstances but also to those circumstances as they were an indication of, and related to, the larger antiblack world that structured all of our lives." Sharpe asks us to consider Black being in the wake, and she grapples with the many meanings of this word, wake: the crashing of water behind a ship, the state of wakefulness, "in the line of recoil of (a gun)," a wake or vigil with someone who has died. Sharpe draws on Frantz Fanon on the "zone of nonbeing," Frank Wilderson, III (2010, p.2) on the need to "stay in the hold of the ship," Saidiya Hartman (2008, p.6) on the afterlives of slavery as "skewed life chances, limited access to health and education, premature death, incarceration, and impoverishment," and Dionne Brand's (2018) poetry on the "door of no return." Building on these foundations, Sharpe (2016, p.18) asks us to consider what it means to do "wake work," that is, to "continue to imagine new ways to live in the wake of slavery, in slavery's afterlives, to survive (and more) the afterlife of property … I mean wake work to be a mode of inhabiting *and* rupturing this episteme with our known lived and un/imaginable lives." To do wake work is not only to mourn, though that might or must be part of any reckoning with the ways that all our lives are entangled in epistemic violence that has shaped all our histories. To do wake work is to recognize that:

> Even if those Africans who were in the holds, who left something of their prior selves in those rooms as a trace to be discovered and who passed through the doors of no return did not survive the holding and the sea, they, like us, are alive in hydrogen, in oxygen; in carbon, in phosphorus, and iron; in sodium and chlorine … they are with us still, in the time of the wake … (Sharpe 2016, p.19)

Writing on an uncovered African Burial Ground in Lower Manhattan, geographer Katherine McKittrick (2013, p.2) describes it as a way to see "spatial continuity between the living and the dead, between science and storytelling, and between past and present," and the ways that the bodies of people who had been buried and forgotten, and then unearthed and memorialized, are "still *there*," and "necessary to thinking about the city as a location where new forms of human life become possible." This opens us for her a way to think in relation to plantation futures, which she defines as, "a conceptualization of time-space that tracks the plantation toward the prison and the impoverished and destroyed city sectors and, consequently, brings into sharp focus the ways the plantation is an ongoing locus of antiblack violence and death that can no longer analytically sustain this violence" (McKittrick 2013, p.2). Remembrance of Black suffering or "scenes of subjection," (Hartman 1997), however, can also fix and naturalize anti-Black violence; this remembering is fraught because it *can* locate the origin of our present in the suffering of an abstracted Black person's body while also imagining "linear progress away from racist violence" (McKittrick 2013, p.9). McKittrick (2013, p.12) asks "what kind of future can the plantation give us?" McKittrick (2013, p.14) reads Dionne Brand's long poem, *Inventory*, not as a catalog of death but of "the struggle *against* death." She uses this to envision, "a conception of the city imbued with a narrative of black history that is neither celebratory nor dissident but rooted in an articulation of city life that accepts that relations of violence and domination have made our existence and presence in the Americas possible as it recasts this knowledge to envision an alternative future."

What do these visions of wake work and plantation futures mean for us, differently situated ordinary people, going about our ordinary lives, in this wake of unintelligible violence? And how do we hold this epistemic violence in our hands and our hearts when we consider other forms of epistemic violence, each incomparable, like the work of settler colonialism to eliminate Indigenous people or the ways that the destruction of nature today is profoundly entangled in the destruction of people's lives and livelihoods? Sharpe asks us to understand the ways that the "semiotics of the slave ship" remain when we see forced migration, uneven and racialized policing, drownings in the Mediterranean Sea, when we see the "reappearances of the slave ship in everyday life in the form of the prison, the camp, and the school" (Sharpe 2016, p.21). She asks us to broaden out our understanding of whom today is in the hold of the ship, to consider "whom the state positions to die ungrievable deaths and live lives meant to be unlivable" (Sharpe 2016, p.22).

The politics that Sharpe invokes is an expansiveness that asks us to recognize the humanity of those drowning in the Mediterranean, to see the echoes of the slave ship in the ships that cross these waters, and for those of us alive today to understand and dismantle the grid of (in)humanity that allows for such deaths. This is a track running parallel to the work of Jacqui Alexander (2005), who speaks to the ways that we allow ourselves to not see the violence of empire even as we participate in it. Of course you will already recognize that these evocations of history to create different ways to live in the present are in stark opposition to other resurgent interpretations of the relationship between our past and our future. Across the globe, the early twenty-first century has witnessed a global turn to the right that seeks to revamp nationalism for the future in ways that evoke a glorious past at risk. We see this in the politics of Brexit, in which racialized discourses drive political narratives even though austerity and economic crisis have disproportionately affected minority communities and minority women (Burrell et al. 2018). We also see it in the US rhetoric of "Make America Great Again" (Gökarıksel and Smith 2016; Steinberg et al. 2018), as well as in sites from Turkey to India to the Philippines (Gökarıksel, Neubert, and Smith 2019; Prashad 2018).

These **temporal** narratives (related to time) are also related to place and people, for example in the ways that specific people and places are represented as turning to the right because of the ways that they have been "left behind," even as on the ground such narratives are too simplistic (Isakjee and Lorne in Burrell et al. 2018)

Our contemporary moment is one in which people of all political perspectives are trying to make sense of what to do with the past as we move into the future: do we work to return to it? Seek to overcome its violences?

As we move forward in this chapter, keep Sharpe's wake work in the back of your mind, and at the end of the chapter we will turn to how we might consider wake work in relation to other ways of thinking about the past, present, future, and our place in the world.

What is the Anthropocene and What Does It Mean for Political Geography?

Polar bears have become a key player in the global iconography of climate change, and not without good reason: they are very "charismatic megafauna," that are important indicators of environmental problems and important to Indigenous people in the Arctic (Manzo 2010; Slocum 2004). The challenges that they face in survival today are a reminder of the degree to which our climate has been changing. Thinking of polar bears, of glaciers, we are brought to an awareness of the immediacy of a changing climate. At the same time, as Rachel Slocum (2004) argues, for those of us living far from polar bears, it is crucial to find ways to acknowledge how "daily life is always already rooted in some place and linked to larger-scale processes," and thus implicated in climate change (Slocum 2004, p.413, see also Kirsch 2015).

Far from polar bears, with his dog, Ginger, as his charismatic animal companion, Chris Neubert (Neubert under review) writes of a mundane but no less revealing signal of the Anthropocene: the smell of liquid pig manure that has been sprayed on fields and now flows down into the pretty, (and smelly) Raccoon River (Figure 13.1). He writes:

> On a hot August evening, I find myself walking with my dog along a muddy bank of the Raccoon River, just before it enters the city of Des Moines, Iowa. There is a deceptive tranquility out here, just outside of the city, where the last remnants of native prairie grass meet with the rare Iowa forest (the largest stand of black walnut in North America, a nearby sign dutifully notes). The sky is blue and the trees are lush, but the water is deep brown and murky, occasionally giving off a scent that can best be described as a stale mix of mold and feces. When the light breeze picks up the scent and carries it to my nostrils, I am reminded that this place is not as idyllic as it superficially appears, and my ears shift their attention from the chattering finches to the cars rumbling along the distant highway.

Neubert asks what odor might tell us about the Anthropocene: what is a sensory experience of intensifying human impact on this planet? Is smell political? What brings Neubert to this unconventional approach? His early research engaged with the role of the Concentrated Animal Feeding Operation (CAFO), in shaping politics and landscapes in the rural US Midwest. Such concentrated animal populations create new forms of waste that are both an ecological disaster and a spatial fix for failing capitalism – turning the toxic sludge that collects underneath giant buildings full of pigs – into a commodity. Neubert writes about a couple who struggle after a CAFO is built near their home.

Figure 13.1 The Raccoon River. Reproduced with permission of Chris Neubert.

Their biggest concern was the stink from the waste being stored under the CAFOs, until they realized that most of that excreta would be spread on the fields surrounding their home, up to the fence-line 100 feet from their back door. Many in the small town near their home told them to get used to this "smell of money." Their concerns were denigrated by politicians who told them "if you don't like it, move to a different state." Elle and Karl's dreams of outdoor cookouts with the grandkids playing outside disappeared. They stopped fishing in the nearby creek, which ran green and frothy with cyanobacteria on the day I visited. Surrounded by feces-covered corn and soybean fields, Elle stopped nursing the injured wildlife that wandered onto their property. There is really no place else for them to go, but as she told me: "this isn't the farm life we were hoping for."

Neubert suggests that the political processes that led to the Anthropocene required bound-edness, and that attention to the unbounded, such as unmanageable and affective sensory experiences, can give us newly ambivalent ways to understand our world. What might help us understand our part in the Anthropocene more than or perhaps in conjunction with the way that we understand our changing Earth through the emotions generated by the knowledge that polar bears are at risk?

While polar bears and smelly rivers might be a sign of risk and change, the phone in your pocket is also a revealing and complex little object that tells us a surprising amount about how we reached the point at which polar bears are in danger. As we think about our global past *and* our global future, we have the opportunity to assess and evaluate what has brought us to this point and consider what kind of future world we want to make and what tools political geography provides us with to move forward. The causes of global environmental change and social and economic inequality transcend national borders, but so do the social movements and political actions that seek to create a different and more just world. Think about how ordinary objects in our lives weave together the ways that old colonial patterns are replicated: e.g., mining of "blood minerals" in the Democratic Republic of Congo, dangerous labor assembly in China, global consumption by the elite, the environmental racism of waste disposal, and how our absorption in tiny screens can both facilitate political activism and networks of solidarity and can isolate and depoliticize us.

Our quick consideration of how our phone comes to bring the world into our pocket or handbag has much in common with the Baloji's and Mutu's visions. Like their art, our phone teaches us that historical patterns of exploitation remain with us today, that our lives are caught up in the life of nature – as we have profound effects upon the natural world, and that through transnational communication via technological development and creativity, there is potential to transcend borders and enact change, though this will not be easy.

The political geography of the Anthropocene is a lens we can use to return to the ideas encountered throughout the book and to consolidate lessons we can take from the political actors, thinkers, and activists that we have encountered in these pages (and of course one thing we have learned is that thinkers *are* activists, and that we are *all* political activists!). How can we apply these ideas to our global responsibility moving forward? What might you take from this book, or the course it is a part of, as you move forward in your life? Let us explore the concept of the Anthropocene in more detail and then return to these questions.

The Anthropocene is a term both old and new. In the 1980s, biologist Eugene Stoermer began using the word, and it was formalized in a publication by Stoermer and Paul Crutzen in 2000 (Crutzen and Stoermer 2000; for an overview of the history of the term see Steffen et al. 2011). Though the term took on a new urgency at this time, in the early years of the twentieth century, directly after the industrial revolution, somewhat similar debates took place, for instance about the possibility of a noösphere – the transformation of the Earth system through human intervention. Steffen et al (2011) suggest that Russian scientist Vladimir Vernadsky was the originator of some of these ideas during a visit to Paris in 1922. In 2002, Paul Crutzen published a short article in the journal *Nature*, titled, "The geology of mankind," writing:

> For the past three centuries, the effects of humans on the global environment have escalated. Because of these anthropogenic emissions of carbon dioxide, global climate may depart significantly from natural behavior for many millennia to come. It seems appropriate to assign the term "Anthropocene" to the present, in many ways human-dominated, geological epoch, supplementing the Holocene – the warm period of the past 10–12 millennia. The Anthropocene could be said to have started in the latter part of the eighteenth century, when analyses of air trapped in polar ice showed the beginning of growing global concentrations of carbon dioxide and methane. This date also happens to coincide with James Watt's design of the steam engine in 1784. (Crutzen 2002, p.23)

One of the key messages of this book is that as we encounter a concept, term, or category, we ought to take care. Foucault's method of genealogy reminds us that we ought to work to unravel when a term comes into being, who uses it and how, and what political work it does in the world. The Anthropocene is a perfect example. We might ask: "What assumptions are embedded in this word?" "What political work does this concept do?" And, "What can we learn by using this word – what does it allow us to understand?" In order to proceed with the ways that the Anthropocene emerges in political geography, let us think through these questions a bit, and then return to some of the questions posed at the onset of the chapter by artists Baloji and Mutu, which also emerge for scholars like Ann Laura Stoler, Arun Saldanha, and Kathryn Yusoff.

First: *What assumptions are embedded in this word?* Ironically, somewhat like the word hybrid, this word connects by dividing. When we describe something as a hybrid, we are both pointing to the qualities that cross borders *and* insisting that there were once two separate entities, that have become one in this "hybrid," thing. Hence, when we discuss postcolonial spaces as "hybrid," we are also strengthening the assumption that colonizer and colonized peoples were once separate – this undermines long-existing global connections and transfers of knowledge, goods, and people, before the process of global colonization that began in earnest in the fifteenth century. In using the term Anthropocene, we must take care that it does not create too firm of a division between humanity and nature; by pointing to the impact of human action we do risk separating out humans too distinctly from other species. Just as pressing, many scholars have argued that the term Anthropocene flattens out the category of human. What does this mean? By arguing for a new relationship between humans (or in some cases, "mankind" [sic]) and geologic forces, Arun Saldanha, Kathryn Yusoff and others (Yusoff 2018; Davis et al. 2019) point out that thinking of "human" as a category impinging on and shaping "nature," is limited in scope. There are two distinct problems here: first, not all humans have the same impact on the earth. Second, we cannot easily separate out humans from nature in the first place!

In 2013, with the spirit of a manifesto, Arun Saldanha (2013) writes,

> Concentration of CO_2 has hit 400 ppm … Hiding their oxymoronic status, green capitalism, ethical consumerism and geo-engineering are convincing everyone ecological disaster can be averted. In the face of the apocalypse it predicts, science remains at worst corrupt and at best spineless, while the left remains hindered by humanist conceptions of political agency. Not the modern city or the nation-state, but *the Anthropocene is now the horizon of revolutionary politics.*

Following this striking statement, Saldanha calls us to denaturalize Marxism and more intentionally politicize science. This call is part of a concert of voices calling for recognition of the Anthropocene as a fundamentally political question, and one that remains open: who is culpable for the conditions we currently inhabit? Jason Moore (2017) and Donna Haraway (2015) have both argued for the designation of the **Capitalocene** as a better term for the era within which we currently reside. This places emphasis not on *people* but on *capital*, suggesting that the drivers of climate change are economic processes, that the capitalist expansion we have discussed at several points in this book is what incentivizes greater use of fossil fuels, increased consumption and waste, and so forth.

These scholars lay the ground for our second question about the Anthropocene: *"What political work does this concept do?"* First, the Anthropocene generates political urgency: it draws attention to the magnitude of the ways in which human life is impacting the environment (particularly through the process of capitalism, as noted earlier). Second, as observed by Lewis and Maslin (2015), when geologists and scientists try to determine *when* the Anthropocene began, this decision will have policy and political implications. For this very reason, they suggest the choice of 1610 as a date for the beginning of the era. This is a year in which forests reforested in North and South America as they underwent a temporary expansion due to the death of millions of native people from disease, enslavement, and warfare. By locating the beginning of the Anthropocene in this time, Lewis and Maslin tie the era to the onset of colonialism and capitalist expansion – thus embedding the question of responsibility and climate justice into the definition of the era itself.

Baldwin (2014, p.525) points to how climate change anxieties reiterate the racial category of the human "at a moment often characterized as simultaneously post-racial *and* post-human." Thus, while post-humanist scholarship has presented an important critique of why it is too simple to try to think of human beings as completely separated from other forms of life, this critique must be held in tension with insights from postcolonial, decolonial and critical race studies. Livingstone and Puar (2011, pp.5–6) suggest that we must take the animals, plants, and microbials seriously as nonhuman actors but that we also must understand how they become racial and sexual proxies, that is, how human differences are reflected in how people talk about nature. This draws our attention to how critical race studies and postcolonial studies, "have continually sought to understand what it means and has meant to be human, given that much of slavery and colonialism operated through and was founded upon legal, medical, intellectual, economic, and political attempts to demarcate the boundaries among species" (Livingston and Puar 2011, p.5) This premise informed much of the discussion in Chapter 8. Our focus on the nonhuman or other forms of life and agency in the Anthropocene must include analysis of race, ethnicity, and other markers of human difference and hierarchy. Angela Last (2015) for instance, focuses on natural disasters in the Caribbean to reveal the environmental foundations of a racist European geopolitics and argue for attention to the geophysical and ecological in the decolonization project.

For Kathryn Yusoff (2013), the "geological turn," that is, the attention to the geological timescale, yields theoretical insights, pushing our focus beyond social relations *with* fossil fuels and human impacts *on* Earth, to think of human *being* as itself geologically composed; the social then emerges as an expression of geology and geochemistry. The Anthropocene debate offers critical scholars a rare opportunity to engage with the scientific community and makes possible "forms of interdisciplinarity that might render geoscience more political" (Castree 2015, p.15).

The Geopolitics of Climate Change and the Politics of Knowledge

Political geographer Simon Dalby asks us to attend to "Anthropocene geopolitics," and the "geopolitics of climate change." He means here the ways that the Anthropocene era is fundamentally linked to and creates a specific form of geopolitics – for example, dependence on oil, the impossibility of separating out questions of humanity from questions of the environment, and the importance of new forms of geopolitical thinking. Politicians, pundits, and scholars have been engaged in vigorous debate over whether climate change can lead to resource wars or other conflicts (McDonald 2013; Reuveny 2007). For instance, Selby et al. (2017) speak back to theories that the Syrian civil war is partly the result of human-induced climate change, and a range of theorists suggest we ought to take care in creating a sense of climate crisis that may make migrants more vulnerable (Baldwin 2016; Farbotko and Lazrus 2012; Hartmann 2010). Meanwhile, political actors cast doubt on the irrefutable science of climate change, in order to slow responses that might have an economic impact.

Militaries have made plans for how to navigate a world of "climate wars," however, scholars have raised concerns that the ways that climate and security are linked naturalizes conflict to the global south and places an emphasis on security without attention to the causality chains that links responsibility for climate change to the very countries that then seek to secure themselves against its impacts. Along the same lines, the possibility of climate migrants sets in motion preparations for an often punitive carceral system that criminalizes migrants (see Mountz 2010, Baldwin 2016, S. Dalby 2013). In Dalby's terms, "in so far as those migrants are set in motion by climate change caused by the fossil fuel consumption of those societies that subsequently incarcerate those in motion, the politics of 'security' become particularly hypocritical" (S. Dalby 2013, p.42).

How then ought climate change affect our understanding of geopolitics? Dalby argues that this is an important time to build on Stuart Elden's (2013a) idea of "the volume," as a way to change how we think about cartographic space in a two dimensional sense. Elden's argument asked us to think through the ways that territory is not only two-dimensional, but also has a volume (the air above, the earth beneath). To these, Dalby adds a material sense of the earth and oceans – the carbon in the atmosphere, the temperature of the air – as important elements that cannot be overlooked.

The qualities of water, ice, and land defy the modernist distinctions upon which political entities are founded. As you will recall for Chapter 4, in their exploration of "Contested sovereignty in a Changing Arctic," Gerhardt et al. (2010) show us that climate change complicates or intensifies the ways that a firm boundary between sea and land has been at the heart of legal sovereignty. Arctic states with coastal claims (Canada, Denmark [Greenland] Norway, Russia, and the United States) look to the Arctic Ocean as a site of concern and potential. Melting sea ice may change coastlines and intensify global warming as the loss of ice decreases the albedo, but it can also mean new shipping routes, changing military strategy, and increased access to mineral resources. Ideals of sovereignty assume a distinction between land and water: with land assumed to be "territorializable," and water more resistant. As they suggest in their study of Arctic sovereignty, this distinction has always been tricky in the Arctic, as a region of islands, water, and ice that functions at times as though it were land, and this distinction is only becoming more complex: "today's ice could become tomorrow's water" (Gerhardt et al. 2010, p.994) (Figure 13.2). The claims of the five states listed earlier are further complicated by the rights of sovereign Indigenous people such as the Inuit and Saami (Figure 13.3).

In 2007, sea ice reached a low enough level that scientists began predicting a Northwest Passage would allow for a new shipping route – in this moment, philosophical questions discussed earlier become legal ones. If new parts of the region become water, are they

Figure 13.2   Chunks of ice melt in the Paris street during the COP21 protests as part of an art installation reminding visitors of the melting icecaps. Reproduced with permission of Erika Wise.

now classified as internal waters? Can Canada thus restrict this route? The "conceptual mapping of land to territory and water to nonterritory fail to resonate with the region's actual materiality," in which it cannot be defined as either one (Gerhardt et al. 2010, p.995). In the same year, 2007, Russian scientists planted a flag on the bottom of the sea to claim this territory (to the dismissal of other states), as though it were land. Against the claims of either Russia or Canada, the Inuit Circumpolar Council demands attention to the region's material indeterminacy and environmental concerns, and the Nordic Saami Convention proposes free travel of Saami people across the national borders of Norway, Sweden, and Finland, and other proposals suggest Indigenous people also have the right to cross the Bering Strait.

These complex geographies demonstrate the importance of some of the questions we began with: attending to the points of tension and inequality embedded in political-environmental questions, thinking through the implicit assumptions in categories, and remembering the importance of the material qualities and agency of the earth itself. As political geographers working on questions of climate change and the Anthropocene suggest, geophysical changes

Figure 13.3   In their series "Leaving Impossible Things Unattended," (#LITU) Ginger Wagg and Mike Dimpfl trace "the relationship between our bodies, the body politic, and the garbage we think we can leave behind." Photo courtesy of Leaving Impossible Things Unattended (LITU).

present us with new political questions that we may not yet have the theoretical capacity or political structures to understand and manage.

Scholars like Hartmann (2010), Farbotko and Lazrus (2012), and Baldwin (2014, 2016) call for care and attention as policy develops from these political questions. How are we to deal with **climate justice**? That is, how ought we distribute responsibility for environmental impacts, protect those affected, and balance the need for equity without running against the limits of the planet's capacity? Following on points raised earlier in the chapter, how do we ensure that climate migration (or the *fear* of climate migration) does not lead to further securitization that harms those who are affected by a changing environment but protects people in places bearing primary responsibility for those changes? In considering how we might begin to study the geopolitics of climate justice and the Anthropocene, we would do well to keep in mind some of the themes of this book. We might keep in mind that the production of knowledge is political, and never neutral, and that we ought to consider what the knowledge that we create enables or forecloses. We might also remember the many ways in which global politics is not something that is "out there," but is always situated in our everyday and intimate life, that we are already entangled in the production of global politics whether we like it or not. We might also do well to begin from the lives of those who are experiencing the effects and processes of global change firsthand, and think of how we can align our work in the service of their struggles.

Work, Extraction, and Sovereignty

The ways that the geopolitics of the Anthropocene is deeply embedded into our daily lives makes an easy fix or neat solution to environmental challenges deeply complicated. This is underlined in work on the relationship between Indigenous geographies and the geographies of resource extraction, which are of course deeply implicated in global warming and the other ecological changes designated in the Anthropocene. The imperial and capitalist drive to extract resources from the earth is inseparable from the compromising of Indigenous sovereignty (and the subjection of people of African descent. Simultaneously, Indigenous people are often simplistically positioned as being homogenous, close to nature, and naturally in opposition to extractive industry. Yet, as we look toward the future, it is important to have more careful accountings of our relationships between environment, resources, and sovereignty. This is demonstrated by Andrew Curley's (2019a; 2019b) careful work on the geographies of extraction in the Navajo Nation. His research with Navajo coal workers and environmentalists demonstrate that the decisions we make today cannot but be inflected by settler colonialism and questions of sovereignty, and yet, at the same time, it is easy to let unitary and overly simplistic visions of Indigenous actors override complexity on the ground.

The relationship between the US government and the Navajo Nation has been one of violence and extraction, with Navajo land exploited for coal, water, and these twinned resources (themselves bound together in the operation of coal-fired power plants and the pumping of water for the Central Arizona Project, which transported water across the state of Arizona and made urban growth possible). Alongside this extraction is the extraction of labor from the bodies of Navajo people, who have worked both in uranium extraction and in coal mining, both on Navajo land. We might understand Navajo coal through the lenses of the resource curse, dependency theory, and settler colonialism, and yet, Curley (2019a) argues, this is not enough. He demonstrates first of all that Navajo people do not have only one political orientation to coal, and that their relationship to coal is in part formed through the ways that coal is important for Navajo sovereignty and for what coal enables. Even as coal mining is difficult and dangerous work, it enables coal workers to support their families and to stay on Navajo land. In this, it becomes part of a subsistence ethic of hard work, *t'áá hwó ají t'éego*, meaning, "you are responsible for your own well-being." This means that even as the state shifts to cheaper alternatives to coal, and younger Navajo activists raise concerns about coal, in 2013, coal workers protested at the Navajo Nation Council to express their frustration at the potential closure of the Navajo Power Generating Station, which would put the Kayenta Mine and its 800 workers in jeopardy. As Curley points out, coal is not an abstraction for the coal workers, but part of daily life, from how they understand their masculinity and family roles, to a paradoxical claim to Navajo sovereignty, as it is coal that makes it possible for them to remain connected to the Nation's territory, and it is through negotiating resource sovereignty that the nation maintains its sovereignty claims. Their response to the changing fortunes of coal is thus also a moral economy, a "response to social change that tribal actors intuitively recognize as unjust" (Curley 2019a, p.83). Given this complex terrain, what comes next in our relations between earth, resources, and the ongoing and unfolding legacies of colonial extraction?

Can Anthropocene Futures be Abundant?

We live in an anxious age, and an age of ecological anxiety (Robbins and Moore 2013), but what are the political consequences of this anxiety (Baldwin 2012; Ginn 2015; Katz 1995; e.g., Schlosser 2015; Skrimshire 2010; Swyngedouw 2013)? When we think of the Anthropocene, and when we think of the future more broadly, we might center the imaginaries of Baloji and Mutu from the opening of this chapter, as their fantastical worlds suggest ways that time is cyclical, not linear, and smudge the boundaries between nature and humanity (for a call for such abundant futures, see Collard, Dempsey, and Sundberg 2015). We might also think carefully about the **temporality** of crisis thinking, that is, the ways that time operates and the quality of time that is implied. That is, is time linear? Does it proceed in cycles? What does the temporality of apocalypse tell us? When you think of the word apocalypse, what comes to mind? Do you imagine a disastrous future? Do you think of the present moment as a kind of apocalypse? Does the apocalypse happen for all of us at the same moment? Indigenous scholars (e.g., Davis and Todd 2017; Tuck and Ree 2013; Whyte 2018; 2016) have suggested we consider whether the apocalypse began many hundreds of years ago. Davis and Todd (2017, p.671; referencing Whyte 2016) mark the colonization of the Americas as the beginning of Anthropocene: "the current environmental crisis which are named through the designation of the Anthropocene, can be viewed as a continuation of, rather than a break from, previous eras that begin with colonialism and extend through advanced capitalism." Baldwin (2012, p.172; 2016) has written that climate change engenders fears specific to race and whiteness, that whiteness emerges in tropes about the future that include, "uncertainty, Utopia, apocalypse, prophesy, hope, fear, possibility and potentiality," in short that the changing climate and the possibility of climate-driven migration creates narratives of fear and decline that cannot be separated from how people are racialized.

When we think on our rapidly changing earth and our responsibilities to it, we would do well to avoid the kind of tropes that are common in the popular representations of apocalypse that we often consume. That is, in film versions of climate catastrophe, we get the impression that science will save us (without related political action), that a band of quick-thinking heroes will rescue us from ourselves and save the planet, that we can ignore the fundamental inequalities that are at the heart of the political and economic processes that got us to this place (see Gergan, Smith, and Vasudevan 2020 for the expansion of these ideas). We might, however, look to the fictive worlds of Afrofuturism and Indigenous futurity, which create forward-looking imaginaries in which the wake work that Christina Sharpe proposes carries through in imagining a future in which present social formations are broken down and realigned, sometimes *through* apocalypse itself.

Geographer at Work: Mabel Gergan

Mabel Gergan is an assistant professor of geography at Florida State University. She received her PhD in Geography from the University of North Carolina at Chapel Hill in 2016.

Causality, Culpability, and Responsibility in the Anthropocene

While the vote is still out on whether we're in a new geological epoch or if we're still in the Holocene; one thing is for certain, anthropogenic climate change – one of the defining features of this proposed new epoch – has led to a global intensification of hazard events (Clark 2011). Critical scholars have argued that there is no such thing as a *natural* disaster since conditions of vulnerability are socially produced, i.e. they are a product of longer histories of marginalization. For instance, while Puerto Rico will always be in the path of hurricanes – its ability to respond to Hurricane Maria in 2017 was severely undermined by its debt crisis that many argue is a by-product of its neo-colonial relationship with the United States. While hazards worsen existing inequalities they can also reveal historical patterns of risk and vulnerability, allowing local communities, activists, and scholars to critique those in power and devise strategies for the future. The Anthropocene then is not just a debate about stratigraphy but also about causality, culpability, and responsibility.

My doctoral research in the Indian Himalayan borderlands was located in Sikkim, the site of controversial hydropower projects, an Indigenous anti-dam protest, and a 6.9 magnitude earthquake. The Himalayan region is a seismically active climate change hotspot where global warming has resulted in shifting monsoon patterns, unseasonal floods, and landslides. While earthquakes are not (yet) linked to climate change, they add to existing ecological and infrastructural vulnerabilities. The epicenter of the Sikkim earthquake in 2011 was located close to an under-construction dam site; subsequent aftershocks and landslides made local communities question the viability of these projects. In interviews with Indigenous anti-dam activists, communities residing near dams, and regional scientists, I found there was growing consensus that dams were exacerbating the impact of earthquakes. Many even believed that dams were causing earthquakes (while there is no evidence to prove this was the case in Sikkim, dam-induced earthquakes are a real thing!). Several locals who held Buddhist and Indigenous shamanic beliefs also believed that dams had desecrated scared landscapes and angered local deities.

In my research, hazards served as a lens to understand uneven regional development, differential vulnerability, and histories of marginalization. Since the early 1980s, India's climate change anxieties have fueled massive biodiversity and wildlife conservation efforts. While these measure are commendable on paper, in reality conservation zones led to the expulsion of marginalized Indigenous tribes and nomadic groups who depended on forests for their livelihood and sustenance. And now Himalayan hydropower is being touted as the latest fix to India's fossil fuel addiction. However, on the ground, hydropower infrastructure is producing patterns of risk and vulnerability that are disturbingly familiar. As with the conservation zones, the actual burden of fixing environmental crisis falls on the most marginalized regions and people. Many Himalayan states including Sikkim, were independent kingdoms and tribes which were incorporated into the Indian Union after it gained independence from the British in 1947. Since Himalayan states are geographically peripheral to and culturally distinct from mainland India, hydropower infrastructure serves to secure a geo-politically sensitive and politically intractable borderland region. However, growing ecological precarity as in the case of Sikkim, has created an opening for local communities and anti-dam activists to critique the Indian state and disastrous infrastructure that jeopardizes their well-being.

My research in the Indian Himalayas questions the "newness" of ecological crisis and centers the voices of local communities who bear the brunt of socially produced disasters. In doing so, it pushes back against the pervasive belief that a universal humanity is to blame for climate change and the Anthropocene in generating concern about an impending apocalypse might avert a dystopian future. Instead my research affirms what Indigenous scholar-activist Kyle Whyte (2018) has pointed out: an ecological apocalypse is not a future or impending scenario for most Indigenous groups, it is their *ongoing* reality, he calls this "our ancestors' dystopia." Addressing climate change requires innovation and creativity but we must fight the impulse to turn to the state or private entrepreneurs for technocratic interventions. Instead, we might want to turn to communities that have *already* lived through the apocalypse, and listen to their stories of survival and resistance.

What Have We Learned and Where Do We Go From Here?

Within the colonizing university also exists a decolonizing education. Occupying the same space and time are the colonizer's territories and institutions and colonized time, but also Indigenous land and life before and beyond occupation. Colonial schools are machines running on desires for a colonizer's future and, paradoxically, desires for Indigenous futures … The bits of machinery that make up a decolonizing university are driven by decolonial desires, with decolonizing dreams who are subversively part of the machinery and part machine themselves. These subversive beings wreck, scavenge, retool, and reassemble the colonizing university into decolonizing contraptions. They are scyborgs with a decolonizing desire. You might choose to be one of them. (paperson 2018, p.1)

In the closing to the first chapter of *In the Wake*, Sharpe (2016, p.22) writes, "if we are lucky, we live in the knowledge that the wake has positioned us as no-citizen." She goes on to appeal directly to the reader, writing:

I want *In the Wake* to declare that we are Black peoples in the wake with no state or nation to protect us, with no citizenship bound to be respected, and to position us in the modalities of Black life lived in, as, under, despite Black death: to think and be and act from there.

Sharpe is writing for and about Black being, a position and evocation that may speak to you directly. But each of us can also take up Weheliye's (2014) call to consider who theorizes for the global human experience, and understand that we are all living in the wake of a multitude of political processes and histories that have dehumanized and excluded people from life's abundance. To understand the processes of space, place, and power is to understand our own position within these constellations, and thus to take an accounting of our own responsibility in the world. What would it mean to approach the study of political geography with a spirit of abundance, with a refusal of citizenship if citizenship fails so many, with the commitment to take up the work of wakefulness?

Earlier in this book we encountered the writing of Tuck and Yang (2012) who exhorted us to remember and insist that "decolonization is not a metaphor." Writing in his alternate persona, la paperson (2018), K. Wayne Yang followed that call with a treatise on becoming a "ghost in the machine" of academic knowledge production. paperson describes the university as world-*making*, and as a colonial space, yet for paperson, "colonial schools carry decolonial riders." What does he mean by this? He goes on to describe the navigation and depiction of colonial schools in Kenya by Ngugi wa Thiong'o (2012), and in Indian boarding schools in the Dakotas by Scott Lyons (2010), among others. paperson observes that wa Thiong'o's and Lyons's (and their ancestors') lines of flight and tracks through school, beyond school, escaping from school, and occupying school cannot be contained, but rather, at times enable what Harney and Moten (2013) term fugitivity: a refusal to be contained. As you close this book and return to your life, I would encourage you to follow the bread crumbs of inspiration left by these thinkers, and to consider the ways in which we are making the world together through our day-to-day practices, and to move forward into the future in that spirit.

Keywords

Anthropocene   The Anthropocene is a term being considered by geologists and other scientists to mark a new geologic era in which humans are an integral aspect of the earth as a system, shaping its climate, geology, and ecosystems in profound ways and leading to a break with the past.

Climate justice   Climate justice draws attention to the need for responses to climate change to be treated as a problem of environmental justice – that is, with attention to who has caused the harm and who will be most impacted.

Prefigurative politics   Prefigurative politics describes the ways that people work to enact in the present the kinds of social and political relationships they wish to create for the future.

Temporality   Relating to how time operates and its qualities.

Further Reading

Anthropocene geopolitics

Ahuja, N. 2016. The Anthropocene Debate: On the Limits of Colonial Geology. September 9. https://ahuja.sites.ucsc.edu/2016/09/09/the-anthropocene-debate-on-the-limits-of-colonial-geology (accesed 27 September 2019).

Baldwin, A. 2014. Pluralising Climate Change and Migration: An Argument in Favour of Open Futures. *Geography Compass* 8(8): 516–528.

Baldwin, A. 2016. Premediation and White Affect: Climate Change and Migration in Critical Perspective. *Transactions of the Institute of British Geographers* 41: 78–90.

Barnett, J. and Adger, W.N. 2007. Climate Change, Human Security and Violent Conflict. *Political Geography* 26(6): 639–655.

Chaturvedi, S. and Doyle, T. 2016. *Climate Terror: A Critical Geopolitics of Climate Change.* Cham: Springer.

Clark, N. 2011. *Inhuman Nature: Sociable Life on a Dynamic Planet.* London: Sage.

Dalby, S. 2007. Anthropocene Geopolitics: Globalisation, Empire, Environment and Critique. *Geography Compass* 1(1): 103–118.

Dalby, S. 2013. The Geopolitics of Climate Change. *Political Geography* 37: 38–47.

Derickson, K.D. and MacKinnon, D. 2015. Toward an Interim Politics of Resourcefulness for the Anthropocene. *Annals of the Association of American Geographers* 105(2): 304–312.

Elden, S. 2013. Secure the Volume: Vertical Geopolitics and the Depth of Power. *Political Geography* 34: 35–51.

Farbotko, C. and Lazrus, H. 2012. The First Climate Refugees? Contesting Global Narratives of Climate Change in Tuvalu. *Global Environmental Change* 22(2): 382–390.

Gerhardt, H., Steinberg, P.E., Tasch, J. et al. 2010. Contested Sovereignty in a Changing Arctic. *Annals of the Association of American Geographers* 100(4): 992–1002.

Ginn, F. 2015. When Horses Won't Eat: Apocalypse and the Anthropocene. *Annals of the Association of American Geographers* 105(2): 351–359.

Hartmann, B. 2010. Rethinking Climate Refugees and Climate Conflict: Rhetoric, Reality and the Politics of Policy Discourse. *Journal of International Development* 22(2): 233–246.

Katz, C. 1995. Under the Falling Sky: Apocalyptic Environmentalism and the Production of Nature. In A. Callari, S. Cullenberg, and C. Biewener (eds), *Marxism in the Postmodern Age*. New York: Guilford Press, pp.276–282.

McDonald, M. 2013. Discourses of Climate Security. *Political Geography* 33: 42–51.

Selby, J., Dahi, O.S., Fröhlich, C. et al. 2017. Climate Change and the Syrian Civil War Revisited. *Political Geography* 60: 232–244.

Swyngedouw, E. 2013. Apocalypse Now! Fear and Doomsday Pleasures. *Capitalism Nature Socialism* 24(1): 9–18.

Decolonizing futurities and prefigurative politics

Belcourt, B.-R. 2016. A Poltergeist Manifesto. *Feral Feminisms* 6.

Butler, O.E. 1993. *Parable of the Sower.* New York: Four Walls Eight Windows.

Collard, R.-C., Dempsey, J., and Sundberg, J. 2015. A Manifesto for Abundant Futures. *Annals of the Association of American Geographers* 105(2): 322–330.

Davis, H. and Todd, Z. 2017. On the Importance of a Date, or, Decolonizing the Anthropocene. *ACME: An International Journal for Critical Geographies* 16(4): 761–780.

Dyson, J. and Jeffrey, C. 2018. Everyday Prefiguration: Youth Social Action in North India. *Transactions of the Institute of British Geographers* 43(4): 573–585.

English, D.K. and Kim, A. 2013. Now We Want Our Funk Cut: Janelle Monáe's Neo-Afrofuturism. *American Studies* 52(4): 217–230.

Frazier, C.M. 2016. Troubling Ecology: Wangechi Mutu, Octavia Butler, and Black Feminist Interventions in Environmentalism. *Critical Ethnic Studies* 2(1): 40–72.

Gergan, M., Smith, S., and Vasudevan, P. 2018. Earth Beyond Repair. *Environment and Planning D: Society and Space.* doi: 10.1177/0263775818756079.

Gilroy, P. 2018. "Where Every Breeze Speaks of Courage and Liberty": Offshore Humanism and Marine Xenology, or, Racism and the Problem of Critique at Sea Level. *Antipode* 50(1): 3–22.

Gumbs, A.P. 2018. *M Archive: After the End of the World.* Durham, NC: Duke University Press.

Gumbs, A.P. Martens, C., and Williams, M., eds. 2016. *Revolutionary Mothering: Love on the Front Lines.* Oakland, CA: PM Press.

Hage, G. 2017. *Is Racism an Environmental Threat.* Cambridge: Polity Press.

Hunt, D. 2018. "In Search of Our Better Selves": Totem Transfer Narratives and Indigenous Futurities. *American Indian Culture and Research Journal* 42(1): 71–90.

Harney, S. and Moten, F. 2013. *The Undercommons: Fugitive Planning & Black Study.* Brooklyn, NY: Minor Compositions.

Houston, D. 2013. Environmental Justice Storytelling: Angels and Isotopes at Yucca Mountain, Nevada. *Antipode* 45(2): 417–435.

Krug, J.A. 2018. *Fugitive Modernities: Kisama and the Politics of Freedom.* Durham, NC: Duke University Press.

McKittrick, K. 2013. Plantation Futures. *Small Axe* 17(342): 1–15.

Muñoz, J.E. 2009. *Cruising Utopia: The Then and There of Queer Futurity.* New York City: New York University Press.

Paperson, la. 2018. *A Third University Is Possible.* Minneapolis, MN: University of Minnesota Press.

Pulido, L. 2012. The Future Is Now: Climate Change and Environmental Justice. *Social Text: Periscope,* January. https://socialtextjournal.org/periscope_article/the_future_is_now_climate_change_and_environmental_justice/ (accessed 27 September 2019).

Robbins, P. and Moore, S.A. 2013. Ecological Anxiety Disorder: Diagnosing the Politics of the Anthropocene. *Cultural Geographies* 20(1): 3–19.

Schlosser, K. 2015. Apocalyptic Imaginaries, Gramsci, and the Last Man on Earth. *GeoHumanities,* 1(2): 307–320.

Sharpe, C. 2016. *In the Wake: On Blackness and Being.* Durham, NC: Duke University Press.

Strauss, K. 2015. These Overheating Worlds. *Annals of the Association of American Geographers* 105(2): 342–350.

Tuck, E. and Ree, C. 2013. A Glossary of Haunting. In S.L. Holman Jones, T.E. Adams, and C. Ellis (eds), *Handbook of Autoethnography.* New York: Routledge, pp.639–658.

Vimalassery, M. 2016. Fugitive Decolonization. *Theory & Event* 19(4). Online at: https://muse.jhu.edu/article/633284 (accessed October 1, 2019).

Weheliye, A. 2014. *Habeas Viscus: Racializing Assemblages, Biopolitics, and Black Feminist Theories of the Human.* Durham, NC: Duke University Press.

Whyte, K.P. 2016. Our Ancestors' Dystopia Now: Indigenous Conservation and the Anthropocene. In U. Heise, J. Christensen, and M. Niemann (eds), *Routledge Companion to the Environmental Humanities.* New York: Routledge.

Whyte, K.P. 2018. Indigenous Science (Fiction) for the Anthropocene: Ancestral Dystopias and Fantasies of Climate Change Crises. *Environment and Planning E: Nature and Space,* 1: 224–242.

References

Aalbers, M.B. 2016. *The Financialization of Home and the Mortgage Market Crisis*. New York: Routledge.

Abrams, P. 1988. Notes on the Difficulty of Studying the State. *Journal of Historical Sociology* 1: 58–89.

Abu-Lughod, J. 1989. On the Remaking of History: How to Reinvent the Past. *Remaking History*, 111–129.

Abu-Lughod, L. 2002. Do Muslim Women Really Need Saving? Anthropological Reflections on Cultural Relativism and Its Others. *American Anthropologist* 104(3): 783–790.

Abu-Lughod, L. 2013. *Do Muslim Women Need Saving?* Cambridge, MA: Harvard University Press.

Achcar, G. 2016. *Morbid Symptoms: Relapse in the Arab Uprising*. Stanford, CA: Stanford University Press.

Acharya, A. 2014. Global International Relations (IR) and Regional Worlds: A New Agenda for International Studies. *International Studies Quarterly* 58(4): 647–659.

Acharya, A. and Buzan, B. 2009. *Non-Western International Relations Theory: Perspectives on and Beyond Asia*. Abingdon: Routledge.

Adey, P. 2009. Facing Airport Security: Affect, Biopolitics, and the Preemptive Securitization of the Mobile Body. *Environment and Planning D: Society and Space* 27(2): 274–295.

Agamben, G. 1998. *Homo Sacer: Sovereign Power and Bare Life*. Stanford, CA: Stanford University Press.

Agamben, G. 2005. *State of Exception*. Chicago: University of Chicago Press.

Agbola, T. 1997. *The Architecture of Fear: Urban Design and Construction Response to Urban Violence in Lagos, Nigeria*. Ibadan: Institut français de recherche en Afrique (Ifra).

Political Geography: A Critical Introduction, First Edition. Sara Smith.
© 2020 John Wiley & Sons Ltd. Published 2020 by John Wiley & Sons Ltd.

Aggarwal, R. 2004. *Beyond Lines of Control: Performance and Politics on the Disputed Borders of Ladakh, India*. Durham, NC: Duke University Press.

Agnew, J.A. 1994. The Territorial Trap: The Geographical Assumptions of International Relations Theory. *Review of International Political Economy* 1: 53–80.

Agnew, J.A. 2003. *Geopolitics: Re-Visioning Word Politics*. London: Routledge.

Agnew, J. and Muscarà, L. 2002. *Making Political Geography*. Lanham, MD: Rowman & Littlefield.

Ahmed, S. 2004. *The Cultural Politics of Emotion*. New York: Routledge.

Ahmed, S. 2010. *The Promise of Happiness*. Durham, NC: Duke University Press.

Ahmed, S. 2017. *Living a Feminist Life*. Durham, NC: Duke University Press.

Ahuja, N. 2011. Abu Zubaydah and the Caterpillar. *Social Text* 29(1 [106]): 127–149.

Akhter, M. 2019. The Proliferation of Peripheries: Militarized Drones and the Reconfiguration of Global Space. *Progress in Human Geography* 43(1): 64–80.

Alderman, D.H. 2000. A Street Fit for a King: Naming Places and Commemoration in the American South. *The Professional Geographer* 52(4): 672–684.

Alexander, M. 2012. *The New Jim Crow: Mass Incarceration in the Age of Colorblindness*. New York: The New Press.

Alexander, M.J. 2005. *Pedagogies of Crossing: Meditations on Feminism, Sexual Politics, Memory, and the Sacred*. Durham, NC: Duke University Press.

Allard, L.B.B. 2016. Why the Founder of Standing Rock Sioux Camp Can't Forget the Whitestone Massacre. *Yes! Magazine* September 3.

Allen, J. 2003. *Lost Geographies of Power*. Malden, MA: Blackwell Publishing.

Amin, A. 2004. Regions Unbound: Towards a New Politics of Place. *Geografiska Annaler: Series B, Human Geography* 86(1): 33–44.

Amin, S. 1974. Accumulation and Development: A Theoretical Model. *Review of African Political Economy* 1(1): 9–26.

Amoore, L. 2006. Biometric Borders: Governing Mobilities in the War on Terror. *Political Geography* 25(3): 336–351.

Amoore, L. and Hall, A. 2009. Taking People Apart: Digitized Dissection and the Body at the Border. *Environment and Planning D: Society and Space* 27(3): 444–464.

Amos, V. and Parmar, P. 1984. Challenging Imperial Feminism. *Feminist Review* 17: 3–19.

An, N., Liu, C., and Zhu, H. 2016. Popular Geopolitics of Chinese Nanjing Massacre Films: A Feminist Approach. *Gender, Place & Culture* 23(6): 786–800.

An, N. and Zhu, H. 2018. Conceptual and Theoretical Debates in Modern Geopolitics and Their Implications for Chinese Geopolitics. *Area Development and Policy* 3(3): 368–382.

Anand, N. 2011. Pressure: The PoliTechnics of Water Supply in Mumbai. *Cultural Anthropology* 26(4): 542–564.

Anand, N. 2017. *Hydraulic City: Water and the Infrastructures of Citizenship in Mumbai*. Durham, NC: Duke University Press.

Anand, N., Agaaz, A.S.S., and CAMP. 2008. *Ek Dozen Paani*. Documentary. https://vimeo.com/channels/ekdozenpaani.

Anderson, B. 2006. *Imagined Communities: Reflections on the Origin and Spread of Nationalism*. London: Verso.

Anderson, B. 2010. Preemption, Precaution, Preparedness: Anticipatory Action and Future Geographies. *Progress in Human Geography* 34(6): 777–798.

Anderson, B., Kearnes, M., McFarlane, C. et al. 2012. On Assemblages and Geography. *Dialogues in Human Geography* 2(2): 171–189.

Anderson, C. 2016. *White Rage: The Unspoken Truth of Our Racial Divide*. New York: Bloomsbury Publishing.

Anderson, K.J. 1987. The Idea of Chinatown: The Power of Place and Institutional Practice in the Making of a Racial Category. *Annals of the Association of American Geographers* 77(4): 580–598.

Anderson, M. 2013. The Beginnings of the Embassy (January 1972) Michael Anderson, "Founding of the Embassy" [Interview with Brenda Gifford, Recorded at the National Film and Sound Archive, 17 June 2011]. In G. Foley, A. Schaap, and E. Howell (eds). *The Aboriginal Tent Embassy: Sovereignty, Black Power, Land Rights and the State*. London: Routledge, pp.117–122.

Anzaldúa, G.B. 1987. *La Frontera: The New Mestiza*. San Francisco: Aunt Lute.

Arendt, H. 1973. *The Origins of Totalitarianism*. New York: Houghton Mifflin Harcourt.

Asad, T. 2003. *Formations of the Secular: Christianity, Islam, Modernity*. Stanford, CA: Stanford University Press.

Ashiq, P. 2015. Now, Buddhist Group Seeks Modi's Intervention to Stop "Love Jehad" in Ladakh. *Hindustan Times,* January 18, 2015. http://www.hindustantimes.com/jandk/now-buddhist-group-seeks-modi-s-intervention-to-stop-love-jehad-in-ladakh/article1-1307914.aspx (accessed October 1, 2019).

Austen, I. 2015. Aylan Kurdi's Death Resonates in Canadian Election Campaign. *New York Times,* September 3, 2015. https://www.nytimes.com/2015/09/04/world/americas/aylan-kurdis-death-raises-resonates-in-canadian-election-campaign.html?_r=1 (accessed October 1, 2019).

Ayoob, M. 2002. Inequality and Theorizing in International Relations: The Case for Subaltern Realism. *International Studies Review* 4(3): 27–48.

Bacchetta, P. 2000. Sacred Space in Conflict in India: The Babri Masjid Affair. *Growth and Change* 31: 255–284.

Bahng, A. 2018. *Migrant Futures: Decolonizing Speculation in Financial Times*. Durham, NC: Duke University Press.

Baldwin, A. 2012. Whiteness and Futurity. *Progress in Human Geography* 36(2): 172–187.

Baldwin, A. 2014. Pluralising Climate Change and Migration: An Argument in Favour of Open Futures. *Geography Compass* 8(8): 516–528.

Baldwin, A. 2016. Premediation and White Affect: Climate Change and Migration in Critical Perspective. *Transactions of the Institute of British Geographers* 41: 78–90.

Ballard, R. 2015. Geographies of Development III: Militancy, Insurgency, Encroachment and Development by the Poor. *Progress in Human Geography* 39(2): 214–224.

Bannerji, H. 2000. *The Dark Side of the Nation: Essays on Multiculturalism, Nationalism and Gender*. Toronto: Canadian Scholars' Press.

Barker, A.J. 2015. "A Direct Act of Resurgence, a Direct Act of Sovereignty": Reflections on Idle No More, Indigenous Activism, and Canadian Settler Colonialism. *Globalizations* 12(1): 43–65.

Basham, V.M. 2018. Liberal Militarism as Insecurity, Desire and Ambivalence: Gender, Race and the Everyday Geopolitics of War. *Security Dialogue* 49: 32–43.

Bauman, Z. 1989. *Modernity and the Holocaust*. Ithaca, NY: Cornell University Press.

Bausells, M. and Shearlaw, M. 2015. Poets Speak out for Refugees: "No One Leaves Home, Unless Home Is the Mouth of a Shark." *The Guardian*, September 16. http://www.theguardian.com/books/2015/sep/16/poets-speak-out-for-refugees- (accessed October 1, 2019).

Bayat, A. 2009. *Life as Politics: How Ordinary People Change the Middle East*. Stanford, CA: Stanford University Press.

Beaumont, J., Miller, B., and Nicholls, W. 2016. Introduction: Conceptualizing the Spatialities of Social Movements. In J. Beaumont, B. Miller, and W. Nicholls (eds), *Spaces of Contention*. New York: Routledge, pp.1–24.

Beck, U. 1992. *Risk Society: Towards a New Modernity*. London: Sage.

Beek, M. van. 2000. Beyond Identity Fetishism: "Communal" Conflict in Ladakh and the Limits of Autonomy. *Cultural Anthropology* 15: 525–569.

Behera, N.C. 2000. *State, Identity and Violence: Jammu, Kashmir and Ladakh*. New Delhi: Manohar.

Belcher, O. 2018. Anatomy of a Village Razing: Counterinsurgency, Violence, and Securing the Intimate in Afghanistan. *Political Geography* 62: 94–105.

Bell, D. and Binnie, J. 2000. *The Sexual Citizen: Queer Politics and Beyond*. Cambridge: Polity.

Bellamy, A.J., Bleiker, R., Davies, S.E. et al. 2007. *Security and the War on Terror*. New York: Routledge.

Bender-Baird, K. 2016. Peeing under Surveillance: Bathrooms, Gender Policing, and Hate Violence. *Gender, Place & Culture* 23(7): 983–988.

Berlant, L. 1997. *The Queen of America Goes to Washington: Essays on Sex and Citizenship*. Durham, NC: Duke University Press.

Berlant, L. 2011. *Cruel Optimism*. Durham, NC: Duke University Press.

Berlant, L. and Warner, M. 1998. Sex in Public. *Critical Inquiry* 24(2): 547–566.

Bhan, M., Duschinski, H., and Osuri, G. 2019. The International Community Must Intervene on Kashmir. *Open Democracy*. https://www.opendemocracy.net/en/international-community-must-intervene-kashmir (accessed October 1, 2019).

Bialasiewicz, L. 2006. "The Death of the West": Samuel Huntington, Oriana Fallaci and a New "Moral" Geopolitics of Births and Bodies. *Geopolitics* 11(4): 701–724.

Bialasiewicz, L. 2012. Off-Shoring and Out-Sourcing the Borders of Europe: Libya and EU Border Work in the Mediterranean. *Geopolitics* 17(4): 843–866.

Biehl, J. 2013. *Vita: Life in a Zone of Social Abandonment*. Berkeley: University of California Press.

Billig, M. 1995. *Banal Nationalism*. Los Angeles: Sage.

Blake, S. 2018. We Talked to Maya Little about Protesting Silent Sam and Her Arrest Monday. *The Daily Tar Heel*. May 1, 2018. http://www.dailytarheel.com/article/2018/05/maya-little-quanda-0501 (accessed October 1, 2019).

Blaut, J.M. 1999. Environmentalism and Eurocentrism. *Geographical Review* 89(3): 391–408.

Bledsoe, A. 2016. Defender Nosso Pedaço De Chão: Quilombola Struggles in Bahia. PhD Dissertation, The University of North Carolina at Chapel Hill.

Bledsoe, A. 2017. Marronage as a Past and Present Geography in the Americas. *Southeastern Geographer* 57(1): 30–50.

Bledsoe, A. 2019. Afro-Brazilian Resistance to Extractivism in the Bay of Aratu. *Annals of the American Association of Geographers* 109(2): 492–501.

Boesche, R. 2002. *The First Great Political Realist: Kautilya and His Arthashastra*. Lanham, MD: Lexington Books.

Borderline Europe. 2013. At the Limen: The Implementation of the Return Directive in Italy, Cyprus and Spain. http://www.borderline-europe.de/sites/default/files/features/2014_Final_brochure_at-the-limen.pdf.

Borrows, J. 2010. *Canada's Indigenous Constitution*. Toronto: University of Toronto Press.

Botterill, K., Hopkins, P., and Sanghera, G. 2018. Familial Geopolitics and Ontological Security: Intergenerational Relations, Migration and Minority Youth (in) Securities in Scotland. *Geopolitics*, 1–26.

Botterill, K., Hopkins, P., Sanghera, G. et al. 2016. Securing Disunion: Young People's Nationalism, Identities and (in) Securities in the Campaign for an Independent Scotland. *Political Geography* 55: 124–134.

Bourdieu, P. 1990. *Outline of a Theory of Practice*. Stanford, CA: Stanford University Press.

Brand, D. 2018. Verso 55. In *The Blue Clerk: Ars Poetica in 59 Versos*. Durham, NC: Duke University Press.

Brenner, N. and Schmid, C. 2014. Planetary Urbanization. In N. Brenner (ed.), *Implosions / Explosions: Towards a Study of Planetary Urbanization*. Berlin: Jovis, pp.160–165.

Brickell, K. 2014. "The Whole World Is Watching": Intimate Geopolitics of Forced Eviction and Women's Activism in Cambodia. *Annals of the Association of American Geographers* 104(6): 1256–1272.

Brown, M.P. 2005. *Closet Space: Geographies of Metaphor from the Body to the Globe*. New York: Routledge.

Browne, K. 2004. Genderism and the Bathroom Problem: (Re) Materialising Sexed Sites, (Re) Creating Sexed Bodies. *Gender, Place & Culture* 11(3): 331–346.

Browne, K., Nash, C.J., and Hines, S. 2010. Introduction: Towards Trans Geographies. *Gender, Place & Culture* 17(5): 573–577.

Buckley, M. and Strauss, K. 2016. With, Against, and Beyond Lefebvre: Planetary Urbanization and Epistemic Plurality. *Environment and Planning D: Society and Space* 34(4): 617–636.

Bullard, R.D. 2008. *Dumping in Dixie: Race, Class, and Environmental Quality*. Boulder, CO: Westview.

Burrell, K., Hopkins, P., Isakjee, A. et al. 2018. Brexit, Race and Migration. *Environment and Planning C: Politics and Space* 37(1): 3–40.

Burton, A.M. 1994. *Burdens of History: British Feminists, Indian Women, and Imperial Culture, 1865–1915*. Chapel Hill: University of North Carolina Press.

Butalia, U. 2000. *The Other Side of Silence: Voices from the Partition of India*. Durham, NC: Duke University Press.

Butler, S.K. 2014. Real Silent Sam Group Draws Attention to Memorials. *The Daily Tar Heel*, September 25, 2014. http://www.dailytarheel.com/article/2014/09/real-silent-sam%20group%20draws%20attention%20to%20memorials (accessed Ocober 1, 2019).

Byrd, J.A. 2011. *The Transit of Empire: Indigenous Critiques of Colonialism*. Minneapolis: University of Minnesota Press.

Cabnal, L. 2012. Documento En Construcción Para Aportar a Las Reflexiones Continentales Desde El Feminismo Comunitario, Al Paradigma Ancestral Originario Del Sumak Kawsay-Buen Vivir. *Sumak Kawsay"–Buen Vivir"* http://Amismaxaj.Files.Wordpress.Com/2012/09/Buen-Vivir-Desde-El-Feminismo-Comunitario.pdf (accessed February 2, 2014).

Cahill, C., Stoudt, B.G., Matles, A. et al. 2017. The Right to the Sidewalk. in J. Hou amd S. Knierbein (eds), *City Unsilenced: Urban Resistance and Public Space in the Age of Shrinking Democracy*. New York: Routledge, pp.94–106.

Cahuas, M.C. 2019a. Burned, Broke, and Brilliant: Latinx Community Workers' Experiences Across the Greater Toronto Area's Non-Profit Sector. *Antipode* 51(1): 66–86.

Cahuas, M.C. 2019b. Interrogating Absences in Latinx Theory and Placing Blackness in Latinx Geographical Thought: A Critical Reflection. *Society & Space.*

Caldwell, K. 2007. *Negras in Brazil: Re-Envisioning Black Women, Citizenship, and the Politics of Identity.* Princeton, NJ: Rutgers University Press.

Caldwell, K.L. 2018. Sexism, Racism Drive Black Women to Run for Office in both Brazil and US. *The Conversation,* October 4, 2018. http://theconversation.com/sexism-racism-drive-more-black-women-to-run-for-office-in-both-brazil-and-us-104208 (accessed October 1, 2019)

Carter, D. 2005. *Stonewall: The Riots That Sparked the Gay Revolution.* Princeton, NJ: Macmillan.

Casas-Cortes, M., Cobarrubias, S., and Pickles, J. 2015. Changing Borders, Rethinking Sovereignty: Towards a Right to Migrate. *REMHU: Revista Interdisciplinar Da Mobilidade Humana* 23(44): 47–60.

Casolo, J. and Doshi, S. 2013. Domesticated Dispossessions? Towards a Transnational Feminist Geopolitics of Development. *Geopolitics* 18(4): 800–834.

Castaño, P. 2007. América Latina y La Producción Transnacional de Sus Imágenes y Representaciones. Algunas Perspectivas Preliminares. In D. Mato and A. Maldonado Fermín (eds), *Cultura y Transformaciones Sociales En Tiempos de Globalización.* Buenos Aires: CLACSO, pp. 213--232.

Castells, M. 1977. *The Urban Question: A Marxist Approach,* trans A. Sheridan. London: Edward Arnold.

Castells, M. 1983. *The City and the Grassroots: A Cross-Cultural Theory of Urban Social Movements.* Berkeley, CA: University of California Press.

Castells, M. 1996. *The Rise of Network Society.* Oxford: Blackwell.

Castree, N. 2015. Unfree Radicals: Geoscientists, the Anthropocene, and Left Politics. *Antipode* 49: 52–74.

Cavallaro, J., Sonnenberg, S., and Knuckey, S. 2012. Living under Drones: Death, Injury and Trauma to Civilians from US Drone Practices in Pakistan. *International Human Rights and Conflict Resolution Clinic at Stanford Law School and Global Justice Clinic at NYU School of Law.*

Certeau, M. de. 1984. *The Practice of Everyday Life.* Berkeley: University of California Press.

Césaire, A. 2000. *Discourse on Colonialism.* New York: New York University Press.

Cháirez-Garza, J.F. 2014. Touching Space: Ambedkar on the Spatial Features of Untouchability. *Contemporary South Asia* 22(1): 37–50.

Chakrabarti, S. and Patnaik, U., eds 2018. *Agrarian and Other Histories: Essays for Binay Bhushan Chaudhuri.* New Delhi: Tulika Books.

Chakrabarty, D. 2008. *Provincializing Europe: Postcolonial Thought and Historical Difference.* Princeton, NJ: Princeton University Press.

Chatterton, P. 2010. SYMPOSIUM Autonomy: The Struggle for Survival, Self-Management and the Common Organiser: Paul Chatterton: Introduction. *Antipode* 42(4): 897–908.

Clark, J.H. 2017. Feminist Geopolitics and the Middle East: Refuge, Belief, and Peace. *Geography Compass* 11(2): e12304.

Clark, N. 2011. *Inhuman Nature: Sociable Life on a Dynamic Planet.* London: Sage.

Cofield, R. and Doan P. In press. Toilets and the Public Imagination: Planning for Safe and Inclusive Spaces. In B. Gökarıksel, M. Hawkins, C. Neubert et al. *Geography*

Unbound: Discomfort, Bodies, and Prefigured Futures. Morgantown, WV: West Virginia University Press.

Collard, R.-C., Dempsey, J., and Sundberg, J. 2015. A Manifesto for Abundant Futures. *Annals of the Association of American Geographers* 105(2): 322–330.

Collins, P.H. 1990. *Black Feminist Thought: Knowledge, Consciousness, and the Politics of Empowerment*. New York: Routledge.

Collins, P.H. 1999. Producing the Mothers of the Nation: Race, Class and Contemporary US Population Policies. In N. Yuval-Davis (ed.), *Women, Citizenship and Difference*. London: Zed Books, pp.118–129.

Combahee River Collective 1977. *A Black Feminist Statement*. https://americanstudies. yale.edu/sites/default/files/files/Keyword%20Coalition_Readings.pdf (accessed October 1, 2019).

Commemorative Landscapes of North Carolina. 2010. March 19, 2010. http://docsouth. unc.edu/commland/monument/41/ (accessed October 1, 2019).

Comissão Pastoral da Terra (CPT) 2000. *Assassinatos no campo Brasil 1985–2000: Violência e impunidade*, Goiânia, MT: CPT Press.

Conrad, R. 2014. *Against Equality: Queer Revolution, Not Mere Inclusion*. Edinburgh: AK Press.

Consolidated Federal Laws of Canada, Canadian Multiculturalism Act 2014. *Code 24*. Vol. Supplement 4. http://laws-lois.justice.gc.ca/eng/acts/c-18.7/page-1.html#h-3 (accessed October 1, 2019).

Coulthard, G.S. 2007. Subjects of Empire: Indigenous Peoples and the "Politics of Recognition" in Canada. *Contemporary Political Theory* 6(4): 437–460.

Coulthard, G.S. 2012. #IdleNoMore in Historical Context. *Decolonization: Indigeneity, Education & Society* December 24.

Coulthard, G.S. 2014. *Red Skin, White Masks: Rejecting the Colonial Politics of Recognition*. Minneapolis: University of Minnesota Press.

Cowen, D. and Gilbert, E., eds 2008. *War, Citizenship, Territory*. New York: Routledge.

Crenshaw, K. 1989. Demarginalizing the Intersection of Race and Sex: A Black Feminist Critique of Antidiscrimination Doctrine, Feminist Theory and Antiracist Politics. *University of Chicago Legal Forum* 1: 139–167.

Crenshaw, K. 1991. Mapping the Margins: Intersectionality, Identity Politics, and Violence against Women of Color. *Stanford Law Review* 43(6): 1241–1299.

Cresswell, T. 2006. *On the Move: Mobility in the Modern Western World*. New York: Routledge.

Cresswell, T. 2012. *Geographic Thought: A Critical Introduction*. Chichester: John Wiley & Sons.

Critical Resistance 2008. *Abolition Now! Ten Years of Strategy and Struggle against the Prison Industrial Complex*. Oakland, CA: AK Press.

Crutzen, P.J. 2002. The Anthropocene: Geology of Mankind. *Nature* 415(6867): 23–24.

Crutzen, P.J. and Stoermer, E.F. 2000. The Anthropocene. *Global Change Newsletter* 41: 17–18.

Culcasi, K. 2014. Disordered Ordering: Mapping the Divisions of the Ottoman Empire. *Cartographica: The International Journal for Geographic Information and Geovisualization* 49(1): 2–17.

Curley, A. 2016. Intervention – "Water Is Life and Life Is Sovereignty: Context and Considerations for Critical Geographers." *Antipode Interventions*, December. https://antipodefoundation. org/2016/12/13/water-is-life-and-life-is-sovereignty/ (accessed October 1, 2019).

Curley, A. 2019a. T'áá hwó ají t'éego and the Moral Economy of Navajo Coal Workers. *Annals of the American Association of Geographers* 109(1): 71–86.

Curley, A. 2019b. Unsettling Indian Water Settlements: The Little Colorado River, the San Juan River, and Colonial Enclosures. *Antipode.* doi: 10.1111/anti.12535.

Dahlman, C.T. 2009. Territory. In C. Gallaher, C.T. Dahlman, M. Gilmartin et al (eds), *Concepts in Political Geography*. Thousand Oaks, CA: Sage, pp.77–86.

Daigle, M. 2016. Awawanenitakik: The Spatial Politics of Recognition and Relational Geographies of Indigenous Self-determination. *The Canadian Geographer/Le Géographe Canadien* 60(2): 259–269.

Daigle, M. 2018. Resurging through Kishiichiwan: The Spatial Politics of Indigenous Water Relations. *Decolonization: Indigeneity, Education & Society* 7(1): 159–172.

Daigle, M. 2019. The Spectacle of Reconciliation: On (the) Unsettling Responsibilities to Indigenous Peoples in the Academy. *Environment and Planning D: Society and Space* 37(4): 703–721.

Dalby, S. 2007. Anthropocene Geopolitics: Globalisation, Empire, Environment and Critique. *Geography Compass* 1(1): 103–118.

Dalby, S. 2010. Recontextualising Violence, Power and Nature: The next Twenty Years of Critical Geopolitics? *Political Geography* 29(5): 280–288.

Dalby, S. 2013. The Geopolitics of Climate Change. *Political Geography* 37: 38–47.

Daley, P. 2013. Refugees, IDPS and Citizenship Rights: The Perils of Humanitarianism in the African Great Lakes Region. *Third World Quarterly* 34(5): 893–912.

Darling, J. 2017. Forced Migration and the City: Irregularity, Informality, and the Politics of Presence. *Progress in Human Geography* 41(2): 178–198.

Das, V. 1995. *Critical Events: An Anthropological Perspective on Contemporary India*. New Delhi: Oxford University Press.

Das, V. 2007. *Life and Words: Violence and the Descent into the Ordinary*. Berkeley: University of California Press.

Datta, A. 2016. The Intimate City: Violence, Gender and Ordinary Life in Delhi Slums. *Urban Geography* 37(3): 323–342.

Davies, C.B. 2007. *Left of Karl Marx: The Political Life of Black Communist Claudia Jones*. Durham, NC: Duke University Press.

Davis, A. and Dent, G. 2001. Prison as a Border: A Conversation on Gender, Globalization, and Punishment. *Signs: Journal of Women in Culture and Society* 26(4): 1235–1241.

Davis, A.Y. 1996. Gender, Class, and Multiculturalism: Rethinking "Race" Politics. In A. Gordon and C. Newfield (eds), *Mapping Multiculturalism*. Minneapolis, MN: University of Minnesota Press, pp.40–48.

Davis, A.Y. 1998. Racialized Punishment and Prison Abolition. In J. James (ed.), *The Angela Y. Davis Reader*. Malden, MA: Wiley Blackwell, pp.96–107.

Davis, A.Y. 2011. *Women, Race, & Class*. New York: Vintage.

Davis, H. and Todd, Z. 2017. On the Importance of a Date, or, Decolonizing the Anthropocene. *ACME: An International Journal for Critical Geographies* 16(4): 761–780.

Davis, J., Moulton, A.A., Van Sant, L. et al. 2019. Anthropocene, Capitalocene, … Plantationocene?: A Manifesto for Ecological Justice in an Age of Global Crises. *Geography Compass* 13(5): e12438.

Davis, M. 2002. *Late Victorian Holocausts: El Niño Famines and the Making of the Third World*. London: Verso.

Davis, S. 2015. *The Empires' Edge: Militarization, Resistance, and Transcending Hegemony in the Pacific*. Athens, GA: University of Georgia Press.

Davis, S. 2017. Apparatuses of Occupation: Translocal Social Movements, States and the Archipelagic Spatialities of Power. *Transactions of the Institute of British Geographers* 42(1): 110–122.

Deitcher, D. 1995. *The Question of Equality: Lesbian and Gay Politics in America since Stonewall*. New York: Scribner.

Deleuze, G. 1988. *Foucault*. Minneapolis, MN: University of Minnesota Press.

Deleuze, G. and Guattari, F. 1987. *A Thousand Plateaus*, trans. B. Massumi. Minneapolis: University of Minnesota Press. (Original Work Published 1980.)

Dennison, J. 2012. *Colonial Entanglement: Constituting a Twenty-First-Century Osage Nation*. Chapel Hill, NC: University of North Carolina Press.

Derickson, K.D. 2017. Masters of the Universe. *Environment and Planning D: Society and Space* 36(3): 556–562.

Detention Watch Network 2017. Immigration Detention 101. Detention Watch Network. https://www.detentionwatchnetwork.org/ (accessed October 1, 2019).

Dhillon, J. and Estes, N. 2016. Introduction: Standing Rock,# NoDAPL, and Mni Wiconi. *Cultural Anthropology, Hot Spots*. https://culanth.org/fieldsights/introduction-standing-rock-no-dapl-and-mni-wiconi (accessed October 1, 2019).

DiAngelo, R. 2011. White Fragility. *The International Journal of Critical Pedagogy* 3(3): 54–70.

Dimpfl, M. 2017. Micro (Bial) Management: Everyday Cleanliness and the Divisive Power of Hygienic Worries. *Cultural Geographies* 25(1): 201–216.

Dimpfl, M. and Smith, S. 2018. Cosmopolitan Sidestep: University Life, Intimate Geopolitics and the Hidden Costs of "Global" Citizenship. *Area* https://doi.org/10.1111/area.12497.

Dittmer, J. 2010. *Popular Culture, Geopolitics, and Identity*. Blue Ridge Summit, US: Rowman & Littlefield.

Dittmer, J. 2012. *Captain America and the Nationalist Superhero: Metaphors, Narratives, and Geopolitics*. Philadelphia: Temple University Press.

Dittmer, J. 2014. Geopolitical Assemblages and Complexity. *Progress in Human Geography* 38(3): 385–401.

Dittmer, J. and Gray, N. 2010. Popular Geopolitics 2.0: Towards New Methodologies of the Everyday. *Geography Compass* 4(11): 1664–1677.

Dixon, D.P. 2015. *Feminist Geopolitics: Material States*. Farnham: Ashgate.

Doan, P.L. 2007. Queers in the American City: Transgendered Perceptions of Urban Space. *Gender, Place and Culture* 14(1): 57–74.

Doan, P.L. 2010. The Tyranny of Gendered Spaces – Reflections from beyond the Gender Dichotomy. *Gender, Place & Culture* 17(5): 635–654.

Dodds, K. 2008. Icy Geopolitics. *Environment and Planning D: Society and Space* 26(1): 1–6.

Dodds, K. 2010a. Flag Planting and Finger Pointing: The Law of the Sea, the Arctic and the Political Geographies of the Outer Continental Shelf. *Political Geography* 29(2): 63–73.

Dodds, K. 2010b. Jason Bourne: Gender, Geopolitics, and Contemporary Representations of National Security. *Journal of Popular Film & Television* 38(1): 21–33.

Dodds, K. and Sidaway, J.D. 1994. Locating Critical Geopolitics. *Environment and Planning D: Society and Space* 12(5): 515–524.

Domosh, M. 2015. President's Column: Why Is Our Geography Curriculum so White? AAG Newsletter. http://news.aag.org/2015/06/why-is-our-geography-curriculum-so-white/ (accessed October 1, 2019).

Doshi, S. 2013. The Politics of the Evicted: Redevelopment, Subjectivity, and Difference in Mumbai's Slum Frontier. *Antipode* 45(4): 844–865.

Dowler, L. and Sharp, J.P. 2001. A Feminist Geopolitics? *Space & Polity* 5: 165–176.

Dunbar-Ortiz, R. 2014. *An Indigenous Peoples' History of the United States*. Boston, MA: Beacon Press.

Duschinski, H., Bhan, M., Zia, A. et al. (eds) 2018. *Resisting Occupation in Kashmir*. Philadelphia: University of Pennsylvania Press.

Dyson, J. and Jeffrey, C. 2018. Everyday Prefiguration: Youth Social Action in North India. *Transactions of the Institute of British Geographers* 43(4): 573–585.

Eaves, L.E. 2019. The Imperative of Struggle: Feminist and Gender Geographies in the United States. *Gender, Place & Culture* 26(7–9): 1314–1321.

Elden, S. 2009. *Terror and Territory: The Spatial Extent of Sovereignty*. Minneapolis, MN: University of Minnesota Press.

Elden, S. 2013a. Secure the Volume: Vertical Geopolitics and the Depth of Power. *Political Geography* 34: 35–51.

Elden, S. 2013b. *The Birth of Territory*. Chicago: University of Chicago Press.

Elliott-Cooper, A. 2018. "Free, Decolonised Education" – A Lesson from the South African Student Struggle. In J. Arday and H.S. Mirza (eds), *Dismantling Race in Higher Education*. London: Palgrave Macmillan, pp. 289–296.

Emanuel, R.E. 2017. Flawed Environmental Justice Analyses. *Science* 357(6348): 260.

Emanuel, R.E. 2018. Water in the Lumbee World: A River and Its People in a Time of Change. *Environmental History* 24(1): 25–51.

Enloe, C. 1989. *Bananas, Beaches and Bases: Making Feminist Sense of International Politics*. London: Pandora.

Esson, J., Noxolo, P., Baxter, R. et al. 2017. The 2017 RGS-IBG Chair's Theme: Decolonising Geographical Knowledges, or Reproducing Coloniality? *Area* 49(3): 384–388.

Estes, N. 2017. Fighting for Our Lives:# NoDAPL in Historical Context. *Wicazo Sa Review* 32(2): 115–122.

Evans, B. and Colls, R. 2009. Measuring Fatness, Governing Bodies: The Spatialities of the Body Mass Index (BMI) in Anti-obesity Politics. *Antipode* 41(5): 1051–1083.

Fanon, F. 1963. *The Wretched of the Earth*. New York: Grove Press.

Fanon, F. 2008. *Black Skin, White Masks*. New York: Grove Press.

Farbotko, C. and Lazrus, H. 2012. The First Climate Refugees? Contesting Global Narratives of Climate Change in Tuvalu. *Global Environmental Change* 22(2): 382–390.

Faria, C. 2010. Contesting Miss South Sudan: Gender and Nation-Building in Diasporic Discourse. *International Feminist Journal of Politics* 12(2): 222–243.

Faria, C. 2014. Styling the Nation: Fear and Desire in the South Sudanese Beauty Trade. *Transactions of the Institute of British Geographers* 39(2): 318–330.

Farmer, P. 2003. *Pathologies of Power: Health, Human Rights, and the New War on the Poor*. Berkeley, CA: University of California Press.

Featherstone, D. 2003. Spatialities of Transnational Resistance to Globalization: The Maps of Grievance of the Inter-Continental Caravan. *Transactions of the Institute of British Geographers* 28(4): 404–421.

Federici, S. 2012. *Revolution at Point Zero: Housework, Reproduction, and Feminist Struggle.* Oakland: PM Press.

Fine, M. 1994. Working the Hyphens. *Handbook of Qualitative Research.* Thousand Oaks, CA: Sage.

Fluri, J. 2011a. Armored Peacocks and Proxy Bodies: Gender Geopolitics in Aid/Development Spaces of Afghanistan. *Gender, Place & Culture* 18(4): 519–536.

Fluri, J. 2011b. Bodies, Bombs and Barricades: Geographies of Conflict and Civilian (in) Security. *Transactions of the Institute of British Geographers* 36(2): 280–296.

Fluri, J.L. 2014. "States of (in)Security: Corporeal Geographies and the Elsewhere War. *Environment and Planning D: Society and Space* 32(5): 795–814.

Fojas, C. 2017. *Zombies, Migrants, and Queers: Race and Crisis Capitalism in Pop Culture.* Urbana, IL: University of Illinois Press.

Foley, G. 2013. Reflection on the First Thirty Days. In G. Foley, A. Schaap, and E. Howell (eds), *The Aboriginal Tent Embassy: Sovereignty, Black Power, Land Rights and the State.* London: Routledge, pp.22–40.

Foley, G., Schaap, A., and Howell, E. 2013. *The Aboriginal Tent Embassy: Sovereignty, Black Power, Land Rights and the State.* London: Routledge.

Foran, C. 2017. The Canada Experiment: Is This the World's First "postnational" Country? *The Guardian,* January 4, 2017, sec. World News. https://www.theguardian.com/world/2017/jan/04/the-canada-experiment-is-this-the-worlds-first-postnational-country (accessed October 1, 2019).

Foucault, M. 1978a. *Discipline and Punish: The Birth of the Prison.* New York: Vintage.

Foucault, M. 1978b. *History of Sexuality, Volume One: An Introduction.* New York: Random House.

Foucault, M. 1978c. *The History of Sexuality.* New York: Pantheon Books.

Foucault, M. 1980. *Power/Knowledge: Selected Interviews and Other Writings 1972–1977.* New York: Pantheon.

Foucault, M. 1991. Governmentality. In G. Burchell, P. Miller, and C. Gordon (eds), *The Foucault Effect: Studies in Governmentality.* Chicago: University of Chicago Press, pp.87–104.

Foucault, M. 1997. Subjectivity and Truth. In P. Rabinow (ed.), *Ethics: Subjectivity and Truth. Essential Works of Michel Foucault, 1954–1984. Vol. 1.* London: Allen Lane.

Foucault, M. 2003. *"Society Must Be Defended": Lectures at the College de France 1975–1976,* trans. D. Macey. New York: Picador.

Foucault, M. 2007. *Security, Territory, Population: Lectures at the College de France 1977–1978,* trans. G. Burchell. New York: Palgrave Macmillan.

Foucault, M. and Simon, J.K. 1991. Michel Foucault on Attica: An Interview. *Social Justice* 18(3): 26–34.

Foxall, A. 2013. Photographing Vladimir Putin: Masculinity, Nationalism and Visuality in Russian Political Culture" *Geopolitics* 18(1): 132–156.

Frazier, C.M. 2016. Troubling Ecology: Wangechi Mutu, Octavia Butler, and Black Feminist Interventions in Environmentalism. *Critical Ethnic Studies* 2(1): 40–72.

Fregonese, S. 2009. The Urbicide of Beirut? Geopolitics and the Built Environment in the Lebanese Civil War (1975–1976). *Political Geography* 28(5): 309–318.

Fregonese, S. 2012. Urban Geopolitics 8 Years on. Hybrid Sovereignties, the Everyday, and Geographies of Peace. *Geography Compass* 6(5): 290–303.

Fregonese, S. and Ramadan. A. 2015. Hotel Geopolitics: A Research Agenda. *Geopolitics* 20(4): 793–813.

Friedman, S. 2000. Spoken Pleasures and Dangerous Desires: Sexuality, Marriage, and the State in Rural Southeastern China." *East Asia* 18: 13–39.

Frontieres, Medecins Sans. 2013. *Violence, Vulnerability and Migration: Trapped at the Gates of Europe. A Report on the Situation of Sub-Saharan Migrants in an Irregular Situation in Morocco. 2013*. Geneva: MSF.

Gaerlan Jr, C. 2013. *The Role of Media: The Mindanao War and the Moro Peoples/Internal Refugees*. http://kalilintad.tripod.com/role_of_media.htm (accessed October 1, 2019).

Gandhi, L. 2005. *Affective Communities: Anticolonial Thought, Fin-de-Siècle Radicalism, and the Politics of Friendship*. Durham, NC: Duke University Press.

Gandhi, M.K. 1931. Power Is Not an End. *Young India* 2 (February): 91.

Gandhi, M.K. 1938. *Hind Swaraj*. Ahmadebad: Navajivan Publishing House.

García-Deister, V. and López-Beltrán, C. 2015. País de Gordos/País de Muertos: Obesity, Death and Nation in Biomedical and Forensic Genetics in Mexico. *Social Studies of Science* 45(6): 797–815.

Gellner, E. 1983. *Nations and Nationalism*. Ithaca, NY: Cornell University Press.

Gergan, M.D. 2014. Precarity and Possibility: On Being Young and Indigenous in Sikkim, India. *Himalaya* 34(2): 67–80.

Gergan, M.D. 2015. Animating the Sacred, Sentient and Spiritual in Post-Humanist and Material Geographies. *Geography Compass* 9: 262–275.

Gergan, M.D. 2017. Living with Earthquakes and Angry Deities at the Himalayan Borderlands. *Annals of the American Association of Geographers* 107(2): 490–498.

Gergan, M.D., Smith, S., and Vasudevan, P. 2020. Earth Beyond Repair. *Environment and Planning D: Society and Space*. doi: 10.1177/0263775818756079.

Gerhardt, H., Steinberg, P.E., Tasch, J. et al. 2010. Contested Sovereignty in a Changing Arctic. *Annals of the Association of American Geographers* 100(4): 992–1002.

Giddens, A. 1990. *The Consequences of Modernity*. Stanford: Stanford University Press.

Giddens, A. 1991. *Modernity and Self-Identity: Self and Society in the Late Modern Age*. Stanford: Stanford University Press.

Gidwani, V.K. 2006. Subaltern Cosmopolitanism as Politics. *Antipode* 38(1): 7–21.

Gidwani, V.K. and Reddy, R.N. 2011. The Afterlives of "Waste": Notes from India for a Minor History of Capitalist Surplus. *Antipode* 43(5): 1625–1658.

Gieseking, J.J. 2015. Crossing over into Neighbourhoods of the Body: Urban Territories, Borders and Lesbian-Queer Bodies in New York City. *Area* 48(3): 262–270.

Gilmartin, M. 2009. Nation-State. In C. Gallaher, C.T. Dahlman, M. Gilmartin et al. (eds), *Key Concepts in Political Geography*. Thousand Oaks, CA: Sage, pp.19–27.

Gilmore, R.W. 2002. Fatal Couplings of Power and Difference: Notes on Racism and Geography. *Professional Geographer* 54(1): 15–24.

Gilmore, R.W. 2007. *Golden Gulag: Prisons, Surplus, Crisis, and Opposition in Globalizing California*. Berkeley, CA: University of California Press.

Gilroy, P. 1993. *The Black Atlantic: Modernity and Double Consciousness*. Cambridge, MA: Harvard University Press.

Ginn, F. 2015. When Horses Won't Eat: Apocalypse and the Anthropocene. *Annals of the Association of American Geographers* 105(2): 351–359.

Gökarıksel, B. 2012. The Intimate Politics of Secularism and the Headscarf: The Mall, the Neighborhood, and the Public Square in Istanbul. *Gender, Place & Culture* 19(1): 1–20.

Gökarıksel, B., Neubert, C., and Smith, S. 2019. Demographic Fever Dreams: Fragile Masculinity and Population Politics in the Rise of the Global Right. *Signs: Journal of Women in Culture and Society* 44(3): 561–587.

Gökarıksel, B. and Secor, A. 2010. Islamic-Ness in the Life of a Commodity: Veiling-Fashion in Turkey. *Transactions of the Institute of British Geographers* 35: 313–333.

Gökarıksel, B. and Secor, A. 2012. "Even I Was Tempted": The Moral Ambivalence and Ethical Practice of Veiling-Fashion in Turkey. *Annals of the Association of American Geographers* 102(4): 847–862.

Gökarıksel, B. and Secor, A. 2014. The Veil, Desire, and the Gaze: Turning the inside Out. *Signs: Journal of Women in Culture and Society* 40(1): 177–200.

Gökarıksel, B. and Smith, S. 2016. "Making America Great Again"?: The Fascist Body Politics of Donald Trump. *Political Geography* 54: 79–81.

González, A.C. 2012. Mujeres Indígenas Constructoras de Región: Desde América Latina Hasta Abya Yala. *Scientific Journal of Humanistic Studies* 4(6): 12–34.

Gordon, A.F. 2008. *Ghostly Matters: Haunting and the Sociological Imagination*. Minneapolis, MN: University of Minnesota Press.

Graham, N. 2017. Remembering Gwendolyn Harrison, the First African American Woman to Attend UNC. *For the Record: News and Perspectives from University Archives and Records Management Services* (blog). April 17. https://blogs.lib.unc.edu/uarms/index.php/2017/04/remembering-gwendolyn-harrison-the-first-african-american-woman-to-attend-unc/ (accessed October 1, 2019).

Graham, S. 2004a. Cities as Strategic Sites: Place Annihilation and Urban Geopolitics. In S. Graham, *Cities, War, and Terrorism: Towards an Urban Geopolitics*. Oxford: Blackwell, 31–53.

Graham, S. 2004b. Postmortem City: Towards an Urban Geopolitics. *City* 8(2): 165–196.

Graham, S. 2005. Remember Fallujah: Demonising Place, Constructing Atrocity. *Environment and Planning D: Society and Space* 23(1): 1–10.

Graham, S. 2006. Cities and the "War on Terror." *International Journal of Urban and Regional Research* 30(2): 255–276.

Gramsci, A. 1992. *Prison Notebooks*. New York: Columbia University Press.

Grayson, K., Davies, M., and Philpott, S. 2009. Pop Goes IR? Researching the Popular Culture–World Politics Continuum. *Politics* 29(3): 155–163.

Gregory, D. 2004. *The Colonial Present*. Oxford: Blackwell Publishers.

Gupta, A. 1995. Blurred Boundaries: The Discourse of Corruption, the Culture of Politics, and the Imagined State. *American Ethnologist* 22: 375–402.

Gupta, C. 2009. Hindu Women, Muslim Men: Love Jihad and Conversions. *Economic and Political Weekly* 44(51): 13–15.

Guthman, J. 2007. Can't Stomach It: How Michael Pollan et al. Made Me Want to Eat Cheetos. *Gastronomica* 7(3): 75–79.

Guthman, J. 2009. Teaching the Politics of Obesity: Insights into Neoliberal Embodiment and Contemporary Biopolitics. *Antipode* 41(5): 1110–1133.

Guthman, J. and DuPuis, M. 2006. Embodying Neoliberalism: Economy, Culture, and the Politics of Fat. *Environment and Planning D: Society and Space* 24(3): 427–448.

Halberstam, J. 2005. *In a Queer Time and Place: Transgender Bodies, Subcultural Lives*. New York: New York University Press.

Halberstam, J. 2008. The Anti-Social Turn in Queer Studies. *Graduate Journal of Social Science* 5(2): 140–156.

Hall, S., Critcher, C., Jefferson, T. et al. 2013. *Policing the Crisis: Mugging, the State and Law and Order*. London: Macmillan International Higher Education.

Hamdan, A.N. 2016. Breaker of Barriers? Notes on the Geopolitics of the Islamic State in Iraq and Sham. *Geopolitics* 21(3): 605–627.

Hannah, M.G. 2000. *Governmentality and the Mastery of Territory in Nineteenth-Century America*. Cambridge: Cambridge University Press.

Hannah, M.G. 2001. Sampling and the Politics of Representation in US Census 2000. *Environment and Planning D: Society and Space* 19(5): 515–534.

Haraway, D. 2015. Anthropocene, Capitalocene, Plantationocene, Chthulucene: Making Kin. *Environmental Humanities* 6(1): 159–165.

Haraway, D.J. 1991. Situated Knowledges: The Science Question in Feminism and the Privilege of Partial Knowledge. In D.J. Haraway, *Simians, Cyborgs, and Women*. London: Routledge, pp.183–202.

Harding, S. 1986. *The Science Question in Feminism*. Ithaca, NY: Cornell University Press.

Harney, S. and Moten, F. 2013. *The Undercommons: Fugitive Planning & Black Study*. Brooklyn, NY: Minor Compositions.

Hartman, S. 1997. *Scenes of Subjection: Terror, Slavery, and Self-Making in Nineteenth-Century America*. Oxford: Oxford University Press.

Hartman, S. 2008. *Lose Your Mother: A Journey along the Atlantic Slave Route*. New York: Farrar, Strauss, and Giroux.

Hartmann, B. 2010."Rethinking Climate Refugees and Climate Conflict: Rhetoric, Reality and the Politics of Policy Discourse. *Journal of International Development* 22(2): 233–246.

Harvey, D. 1973. *Social Justice and the City*. Baltimore: Johns Hopkins University Press.

Harvey, D. 1982. *The Limits to Capital*. Oxford: Blackwell Publishers.

Harvey, D. 1989. *The Condition of Postmodernity: An Enquiry into the Conditions of Cultural Change*. Oxford: Blackwell.

Harvey, D. 1999. *The Limits to Capital*. New York: Verso.

Harvey, D. 2003. *The New Imperialism*. New York: Oxford University Press.

Harvey, D. 2008. The Right to the City. In R.T. LeGates and F. Stout (eds), *The City Reader*. London: Routledge, pp.270–278.

Harvey, S. 2016. Remembering Zora Neale Hurston at UNC. *UNC Global.* February 24. http://uncglobal.tumblr.com/post/139916856983/remembering-zora-neale-hurston-at-unc (accessed October 1, 2019).

Hayes-Conroy, A. and Hayes-Conroy, J. 2008. Taking Back Taste: Feminism, Food and Visceral Politics. *Gender Place and Culture* 15: 461–473.

Hayes-Conroy, J. and Hayes-Conroy, A. 2013. Veggies and Visceralities: A Political Ecology of Food and Feeling. *Emotion, Space and Society* 6: 81–90.

Heininen, L. 2004. Circumpolar International Relations and Geopolitics. In *Arctic Human Development Report*. Akureyri: Stefansson Arctic Institute, pp.207–225.

Hendre, S.L. 1971. *Hindus and Family Planning: A Socio-Political Demography*. Bombay: Supraja Prakashan.

Herbst, J. 2014. *States and Power in Africa: Comparative Lessons in Authority and Control*. Princeton, NJ: Princeton University Press.

Hewitt, K. 1983. Place Annihilation: Area Bombing and the Fate of Urban Places. *Annals of the Association of American Geographers* 73(2): 257–284.

Heyes, C.J. 2006. Foucault Goes to Weight Watchers. *Hypatia* 21(2): 126–149.

Hickel, J. 2018. How Britain Stole $45 Trillion from India. December 19. https://www.aljazeera.com/indepth/opinion/britain-stole-45-trillion-india-181206124830851.html (accessed October 1, 2019).

Hirschkind, C. and Mahmood, S. 2002. Feminism, the Taliban, and Politics of Counter-Insurgency. *Anthropological Quarterly* 75(2): 339–354.

Ho, E.L.E. and McConnell, F. 2017. Conceptualizing "Diaspora Diplomacy" Territory and Populations Betwixt the Domestic and Foreign. *Progress in Human Geography* 43(2): 235–255.

Holston, J. 2008. *Insurgent Citizenship: Disjunctions of Democracy and Modernity in Brazil.* Princeton, NJ: Princeton University Press.

hooks, b. 1981. *Ain't I a Woman: Black Women and Feminism.* London: South End Press.

hooks, b. 1984. *Feminist Theory: From Margin to Center.* Boston: South End Press.

Huang, R.T. 1925. Consular Courts in China: A Legal Joke. *The Chinese Students' Monthly* 21(2): 25–26.

Hubbard, P. 2013. Kissing Is Not a Universal Right: Sexuality, Law and the Scales of Citizenship. *Geoforum* 49: 224–232.

Hübinette, T. 2012. The Reception and Consumption of Hallyu in Sweden: Preliminary Findings and Reflections. *Korea Observer* 43(3): 503.

Hudson, S. 2017. UNC Prepares to Share the Story of the Area's Indigenous People – UNC Global. *University Gazette*, November. https://global.unc.edu/news/unc-prepares-to-tell-the-story-of-the-areas-indigenous-people/ (accessed October 1, 2019).

Hunt, S. 2014. Ontologies of Indigeneity: The Politics of Embodying a Concept. *Cultural Geographies* 21(1): 27–32.

Hunt, S. and Holmes, C. 2015. Everyday Decolonization: Living a Decolonizing Queer Politics. *Journal of Lesbian Studies* 19(2): 154–172.

Hurston, Z.N. 1937. *Their Eyes Were Watching God.* New York: JB Lippincott.

Hyndman, J. 2001. Towards a Feminist Geopolitics. *The Canadian Geographer* 45: 210–222.

Hyndman, J. 2004. Mind the Gap: Bridging Feminist and Political Geography through Geopolitics. *Political Geography* 23: 307–322.

Ingram, A. 2005. The New Geopolitics of Disease: Between Global Health and Global Security. *Geopolitics* 10: 522–545.

Inuit Circumpolar Conference 2009. A Circumpolar Inuit Declaration on Sovereignty in the Arctic. Inuit Circumpolar Council. https://iccalaska.org/wp-icc/wp-content/uploads/2016/01/Signed-Inuit-Sovereignty-Declaration-11x17.pdf (accessed October 1, 2019).

Isin, E.F. 2004. The Neurotic Citizen. *Citizenship Studies* 8(3): 217–235.

Iveson, K. 2017. "Making Space Public" through Occupation: The Aboriginal Tent Embassy, Canberra. *Environment and Planning A* 49(3): 537–554.

Jazeel, T. 2014. Subaltern Geographies: Geographical Knowledge and Postcolonial Strategy. *Singapore Journal of Tropical Geography* 35(1): 88–103.

Jazeel, T. 2017. Mainstreaming Geography's Decolonial Imperative. *Transactions of the Institute of British Geographers* 42(3): 334–337.

Jefferson, B.J. 2016. Broken Windows Policing and Constructions of Space and Crime: Flatbush, Brooklyn. *Antipode* 48(5): 1270–1291.

Jefferson, B.J. 2018. Predictable Policing: Predictive Crime Mapping and Geographies of Policing and Race. *Annals of the American Association of Geographers* 108(1): 1–16.

Jeffries, M. 2015. Re-Membering Our Own Power: Occaneechi Activism, Feminism, and Political Action Theories. *Frontiers: A Journal of Women Studies* 36(1): 160–195.

Johnson, A. 2017. Getting Comfortable to Feel at Home: Clothing Practices of Black Muslim Women in Britain. *Gender, Place & Culture* 24(2): 274–287.

Johnson, A., Joseph-Salisbury, R., and Kamunge, B., eds 2019. *The Fire Now: Anti-Racist Scholarship in Times of Explicit Racial Violence*. London: Zed.

Johnson, C., Jones, R., Paasi, A. et al. 2011. Interventions on Rethinking "the Border" in Border Studies. *Political Geography* 30(2): 61–69.

Jones, M., Jones, R., Woods, M. 2015. *An Introduction to Political Geography*, 2e. London: Routledge.

Jones, R. 2009. Sovereignty and Statelessness in the Border Enclaves of India and Bangladesh. *Political Geography* 28(6): 373–381.

Jones, R. 2012. Spaces of Refusal: Rethinking Sovereign Power and Resistance at the Border. *Annals of the Association of American Geographers* 102(3): 685–699.

Jones, R. 2016. *Violent Borders: Refugees and the Right to Move*. London: Verso.

Joo, J. 2011. Transnationalization of Korean Popular Culture and the Rise of "Pop Nationalism" in Korea. *The Journal of Popular Culture* 44(3): 489–504.

Joseph-Salisbury, R. 2019. Institutionalised Whiteness, Racial Microaggressions and Black Bodies out of Place in Higher Education. *Whiteness and Education* 4(1): 1–17.

Kaba, M. 2012. Prison Culture: Transformative Justice. *Prison Culture* (blog). 2012. http://www.usprisonculture.com/blog/transformative-justice (accessed October 1, 2019).

Kabachnik, P. 2012. Wounds That Won't Heal: Cartographic Anxieties and the Quest for Territorial Integrity in Georgia. *Central Asian Survey* 31(1): 45–60.

Kapoor, S.D. 2003. BR Ambedkar, WEB DuBois and the Process of Liberation. *Economic and Political Weekly*, 5344–5349.

Katz, C. 1995. Under the Falling Sky: Apocalyptic Environmentalism and the Production of Nature. In A. Callari, C. Biewener, and S. Cullenberg (eds), *Marxism in the Postmodern Age*. New York: Guilford, pp.276–282.

Katz, C. 2001. On the Grounds of Globalization: A Topography for Feminist Political Engagement. *Signs* 26(4): 1213–1234.

Katz, C. 2008. Me and My Monkey: What's Hiding in the Security State. In R. Pain and S. Smith (eds), *Fear: Critical Geopolitics and Everyday Life*. London: Ashgate, pp.59–68.

Kayaoğlu, T. 2010. *Legal Imperialism: Sovereignty and Extraterritoriality in Japan, the Ottoman Empire, and China*. Cambridge: Cambridge University Press.

Kautilya. 1915. *Arthashastra*, trans. R. Shamasastry. Bangalore: Government Press.

Keil, R. 2009. City. In D. Gregory (ed.), *Dictionary of Human Geography*. Oxford: Blackwell, p.86.

Kelley, R.D.G. 2015. *Hammer and Hoe: Alabama Communists during the Great Depression*. Chapel Hill: University of North Carolina Press.

Kim, Y. 2013. *The Korean Wave: Korean Media Go Global*. London: Routledge.

King, L. and Johnson, G. 2015. Death of Syrian Toddler Throws Global Spotlight onto Refugees Crisis – LA Times. *Los Angeles Times*, September 3. http://www.latimes.com/world/europe/la-fg-syria-refugee-toddler-drowned-20150903-story.html (accessed October 1, 2019).

Kirsch, S. 2015. Cultural Geography III Objects of Culture and Humanity, or, Re-"Thinging" the Anthropocene Landscape. *Progress in Human Geography* 39(6): 818–826.

Kobayashi, A. and Peake, L. 2000. Racism out of Place: Thoughts on Whiteness and an Antiracist Geography in the New Millennium. *Annals of the Association of American Geographers* 90(2): 392–403.

Koch, N. 2013. Sport and Soft Authoritarian Nation-Building. *Political Geography* 32: 42–51.

Kocher, A. 2017. The New Resistance: Immigrant Rights Mobilization in an Era of Trump. *Journal of Latin American Geography* 16(2): 165–171.

Koopman, S. 2009. Alter-Geopolitics: Another Geopolitics Is Possible. Presented at the Annual Meeting of the Association of American Geographers. Las Vegas.

Koopman, S. 2011. Alter-Geopolitics: Other Securities are Happening. *Geoforum* 42(3): 274–284.

Koopman, S. 2017. Social Movements. In J. Agnew, V. Mamadouh, A.J. Secor et al. (eds), *The Wiley Blackwell Companion to Political Geography*. Hoboken, NJ: John Wiley and Sons, pp.339–351.

Kovras, I. and Robins, S. 2016. Death as the Border: Managing Missing Migrants and Unidentified Bodies at the EU's Mediterranean Frontier. *Political Geography* 55: 40–49.

Krasner, S.D. 1999. *Sovereignty: Organized Hypocrisy*. Princeton, NJ: Princeton University Press.

Krasner, S.D. 2001. Rethinking the Sovereign State Model. *Review of International Studies* 27(5): 17–42.

Krishna, S. 1994. Cartographic Anxiety: Mapping the Body Politic in India. *Alternatives: Social Transformation and Humane Governance* 19: 507–521.

Krishna, S. 2014. A Postcolonial Racial/Spatial Order: Gandhi, Ambedkar, and the Construction of the International. In A. Anievas, N. Manchanda, and R. Shilliam (eds), *Race and Racism in International Relations*. London: Routledge, pp.151–168.

Kuotsu, N. 2013. Architectures of Pirate Film Cultures: Encounters with Korean Wave in "Northeast" India. *Inter-Asia Cultural Studies* 14(4): 579–599.

Kuus, M. 2015a. Symbolic Power in Diplomatic Practice: Matters of Style in Brussels. *Cooperation and Conflict* 50(3): 368–384.

Kuus, M. 2015b. Transnational Bureaucracies: How Do We Know What They Know? *Progress in Human Geography* 39(4): 432–448.

Kwan, M.-P. 2002. Feminist Visualization: Re-Envisioning GIS as a Method in Feminist Geographic Research. *Annals of the Association of American Geographers* 92(4): 645–661.

Last, A. 2015. Fruit of the Cyclone: Undoing Geopolitics through Geopoetics. *Geoforum* 64: 56–64.

Laws, G. 1994. Oppression, Knowledge and the Built Environment. *Political Geography* 13(1): 7–32.

Lawson, G. 2015. Trudeau's Canada, Again. *The New York Times*, December 8, sec. Magazine. https://www.nytimes.com/2015/12/13/magazine/trudeaus-canada-again.html (accessed October 1, 2019).

LeBesco, K. 2004. *Revolting Bodies?: The Struggle to Redefine Fat Identity*. Boston: University of Massachusetts Press.

Lefebvre, H. 2003. *The Urban Revolution*. Minneapolis, MN: University of Minnesota Press.

Lefebvre, H. 2004. *The Production of Space*. Oxford: Blackwell Publishing.

Legg, S. 2005. Foucault's Population Geographies: Classifications, Biopolitics and Governmental Spaces. *Population, Space and Place* 11: 137–156.

Legg, S. 2010."An Intimate and Imperial Feminism: Meliscent Shephard and the Regulation of Prostitution in Colonial India. *Environment and Planning D: Society and Space* 28: 68–94.

Legg, S. 2011. Assemblage/Apparatus: Using Deleuze and Foucault. *Area* 43(2): 128–133.

Legg, S. 2014. *Prostitution and the Ends of Empire: Scale, Governmentalities, and Interwar India*. Durham, NC: Duke University Press.

Leitner, H. and Ehrkamp, P. 2006. Transnationalism and Migrants' Imaginings of Citizenship. *Environment and Planning A* 38(9): 1615–1632.

Leloudis, J. 2017. History Speaks on Intentions behind Confederate Statues. Newsobserver. August 23. http://www.newsobserver.com/opinion/op-ed/article168971292.html (accessed October 1, 2019).

Lemanski, C. 2004. A New Apartheid? The Spatial Implications of Fear of Crime in Cape Town, South Africa. *Environment and Urbanization* 16(2): 101–112.

Lerner, S. 2010. *Sacrifice Zones: The Front Lines of Toxic Chemical Exposure in the United States*. Cambridge, MA: MIT Press.

Leroux, D. 2018. "We've Been Here for 2,000 Years": White Settlers, Native American DNA and the Phenomenon of Indigenization. *Social Studies of Science* 48(1): 80–100.

Letter, An Open. 2018. A Call to Defend Rojava. *The New York Review of Books* (blog). April 23. https://www.nybooks.com/daily/2018/04/23/a-call-to-defend-rojava/ (accessed October 1, 2019).

Lewis, S.L. and Maslin, M.A. 2015. Defining the Anthropocene. *Nature* 519(7542): 171–180.

Lilla, M. 2016. The End of Identity Liberalism. *New York Times*, November 18, sec. Opinion. https://www.nytimes.com/2016/11/20/opinion/sunday/the-end-of-identity-liberalism.html (accessed October 1, 2019).

Lipsitz, G. 2011. *How Racism Takes Place*. Philadelphia: Temple University Press.

Livingston, J. and Puar, J.K. 2011. Interspecies. *Social Text* 29(1 106): 3–14.

Long, J.S. 2010. *Treaty No. 9: Making the Agreement to Share the Land in Far Northern Ontario in 1905*. Montreal: McGill-Queen's Press.

Longhurst, R. 2005. Fat Bodies: Developing Geographical Research Agendas. *Progress in Human Geography* 29: 247–259.

Longhurst, R. 2012. Becoming Smaller: Autobiographical Spaces of Weight Loss. *Antipode* 44(3): 871–888.

Lorde, A. 1984. *Sister Outsider: Essays and Speeches*. Fredom, CA: Crossing Press.

Lorde, A. 1996. *The Audre Lorde Compendium: Essays, Speeches and Journals*. London: Pandora.

Lowery, M.M. 2018. Opinion: We Are the Original Southerners. *The New York Times*, May 22, sec. Opinion. https://www.nytimes.com/2018/05/22/opinion/confederate-monuments-indians-original-southerners.html (accessed October 1, 2019).

Loyd, J.M. 2009. "A Microscopic Insurgent": Militarization, Health, and Critical Geographies of Violence. *Annals of the Association of American Geographers* 99(5): 863–873.

Loyd, J.M. 2012. Geographies of Peace and Antiviolence. *Geography Compass* 6(8): 477–489.

Loyd, J.M. and Gilmore, R.W. 2012. Race, Capitalist Crisis, and Abolitionist Organizing. In J.M. Loyd, M. Mitchelson, and A. Burridge (eds), *Beyond Walls and Cages: Prisons, Borders, and Global Crisis*. Athens, GA: University of Georgia Press, pp.42–54.

Loyd, J.M., Mitchelson, M., and Burridge, A. 2013. Introduction: Borders, Prisons, and Abolitionist Visions. In J.M. Loyd, M. Mitchelson, and A. Burridge (eds), *Beyond Walls and Cages: Prisons, Borders, and Global Crisis.* Athens, GA: University of Georgia Press, pp.1–15.

Lugones, M. 2010. Toward a Decolonial Feminism. *Hypatia* 25(4): 742–759.

Lyons, H. 2018. The Intangible Nation: Spatializing Experiences of Britishness and Belonging for Young British Muslim Women. *Geoforum* 90: 55–63.

Lyons, S.R. 2010. *X-Marks: Native Signatures of Assent.* Minneapolis, MN: University of Minnesota Press.

Macharia, K. 2016. On Being Area-Studied: A Litany of Complaint. *GLQ: A Journal of Lesbian and Gay Studies* 22(2): 183–190.

Mackinder, H. 1919. *Democratic Ideals and Reality: A Study in the Politics of Reconstruction.* London: Constable and Company.

Mahmood, S. 2011. *Politics of Piety: The Islamic Revival and the Feminist Subject.* Princeton, NJ: Princeton University Press.

Mahtani, M. 2014. Toxic Geographies: Absences in Critical Race Thought and Practice in Social and Cultural Geography. *Social & Cultural Geography* 15(4): 359–367.

Mamdani, M. 2004. *Good Muslim, Bad Muslim: America, the Cold War, and the Roots of Terror.* New York: Pantheon Books.

Manzo, K. 2010. Beyond Polar Bears? Re-envisioning Climate Change. *Meteorological Applications* 17(2): 196–208.

Marston, S.A. 2002. The Social Construction of Scale. *Progress in Human Geography* 24: 219–242.

Marston, S.A., Jones, J.P., III, and Woodward, K. 2005. Human Geography without Scale. *Transactions of the Institute of British Geographers* 30: 415–432.

Martin, L. 2010. Bombs, Bodies, and Biopolitics: Securitizing the Subject at the Airport Security Checkpoint. *Social & Cultural Geography* 11: 17–34.

Martin, L. 2011. The Geopolitics of Vulnerability: Children's Legal Subjectivity, Immigrant Family Detention and US Immigration Law and Enforcement Policy. *Gender, Place and Culture* 18(4): 477–498.

Marx, K. 1990. *Capital: A Critique of Political Economy, Volume I.* New York: Penguin Books.

Marx, K. and Engels, F. 1967. *The Communist Manifesto*, trans. S. Moore. London: Penguin. (Original work published 1848.)

Massaro, V.A. 2015. The Intimate Entrenchment of Philadelphia's Drug War. *Territory, Politics, Governance* 3(4): 369–386.

Massey, D. 1993. Power-Geometry and a Progressive Sense of Place. In J. Bird, B. Curtis, T. Putnam et al. (eds), *Mapping the Futures: Local Cultures, Global Change*, London: Routledge, pp.61–70.

Massey, D. 1994. *Space, Place and Gender.* Cambridge: Polity Press.

Massey, D. 2004. Geographies of Responsibility. *Geografiska Annaler: Series B, Human Geography* 86(1): 5–18.

Massey, D. 2005. *For Space.* London: Sage.

Mawdsley, E. 2018. Development Geography II: Financialization. *Progress in Human Geography* 42(2): 264–274.

Mayer, T. 2000. *Gender Ironies of Nationalism: Sexing the Nation.* Hove: Psychology Press.

Mays, K.T. 2016. From Flint to Standing Rock: The Aligned Struggles of Black and Indigenous People – Cultural Anthropology. *Cultural Anthropology: Hot Spots.* https://

culanth.org/fieldsights/from-flint-to-standing-rock-the-aligned-struggles-of-black-and-indigenous-people (accessed October 1, 2019).

McCarthy, J. 2009. Social Movement. In D. Gregory (ed.), *Dictionary of Human Geography*. Chichester: Blackwell, p.695.

McClintock, A. 1995. *Imperial Leather: Race, Gender and Sexuality in the Colonial Contest*. New York: Routledge.

McConnell, F. 2017. Liminal Geopolitics: The Subjectivity and Spatiality of Diplomacy at the Margins. *Transactions of the Institute of British Geographers* 42(1): 139–152.

McDonald, M. 2013. Discourses of Climate Security. *Political Geography* 33: 42–51.

McGee. C. 2019. Beyond Forced Labor: How UNC Made its Founding Investments on Slavery, Stolen Property. *The Daily Tar Heel*. September 23.

McKittrick, K. 2006. *Demonic Grounds: Black Women and the Cartographies of Struggle*. Minneapolis, MN: University of Minnesota Press.

McKittrick, K. 2011. On Plantations, Prisons, and a Black Sense of Place. *Social & Cultural Geography* 12(8): 947–962.

McKittrick, K. 2013. Plantation Futures" *Small Axe* 17(3 42): 1–15.

McKittrick, K. 2017. Commentary: Worn Out. *Southeastern Geographer* 57(1): 96–100.

McKittrick, K. and Woods, C. 2007. No One Knows the Mysteries at the Bottom of the Ocean. In K. McKittrick and C. Woods (eds), *Black Geographies and the Politics of Place*. Cambridge, MA: South End Press, pp.–13.

McSweeney, K. and Pearson, Z. 2013. Vaccines, Fertility, and Power: The Political Ecology of Indigenous Health and Well-Being in Lowland Latin America. In B. King and K.A. Crews (eds), *Ecologies and Politics of Health*. New York: Routledge, pp.139–158.

Mehta, S. 2009. *Maximum City: Bombay Lost and Found*. New York: Vintage.

Merrifield, A. 2013. The Urban Question under Planetary Urbanization. *International Journal of Urban and Regional Research* 37(3): 909–922.

Metcalf, B.D. and Metcalf, T.R. 2006. *A Concise History of Modern India*. Cambridge: Cambridge University Press.

Mignolo, W.D. 2002. *Local Histories/Global Designs: Coloniality, Subaltern Knowledges, and Border Thinking*. Princeton, NJ: Princeton University Press.

Militz, E. and Schurr, C. 2016. Affective Nationalism: Banalities of Belonging in Azerbaijan. *Political Geography* 54: 54–63.

Miñoso, Y.E., Correal, D.G., and Muñoz, K.O. 2014. *Tejiendo de Otro Modo: Feminismo, Epistemología y Apuestas Descoloniales En Abya Yala*. Popayán: Universidad del Cauca.

Miradas Criticas del territorio desde el Feminismo. 2017. *Mapeando El Cuerpo- Territorio. Guía Metodologica Para Mujeres Que Defienden Sus Territorios*. Quito: Abya Yala.

Miraftab, F. 2007. Governing Post Apartheid Spatiality: Implementing City Improvement Districts in Cape Town. *Antipode* 39(4): 602–626.

Mitchell, T. 1991. The Limits of the State – Beyond Statist Approaches and Their Critics. *American Political Science Review* 85: 77–96.

Mitchell, T. 1999. Society, Economy, and the State Effect. In G. Steinmetz (ed.), *State/Culture: State-Formation After the Cultural Turn*. Ithaca, NY: Cornell University Press, pp.76–87.

Mohan, R. 2011. Love Jihad and Demographic Fears. *Indian Journal of Gender Studies* 18(3): 425–430.

Mohanty, C.T. 1991. Under Western Eyes: Feminist Scholarship and Colonial Discourses. In C.T. Mohanty, A, Russo, and L. Torres (eds), *Third World Women and the Politics of Feminism*. Bloomington, IN: Indiana University Press, pp.51–80.

Mohanty, C.T. 2003. *Feminism without Borders: Decolonizing Theory, Practicing Solidarity*. Durham, NC: Duke University Press.

Mollett, S. 2010. Está Listo (Are You Ready)? Gender, Race and Land Registration in the Río Plátano Biosphere Reserve. *Gender, Place and Culture* 17(3): 357–375.

Mollett, S. 2011. Racial Narratives: Miskito and Colono Land Struggles in the Honduran Mosquitia. *Cultural Geographies* 18(1): 43–62.

Mollett, S. 2013. Mapping Deception: The Politics of Mapping Miskito and Garifuna Space in Honduras. *Annals of the Association of American Geographers* 103(5): 1227–1241.

Mollett, S. 2015. "Displaced Futures": Indigeneity, Land Struggle, and Mothering in Honduras. *Politics, Groups, and Identities* 3(4): 678–683.

Monkman, L. 2017. "No Ban on Stolen Land," Say Indigenous Activists in U.S."*CBC News*, February 6. http://www.cbc.ca/news/indigenous/indigenous-activists-immigration-ban-1.3960814 (accessed October 1, 2019).

Moore, J. 2018. Constellating Queer Spaces: An Interview with Jen Jack Gieseking. *Urban Omnibus: A Publication of the Architectural League of New York*, February 9. https://urbanomnibus.net/2018/02/constellating-queer-spaces/ (accessed October 1, 2019).

Moore, J.W. 2017. The Capitalocene Part I: On the Nature & Origins of Our Ecological Crisis. *Journal of Peasant Studies* 44(3): 594–630.

Morgensen, S.L. 2012. Theorising Gender, Sexuality and Settler Colonialism: An Introduction. *Settler Colonial Studies* 2(2): 2–22.

Mott, C. and Cockayne, D. 2017. Citation Matters: Mobilizing the Politics of Citation Toward a Practice of "Conscientious Engagement." *Gender, Place & Culture* 24(7): 954–973.

Mountz, A. 2004. Embodying the Nation-State: Canada's Response to Human Smuggling. *Political Geography* 23(3): 323–345.

Mountz, A. 2010. *Seeking Asylum: Human Smuggling and Bureaucracy at the Border*. Minneapolis: University of Minnesota Press.

Mountz, A. 2013. Political Geography I: Reconfiguring Geographies of Sovereignty. *Progress in Human Geography* 37(6): 829–841.

Mountz, A. 2015. In/Visibility and the Securitization of Migration: Shaping Publics through Border Enforcement on Islands. *Cultural Politics* 11(2): 184–200.

Mountz, A. 2017. Island Detention: Affective Eruption as Trauma's Disruption. *Emotion, Space and Society* 24: 74–82.

Mountz, A. and Hiemstra, N. 2014. Chaos and Crisis: Dissecting the Spatiotemporal Logics of Contemporary Migrations and State Practices. *Annals of the Association of American Geographers* 104(2): 382–390.

Mountz, A. and Hyndman, J. 2006. Feminist Approaches to the Global Intimate. *Women's Studies Quarterly* 34(1/2): 446–463.

Mowl, G. and Fuller, D. 2014. Geographies of Disability. In R. Pain, J. Gough, G. Mowl et al. (eds), *Introducing Social Geographies*. London: Routledge, pp.164–186.

Murray, S. 2008. Fattening Up Foucault: A "Fat"Counter-Aesthetic? In S. Murray, *The "Fat"Female Body*. London: Palgrave Macmillan, pp.122–134.

Mutu, W. 2014. BOMB – Artists in Conversation. Interview by Deborah Willis. http://bombmagazine.org/article/1000052/wangechi-mutu (accessed October 1, 2019).

Nagar, R. 1998. Communal Discourses, Marriage, and the Politics of Gendered Social Boundaries among South Asian Immigrants in Tanzania. *Gender, Place and Culture: A Journal of Feminist Geography* 5: 117–139.

Nagar, R. 2014. *Muddying the Waters: Coauthoring Feminisms across Scholarship and Activism.* Champaign: University of Illinois Press.

Naoroji, D. 1887. *Essays, Speeches, Addresses and Writings of Dadabhai Naoroji,* ed. C.L. Parekh. Bombay: Caxton.

Napoleon, V. 2013. Thinking about Indigenous Legal Orders. In R, Poost and C. Sheppard (eds), *Dialogues on Human Rights and Legal Pluralism.* Dordrecht: Springer, pp.229–245.

Nash, C.J. and Browne, K. 2015. Sexual Politics. In J. Agnew, V. Mamadouh, A.J. Secor et al. (eds), *The Wiley Blackwell Companion to Political Geography.* Chichester: Wiley-Blackwell, pp.366–379.

Nast, H. 2000. Mapping the "Unconscious": Racism and the Oedipal Family. *Annals of the Association of American Geographers* 90: 215–255.

Nast, H.J. 1998. Unsexy Geographies. *Gender, Place and Culture* 5(2): 191–206.

Nayak, A. 2010. Race, Affect, and Emotion: Young People, Racism, and Graffiti in Postcolonial English Suburbs. *Environment and Planning A* 42(10): 2370–2392.

Naylor, L. 2017. Reframing Autonomy in Political Geography: A Feminist Geopolitics of Autonomous Resistance. *Political Geography* 58: 24–35.

Naylor, L., Daigle, M., Zaragocin, S. et al. 2018. Interventions: Bringing the Decolonial to Political Geography. *Political Geography* 66: 199–209.

Neubert, C. Under review. The Anthropocene Stinks! Odor, Affect, and the Entangled Politics of Livestock Waste in a Rural Iowa Watershed. *Environment and Planning D: Society and Space.*

Nevins, J. 2013. Policing Mobility: Maintaining Global Apartheid from South Africa to the United States. In J.M. Loyd, M. Mitchelson, and A. Burridge (eds), *Beyond Walls and Cages: Prisons, Borders, and Global Crisis.* Athens, GA: University of Georgia Press, pp.1–15.

Ngai, M.M. 2014. *Impossible Subjects: Illegal Aliens and the Making of Modern America.* Princeton, NJ: Princeton University Press.

Nicholls, W.J. 2007. The Geographies of Social Movements. *Geography Compass* 1(3): 607–622.

Nicholls, W.J. 2013. *The DREAMers: How the Undocumented Youth Movement Transformed the Immigrant Rights Debate.* Berkeley: Stanford University Press.

Nicol, H. 2010. Reframing Sovereignty: Indigenous Peoples and Arctic States. *Political Geography* 29(2): 78–80.

Nicol, H., Weber, B., Barkan, J. et al. 2016. Book Review Forum on Contesting the Arctic: Politics and Imaginaries in the Circumpolar North. *The AAG Review of Books* 4(3): 170–178.

Noble, S.U. 2018. *Algorithms of Oppression: How Search Engines Reinforce Racism.* New York: New York University Press.

Noxolo, P. 2017a. Decolonial Theory in a Time of the Re-colonisation of UK Research. *Transactions of the Institute of British Geographers* 42(3): 342–344.

Noxolo, P. 2017b. Introduction: Decolonising Geographical Knowledge in a Colonised and Re-colonising Postcolonial World. *Area* 49(3): 317–319.

Noxolo, P., Raghuram, P., and Madge, C. 2008. "Geography Is Pregnant" and "Geography's Milk Is Flowing": Metaphors for a Postcolonial Discipline? *Environment and Planning D: Society and Space* 26(1): 146–168.

Noxolo, P., Raghuram, P., and Madge, C. 2012. Unsettling Responsibility: Postcolonial Interventions. *Transactions of the Institute of British Geographers* 37(3): 418–429.

Nugent, P., Hammett, D., and Dorman, S. 2007. *Making Nations, Creating Strangers: States and Citizenship in Africa.* Leiden: Brill.

Omi, M. and Winant, H. 2014. *Racial Formation in the United States.* New York: Routledge.

Oza, R. 2007. The Geography of Hindu Right-Wing Violence in India. In D. Gregory and A. Pred (eds), *Violent Geographies: Fear, Terror, and Political Violence.* New York: Routledge, pp.153–174.

Paasche, T.F., Yarwood, R., and Sidaway, J. D. 2014. "Territorial Tactics: The Socio-Spatial Significance of Private Policing Strategies in Cape Town. *Urban Studies* 51(8): 1559–1575.

Pain, R. 2009. Globalized Fear? Towards an Emotional Geopolitics. *Progress in Human Geography* 33(4): 466–486.

Pain, R. and Smith, S.J. 2008. Fear: Critical Geopolitics and Everyday Life. In R. Pain and S.J. Smith (eds), *Fear: Critical Geopolitics and Everyday Life,* 1–19. Burlington, VT: Ashgate, pp.1–19.

Painter, J. 2006. Prosaic Geographies of Stateness. *Political Geography* 25(7): 752–774.

Painter, J. and Jeffrey, A. 2009. *Political Geography.* Thousand Oaks, CA: Sage.

paperson, la. 2018. *A Third University Is Possible.* Minneapolis, MN: University of Minnesota Press.

Parr, H. and Butler, R. 1999. New Geographies of Illness, Impairment and Disability. In R. Butler and H. Parr (eds), *Mind and Body Spaces: Geographies of Illness, Impairment and Disability.* London: Routledge, pp.1–24.

Peake, L. and Kobayashi, A. 2002. Policies and Practices for an Antiracist Geography at the Millennium. *The Professional Geographer* 54(1): 50–61.

Pelletier, I.R., Lundmark, L., Gardner, R. et al. 2016. Why ISIS's Message Resonates: Leveraging Islam, Sociopolitical Catalysts, and Adaptive Messaging. *Studies in Conflict & Terrorism* 39(10): 871–899.

Pérez, M.A. 2016. Yearnings for Guácharo Cave: Affect, Absence, and Science in Venezuelan Speleology. *Cultural Geographies* 23(4): 693–714.

Perry, K.-K.Y. 2012. State Violence and the Ethnographic Encounter: Feminist Research and Racial Embodiment. *African and Black Diaspora: An International Journal* 5(1): 135–154.

Perry, K.-K.Y. 2013. *Black Women against the Land Grab: The Fight for Racial Justice in Brazil.* Minneapolis, MN: University of Minnesota Press.

Phadke, S., Khan, S., and Ranade, S.. 2011. *Why Loiter?: Women and Risk on Mumbai Streets.* New Delhi: Penguin Books India.

Pickerill, J. and Chatterton, P. 2006. Notes towards Autonomous Geographies: Creation, Resistance and Self-Management as Survival Tactics. *Progress in Human Geography* 30(6): 730–746.

Pollan, M. 2007. You Are What You Grow. *The New York Times Magazine* April 22.

Porteous, D. and Smith, S.E. 2001. *Domicide: The Global Destruction of Home.* Montreal: McGill-Queen's Press.

Povinelli, E.A. 2002. *The Cunning of Recognition: Indigenous Alterities and the Making of Australian Multiculturalism*. Durham, NC: Duke University Press.

Powell, R.C. 2010. Lines of Possession? The Anxious Constitution of a Polar Geopolitics. *Political Geography* 29(2): 74–77.

Prashad, V. 2008. *The Darker Nations: A People's History of the Third World*. New York: The New Press.

Prashad, V., ed. 2018. *Strongmen: Putin • Erdoğan • Duterte • Trump • Modi*. New York: OR Books.

Pratt, G. 1982. Class Analysis and Urban Domestic Property: A Critical Reexamination. *International Journal of Urban and Regional Research* 6(4): 481–502.

Pratt, G. and Rosner, V. 2012. *The Global and the Intimate: Feminism in Our Time*. New York: Columbia University Press.

Puar, J. 2007. *Terrorist Assemblages: Homonationalism in Queer Times*. Durham, NC: Duke University Press.

Puar, J. 2013. Rethinking Homonationalism. *International Journal of Middle East Studies* 45(2): 336–339.

Pulido, L. 2002. Reflections on a White Discipline. *The Professional Geographer* 54(1): 42–49.

Pulido, L. 2017. Geographies of Race and Ethnicity II: Environmental Racism, Racial Capitalism and State-Sanctioned Violence. *Progress in Human Geography* 41(4): 524–533.

Quijano, A. 1992. Colonialidad y Modernidad/Racionalidad. *Perú Indígena* 13(29): 11–20.

Quijano, A. 2007. Coloniality and Modernity/Rationality. *Cultural Studies* 21(2–3): 168–178.

Rai, M. 2004. *Hindu Rulers, Muslim Subjects: Islam, Rights, and the History of Kashmir*. Princeton, NJ: Princeton University Press.

Ramadan, A. 2009. Destroying Nahr El-Bared: Sovereignty and Urbicide in the Space of Exception. *Political Geography* 28(3): 153–163.

Rånes, B.C.N. 2014. Chocolate, Mustard and a Fox-Norwegian K-Pop, Its Production and Performance. Master's thesis, Norwegian University of Science and Technology.

Ranganathan, M. 2015. Storm Drains as Assemblages: The Political Ecology of Flood Risk in Post-colonial Bangalore. *Antipode* 47(5): 1300–1320.

Ranganathan, M. 2018. Rule by Difference: Empire, Liberalism, and the Legacies of Urban "Improvement." *Environment and Planning A: Economy and Space* 50(7): 1386–1406.

Reardon, J. and TallBear, K. 2012. "Your DNA Is Our History" Genomics, Anthropology, and the Construction of Whiteness as Property. *Current Anthropology* 53: S233–245.

Reese, A.M. 2018. "We Will Not Perish; We're Going to Keep Flourishing": Race, Food Access, and Geographies of Self-Reliance. *Antipode* 50(2): 407–424.

Reese, A.M. 2019. *Black Food Geographies: Race, Self-Reliance, and Food Access in Washington*. Chapel Hill, NC: University of North Carolina Press.

Reid-Henry, S. 2007. Exceptional Sovereignty? Guantánamo Bay and the Re-colonial Present. *Antipode* 39(4): 627–648.

Reuveny, R. 2007. "Climate Change-Induced Migration and Violent Conflict. *Political Geography* 26(6): 656–673.

Reyes, A. 2015. Zapatismo: Other Geographies circa "the End of the World." *Environment and Planning D: Society and Space* 33(3): 408–424.

Reyes, A. and Kaufman, M. 2011. Sovereignty, Indigeneity, Territory: Zapatista Autonomy and the New Practices of Decolonization. *South Atlantic Quarterly* 110(2): 505–525.

Ridgley, J. 2008. Cities of Refuge: Immigration Enforcement, Police, and the Insurgent Genealogies of Citizenship in US Sanctuary Cities. *Urban Geography* 29(1): 53–77.

Robbins, P. and Moore, S.A. 2013. Ecological Anxiety Disorder: Diagnosing the Politics of the Anthropocene. *Cultural Geographies* 20(1): 3–19.

Robeson, P. 1988. *Here I Stand*. Boston: Beacon Press.

Robinson, C.J. 1983. *Black Marxism: The Making of the Black Radical Tradition*. Chapel Hill, NC: University of North Carolina Press.

Robinson, J. 1997. The Geopolitics of South African Cities: States, Citizens, Territory. *Political Geography* 16(5): 365–386.

Robinson, S. 1994. The Aboriginal Embassy: An Account of the Protests of 1972. *Aboriginal History* 18(1): 49–63.

Rokem, J. 2016. Learning from Jerusalem: Rethinking Urban Conflicts in the 21st Century: Introduction. *City* 20(3): 407–411.

Rokem, J., Fregonese, S., Ramadan, A. et al. 2017. Interventions in Urban Geopolitics. *Political Geography* 61: 253–262.

Roman, M.L. 2012. *Opposing Jim Crow: African Americans and the Soviet Indictment of US Racism, 1928–1937*. Omaha: University of Nebraska Press.

Rose, D.B. 1991. *Hidden Histories: Black Stories from Victoria River Downs, Humbert River and Wave Hill Stations*. Canberra: Aboriginal Studies Press.

Rose, G. 2016. *Visual Methodologies: An Introduction to Researching with Visual Materials*. Thousand Oaks, CA: Sage.

Rose, N. 1996. Governing "Advanced" Liberal Democracies. In A. Bary, T. Osborne, and N. Rose (eds), *Foucault and Political Reason: Liberalism, Neo-Liberalism, and Rationalities of Government*. Chicago: University Of Chicago Press, pp.37–64.

Rose-Redwood, R., Alderman, D., and Azaryahu, M. 2008. Collective Memory and the Politics of Urban Space: An Introduction. *GeoJournal* 73: 161–164.

Rose-Redwood, R., Alderman, D., and Azaryahu, M. 2010. Geographies of Toponymic Inscription: New Directions in Critical Place-Name Studies. *Progress in Human Geography* 34(4): 453–470.

Rostow, W.W. 1990. *The Stages of Economic Growth: A Non-Communist Manifesto*. Cambridge: Cambridge University Press.

Routledge, P. 2003. Anti-Geopolitics. In J.A. Agnew, K. Mitchell, and G. Toal (eds), *A Companion to Political Geography*, Malden, MA: Wiley-Blackwell, pp.236–248.

Roy, A. 2003. *City Requiem, Calcutta: Gender and the Politics of Poverty*. Minneapolis, MN: University of Minnesota Press.

Roy, A. 2016. What Is Urban about Critical Urban Theory? *Urban Geography* 37(6): 810–823.

Ruddick, S., Peake, L., Tanyildiz, G. et al. 2018. Planetary Urbanization: An Urban Theory for Our Time? *Environment and Planning D: Society and Space* 35(3): 387–404.

Said, E. 1979. *Orientalism*. New York: Vintage.

Saktanber, A. 2006. Women and the Iconography of Fear: Islamization in Post-Islamist Turkey. *Signs: Journal of Women in Culture and Society* 32(1): 21–31.

Salama, M. 2011. *Islam, Orientalism and Intellectual History: Modernity and the Politics of Exclusion Since Ibn Khaldun*. London: IB Tauris.

Saldanha, A. 2007. *Psychedelic White: Goa Trance and the Viscosity of Race*. Minneapolis, MN: University of Minnesota Press.

Saldanha, A. 2013. Some Principles of Geocommunism. blog, July. https:// progressivegeographies.com/2013/07/31/arun-saldanha-some-principles-of-geocommunism/ (accessed October 1, 2019).

Saldon, S.. 2017. I Am Saldon I Am Shifah. *Indian Express*, September 19, sec. Opinion. http://indianexpress.com/article/opinion/columns/i-am-saldon-i-am-shifah-4850000 (accessed October1, 2019).

Sandoval, E. 2019. More than Violence: UndocuQueers' Narratives of Disidentification and World-Making in Seattle, Washington, USA. *Gender, Place & Culture* 25(12): 1759–1780.

Sangtin Writers Collective and Nagar, R. 2006. *Playing with Fire: Feminist Thought and Activism through Seven Lives in India*. Minneapolis, MN: University of Minnesota Press.

Schlosser, K. 2015. Apocalyptic Imaginaries, Gramsci, and the Last Man on Earth. *GeoHumanities* 1(2): 307–320.

Schmitt, C. 1996. *The Concept of the Political*, trans. G. Schwab. Chicago: University of Chicago Press.

Schultz, D. 2017. Tax, Class, and the Limits of Identity Politics. *Huffington Post* (blog). December 19. https://www.huffingtonpost.com/entry/tax-class-and-the-limits-of-identity-politics_us_5a3923b1e4b0578d1beb7306 (accessed October 1, 2019).

Schumpeter, J.A. 1942. *Socialism, Capitalism and Democracy*. New York: Harper and Brothers.

Scott, J. 1998. *Seeing like a State: How Certain Schemes to Improve the Human Condition Have Failed*. New Haven, CT: Yale University Press.

Scott, J. 2009. *The Art of Not Being Governed: An Anarchist History of Upland Southeast Asia*. New Haven: Yale University Press.

Scully, E.P. 2001. *Bargaining with the State from Afar: American Citizenship in Treaty Port China, 1844-1942*. New York: Columbia University Press.

Selby, J., Dahi, O.S, Fröhlich, C. et al. 2017. Climate Change and the Syrian Civil War Revisited. *Political Geography* 60: 232–244.

Semple, E.C. 1911. *Influences of Geographic Environment, on the Basis of Ratzel's System of Anthropo-Geography*. London: H. Holt.

Shabazz, R. 2015. *Spatializing Blackness: Architectures of Confinement and Black Masculinity in Chicago*. Chicago: University of Illinois Press.

Shah, N. 2012. *Stranger Intimacy: Contesting Race, Sexuality and the Law in the North American West*. Berkeley: University of California Press.

Sharp, J.P. 1998. Reel Geographies of the New World Order: Patriotism, Masculinity, and Geopolitics in Post-Cold War American Movies. In G. ÓTuathail and S. Dalby (eds), *Rethinking Geopolitics*. London: Routledge, pp.170–197.

Sharp, J.P. 2000. *Condensing the Cold War: Reader's Digest and American Identity*. Minneapolis: University of Minnesota Press.

Sharp, J.P. 2011. A Subaltern Critical Geopolitics of the War on Terror: Postcolonial Security in Tanzania. *Geoforum* 42(3): 297–305.

Sharp, J.P. 2013. Geopolitics at the Margins? Reconsidering Genealogies of Critical Geopolitics. *Political Geography* 37: 20–29.

Sharpe, C. 2016. *In the Wake: On Blackness and Being*. Durham, NC: Duke University Press.

Shaw, I. and Akhter, M. 2012. The Unbearable Humanness of Drone Warfare in FATA, Pakistan. *Antipode* 44(4): 1490–1509.

Shaw, I. and Akhter, M. 2014. The Dronification of State Violence. *Critical Asian Studies* 46(2): 211–234.

Sheller, M. 2014. *Aluminum Dreams: The Making of Light Modernity*. Cambridge, MA: MIT Press.

Shim, D. 2006. Hybridity and the Rise of Korean Popular Culture in Asia. *Media, Culture & Society* 28(1): 25–44.

Shivani, A. 2017. Time to Give up on Identity Politics: It's Dragging the Progressive Agenda down. *Salon* (blog). September 2. https://www.salon.com/2017/09/02/time-to-give-up-on-identity-politics-its-dragging-the-progressive-agenda-down (accessed October 1, 2019).

Silva, D.F da. 2011. Note for a Critique of the "Metaphysics of Race." *Theory, Culture & Society* 28: 138–148.

Silva, K. 2016. *Brown Threat: Identification in the Security State*. Minneapolis, MN: University of Minnesota Press.

Simone, A. (2011) The Surfacing of Urban Life: A Response to Colin McFarlane and Neil Brenner, David Madden and David Wachsmuth. *City* 15(3–4): 355–364.

Simpson, A. 2007. On Ethnographic Refusal: Indigeneity, "Voice" and Colonial Citizenship. *Junctures: The Journal for Thematic Dialogue*, 9: 67–80.

Simpson, A. 2014. *Mohawk Interruptus: Political Life across the Borders of Settler States*. Durham, NC: Duke University Press.

Simpson, L. 2011. *Dancing on Our Turtle's Back: Stories of Nishnaabeg Re-Creation, Resurgence and a New Emergence*. Winnipeg: Arbeiter Ring Pubublishers.

Sinha, M. 2000. Mapping the Imperial Social Formation: A Modest Proposal for Feminist History. *Signs: Journal of Women in Culture and Society* 25(4): 1077–1082.

Skrimshire, S. 2010. *Future Ethics: Climate Change and Apocalyptic Imagination*. London: Continuum Books.

Slack, J. 2016. Captive Bodies: Migrant Kidnapping and Deportation in Mexico. *Area* 48(3): 271–277.

Slack, J. and Whiteford, S. 2011. Violence and Migration on the Arizona-Sonora Border. *Human Organization* 70(1): 11–21.

Slocum, R. 2004. Polar Bears and Energy-Efficient Lightbulbs: Strategies to Bring Climate Change Home. *Environment and Planning D: Society and Space* 22(3): 413–438.

Slocum, R. 2008. Thinking Race through Corporeal Feminist Theory: Divisions and Intimacies at the Minneapolis Farmers' Market. *Social & Cultural Geography* 9: 849–869.

Smiles, D. 2018. "… to the Grave"—Autopsy, Settler Structures, and Indigenous Counter-Conduct. *Geoforum* 91: 141–150.

Smith, A.D. 1991. *National Identity*. Reno: University of Nevada Press.

Smith, C.A.. 2015. Blackness, Citizenship, and the Transnational Vertigo of Violence in the Americas. *American Anthropologist* 117(2): 384–387.

Smith, C.A.. 2016. Towards a Black Feminist Model of Black Atlantic Liberation: Remembering Beatriz Nascimento. *Meridians* 14(2): 71–87.

Smith, D.E. 1974. Women's Perspective as a Radical Critique of Sociology. *Sociological Inquiry* 44(1): 7–13.

Smith, L.T. 2012. *Decolonizing Methodologies: Research and Indigenous Peoples.* 2e. New York: Zed.

Smith, M.P. 1979. *The City and Social Theory.* New York: St. Martin's Press.

Smith, N. 1979. Toward a Theory of Gentrification a Back to the City Movement by Capital, Not People. *Journal of the American Planning Association* 45(4): 538–548.

Smith, N. 2005. *The New Urban Frontier: Gentrification and the Revanchist City.* New York: Routledge.

Smith, S. and Gergan, M.D. 2015. The Diaspora Within: Himalayan Youth, Education-Driven Migration, and Future Aspirations in India. *Environment and Planning D: Society and Space* 33(1): 119–135.

Smith, S., Swanson, N.W., and Gökarıksel, B. 2016. Territory, Bodies and Borders. *Area* 48(3): 258–261.

Smith, S. and Vasudevan, P. 2017. Race, Biopolitics, and the Future: Introduction to the Special Section. *Environment and Planning D: Society and Space* 35(2): 210–221.

Solomon, H. 2016. *Metabolic Living: Food, Fat, and the Absorption of Illness in India.* Durham, NC: Duke University Press.

Spivak, G.C. 1988. Can the Subaltern Speak? Speculations on Widow Sacrifice. In C. Nelson (ed.), *Marxism and the Interpretation of Culture*, London: Macmillan, pp.271–313.

Springer, S. 2012. Anarchism! What Geography Still Ought to Be. *Antipode* 44(5): 1605–1624.

Squire, V. 2016. *The Exclusionary Politics of Asylum.* Basingstoke: PalgraveMacmillan.

Srinivas, S.V. 2016. Chinaman, Not Hindustani: Stereotypes and Solidarity in a Hong Kong Film on India. In J.T.-H. Lee and S. Kolluri (eds), *Hong Kong and Bollywood.* London, Macmillan, pp.85–103.

Staeheli, L.A., Ehrkamp, P., Leitner, H. et al. 2012. Dreaming the Ordinary: Daily Life and the Complex Geographies of Citizenship. *Progress in Human Geography* 36(5): 628–644.

Staples, B. 2018. Opinion: How the Suffrage Movement Betrayed Black Women. *The New York Times*, July 28. https://www.nytimes.com/2018/07/28/opinion/sunday/suffrage-movement-racism-black-women.html (accessed October 1, 2019).

Stark, H. 2010. Respect, Responsibility, and Renewal: The Foundations of Anishinaabe Treaty Making with the United States and Canada. *American Indian Culture and Research Journal* 34(2): 145–164.

Steffen, W., Grinevald, J., Crutzen, P. et al. 2011. The Anthropocene: Conceptual and Historical Perspectives. *Philosophical Transactions of the Roayal Society A* 369: 842–867.

Steinberg, P.E., Page, S., Dittmer, J. et al. 2018. Reassessing the Trump Presidency, One Year On. *Political Geography* 62: 207–215.

Steinberg, P.E., Tasch, J., and Gerhardt, H. 2015. *Contesting the Arctic: Rethinking Politics in the Circumpolar North.* London: IB Tauris.

Stelter, B. 2010. For Fox's "24," Terror Fight and Series Near End. *New York Times*, March 26. http://www.nytimes.com/2010/03/27/arts/television/27twentyfour.html (accessed October 1, 2019).

Stephen, C. 2013. Libya Turns Zoo into Migrant Processing Centre as More Head for EU. *The Guardian.* October 13. http://www.theguardian.com/world/2013/oct/13/libya-zoo-migrant-centre-eu-refugee (accessed October 1, 2019).

Stojevich, S. 2017. Reader's View: Neighborhood Victimized by Construction Delay. *Duluth News Tribune*, 2017.

Stoler, A.L. 1995. *Race and the Education of Desire: Foucault's History of Sexuality and the Colonial Order of Things*. Durham, NC: Duke University Press.

Stoler, A.L. 2002. *Carnal Knowledge and Imperial Power: Race and the Intimate in Colonial Rule*. Berkeley, CA: University of California Press.

Stoler, A.L. 2013. *Imperial Debris: On Ruins and Ruination*. Durham, NC: Duke University Press.

Sturkey, W. 2017. Carr Was Indeed Much More than Silent Sam. *Heraldsun*. October 31. http://www.heraldsun.com/opinion/article181567401.html (accessed October 1, 2019).

Sultana, F. 2009. Fluid Lives: Subjectivities, Gender and Water in Rural Bangladesh. *Gender, Place and Culture* 16(4): 427–444.

Sultana, F. and Loftus, A. 2013. *The Right to Water*. London: Routledge.

Swyngedouw, E. 2013. Apocalypse Now! Fear and Doomsday Pleasures. *Capitalism Nature Socialism* 24(1): 9–18.

Sycamore, M.B. 2008. *That's Revolting!: Queer Strategies for Resisting Assimilation*. Berkeley, CA: Soft Skull Press.

Tadiar, N.X.M. 2016. City Everywhere. *Theory, Culture & Society* 33(7–8): 57–83.

Talaga, T. 2017. *Seven Fallen Feathers: Racism, Death, and Hard Truths in a Northern City*. Toronto, ON: Anansi.

Taylor, D. 2014. *Toxic Communities: Environmental Racism, Industrial Pollution, and Residential Mobility*. New York: New York University Press.

Teal, D. 1971. *The Gay Militants*. New York: St. Martin's Press.

Teschke, B. 2003. *The Myth of 1648: Class, Geopolitics and the Making of Modern International Relations*. London: Verso.

Thiong'o, Ngugi wa. 2012. *In the House of the Interpreter: A Memoir*. New York: Random House.

Thomas, W. and Jacobs, S.-E. 1999. "… And We Are Still Here": From Berdache to Two-Spirit People. *American Indian Culture and Research Journal* 23(2): 91–107.

Tilly, C. 1975. *The Formation of National States in Europe*. Princeton, NJ: Princeton University Press.

Toal, G. 1996. *Critical Geopolitics: The Politics of Writing Global Space*. Minneapolis, MN: University of Minnesota Press.

Toal, G. and O'Loughlin, J. 2013. Inside South Ossetia: A Survey of Attitudes in a de Facto State. *Post-Soviet Affairs* 29(2): 136–172.

Toal, G., Ó Tuathail, G., Dalby, S. et al. 1998. *The Geopolitics Reader*. New York: Routldege.

Todd, Z. 2016. An Indigenous Feminist's Take on the Ontological Turn: "Ontology" is Just Another Word for Colonialism. *Journal of Historical Sociology* 29(1): 4–22.

Tolia-Kelly, D.P. 2006. Mobility/Stability: British Asian Cultures of Landscape and Englishness. *Environment and Planning A* 38(2): 341–358.

Tolia-Kelly, D.P. 2017. A Day in the Life of a Geographer: "Lone," Black, Female. *Area* 49(3): 324–328.

Torres, R.M. 2018. A Crisis of Rights and Responsibility: Feminist Geopolitical Perspectives on Latin American Refugees and Migrants. *Gender, Place & Culture* 25(1): 13–36.

Trask, H.-K. 1996. Feminism and Indigenous Hawaiian Nationalism. *Signs: Journal of Women in Culture and Society* 21(4): 906–916.

Tuck, E. and Ree, C. 2013. A Glossary of Haunting. In S.L. Holman Jones, T.E. Adams, and C. Ellis (eds), *Handbook of Autoethnography*. New York: Routledge, pp.639–658.

Tuck, E. and Yang, K.W. 2012. Decolonization Is Not a Metaphor. *Decolonization: Indigeneity, Education & Society* 1(1): 1–40.

Tyner, J.A. 2008. *The Killing of Cambodia: Geography, Genocide and the Unmaking of Space.* Burlington, VT: Ashgate.

Ul-Qamrain, N. 2015. Buddhists in Ladakh Allege Love Jihad. *The Sunday Guardian* January 31. http://www.sunday-guardian.com/news/buddhists-in-ladakh-allege-love-jihad (accessed October 1, 2019).

Valdivia, G. 2008. Governing Relations Between People and Things: Citizenship, Territory, and the Political Economy of Petroleum in Ecuador. *Political Geography* 27(4): 456–477.

Varma, S. 2019. Kashmir Has Become a Zone of Permanent, Limitless War. *The Nation.* September 4.

Vasudevan, A., McFarlane, C., and Jeffrey, A. 2008. Spaces of Enclosure. *Geoforum* 39(5): 1641–1646.

Vasudevan, P. 2019. An Intimate Inventory of Race and Waste. *Antipode*, https://doi.org/10.1111/anti.12501 .

Vaughan-Williams, N. 2015. "We Are Not Animals!" Humanitarian Border Security and Zoopolitical Spaces in EUrope1. *Political Geography* 45: 1–10.

Vaz, P. 2018. City of God(Desses): From a Place of Necessity to a Space of Politics. PhD Dissertation, Chapel Hill: University of North Carolina at Chapel Hill.

Veracini, L. 2010. *Settler Colonialism.* New York: Springer.

Veracini, L. 2011. Introducing: Settler Colonial Studies. *Settler Colonial Studies* 1(1): 1–12.

Wacquant, L. 2002. From Slavery to Mass Incarceration. *New Left Review* 13: 41–60.

Wallerstein, I. 1974. *The Modern World-System I: Capitalist Agriculture and the Origins of the European World-Economy in the Sixteenth Century.* Berkeley: University of California Press.

Wallerstein, I. 2003. *The Decline of American Power: The US in a Chaotic World.* New York: The New Press.

Walmsley, R. 2013. World Prison Population List. London: International Centre for Prison Studies. http://www.prisonstudies.org/research-publications?shs_term_node_tid_depth=27 (accessed October1, 2019).

Wang, S.H. 2017. Fetal Citizens? Birthright Citizenship, Reproductive Futurism, and the "Panic" over Chinese Birth Tourism in Southern California. *Environment and Planning D: Society and Space* 35(2): 263–280.

Ward, K. 2017. Financialization and Urban Politics: Expanding the Optic. *Urban Geography* 38(1): 1–4.

Warner, M. 1991. Introduction: Fear of a Queer Planet. *Social Text* 9: 3–17.

Washburne, C.W. 1932. *Remakers of Mankind.* The John Day Company.

Weber, M. 1946. *From Max Weber: Essays in Sociology*, trans. by Hans H. Gerth and C. Wright Mills. New York: Oxford University Press.

Weheliye, A. 2014. *Habeas Viscus: Racializing Assemblages, Biopolitics, and Black Feminist Theories of the Human.* Durham, NC: Duke University Press.

Whyte, K. 2017. The Dakota Access Pipeline, Environmental Injustice, and US Colonialism. *Red Ink* 19(1): 154–69.

Whyte, K.P. 2016. Our Ancestors' Dystopia Now: Indigenous Conservation and the Anthropocene. In U. Heise, J. Christensen and M.N. *Companion to the Environmental Humanities.* New York: Routledge, pp.206–215.

Whyte, K.P. 2018. Indigenous Science (Fiction) for the Anthropocene: Ancestral Dystopias and Fantasies of Climate Change Crises. *Environment and Planning E: Nature and Space* 1: 224–242.

Wilderson III, F.B. 2010. *Red, White & Black: Cinema and the Structure of US Antagonisms.* Durham, NC: Duke University Press.

Williams, B.H. 1922. The Protection of American Citizens in China: Extraterritoriality. *American Journal of International Law* 16(1): 43–58.

Williams, J. and Boyce, G.A. 2013. Fear, Loathing and the Everyday Geopolitics of Encounter in the Arizona Borderlands. *Geopolitics* 18(4): 895–916.

Williams, J. and Boyce, G.A. 2016. The Safety/Security Nexus and the Humanitarianisation of Border Enforcement. *The Geographical Journal* 182: 27–37.

Williams, J. and Massaro, V. 2013. Feminist Geopolitics: Unpacking (in) Security, Animating Social Change. *Geopolitics* 18(4): 751–758.

Williams, W. 2016. The Limits of Identity Politics. *The New York Times*, December 16, sec. Opinion Letter to the editor. https://www.nytimes.com/2016/12/16/opinion/the-limits-of-identity-politics.html (accessed October 1, 2019).

Wolfe, P. 2006. Settler Colonialism and the Elimination of the Native. *Journal of Genocide Research* 8(4): 387–409.

Wolfe, P. 2011. Race and the Trace of History: For Henry Reynolds. In F. Bateman and L. Pilkington (eds), *Studies in Settler Colonialism*. Basingstoke: Palgrave Macmillan, pp. 272–296.

Wolford, W. 2004. This Land Is Ours Now: Spatial Imaginaries and the Struggle for Land in Brazil. *Annals of the Association of American Geographers* 94(2): 409–424.

Wong, J.C. 2016. Dakota Access Pipeline: 300 Protesters Injured after Police Use Water Cannons. *The Guardian*, November 21, sec. US news. https://www.theguardian.com/us-news/2016/nov/21/dakota-access-pipeline-water-cannon-police-standing-rock-protest (accessed October 1, 2019).

Woon, C.Y. 2014. Popular Geopolitics, Audiences and Identities: Reading the "War on Terror" in the Philippines. *Geopolitics* 19(3): 656–683.

Wouters, J.J.P. and Subba, T.B. 2013. The "Indian Face," India's Northeast, and "the Idea of India." *Asian Anthropology* 12(2): 126–140.

Wynter, S. 1994. "No Humans Involved." An Open Letter to My Colleagues. *Forum N.H.I. Knowledge for the 21st Century* 1(1): 42–73.

Wynter, S. 2003. Unsettling the Coloniality of Being/Power/Truth/Freedom: Towards the Human, After Man, Its Overrepresentation--An Argument. *The New Centennial Review* 3(3): 257–337.

Ybarra, M. 2019. "We Are Not Ignorant" Transnational Migrants' Experiences of Racialized Securitization. *Environment and Planning D: Society and Space* 37(2): 197–215.

Ybarra, M. and Peña, I.L. 2017. "We Don't Need Money, We Need to Be Together": Forced Transnationality in Deportation's Afterlives. *Geopolitics* 22(1): 34–50.

Yeh, E. 2009. Living Together in Lhasa: Ethnic Relations, Coercive Amity, and Subaltern Cosmopolitanism. In S. Mayaram (ed.), *The Other Global City*. New York: Routledge.

Yin, K.F.S. and Liew. K.K. 2005. Hallyu in Singapore: Korean Cosmopolitanism or the Consumption. *Korea Journal* Winter: 206–232.

Yoo, J. 2006. *War by Other Means: An Insider's Account of the War on Terror*. New York: Atlantic Monthly Press.

Young, R. 2004. *White Mythologies*. London: Routledge.

Young, R. 2016. *Postcolonialism: An Historical Introduction*. Chichester: John Wiley & Sons.

Yusoff, K. 2013. Geologic Life: Prehistory, Climate, Futures in the Anthropocene. *Environment and Planning D: Society and Space* 31: 779–795.

Yusoff, K. 2018. *A Billion Black Anthropocenes or None*. Minneapolis: University of Minnesota Press.

Zaragocin, S. in press. Challenging the Epistemic Authority of Anglophone Feminist Geography from Latin American Feminist Debates on Territoriality. In B. Gökarıksel, M. Hawkins, C. Neubert et al. *Feminist Geography Unbound: Intimacy, Territory, and Embodied Power*. Morgantown, WV: West Virginia University Press.

Zenko, M. 2013. If Trayvon Were Pakistani … *Foreign Policy*, July 22.

Zutshi, C. 2010. Rethinking Kashmir's History from a Borderlands Perspective. *History Compass* 8(7): 594–608.

Index

Note: A page number in boldface denotes a definition of the term.